SUITS AND UNIFORMS

PHILIP ROBINS

Suits and Uniforms

Turkish Foreign Policy
since the Cold War

University of Washington Press
Seattle

First published in the United Kingdom by
C. Hurst & Co. (Publishers) Ltd, London
Published simultaneously in the United States of America by
University of Washington Press
PO Box 50096
Seattle, WA 98145-5096
www.washington.edu/uwpress

Printed by Bell & Bain Ltd., Glasgow

Library of Congress Cataloging-in-Publication Data
Robins, Philip.
Suits and Uniforms: Turkish Foreign Policy since the Cold War/Philip Robins.
p. cm.
Includes bibliographical references (p.) and index.
ISBN 0-295-98281-0
1. Turkey—Foreign relations—1960–1980. 2. Turkey—Foreign relations—1980–.
I. Title.
DR477.R63 2002
327.561—dc21   2002069559

The central figure in the cover photograph is Ismail Cem, Foreign
Minister of Turkey 1997–2002. Reproduced by courtesy of *Hurriyet*.

To my mother, Muriel,
and in memory of
my father, Calvert

ACKNOWLEDGEMENTS

This book is the product of more than a dozen years of work. My most sincere thanks are therefore reserved for those whom I met early on in my research on Turkey and with whom I have had countless discussions about Turkish foreign policy, and the domestic politics that lies behind it. Special mention here is due to Mensur Akgun, Sahin Alpay, Suha Bolukbasi, Andy and Caroline Finkel, Bill Hale, Semih Idiz, Gun and Sule Kut, Hugh Pope and Nicole Pope. I would also like to thank a much longer list of people, too numerous to name, both inside and outside Turkey, who have shared their thoughts, ideas and criticisms with me since then. Included in this number are many officials and representatives, most of whom were happy to debate but strictly on the condition of confidentiality. The fact that they are not individually named in no way diminishes my gratitude to them.

The study itself was made possible due to a generous grant from the Levehulme Trust, which financed much of the fieldwork. I would also like to thank Ekavi Athanassopoulou and Gordon Peake, who worked as research assistants at various stages of the work, and who have since moved on to higher things.

I have also had cause to be grateful to the principal institutions with which I have been affiliated during this time. At Chatham House, Keith Kyle, John Moberly and William Wallace, who initially encouraged me to work on Turkey, were helpful and supportive, and the Institute's library staff under the successive leadership of Susan Boyde and Mary Bone gave extensive advice and assistance on sources. I thank my colleagues at St Antony's College, Oxford, where I have been based for the last seven years, for their unfailing stimulation as well as the calm, studious atmosphere that exists at that institution, so facilitating of research and scholarly interaction. Lastly, I thank academic staff members at Bogazici University in Istanbul, with whom I spent an enjoyable sabbatical semester in the mid 1990s, notably members of the Department of Politics and International Relations, Yesim Arat, Ali Carkoglu, Ustun Erguder, Ersin Kalaycioglu, Kemal Kirisci, Ziya Onis (now at Koc University), Binnaz Toprak and Gareth Winrow (now at Bilgi University).

I also thank those who were good enough to make space in their busy schedules to read and comment on the manuscript. Gun Kut, Neil McFarlane, Bob O'Neil, Soli Ozel and Laurence Whitehead read all or most of the work, and made extensive and valuable comments. Hussein Agha, Chris Cviic, Brian Daves, Ahmad Khalidi, Ariel Levite, Hugh Pope and Avi Shlaim read selected chapters. I am very grateful to them all; the usual caveats regarding my exclusive responsibility for the final work naturally apply.

Thanks are also due to Michael Dwyer of Hurst & Co, who signed up the manuscript for publication, and to Christopher Hurst and Fintan McCullagh for their help in guiding it through to book form.

Finally, on a personal note, I thank my family—Helen, Verity, Isabel and Edmund—for their love, support and joyous diversions during this lengthy project, as I do my parents, Muriel and Calvert, to whom the book is dedicated.

July 2002 PHILIP ROBINS

CONTENTS

Part II. DOMESTIC MOTIVATORS OF TURKISH FOREIGN POLICY

MAPS

Turkey and the Near East

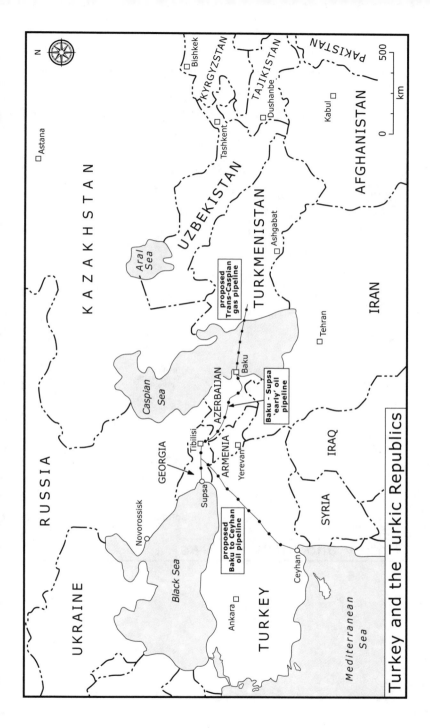

Turkey and the Turkic Republics

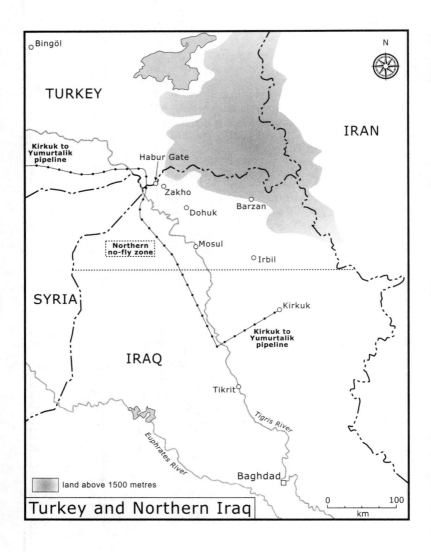

Turkey and Northern Iraq

xviii

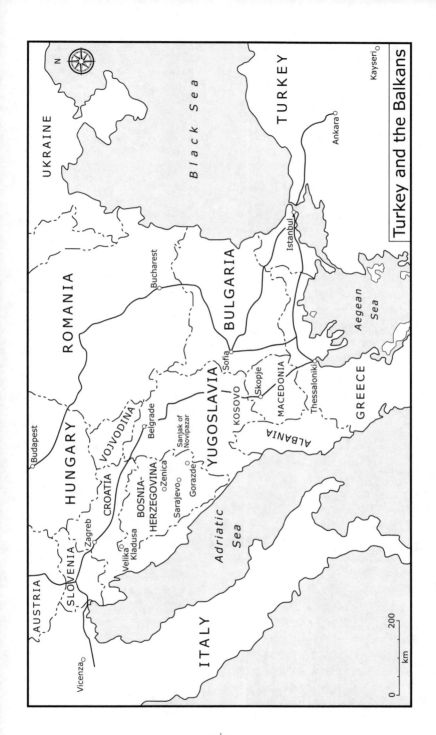

Turkey and the Balkans

xix

INTRODUCTION

Over the eight decades of its existence, Turkey has faced four major foreign policy challenges. The first, in the early and mid 1920s, saw the challenge of consolidating the emerging state of Turkey, especially through external recognition; the second came with the Second World War and the need to remain outside a conflict that raged all around, spanning most of Europe and the Middle East; the third came with the territorial and security challenge from the Soviet Union, especially during the early period of the Cold War; and the fourth coincided with the end of the Cold War and the collapse of bipolarity, and the need to navigate carefully through the transitional period in the international system. It is with this fourth period and its related challenges that this book is concerned.

Before 1989 international relations experts and practitioners tended to view Turkey as a bit player in a global game played between two blocs operating within one main international relations system. Turkey's loyal membership of NATO and earnest desire to deepen its relations with the European Community (EC) tended to confirm this impression. Turks hardly encouraged a more textured view of their own country, with their parochial fixation with Cyprus and Greece, a fixation that has been generously reciprocated over time. Consequently, would-be foreign policy commentators and international relations experts gravitated towards the Arab World, Western Europe and the Soviet Union as more stimulating and complex fields of study.[1] It is little wonder that few bothered to write about Turkey's external relations.

There was of course always more to say about Turkish foreign policy than those wearing either fish-eye lenses or blinkers would

---

[1] For two good examples with respect to the Arab World, see Michael N. Barnett, *Dialogues in Arab Politics, Negotiations in Regional Order* (Columbia University Press, New York, 1998) and Stephen M. Walt, *The Origins of Alliances* (Cornell University Press, Ithaca, NY, 1987).

have had us believe. My own interest in the field began in 1987 in the course of a study of the Iran-Iraq war. A number of issues arose in relation to that conflict which had direct and major relevance for Turkey and raised wider questions. These included: how Turkey managed to develop excellent commercial relations simultaneously with both protagonists; the Kurdish issue, which overlapped all three states; the spread of political Islam as a transnational phenomenon; the implications for Turkey of the defeat of either of the warring states. Not only was there a dearth of answers to such questions, but no one seemed even to be posing them. It was in such a context that I began my study of Turkey's relations with the Middle East, leading to the first such book on the subject in any language.[2]

On the whole, international relations experts were slow to appreciate the new importance of Turkey, even after 1989. At first, it tended to be assumed that systemic breakdown would devalue even further the importance of a state that had only been of peripheral significance before. Even the Gulf crisis, where Turkey's failure to send troops to join the international coalition assembled in Saudi Arabia gave a misleading view of its importance, did little to reverse this impression, save, most importantly, among policy insiders within the Washington beltway. If the disciplinary generalists assumed that any need for a wake-up call would be administered from the field of area studies they were mistaken. Arabists, Europeanists and specialists in the former Soviet bloc had too much to grapple with within their own domains of expertise to take on a large, new country that never seemed quite to fit in; meanwhile, there were few Turkey specialists left after years of funding neglect in universities and think tanks, and they were spread thinly across the disciplines.

It was then only slowly and fitfully through the course of the 1990s that interest in Turkey picked up. In the West, this has taken place as a function of three things: the need to expand and redesign the architecture of Western institutions such as NATO and the EU, membership of which Turkey values and aspires to respectively; the outbreak of a rash of conflicts in regions to which Turkey lies adjacent, that is to say the Balkans, the north and south Caucasus and the Middle East; the growing importance of the politics of

---

[2] Philip Robins, *Turkey and the Middle East* (Pinter/RIIA, London, 1991).

resources and resource transportation in the former Soviet south and the Persian Gulf sub-system, in relation to which Turkey occupies a potentially key location. Nevertheless, even more than a decade after the end of the Cold War it is still highly unusual to see international relations generalists taking Turkey seriously, even as a country case study among many, let alone as a central focus.[3] This is a book written in order to try to rectify this situation.

In order to view Turkish foreign policy from different vantage points I have adopted a three-part approach to this study. In the first section I have attempted to engage with both the international systemic and the domestic institutional context in which Turkish foreign policy takes place. In so doing, I subscribe to a rising view in international relations, summarised succinctly by Thomas Risse-Kappen, that *'interactive approaches* integrating external and internal factors offer a better and richer understanding of foreign policy than accounts exclusively relying on one aspect'.[4] This section also includes a three phase analytical typology of Turkish foreign policy since 1985, the beginning of the end of the Cold War.

In the second part, I have focused on the material and ideational (that is to say the ideological and identity related) origins of Turkish foreign policy during this phase of Cold War transition, from 1985 to 2000. In doing so, I have placed considerable emphasis on domestic drivers of policy, both as a corrective to the perennially more systemic analysis of international relations generalists, and because among Turkey specialists these elements are rarely aired critically. In order to ensure that this book does not turn into a work principally on Turkish domestic politics, I have peppered this section with examples from more than a decade of Turkish foreign policy. This, I hope, conveys the complexity and range of Turkey's external relations, and gives at least a flavour of Turkey's relations with a number of different countries, regions and multilateral organisations. What it self-consciously does not do is to take a region by region approach,

[3] A rare and stimulating exception is Barry Buzan, whose article co-authored with Thomas Diez, 'The European Union and Turkey' (*Survival* 00 spring 1999) likened Turkey to Russia, Japan and Israel, as a 'Westernistic state', that is one that can 'never be purely Western or European by definition', p. 49.

[4] 'Introduction' in Thomas Risse-Kappen (ed.), *Bringing Transnational Relations Back In, Non-State Actors, Domestic Structures and International Institutions* (Cambridge University Press, 1995), p. 16.

with its tendency to generate a by now repetitious recitation of dull observations.

In the third part I have taken four cases, the Bosnian conflict, the relationship with Israel, northern Iraq and relations with the so-called 'Turkic' states, in which I examine the emergence and evolution of Turkish foreign policy in some detail through the chronological span of the book. I have purposely selected cases of general importance involving countries that lie adjacent to Turkey, but which tend to have been less extensively addressed by scholarly writings. In so doing, I have avoided focusing unduly on some of Turkey's hoary old involvements, the fleshless bones of which are frequently picked over. I hope that the analysis has a freshness that reflects the recent or transformed nature of their relations for Turkey.

Based on the content briefly outlined above, this book claims to make a contribution to the existing literature in three ways. From an international relations methods perspective the book adds its weight to those who argue for a more systematic treatment of domestic factors in the sub-discipline of foreign policy analysis. It argues that it is not important merely to study domestic factors in the actual and aspirant superpowers of the world, which have a formative impact on the international system, but on major regional powers as well. Moreover, this study shows that when looking at domestic factors there is a need not merely to look at decision-making structures and processes at the state level alone, but also to consider the experiences, ideas and values which help to condition perceptions and create the boundaries of the 'bounded rationality' in question. As such, the work is part of what I perceive to be a new approach to the foreign policy analysis of the developing world that began to emerge in the 1990s, and which attempts to reconcile and integrate both the concepts and methodologies of the discipline with the authoritative case knowledge of area studies.

For a generalist international relations readership the book is designed to provide extensive material from a single country case.[5] This material locates Turkish foreign policy in its broader international relations context; it describes and illustrates the actors, processes and

---

[5] In that sense I see this book as being comparable to similar in-depth studies on other major states, such as Thomas W. Robinson and David Shambaugh (eds), *Chinese Foreign Policy: Theory and Practice* (Clarendon Press, Oxford, 1994).

structures that are important in decision-making; it focuses on the material and ideational drivers that are important in the emergence of foreign policy; it provides a wealth of bilateral, multilateral and functional case material within a framework that maximises the complementary nature of what is often great diversity. Indeed, I would hope that the greatest contribution of the book is in providing ideas and empirical material that can be plundered by those generalists who think broadly and comparatively from a number of sub-disciplinary perspectives, from security studies through European studies and diplomatic history to policy studies.

For the field of Turkish studies the book is an attempt to view that country's foreign policymaking and external relations from a holistic perspective. Such an approach is valuable because the overwhelming majority of studies of Turkish foreign policy, and especially those that have emerged over the last decade, have been much narrower in focus, taking some aspect of bilateral, functional or regional relations, rather than viewing Turkish foreign policy in the round.[6] Though many of these studies have been very useful, and the ideas and observations of these works are to be found referenced in this book, they inevitably suffer from the absence of what one might call the inter-connectivities of foreign policy. Indeed, it was this very absence that was a weakness of my own *Turkey and the Middle East*, and made me want to rectify the shortcoming through this current book. In addition, I hope that this book brings a dispassionate perspective to the study of modern Turkey and its foreign relations that those either too close to the ground or too partisan in their approach will always find difficult to achieve.

Those picking up the book for a fleeting glance will see that it contains no dedicated chapter on Turkey and Cyprus, Turkey and Greece or Turkey and the EU. This is entirely deliberate. It strikes me that writings and publications on bilateral relations with Cyprus and Greece exist in inverse proportion to the substantive developments that have taken place in those two areas during the period under discussion. In consequence, there is much less to say than in many other areas of Turkish foreign policy. It is therefore with a sense of mercy that I release the reader from having to read yet

---

[6] A rare, recent and authoritative exception, taking more of a historical approach, is William Hale, *Turkish Foreign Policy, 1774–2000* (Frank Cass, London, 2000).

another regurgitation of the 'facts' on these subjects, and am happy to direct them towards existing works. This point is not entirely frivolously made. It has long struck me that Turkish foreign policy makers spend an incongruously large amount of time on these two subjects. I should also point out that in spite of the absence of 'a chapter on Cyprus and Greece' there is much to be found on both subjects, in, I hope, a more interpretative, argument-oriented and hence palatable from of presentation. Likewise, the absence of a 'chapter on Turkey and the EU' does not mean that the subject is ignored. I would refer the reader to the chapters on the international system, history, ideology and the economy in particular.

The basic arguments running through the book are threefold. First, in general terms, in the arena of foreign affairs Turkey is a status quo power. This was certainly true during the era of the Cold War, when, for example, Turkey was an enthusiastic and committed member of NATO. Curiously, perhaps, this has continued to be the case since the end of the Cold War. Turkey's foreign policy elites remained wedded to the sanctity of borders, of states, of multilateral institutions and of norms of conduct, even when it became clear that systemic changes had rendered some of these continuities no longer tenable. At the state or unit level, this belief in continuity was generated by a strong commitment to ideological and territorial continuity at home; looking outward, it was a reflection of a sense of foreboding at the impact that the forces of change could and did have in adjacent regions. Yet while Turkey's commitment to the status quo may have been understandable, it often tended to ignore the uncontainable dynamics released by the end of the Cold War. In often being impervious to such forces for change, Turkey showed just to what extent it was a passive player rather than an initiator of change, to what extent Ankara never really 'owned' the processes of change that have taken place since the mid 1980s.

Second, in spite of the number of times the question 'which way Turkey now?' has been posed over the past decade,[7] Turkey continues

[7] This was actually the title of a one-day seminar organised by myself and my colleague in Turkish studies, Dr Celia Kerslake, at St Antony's College, Oxford, on 27 April 1996. There were of course dozens of gatherings concerned with basically the same set of issues through the 1990s.

to be firmly oriented westwards in terms of its foreign relations.[8] This orientation can be seen institutionally in terms of the premium which Turkey continues to place on its membership of NATO, and in its earnest pursuit of membership of other organisations, notably the EU and, until recently, the WEU; it can certainly be seen economically, with the increasing orientation of trade with Western Europe and the adoption of the regulatory frameworks of the EU; it can also be seen demographically, especially with the growing number of people from Turkey now resident in the EU.

This continuing westward orientation has been the product of three key factors: the residue of history, which forged a close security relationship between the West and Turkey in the face of the military and ideological challenge from the former Soviet Union; the re-emergence of Western Europe as an economic centre of gravity, the pull of which has been irresistible for Turkey as it has been for an arc of countries on Europe's geographical periphery; the need for Turkey's relatively small and embattled Kemalist elite to consolidate itself through the irreversible orientation of the country westwards, as a means of reinforcing both its own values of militant secularism and its own position of privilege. It is the Turkish elite's failure to comprehend the normative changes that have been taking place in Western Europe, and the mismatch of values which has followed, that best explain the uncomfortable bilateral relationship that has existed since the end of the Cold War, in spite of this westward orientation.

Third, to paraphrase Malik Mufti, there has been more caution than daring in Turkish foreign policy since the mid-1980s.[9] It is fashionable to regard Turkey as a more assertive, more interventionist power than was the case during the Cold War.[10] And it is of course

[8] The strong and enduring westward orientation of Turkish foreign policy is a reality which makes the elevation of geography as a fifth major driver deeply problematic. A principally geographical approach might have raised expectations that Turkish foreign policy would indeed have been much more balanced in terms of its adjacent regions in the 1990s than has actually been the case. Moreover, a geographically deterministic approach would not have explained how many of the interior Anatolian 'tiger' cities would end up exporting to the European market.

[9] A Malik Mufti, 'Daring and Caution in Turkish Foreign Policy', *Middle East Journal*, vol. 52, 1998, pp. 32–51.

[10] A leading and highly respected exponent of this view is Ian Lesser of the Rand Corporation, who has written of 'a trend toward more assertive regional policies'.

true that, with the loosening of the shackles of bipolarity and the emergence of multiple successor states in the Balkans and the former Soviet Union, Turkish foreign policy has had to adjust and develop new relationships where none had existed before. But what is actually remarkable is that this large, populous and, at least in the longer run, increasingly prosperous state, which has seen its own position of power relative to its neighbours increase since 1989, has not been more interventionist. On the contrary, Ankara has remained determinedly committed to a multilateral political orientation, whether during the Bosnian war or over Kosovo. The dog of Turkish intervention has tended not to bark, whether during two Chechen crises or over Nagorno-Karabakh; in that way Cyprus in 1974, an event which after all comfortably preceded the end of the Cold War, has been much more the exception than the rule. Indeed, where Ankara has been tempted into unilateral acts of leadership, as with the Black Sea Economic Co-operation organisation or the ill-fated group of eight developing countries, the D-8, they have invariably been unconvincing and ineffectual. Even when Turkey has acted robustly across its borders, its actions have either been based on precedent from an earlier era (military raids into northern Iraq) or been made after repeated and long suffered provocations (Öcalan and Syria from 1987 to 1998). Indeed, it can be argued that it is precisely because Turkey remains rigidly committed to Atatürk's warnings about foreign adventures that the Turkey of the post-Cold War era has been so highly valued in official circles among the major states of the West.

This study was begun in 1993 when I was still at Chatham House, following the award of a generous grant by the Leverhulme Trust. I have continued to work on the project during the past six years as a Fellow of St Antony's College, Oxford, putting back the deadline for completion to take into account such significant developments as the year-long experiment with an Islamist-led government and the 'soft coup' of 1997. In reality, the study is a product of nearly twelve years working on Turkish foreign policy, going back to the commencement of the original study on Turkey and the Middle

---

See his 'Beyond "Bridge or Barrier"': Turkey's Evolving Security Relations with the West' in Alan Makovsky and Sabri Sayarı (ed.), *Turkey's New World, Changing Dynamics in Turkish Foreign Policy* (WINEP, Washington DC, 2000), p. 219.

East, when I began first to try to make sense of the substance and orientation of that country's external relations.

The study is based on a mixture of: extensive secondary published works, mainly in English, but also in French and Turkish; some contemporary primary materials where they have been available; newspaper sources in English, French, Turkish and Arabic, together with press and official transcripts carried in such summaries as the BBC *Summary of World Broadcasts;* and numerous interviews conducted during some twenty-five visits, ranging from one week to five months in duration, that I have made to the country over that time. The interviews have been conducted with Turkish diplomats, senior officers, politicians, journalists, businessmen and academics, Islamists as well as Kemalists, Kurds as well as Turks and others who are less easily categorised; in addition, I have spoken extensively to foreign observers of Turkey and to policymakers responsible for the conduct of relations with Turkey, both in the country and during numerous trips to other relevant multilateral institutions and states, not least those like Greece, Syria, Iran, Israel and others that lie adjacent to Turkey. Finally, I have had adequate opportunity to hear the views of others and to debate with them at an estimated thirty conferences, round tables, seminars and bilateral meetings which have focused on different aspects of Turkey during that time. While the input of others has been invaluable to the development of my own ideas and hence the approach, framework and contents of this book, responsibility for the final product, its strengths and weaknesses, remains my own.

Part I

TURKISH FOREIGN POLICY
IN CONTEXT

1

TURKEY AND THE CHANGING
INTERNATIONAL SYSTEM

With the exception of Germany, surely no other Western state has been as much affected by the recent changes in the international system as Turkey. After all, in the mid 1980s everything seemed relatively set and straightforward: a strategic enemy in the Soviet Union; a strong Western alliance with Turkey as a valued, four-decade-old member; a European aspiration that dared not be rejected outright in Brussels; domestic consensus among those who mattered as to national values and foreign policy priorities. Then came the change: state collapse on three sides; a rash of adjacent ethnic conflicts; the devaluation of NATO; and the vision of an expanded and united Europe, though one in which Turkey appeared not to feature. Turkey's experience of 1989 was not quite the same as Western Europe's: Beethoven's Ninth, but without the Ode to Joy.

Of course that is not to say that Turkey is no longer of strategic importance. Quite the contrary. The think-tank discussions of the early 1990s when experts tried to decide whether Turkey was of greater or lesser strategic importance than before are now redundant.[1]

---

[1] Antony Blinken, President Clinton's special assistant and senior director for European affairs at the National Security Council, referred to this debate when he delivered the Turgut Özal Memorial Lecture at the Washington Institute for Near East Policy on 8 December 1999. Asserting that Turkey's value has appreciated as far as the US is concerned, he noted that 'What seems an obvious point today was not so clear just a decade ago'. For a summary of the speech see WINEP *Special Policy Forum Report*, no. 426, 8 December 1999.

Turkey has gone from being a peripheral player in a global, bipolar conflict to being a central actor in a raft of actual or potential regional conflicts; as a state, it has literally gone from flank to front. The reality then is that Turkey is simultaneously both of less and of more strategic importance than it was before 1989. The United States in particular understands the enduring though changing geostrategic value of Turkey very well. Indeed, in the 1990s Turkish-US relations have often appeared to have been reduced to the level of geostrategy. For those located closer by, such as the Western Europeans, Turkey's importance is also palpable, but not necessarily palatable. For the growing truth is that, without the Cold War to bind them together, Euro–Turkish relations have become as frequently defined by confrontation as by co-operation.

All of this is very unfair on Turkey. Before 1989 Turkey was a *status quo* power par excellence. It neither wanted nor sought change. If anything Turkey, with its efforts to liberalise its economy and to move from an import substitution-led to an export-led economy in the early 1980s, could plausibly have claimed that it was anticipating effectively the changes in the international system, certainly at the economic level. Nevertheless, Turkey had systemic change thrust upon it at the end of the 1980s.

Turkey's experiences of trying to cope with these changes have been mixed. Ankara has navigated effectively through some of the regional conflicts close to its borders. It has coped much less well with the rapid normative changes which have accompanied the end of the Cold War. On big concept issues, such as the diminution of the state, the emergence of civil society and the centrality of human rights Turkey has not only failed to change but has even failed to understand the dynamics of the new milieu.[2] If many Europeans feel Turkey to be 'not like us', it is because of the growing normative gap on issues of liberal values and institutions, rather than for reasons of religion or culture. It is the nature, impact and consequences of 1989, in both strategic and cognitive terms, that this chapter will address.

---

[2] As ever there are honourable exceptions in Turkey, to be found in areas such as academia, business, the media, non-governmental organisations and even politics. But more than a decade after the fall of the Berlin Wall these exceptions are not as numerous as one might have expected.

Faultline 1989

1989 was a turning point in history in which history remembered to turn. The refusal of Gorbachev's Soviet Union any longer to prop up the Communist regimes in Eastern Europe broke the psychology of submission of the peoples concerned, and resulted in regime collapse in rapid time across the remainder of the continent.

Turkey, like the rest of the NATO alliance, was a passive actor in this unfolding drama. There were, however, two ways in which the position of Turkey differed from its allies. First, Turkey could not and did not claim a role in bringing about such change. This contrasted with the United States, which claimed that Communism was broken by the economic strains placed on the system of trying to keep up with American security innovation, such as the Strategic Defence Initiative. It also contrasted with the Western Europeans and the Americans, who claimed that the end of the Cold War marked a decisive victory for the liberal values of democracy, co-operative institution-building and the free market. Finally, it further contrasted with the West Germans, who were able to claim that it was their example of peace, democracy and prosperity that eventually proved to be irresistible for Eastern Europeans in general and East Germans in particular. While Europeans and Americans celebrated the historic victory of the Western value system, Turkey was left, as ever, at the margins.

Turkey was not then part of the normative euphoria which swept through Europe. Thus, with a small number of honourable exceptions, it missed out on the self-confident reaffirmation of core European values like human rights, civil society and real, as opposed to formal, democratisation. Indeed, in many respects, whether in terms of an authoritarian ideology, a deified political leader, the enduring role of the military and the primacy of the state, Turkey appeared more to resemble the former Eastern European states than their post-Communist successors. Even some ten years later, in the late 1990s, diplomats from Western European countries could still be heard to say, *sotto voce*, that Turkey seemed like the last Stalinist regime in Europe.

There was a second, crucial way in which Turkey differed from most of its fellow alliance members. This was in the area of threat perception and threat proximity. The collapse of the Communist regimes in Eastern Europe and the return home of Soviet troops immediately lifted the threat of war from West Germany and Western Europe in general. The profundity and certainty of this threat removal allowed NATO to set about dismantling much of its military infrastructure, the redeployment of both men and materiel being speeded up by the contingency of the August 1990 Gulf crisis, which required the rapid movement of military resources from central Europe to the Middle East.

For Ankara, which hitherto had remained more immune to Gorby-mania than many other NATO allies,[3] the Soviet threat did not evaporate or appreciably recede. As Ian Lesser delicately put it at the time, 'Ankara retains a rather conservative view of the residual military threat to Turkey' from the Soviet Union.[4] Indeed, the Soviet Union remained as a credible external threat until the collapse of the USSR as a state at the end of 1991. It was, for instance, not unusual to witness elite debates in Turkey about the enduring nature of the threat from the USSR long after the collapse of Communism had delivered real peace to the central European theatre. It must be remembered that Soviet forces were to remain on the Turkish border until the end of 1991, when they rematerialised as Russian forces. Thereafter, they hardly even went away, Russian forces remaining in Armenia and Georgia, and patrolling the border between the Commonwealth of Independent States and Turkey until the late 1990s.

For Ankara, the enduring nature of the threat from the Soviet superpower necessitated continued respect for Moscow as the power centre of the Soviet Union. All contacts with the USSR were routed through Moscow, virtually until the collapse of the state, for fear of alienating the centre through the development of relations with the Soviet constituent republics. This contrasted with the approach of the US and the Western Europeans, who much earlier on set out to develop good working relations with the Baltic States and actively sought to prise them away from the Soviet Union.

---

[3] This laconic observation was made by a senior member of the US embassy in Ankara, as he observed that Turkey still perceived the USSR as presenting a military threat, not least on the basis of historical experience. Interview, 15 March 1989.

[4] Graham E. Fuller, Ian O. Lesser *et al.*, *Turkey's New Geopolitics* (Westview Press, Boulder, CO, 1993), p. 117.

The rapidly diverging nature of Turkey's threat perceptions towards Moscow compared with its partners in NATO only served to point out just how unique had been the bipolarity of the Cold War years. It is extraordinary that a world which had been so messy prior to the Second World War had emerged with such discipline, organised along a binary divide, after the war. Geopolitics ought to have made one sceptical that countries as diverse and as distant as Turkey, Norway, Britain and the United States might have identified their core security interests in the same primary terms over such a sustained period, yet that was a prevailing systemic characteristic between the early 1950s and the late 1980s. However, once the external cement of the alliance had been taken away in the form of the collapse of Communism and the Soviet Union, the artificiality of such close relations began to be exposed.

The Gulf Crisis, 1990–1

The cause of residual Western solidarity gained an early respite through the Gulf crisis in 1990–1.[5] Saddam Hussain's invasion of Kuwait and its annexation to Iraq some six days later presented a challenge both to the international norms which had been developed during the previous 40 or more years and to international order itself. Confronting an aggressive, revisionist power in a region of high strategic value was therefore a timely reminder of the utility of military co-operation among those that formed the membership of the Western alliance.

For Turkey, it was the least desirable of challenges. Had the contingency taken place in, say, close proximity to the northern flank of NATO, Turkey could enthusiastically have played an unequivocal role within the organisation, and watched with satisfaction as the existing alliance membership agreed on the retention of the old style alliance. Unfortunately, however, the crisis took place in the Middle East, a region which was formally 'out of area', and where for Turkey the situation was fraught with complications.

---

[5] For a discussion of the impact of the Gulf crisis and its aftermath on Turkish policy towards the Middle East see William Hale, 'Turkey, the Middle East and the Gulf Crisis', *International Affairs*, vol. 68, no. 4, October 1992.

The first complication was that the Iraq-Kuwait crisis took place in a region of the world where Turkey had previously reserved the right to decouple its local interests from those of the wider alliance. Ever since the debacle of the late 1950s, particularly the ignominious collapse of the Baghdad Pact, Turkey had separated its strategic alliance commitments from regional relations in the Middle East. Second, the 1990 crisis took place in a region where the Turkish elite and public alike were chary of involvement, not least because of the bruising experiences of the last years of empire. Whereas Ankara could send Turkish troops thousands of miles to fight in Korea with alacrity in the early 1950s, the giving up of yet more 'Turkish blood to the sands of Arabia' was a move from which the population instinctively recoiled. Third, there was the problem of Turkey's rather lucrative economic relationship with Iraq, which had prospered all through the 1980–88 war with Iran. To support the international ostracism of Iraq, to help implement a tough economic sanctions regime and to facilitate a military bombardment dedicated to the degradation of Iraq's civilian as well as military infrastructure was asking for considerable self-sacrifice from Turkey.

In throwing in its lot with the United States and the growing number of countries which favoured confrontation with Iraq, Turkey showed little hesitation. This, though, owed comparatively little to either public opinion or bureaucratic structures. The speed and aplomb with which Turkey agreed to support the international sanctions and to lead the way in their implementation was much more the product of the strong leadership of the president, Turgut Özal.[6] It has been argued that Turkey would have accepted the Security Council resolutions on Iraq in any case, and this is almost certainly true. The nature of the Chapter Seven resolutions were that they demanded acceptance and compliance; the Turkish Foreign Ministry, which has routinely laid great importance on the letter of international law, would have argued that the state was obliged to endorse and implement them. What such an argument misses, however, was the importance of Turkey in bolstering the

---

[6] For a discussion of Özal's decision-making during the Gulf crisis see Philip Robins, 'Turkish Policy and the Gulf Crisis: Adventurist or Dynamic?' in Clement H. Dodd (ed.), *Turkish Foreign Policy: New Prospects* (Eothen Press, Huntingdon, 1992), pp. 70–87.

nervous indecision of key regional players in the first days of the crisis. Without Özal's swift and unequivocal decision to close the two oil pipelines traversing Turkey from Iraq, Saudi Arabia would have been more likely to have acted cautiously over the IPSA-2 line from Iraq to the Red Sea terminal of Yanbu. Such decisions were, in turn, crucial in the context of the Saudi leadership's decision whether or not to allow the US to use the Kingdom as a springboard for military action to eject Iraq from Kuwait, a decision which could not be demanded by Security Council resolutions.

In the end Özal was only able to carry the day at the start of the crisis. He was able to face down ministers and even generals in his pursuit of a bold strategy towards the crisis. But, as time proceeded, he was increasingly obliged to take into account domestic constraints, most notably that of public opinion, over the issue of the deployment of troops in the Gulf. Consequently, Turkey did not send even a symbolic contingent of soldiers to join the international coalition, even though, ironically, it did subsequently put itself at much greater risk by allowing the US to use the joint air bases in the south-east of the country to fly multiple sorties against targets in Iraq once the bombardment had begun on 17 January 1991.[7] The prejudices and past traumas of the Turkish public therefore prevented Turkey from taking full advantage of the political opportunities provided by the crisis,[8] even though few countries in the region actually took the security risks that Ankara did.

The Iraq-Kuwait crisis proved to be an important success for Turkey, especially in reaffirming the predominance of the geostrategic view of Turkey within policy circles in the United States.[9] Since

---

[7] The attack commenced on 17 January at 01.30, Iraq time.

[8] The fact that Turkish troops never became part of the 30-strong country contingent on the ground in Saudi Arabia meant that in an important symbolic sense Turkey was never fully part of the international coalition. Thus Ankara lost an opportunity to underline its geopolitical importance beyond a relative small group of policy insiders in the US and parts of Western Europe.

[9] Though the US traditionally prizes Turkey's geostrategic location, it should not be assumed that Europe was impervious to such arguments as a result of the important role played by Turkey in the Gulf crisis. For example the Turkey desk officer in the European Commission could write from Brussels in 1991 that the crisis 'has confirmed to doubters Turkey's *permanent and crucial* geostrategic role' [emphasis added] which 'has...won Turkey a new respect in the West and a

then a relatively small number of highly influential serving and former officials and commentators have exercised a disproportionate influence on Turkey's behalf on the inside of policy-making in Washington DC. Many of these, like Richard Perle and Paul Wolfowitz, are leading members of the US defence establishment. Partisans of Turkey have come from other agencies, notably Morton Abramowitz, Marc Grossman and Alan Makovsky from State and Paul Henze from the CIA.

For some members of the Turkish elite the importance of the Gulf crisis in solidifying US support at a moment of transition in the international system has been recognised. For the majority of Turks, however, there is a tendency to view the crisis with a disappointment bordering on brooding resentment. The Gulf crisis is viewed as a gamble by Özal which signally failed to pay off. There exists instead a fixation with the economic costs of the crisis, together with its perceived impact on the Kurdish issue. Turks now routinely believe their own rhetoric in estimating the direct economic loss from the crisis at $5 bn a year. The immediate experience after the crisis of an acute, though short-lived Kurdish refugee influx has further prejudiced the Turkish view. The Turkish interest in the creation of a safe haven in north-eastern Iraq, which allowed Iraqi Kurds to return to their land, has been eclipsed by a preoccupation with the haven as a political vacuum.

The United States in particular and much of the international community in general look back on the Gulf crisis as a test that was passed; a test which helped to reaffirm the principles of international order and convention in conduct among states. In that sense the forces of international order were fortunate that the first challenge to the post-Cold War era was both so flagrant and so clear-cut. Turkey, as a NATO member and US ally, would have been well served to view the crisis in a similar vein, albeit accepting some negative regional consequences. In fact the Turkish view has failed to rise beyond its narrow focus. Ankara has struggled to share this overall view of the impact of the crisis from a long term alliance perspective. Instead, the Turkish attitude has tended to be the more

better appreciation of her importance'. See Michael Cendrowicz, 'The European Community and Turkey. Looking Backwards, Looking Forwards' in Clement H. Dodd (ed.), *Turkish Foreign Policy, op. cit.,* p. 24.

parochial, geostrategic view of a state on the ground which has experienced a persistent and continuing material cost from the crisis, while also grappling with the centrifugal force of Kurdish ethno-nationalism. As such, the Gulf crisis was a missed opportunity to bind Turkey into a new normatively-based solidarity among allies that had been brought together in a Cold War context.

Turkey and 'The West'

The end of the Cold War and the fall of Communism raised a debate on what should be the future of Western institutions, and whether new architecture should be created in such areas as the security field. In the early to mid 1990s debate raged about the future of NATO,[10] not only about its future mission, but whether it should continue to exist at all. At the same time, the issue of the enlargement of the European Union, which had hitherto been rather eclipsed by the preoccupation with 1992 and the building of a single market, became of greater importance. Also within an EU context debates about the need for a common foreign and security policy began to take hold, with such ideas initially focusing on the future of the Western European Union (WEU).

In all of these big issues Turkey had a strong interest, and was to argue its corner robustly. Ankara's interests in many of these issue areas were synonymous with the status quo. This was actually disadvantageous for Ankara because, at a time when the West was excited by the challenge of change, Turkey still appeared to be wedded to the past. For example, while most of Western Europe was celebrating the reunification of the continent, in February 1990 the Turkish military was still preoccupied with the 3:1 conventional force superiority of the Warsaw Pact states over NATO, and the 'well advanced locations' of these forces.[11] Though past arrangements had served

---

[10] Paul Cornish, for example, shows that while the Euro-American relationship within NATO 'took its biggest public battering' in November 1994, by late 1996 the alliance was 'going from strength to strength'. See 'European security: the End of Architecture and the New NATO', *International Affairs*, vol. 72, no. 4, October 1996, p. 755.

[11] See the interview with the Turkish Chief of the General Staff, Necip Torumtay, in *Newspot*, 1 February 1990.

the West well, change was now seen as inevitable and hence desirable. Turkey's position, by contrast, appeared to be increasingly anachronistic.

Turkey was at its most conservative in relation to the future of NATO. For Ankara the organisation was a strong and effective multilateral institution, and one which more effectively than other paler organisations, such as the Council of Europe, locked Turkey into a Western orientation.[12] Together with the US and Britain, Turkey shared an Atlanticist conception of European security; Ankara wished to see NATO remain as a strong organisation with a stable membership. Turkey was therefore naturally chary of those who talked about finding a new role for NATO, especially if that search risked becoming increasingly synonymous with an imagined threat from Islam. It was downright dismissive of those who spoke openly about NATO's time as having passed, and therefore the proper course of action as being to wind up the organisation. Consequently, Turkey was cool towards the Franco-German idea of a European force,[13] and was to remain so through the 1990s,[14] instead believing that all other security institutions should enhance rather than eclipse or substitute for NATO. It was an irony not lost on senior NATO personnel that the NATO member furthest to the east was the one most concerned at preserving connections with the allies to the west.[15]

---

[12] The Turkish establishment's wholehearted commitment to NATO occasionally bursts through in bouts of rhetorical flourish, such as President Demirel's protestation that 'We will continue to be a strong and reliable member of NATO, which undoubtedly is the most successful Alliance that humankind has ever witnessed'. See 'Turkey and NATO at the Threshold of a New Century' in *Perceptions, Journal of International Affairs*, vol. IV, no. 1, March-May 1999, p. 12.

[13] The early to mid 1990s period was punctuated by Franco-German statements on the establishment of some variant of this. The most celebrated examples include: the October 1991 proposal to establish a Eurocorps; the May 1992 La Rochelle summit, at which Chancellor Kohl and President Mitterrand approved the further development of the idea; the March 1996 Freiburg meeting at which both states aired the idea of the creation of a 'European army'.

[14] For a later example, see the speech by Deputy Chief of Staff Çevik Bir to the conference of the New Atlantic Initiative in Istanbul in early May 1998, when he warned against the undermining of NATO and Transatlantic relations by promoting the European Security and Defence Identity.

[15] See, for example, Dr John Barrett, head of the policy planning and speech-writing section at NATO, who observed that 'Turkey's voice is always the first

The London-Washington view of the future of NATO eventually carried the day. The organisation was retained, and its utility in anchoring an American presence in Europe and binding an enduring US interest in European security remained as the orthodox view. Moreover, the emergence of instability and conflict in the Balkans also emphasised the need for a strong security organisation and the wisdom of continuing Euro-US co-operation at the operational level. Hence the experience of Bosnia, where NATO was eventually used as the institution of military intervention, built upon the salutary lesson of the 1990–1 Gulf crisis. There was, in addition, among British and American security experts in particular, a clear sense that the continued presence of a strong NATO was good for future relations with Turkey. NATO was regarded as an institutional anchor which kept Turkey strategically part of the West; consolidated Turkey's Europeanness; and helped to manage the volatile area of relations between Greece and Turkey,[16] 'those perennial antagonists', as Joseph Nye has called them.[17]

However, even in the area of the future of NATO, Turkey's aims were only partially fulfilled. There were two key areas where Ankara was left dissatisfied and perplexed at the impact of systemic change on the alliance. The first was over the issue of arms control vis-à-vis the newly emerging state of Russia; the second was in the area of NATO enlargement.

THE CFE TREATY

The arms control debate concentrated on the issue of the Conventional Forces in Europe (CFE) agreement,[18] the most comprehensive treaty in European history ever to address the issue, which was signed in Paris on 19 November 1990. However, by the time of its

---

one to be heard about the importance of maintaining that [transatlantic link collective defense] connection'. John Barrett, 'Current Political Agenda of the Atlantic Alliance and Turkey' in Mustafa Aydın (ed.), *Turkey at the Threshold of the 21st Century* (International Relations Foundation, Ankara, 1998), p. 35.

[16] Ditchley Park conference of American and British experts, 7 May 1993.

[17] Joseph S. Nye, 'The US and Europe: Continental Drift?', in *International Affairs*, vol. 76, no. 1, January 2000, p. 54.

[18] For an extremely useful precise of the main terms of the treaty, as well as a discussion of its impact and achievements, see Jonathan Dean and Randall Watson Forsberg in 'CFE and Beyond, The Future of Conventional Arms Control', *International Security*, vol. 17, no. 1, summer 1992.

ratification some two years later, it had been overtaken by fast changing circumstances on the ground, notably the dissolution of the Soviet Union. The emergence of secessionist movements in the Caucasus, together with civil war and inter-state tensions within and among the new states in the Transcaucasus, meant that by 1993 Moscow was arguing for a revision of the treaty to allow it to deploy greater levels of tanks, artillery pieces and military aircraft on its southern borders.[19] For example, Russia argued that in the new circumstances of East-West peace and internal instability it was no longer appropriate for Russia to be limited to 250 tanks on its, 1,000-kilometre-long north Caucasus border.[20]

The Turkish reaction to Russia's proposal to revise the treaty was one of acute concern. For Ankara, the CFE represented an important formal guarantee of the limited military presence of Russia in the proximity of its borders. The initial NATO reaction to the Russian special pleading was that it was 'unacceptable'. However, this reflected more an aversion to the practical problems of reopening negotiations on complex and far-reaching treaties than a more urgent concern at the immediate and practical security implications of such a move, which were the cause for Turkish concern.[21] This feature of an earnest and anxious Turkey working within a NATO milieu where concern was rather more notional was to be a recurring theme of the CFE debate.[22]

The issue of the CFE treaty remained as a thorny issue in bilateral relations between Turkey and Russia from the moment President Yeltsin formally raised the issue of amending the CFE in September 1993,[23] through to the end of 1996. Bilateral ties had sufficient ballast,

---

[19] For a contextualisation of the CFE treaty with respect to NATO and the former Soviet south see Robin Bhatty and Rachel Bronson, 'NATO's Mixed Signals in the Caucasus and Central Asia', *Survival*, vol. 42, no. 3, autumn 2000.

[20] Interview with Russian ambassador to Turkey, Albert Chernishev, in *Turkish Daily News*, 17 March 1994.

[21] *Turkish Daily News*, 28 September 1993.

[22] See, for example, *Turkish Probe* no. 126, 28 April 1995.

[23] The first indication of Russian dissatisfaction with the treaty came in March 1993. However, it was President Yeltsin's letter to the heads of state of the contracting parties on 17 September 1993, outlining reasons for lifting the flank ceilings, and a formal Russian proposal to suspend Article V eleven days later that marked the start of Moscow's campaign to revise the treaty. See Richard A. Falkenrath, 'The CFE Flank Dispute, Waiting in the Wings', *International Security*, vol. 19, no. 4, spring 1995, pp. 128–9.

notably the lucrative gas-driven trade, for relations not to become an exclusive function of the issue, nor to decline precipitously as a result of it. Furthermore, Turkey was concerned lest its strenuous objections to Moscow's attempted revisions had a deleterious effect on its own wider relations with NATO.

Nevertheless, attempts to try to forge an acceptable accommodation proved to be difficult. Turkey objected to unilateral Russian attempts in the spring of 1995, led by Defence Minister Pavel Grachev, either to ignore the CFE requirements until the Chechen conflict was over or to take over some of the hardware quota allocated to Georgia under the treaty. A compromise proposal from Moscow to give additional security guarantees to Turkey in exchange for Ankara's agreement for the amendment of the CFE was rejected by the Turks in April 1995. Though apparently inflexible, the Turkish position was hardly surprising as it came just after Russia's use of force in Chechnya, and at a time when Moscow's defence policy was being determined by hard-liners. With Moscow suffering from periodic bouts of political turmoil, Ankara could be forgiven for not valuing its security guarantees very highly. Bilateral relations over the CFE issue appeared to hit their lowest point in May 1995, when Turkey threatened to retaliate should Russia insist on ignoring the treaty's provisions. Ankara reiterated this warning in November more explicitly when it publicly contemplated increasing the military presence of the Third Army in eastern Anatolia in excess of the treaty ceiling.

While Turkish officials became increasingly resentful at Russia's *de facto* ignoring of the treaty's provision on the southern flank, the rest of NATO looked more positively at what was seen as 'Russia's 90 per cent compliance'. This led some Turkish officials to regard the CFE as 'lame'. From September 1995 onwards Turkey came under 'friendly pressure' to agree to a compromise formula. By the end of November Turkey had come to accept the inevitable. Ankara abandoned its view of the treaty as sacrosanct, instead opening the door to compromise by saying that it would not veto a good proposal just because this would entail changes to the treaty. While Turkey remained deeply displeased with Russia's violations, it did not want to harm its standing in NATO by being regarded as a 'spoiler'.[24] In May 1996 NATO countries formally agreed to allow Russia to

[24] *Turkish Daily News,* 29 November 1995.

increase its force levels, and to give Moscow until 1999 to meet these revised objectives.

Turkey's sense of a compromise made at its own expense, however, continued to simmer on. In February 1998 Turkey's second most senior military man, General Çevik Bir, publicly reflected that resentment when he stated that giving 'a green light' to 'prior adversaries' to deploy more forces in the Caucasus means that 'the risks for Turkey are compounded and the newly independent states [of the former Soviet Union] are left under political and military pressure'.[25] In spite of such misgivings, Ankara did not attempt to abandon the compromise. Subsequently the CFE treaty was formally revised without fuss in November 1999. That Turkey had long since become reconciled to the inevitable was seen in the fact that the signing ceremony actually took place on its own territory, during the Istanbul summit of the OSCE.[26]

NATO ENLARGEMENT

The most profound and welcome outcome from the events of 1989 was the reunification of Europe in the name of peace and democracy. Once regime change had fully taken place in such states as Poland, Czechoslovakia and Hungary, from February 1991 known as the Visegrad states, a debate began as to what would be the proper relationship between such countries and the main institutions of the continent, namely NATO and the EU. The Visegrad countries had a clear idea of their own aims. They wanted full membership of NATO in order to extend the alliance principle of common defence eastwards, as an insurance policy against a future resurgence of Russian power. Furthermore, they wanted full membership of the EU in order to raise their levels of prosperity and hence underpin their newly installed democratic systems.

For Turkey the speed and direction of such events elicited shock and increasingly a sense of injustice. With the governments and, perhaps more importantly, the peoples of Western Europe well disposed to the newly liberated states of Eastern Europe, a strong

---

[25] Shortened version of a speech by General Bir to the National Defense University, Washington, DC, on 24 November 1997, published as 'Turkey's Role in the New World Order', *Strategic Forum*, no. 135, February 1998.

[26] For further details on the CFE revision at the summit, see *Briefing*, no. 1269, 22 November 1999.

sentiment began to gather pace that it was right and appropriate for the Visegrad states to join the EU. Suddenly Turkey was faced with the deeply disturbing prospect that states which until recently had been members of a rival and expansionist security organisation, the Warsaw Pact, and which had been ideologically committed to the destruction of Western institutions had overtaken it in the queue for full accession. Moreover, Turkey also faced the prospect that its own decade-old commitment to economic liberalisation, which had placed it far ahead of the economies which had just thrown off the dead hand of centralised state planning, apparently counted for little within the EU.

Turkey's view of NATO enlargement was different to its perspective on the EU. Turkey was already a member of NATO, and was therefore in a less competitive position with the old Eastern European states. Indeed, Turkey was to some extent in a position to exploit the situation to its own advantage. The accession of states in eastern Europe would help to fashion NATO's future threat perceptions, which, in view of the experiences of the old Eastern bloc states, would inevitably be oriented towards the fear of a resurgent Russia. NATO enlargement eastwards would in any case render Russia more proximate to the easternmost states of the alliance, again helping to change the collective consciousness within the organisation. The rise to prominence of the extremist nationalist leader, Vladimir Zhirinovsky, had in any case served to underline the volatility and potential for extremism in Russian domestic politics.[27] Finally, an eastward enlargement that included the likes of Bulgaria and Romania would physically join the central area of the organisation with the southern flank, and hence would counteract the cognitive and spatial marginalisation of Turkey, which had long existed during the Cold War.[28]

Once it had made its calculations, Turkey's view on enlargement had by 1993 crystallised. Ankara's position was that it was not against enlargement in principle, but it feared that a rapid or expansive

---

[27] By the end of 1993 it had also achieved a directly positive impact on Turkey's relations with other Western countries, notably, according to Mehmet Ali Birand, the US and Germany. See *Sabah*, 3 January 1994.

[28] Defence Minister Mehmet Gölhan argued that Bulgaria, Romania and even Albania should be among the first countries to be invited to join NATO. See *Turkish Daily News*, 29 November 1994.

increase in membership might weaken the organisation. Turkey certainly accepted the 'Partnership for Peace' (PfP) programme,[29] which was adopted at the January 1994 Brussels summit, and which embraced most European states. This was a loose framework within which individual states would establish political relationships with NATO, the nature of which would depend on the starting point and aspirations of the states concerned. Though it fell short of membership and of security guarantees, it did hold out the possibility of eventual membership in the distant future as a result of an 'evolutionary process'.

Turkey was confronted with a new situation, as were the rest of NATO's constituent countries, when the Clinton administration unilaterally decided that it wanted to extend full membership of the organisation to some of the former Communist states. Together with the rest of the NATO membership, Ankara was unable and indeed unwilling to be seen to be opposing US policy. Equally, Turkey was ambivalent about full membership for some of the old Eastern European states, especially with the PfP programme now in place. It expressed itself as being 'guarded' in response to President Clinton's wish that the first round of NATO expansion be complete by 1999.[30] Finding itself in such a position, Turkey was increasingly tempted to flirt with the possibility of using its veto power as a member of NATO against future enlargement as a means to further its own, more general foreign policy interests.

One way in which Turkey sought to use the issue of NATO enlargement was ironically in her relations with Russia. Eager to find ways of asserting complementarity rather than competition with its volatile northern neighbour, Turkey presented an empathetic stance towards Russia. Through the mid 1990s Turkish officials underlined the fact that NATO should not once again come to be considered as an alliance against Russia, the implication being that an eastward enlargement would do just that. On some occasions, the Turkish approach to the issue was altogether more explicit. Thus, for example, during her December 1996 visit to Moscow, Turkish foreign minister Tansu Çiller stated that NATO expansion could not proceed without Turkey. In linking this somewhat crudely with

---

[29] Evidence for this includes the establishment of a PfP training centre in Ankara, which was commissioned in June 1998.

[30] *Turkish Daily News*, 24 October 1996.

Russia's decision to sell S-300 missiles to Cyprus, Mrs Çiller appeared to be using the enlargement issue as foreign policy leverage.

Of more profound importance has been the temptation for Turkey to use the issue of NATO enlargement as leverage in support of its own aspirations for EU membership. As early as 1994 some Turkish foreign policy experts were bemoaning the fact that Turkey had not enjoyed more of a *quid pro quo* from NATO or the United States over eastern enlargement.[31] By 1995 Turkish diplomats had begun to link the issues, though in a more subtle and indirect fashion. Speaking on the occasion of the 46th anniversary of the establishment of NATO, the Foreign Ministry under-secretary Özdem Sanberk stated that the goal was the spread of stability, and nothing should be done that contravened this goal. Thus, he said, any offer of full integration of the former Warsaw Pact states into Europe through EU and NATO membership should not exceed that which was on offer to Turkey.[32]

It was, however, during the first half of 1997, in the approach to the Madrid summit at which a decision on the states to be included in the enlargement would be taken, that speculation about a possible Turkish veto became most intense. The month of February 1997 arguably saw the most sustained and explicit threats expressed of a veto on NATO enlargement in the absence of a reciprocal gesture towards Turkey's EU membership. A dalliance with such a linkage even emanated from the Foreign Ministry.[33] The timing was also important because of the domestic political context in which this particular issue was being played out. The Islamist-led coalition of the Refah or Welfare Party (RP) and the Doğru Yol Partisi or True Path Party (DYP) was being subjected to increasing pressure from the Turkish military from mid January onwards. It may have been the case that Premier Erbakan and his deputy, Mrs Çiller, chose to become increasingly strident in their linkage of EU and NATO enlargement because they felt that this was both a populist issue and one which could potentially unite Islamists and Kemalists alike. Consequently, both argued this position in public during the visit of the NATO Secretary-General, Javier Solana, to Turkey on 5 February.

---

[31] For example, Marmara University international relations expert and *Yeni Yüzyil* columnist Mensur Akgün. Interview with author 21 January 1995.

[32] *Turkish Daily News*, 5 April 1995.

[33] *Cumhuriyet*, cited in the *Turkish Press Review*, 4 February 1997.

Whatever the calculations of the government, and the state of Turkish foreign policy, they did not prevent the military from using the National Security Council (NSC) meeting of 28 February to submit an ultimatum on domestic policy which, some three and half months later, was to bring down the coalition.

In spite of more than two years' worth of hints and innuendo, there was always a sense that Turkey was not entirely serious about its threat to veto NATO expansion. As in the case of the CFE, Turkey always seemed to draw back from a position that would jeopardise its entire relationship with the organisation. Even the normally brazen Mrs Çiller seemed to lose her nerve at a Brussels meeting of NATO foreign ministers in February, when she merely stated that the expansion of NATO and EU membership should be 'a parallel process'.[34] This in turn prompted her peers among the other NATO members to conclude that Turkey would not dare to use the veto, and the meeting to concentrate on the more substantive question of Russian opposition to NATO expansion. If confirmation of the real Turkish position was required, it came in May, with President Demirel's state visit to Warsaw. Reluctant to keep up the ambivalence at the expense of bilateral relations, Demirel commenced his trip by reassuring his hosts that Turkey would not block Poland's accession to NATO.[35]

Consequently, it was with little talk of a veto that the Madrid summit in July approved the accession of the Czech Republic, Hungary and Poland as the first wave of new states. Ankara confined its activities in the approach to the meeting to operational matters, notably the creation of a new command structure, and its perennial agenda issue of terrorism. Turkey set aside its lingering misgivings on enlargement belatedly to back France's and Italy's advocacy of the membership credentials of Romania,[36] only to see the bid fail in the face of implacable American opposition.[37] Even

---

[34] *Turkish Probe*, no. 216, 21 February 1997.

[35] *Turkish Probe*, no. 227, 16 May 1997.

[36] For a pithy and succinct discussion of the issue of Romania's inclusion in the enlargement, see Jonathan Eyal, 'NATO'S Enlargement: Anatomy of a Decision', *International Affairs*, vol. 73, no. 4, October 1997, pp. 707–10.

[37] For a detailed discussion of the policy issues surrounding NATO enlargement, with particular emphasis on a southern expansion, see Karl-Heinz Kamp, 'NATO Entrapped: Debating the Next Enlargement Round', *Survival*, vol. 40 no. 3, autumn 1998.

this effort showed all the signs of going through the motions, some commentators even going so far as to say that enlargement beyond the Visegrad group had been a non-starter as early as 1995.[38]

   Both President Demirel and the newly installed foreign minister İsmail Cem attended the Madrid summit, at which the US unveiled a latest attempt to forge a rapprochement in Graeco-Turkish relations.[39] In the end the Americans had played Turkey well. Concern about NATO enlargement was forgotten as the Turkish delegation latched on to the foreign policy comfort blanket of relations with Greece.

Norms and order

The 1980s saw the beginnings of a new norms-based approach to international affairs, especially in Europe and the developed world. These essentially liberal norms were of course ones that had been important even before the end of the Cold War. Turkey, for example, had been heavily criticised in Europe for the September 1980 military intervention, and the armed forces for their conduct at home over the following two and a half years. Nevertheless, the end of the 1980s can be said to represent the beginning of a new era. There were three developments which helped to crystallise this value change, related to three distinct domains, the ideological, the organisational and the systemic. All three were related to the sweeping changes which had taken place on the continent of Europe. And all three left Turkey, to varying degrees, untouched.

   The ideological change related to the emergence of a hegemony of liberal values, with their emphasis, in the political domain, on democracy, pluralism, human rights and civil society. The state was regarded with greater suspicion than had hitherto been the case. Rigid, over-arching state ideologies were regarded with distaste. The US elevated the promotion of democratisation as a core aim of its foreign policy. Changes at the organisational level reflected and in turn complemented this ideological change. There was an increase in the level of activity in international civil society. The notion that

[38] Michael McGwire, 'NATO Expansion: a Policy Error of Historic Importance', *Review of International Studies*, vol. 24, no. 1, January 1998, p. 24.
[39] *Turkish Probe* no. 235, 11 July 1997.

international affairs should not be reduced to interaction among states received a powerful boost. The systemic contribution to the new norms-based approach was predicated on the collapse of global bipolarity. In the absence of two rival blocs cancelling one another out, at least formally at the UN Security Council, there was a greater sense of empowerment. Ideas and values which were rapidly coming to the fore could at last find operational expression through the machinery of international institutions.

Turkey just did not connect with the spirit of these normative changes. This was partly because, as has already been seen, Turkey had no share in helping to bring about the liberal revolutions in Eastern Europe. Not only did Turkey have no stake in them but the newly emerging liberal states of middle Europe represented a threat to Turkey's interests, especially in its aspirations to EU membership.

Just as importantly, the domestic landscape inside the country had no resonance with these changes. Turkey was a country where the state was big, proud and muscular, while society was weak, fragmented and subordinate. Ordinary Turks instinctively deferred to the *memur*, or state official. There was no strong tradition of a robust and independent civil society. Paradoxically, the best developed parts of civil society were those associations which acted as a civil complement to the Kemalist state. Civil society was just as likely to applaud military intervention in domestic politics as it was to protest against it, the elites of state and society often sharing vested interests based on ideology and economic privilege. Turkish participation in international civil society, by contrast, was in its infancy. This character of state-society relations was replicated at the level of governance, where the state was invariably stronger than government.

Perhaps the changes in Eastern Europe came too soon for Turkish political culture. It was certainly not the case that in Turkey things were immutable and fossilised. Indeed, in the late 1980s there was some expectation that a variety of factors would help to redress this imbalance in favour of society over state. Özal's reorientation of the economy towards export markets and international competition and Özal's re-civilianisation of domestic politics from 1983 onwards, together with the successful challenge of the private sector to the state's monopoly of the broadcast media in 1989, all offered the possibility of a diminishing profile for the state, relative to a society that was beginning to acquire economic power and access to information unmediated by the state.

It may still be the case that in the long run the cognitive subservience of Turkish civil society to the state will diminish. By the early 1990s, however, rather than being transformed by liberal, exogenous factors, Turkey was retreating from such values as a process of de-democratisation began to take hold. This de-democratisation would culminate with the indirect military intervention of 1997 to remove the RP-DYP coalition government. In retrospect, the high point of Özal's liberalisation of politics arguably came in 1991, when there was a widespread, though ultimately erroneous, expectation that the military would be brought under the political control of the Defence Ministry.[40]

The reason why Turkey was swimming against the globalist tide lay almost exclusively in domestic political factors, but ones which had themselves been affected by the wider environment. In a broader context of pluralism, Turkish society had begun to discover its other identities. These were primarily ethnic and religious identities, based on the myriad influences accumulated in the territory which became Turkey over many decades up to the 1920s. These rediscovered identities were a potential threat to the official twin identities which had been rigidly laid down by the Kemalist state, namely secularism and Turkish nationalism.

These pluralistic developments would have led to illiberal counter-moves eventually, as the demise of the RP-DYP government proves. That such moves began even during the honeymoon period after the reunification of Europe was evidence of a more tangible and immediate threat, that which was posed by Kurdish ethno-nationalism, which, in the form of the PKK-led insurgency, was by 1989 beginning to threaten the stability if not the integrity of the Turkish state. In its most benign form, Turkey's Kurdish challenge was partly about trying to gain the liberal benefits that had recently accrued in Eastern Europe, such as the right to publish, broadcast and teach in Kurdish—the right in a pluralist society to pronounce

---

[40] For a contemporary discussion of civil-military relations see Philip Robins, 'La Turquie à l'heure des revisions stratégiques' in Bassma Kodmani-Darwish and May Chartouni-Dubarry (eds), *Perceptions de sécurité et stratégies nationales au Moyen-Orient* (Ifri/Masson, Paris, 1994).

oneself as being different. At its most uncompromising, however, Kurdish ethno-nationalism, as increasingly epitomised by the authoritarian structures and methods of the PKK, had overtones of its despised equivalent in Turkey. It was about the imposition of a strong state and a rigid ideology, albeit an alternative and competitive one, on a passive and quiescent population.

At the level of foreign relations, the appearance of Turkey being increasingly out of step as far as the new norms of the age were concerned definitely imposed a cost. This took the form of a growing and disapproving interest in Turkish domestic affairs on the part of foreign actors and an increasing willingness to criticise the performance of the Turkish state on a whole series of issues. These extended from specific issues, such as the widespread use of torture in Turkish police stations and prisons, through general concern about human rights, to a more mixed set of concerns, straddling human, political and other rights, as in the case of the Kurds. Thus, for example, in December 1992 the Council of Europe published a report on torture in Turkey which proved to be the most critical report on a member state ever issued by the Council.[41]

At a state to state level, however, these costs were to some extent mitigated or balanced, especially on the part of larger states with a complex set of interactions with Turkey, notably those encompassing the strategic and commercial.[42] Turkey was then partially successful in staving off criticism resulting from the increasing disparity between its actions and the norms of the age. Nevertheless, it would be wrong to say that these issues were cost free, even where Turkey's relations with its closest friends were concerned. In the corridors of power in the West there was no-one willing to defend Turkey's policy towards the Kurds. Even in the US, such geostrategic hawks and undoubted Turcophiles as Richard Perle shrank from a defence of Turkish policy.

It is at the level of the non-state actor, however, that Turkey has paid a real, deep and enduring cost as a result of the growing

[41] *The Guardian*, 22 December 1992.

[42] For a discussion of the impact of the Kurdish issue on relations between Turkey and a number of EU member states, small as well as large, see Philip Robins, 'More Apparent Than Real? The Impact of the Kurdish Issue on Euro-Turkish Relations' in Robert Olson (ed.), *The Kurdish Nationalist Movement in the 1990s* (University Press of Kentucky, Lexington, 1996).

normative gap. Predictably enough this has been experienced most in relation to European non-governmental organisations. However, it is not just NGOs which have become more critical of and less patient with Turkey. Transnational political structures such as the European Parliament (EP) have taken an increasing interest in Turkey, especially as the EP has developed a human rights niche for itself within the wider EU division of labour. When the proposal for the establishment of a Customs Union between the EU and Turkey was brought to the EP in 1995 the thrust of the debate centred on whether a CU would be a positive or a negative factor in bringing about progress in Turkey on a basket of issues under the heading of democracy and human rights. After the CU was approved, a Surveillance Group was established to monitor whether Turkey was carrying out the undertakings given. The group visits Turkey every nine months, and has included in its membership a leader of the European Socialists, Pauline Green. The general conclusion of the group is that Ankara has not implemented promises made. In the words of Pauline Green, referring to the ineffectiveness of the CU in bringing about human rights reform, 'we feel as if we have been conned'.[43]

The costs imposed on Turkey by such actors as NGOs and the EP are, by the nature of the organisations concerned, less tangible than those imposed by states. It would, however, be misleading to suppose that the generally critical view of Turkey of these actors somehow does not count. This has tended to be the view of Turks towards both leading NGOs, like Amnesty International (AI), and the EP. For instance, the Ministry of Foreign Affairs in Ankara has often simply dismissed the reports of AI by saying that the organisation has long since lost its credibility.[44] Yet, as the 1990s have unfolded, it is precisely such actors that have rapidly increased their influence and impact. The EP has acquired the right to approve EU budgets and external treaties, thereby giving it enormous potential leverage, especially in the area of external relations.[45] The role of

[43] *Turkish Daily News*, 31 March 1997.

[44] See, for example, the response of the ministry to an AI report on the torture of political and criminal suspects. *Turkish Daily News*, 8 July 1995.

[45] For example, in order for the notorious Fourth Financial Protocol with Turkey to be adopted it would have been necessary to marshal 260 votes in the 518-

the EP scaled new heights in March 1999, when it succeeded in precipitating the resignation of the President of the European Commission, Jacques Santer, and the eighteen Commissioners.

It is precisely such NGOs as Amnesty International that have emerged as the benchmark of conscience within the EU. The views and criticisms of AI have in turn become influential in helping to mould elite opinion in Britain and more widely in Europe towards Turkey. Such opinion is often important when issues relating to Turkey arrive at critical policy junctures. It is the growing normative gap—more than, say, diversity in culture and religion—that has helped to instil scepticism on the part of large numbers of decision-makers and opinion formers in Europe towards Turkey.

HUMAN RIGHTS

Of all the issues which have contributed to the sense of an expanding normative gap to Turkey's disadvantage, that of human rights has been the most sustained and visible. Indeed, for the last two decades Turkey has been subject to a veritable mantra of criticism for widespread and officially inspired human rights abuses. The authority and, most of all, the repetitive nature of this chorus of criticism have helped to make the state of Turkey synonymous with the notion of human rights abuses.

Though the criticism of Turkey has been widespread and strong over an extended period, this does not mean that the nature or the basis of such criticism has been the same. One can divide the past 20 years into roughly four phases consisting of two periods marked by intensive human rights abuses, both of which were followed by two periods when human rights abuses, though serious, were not appalling.

The first period of intensive abuses, 'a hellish period' as one activist has described it, coincided with the start of the period of military rule in September 1980 and ran through to the first post-coup general election in May 1983, and the early tentative months of the re-civilianisation of politics. The second period of intensive abuses began with the emergence of the 'deep state' as a powerful and

---

strong European Parliament, in addition to the more publicised unanimity at the Council of Ministers. Interview with European Commission Turkey desk officer Michael Cendrowicz, 13 March 1991.

largely unaccountable force within Turkish politics and the beginning of extra-judicial murders in the summer of 1991. This phase was largely a function of the Kurdish insurgency. The period continued through to the Susurluk affair of November 1996, when the scrutiny of the state increased and those who were part of the 'deep state' could no longer act with impunity.

Of course, it can be argued that both of these high intensity phases were associated with extremely unusual and hence atypical phases in Turkish politics. Neither the period of direct military rule nor that of the Kurdish insurgency can be considered to be the political norm. But what has been particularly demoralising for the human rights community is that the periods that have followed, between 1985 and 1991 and since 1996,[46] have nevertheless been characterised by widespread and serious problems, periods of what one might call the routinisation of human rights abuses.

Criticism of Turkey during the period of the military takeover was predictable enough. It concentrated on three areas. First, the direct intervention of the military and the senior generals' subsequent refusal to return swiftly to the barracks once the street violence of the day had been brought to an end. Second, the suppression of a broad range of civil liberties and rights, from the clampdown on political parties through the suppression of trade unions to the close state supervision of the universities. Third, the use of certain methods to restore order and punish the enemies of the state, most notably the death penalty. AI estimated that 50 executions took place between the coup and 25 October 1984, the date of the most recent execution in Turkey.

Those who campaigned for liberal reform in Turkey during the period between 1985 and 1991 found it to be a frustrating exercise. The cause of reform was caught between the illiberal legacy of the previous period, with its state security courts, military judges and restrictive penal code, and the social and political culture of the country for which physical abuse was very much part of the experiential milieu. In spite of the recivilianisation of government from 1983 onwards there was never much optimism for the immediate future

---

[46] The most recent AI report on Turkey illustrated this point with its title-cum-slogan of 'An End to Torture and Impunity is Overdue!', published 8 November 2001.

at AI. In general, this is seen as a 'stale period', when little really changed. It is no coincidence that AI's first campaign on Turkey came in 1988.

DEATHS IN CUSTODY

1979	4
1980	18
1981	16
1982	13
1983	10
1984	8
1985	9

Source: Ministry of the Interior[47]

The strategy of the government during this period seemed to be to sign up to the formalities of reform and hope that this would assuage international liberal opinion. Invariably, such gestures back-fired, simply creating an even greater gulf between the provisions which Turkey had embraced and the actual experiences on the ground. A good illustration of this, and an enduring problem for the Özal government during this period, was the issue of torture. In January 1988 the Turkish government signed the Council of Europe Convention on the Prevention of Torture, in response to a stinging publication by the Helsinki Watch Group, which maintained that torture was routinely used in police stations. In August 1988 Ankara willingly signed up to the UN convention against torture, only to have more than 20 reports of torture lodged against it within two months of the convention's adoption.[48] The prevalence of torture in Turkey was glimpsed at in a report published in November 1990 and based on interviews with 200 non-political prisoners across the country: while 8% said that they had experienced torture in Turkey's

[47] Reprinted from *Turkey: Brutal and Systematic Abuse of Human Rights* (Amnesty International, London, 1989), p. 42. The report states that: 'It is not possible…to give an exact figure for deaths in custody caused by torture. The official figures are contradictory and unreliable…' It therefore seems safe to assume that while significant in themselves, these figures are under-estimates, especially for the period relating to military rule.

[48] *Turkey Briefing*, November 1988.

jails, a massive 73% reported experiences of beatings and other forms of abuse when in police custody.[49]

Nevertheless, opinions differed about the degree to which torture was institutionalised in Turkey during this time. AI considered torture to be 'widespread and systematically used',[50] claiming that it had 'not observed any fundamental change in the widespread and systematic use of torture' in over five years of civilian rule.[51] By contrast, writing about the same time, the US State Department report on human rights took a notably milder tone, exonerating Turkey of systematic torture, though stating that the practice continued, especially in the first few days of detention. Inevitably, there was NGO suspicion that the US government was soft-pedalling its criticism for wider strategic reasons.[52]

The pressure for reform in Turkey made the country the focus of much international attention. Liberal European institutions were seized of the matter of Turkey's human rights record. For example, after the arrest of two of the country's Communist leaders, Haydar Kutlu and Nihat Sargın, a large group of international observers attended the hearings, in spite of the frequent postponements; the president of the European Parliament, Lord Plumb, campaigned in favour of a fair trial. For many observers, human rights in Turkey was a barometer of the larger political rehabilitation of the country. In the words of one Euro MP at the time, Luc Beyer de Ryke: 'As long as trials such as this [Kutlu & Sargın] continue it is impossible to think that democracy in Turkey is improving.'[53]

That is not to say that real improvements were not also taking place during this phase. The Turkish government accepted the competence of the European Commission for Human Rights in January 1987; in September 1989 it recognised the jurisdiction of the European Court of Human Rights, the last Council of Europe

---

[49] Contemporary Research Centre survey cited in *Turkey Briefing*, December 1990.

[50] Amnesty International, *Continuing Violations of Human Rights in Turkey*, London, June 1987.

[51] Amnesty International, *Turkey: Brutal and Systematic Abuse of Human Rights*, London, January 1989.

[52] See the Bar of the City of New York, 'Torture in Turkey', for a criticism of the State Department and the American Embassy in Ankara over this matter. Report cited in *Turkey Briefing*, January 1990.

[53] *Turkey Briefing*, September 1988.

member so to do. In both cases, however, the Turkish authorities insisted on limiting the recourse of potential complainants. After two previous refusals, a local NGO, the Human Rights Association, was given permission to operate in June 1987. The controversial Articles 141, 142 and 163 of the Penal Code, which failed to distinguish between acts of violence and of thought and which banned activities deemed permissible across the states of the Council of Europe, were repealed in 1991, but only to be replaced by an equally restrictive Anti-Terror Law.[54] In general, then, improvements during this period tended to be spasmodic and faltering. As Jeri Laber of the US Helsinki Watch Committee stated in mid 1987, improvements were not continuous, but a question of two steps forward, one step back.[55]

As the normative changes in Europe swiftly made human rights abuses such as torture and the curtailment of press freedoms much more unacceptable than had previously been the case, Turkey was moving decisively from a period of difficulty in human rights into one of a human rights catastrophe. The situation was not merely worsening relatively, but absolutely too. The reason for this was the rapid deterioration in the situation in south-east Turkey, with the growing intensity of the PKK-led insurgency. By 1991 the Turkish state was suffering from high casualties and the punitive economic cost of the insurgency, while its authority over much of the south-east was becoming increasingly tenuous. Furthermore, the political vacuum which had existed in northern Iraq since the end of the Gulf war in February 1991 provided the perfect springboard for operations by the PKK.

Faced by an increasingly dire situation, the Turkish state's response was to exempt the south-east from many of the freedoms in place elsewhere in the country, through the creation of an emergency rule super-governorate covering 10 provinces. In tandem, it set about using any means at its disposal to combat the PKK. Often this involved the use of shadowy proxy groups, acting in alliance with the state. The actions of this opaque and unaccountable 'deep state' or 'national security state' were to be the focus of human rights

---

[54] See Helsinki Watch, *Turkey: New Restrictive Anti-Terror Law*, New York, June 1991.
[55] *Turkey Briefing*, July 1987.

advocacy through much of the 1990s. The methods of the deep state involved the use of force, physical and psychological intimidation, extra-judicial killings, and the creation of a *cordon sanitaire* through the razing of villages and the displacement of rural populations. In the words of the human rights campaigner Jonathan Sugden, the Turkish state was heavy-handed in its conduct of human rights up to 1991; after 1991, however, it went from being Turkish to South American in the scale and intensity of the abuses.

DEATHS 'IN DETENTION AND PRISONS'

1990	12
1991	21
1992	17/18
1993	29/40
1994	34/53
1995	37
1996	72
1997	52
1998	43

Source: Human Rights Foundation of Turkey[56]

In focusing increasingly on the situation in the south-east of the country, issues of human rights inevitably became blurred with the issue of Kurdish rights. To some extent this was difficult to avoid because it was in the south-east that the greatest concentration of abuses was being felt. However, some human rights campaigners assert that it was the deliberate policy of the Turkish state to confuse the two, as a way of creating ambivalence towards the issue of human rights among the Turkish population.[57] Either way, from a Turkish state or nationalist point of view it could then be argued that foreign organisations were less concerned with abstract rights and more concerned to aid the forces of Kurdish ethno-nationalism. This in turn translated into the perception of an unacceptable and sinister

[56] There appears to be a discrepancy between some of the figures published by the HRFT. Hence the figures on the left are from the *1996 Turkey Human Rights Report* (HRFT, Ankara, 1998), p. 322; the figures on the right are from the *Human Rights Situation in Turkey—Current Trends* (HRFT, Ankara, undated, received electronically 15 November 2000).
[57] Interview with Heidi Wedel, AI desk officer for Turkey, 13 May 1999.

interference in domestic affairs at a time of an existential struggle against the PKK. Consequently, relations between Turkey and the human rights community, which had never been exactly cordial, deteriorated precipitously. Once again, it was the standing of the state of Turkey in a liberal Europe where human rights and other liberal values were becoming increasingly prized that was a casualty of this period.

A good illustration of this was the growing number of organisations that initiated investigations into human rights abuses in Turkey and eventually added their voices of condemnation. At the beginning of the 1990s, it was mostly the small handful of NGOs which had been most active in the late 1980s that exposed the increased activities of the deep state. This included AI, with its increasingly vigorous 'Urgent Action' campaign that highlighted the plight of leading individuals. It also notably included the New York-based Helsinki Watch (soon to be renamed Human Rights Watch), and, at the supranational level, the activities of the various organs of the Council of Europe. By 1994, this small number had grown rapidly to include such organisations as: Article 19, the Bar Human Rights Committee, the British Parliamentary Human Rights Group, the Conference on Security and Co-operation in Europe, the US-based Committee to Protect Journalists, the Brussels-based International Federation of Journalists, the International Press Institute, Medico International, and the US House of Representatives.

Turkey's international reputation was also being increasingly undermined by the sheer volume of cases being made against it. Between 1991 and 1994 some 4,000 claims of torture had been submitted by human rights organisations; up to the end of 1994 there had been 2,000 mystery killings; Turkey was routinely labelled the country with the most journalists behind bars;[58] by the spring of 1996 some 3,000 villages had been razed to the ground; a total of more than 2.1 million people had been displaced as a result of a deliberate effort to, in Maoist parlance, deprive the PKK fish of their water.

Increasingly, the impact of this message was damaging for the country. As one of the most perceptive Turkish foreign affairs

---

[58] According to the Committee for the Protection of Journalists there were 78 in 1997. The Turkish state rejects such accusations by insisting that Kurdish separatists often use the title of journalist as political cover.

journalists, Semih İdiz, noted, writing in March 1994, the notion was taking root in Brussels that 'human rights violations are an unchangeable *a priori*' in Turkey.[59] Two years later İdiz observed that: 'The problem is...that Turkey has put itself in the position in the West of automatically being presumed guilty' as far as human rights accusations are concerned.[60] An ominous confirmation of this view was to be seen around the same time in the assessment of Freedom House, a non-partisan NGO which monitors democratic practice among states. In 1996 it designated Turkey as only being 'partly free', by so doing including it in the same category as Jordan and Kuwait.

Belatedly, inadequately and half-heartedly, successive Turkish governments sought to ameliorate the damage being done to the reputation of the country through presentational management of the human rights issue. In July 1994 President Demirel hastily convened a crisis meeting to discuss the 'mounting pressure' from Western institutions and governments over human rights.[61] In August 1994 a Human Rights Advisory Office was established in the Prime Minister's Office in Ankara to investigate human rights violations. In December 1994 Premier Çiller announced that she was launching a new drive for democracy and human rights in advance of a meeting of the EU–Turkish Association Council; included as part of this initiative was the adoption of a bill for the establishment of a human rights ministry, an objective which had languished, though part of the government's policy agenda, for the past three years.[62]

Even such limited attempts at a positive response were, however, often undermined. Turkish politicians were frequently inclined to complain bitterly that after Bosnia Europe was in no position to lecture Turkey on human rights.[63] Recourse was sometimes made

---

[59] Writing in *Turkish Probe*, no. 68, 10 March 1994.
[60] Writing in *Turkish Probe*, no. 193, 30 August 1996.
[61] This meeting included Murat Karayalçin (leader of the junior coalition partner), Hikmet Çetin (foreign minister), Özdem Sanberk (under-secretary at the Ministry of Foreign Affairs), Erdal İnönü (chair of the parliament's Foreign Affairs Committee) and Sait Kemal Mimaroğlu (chairman of the Turkish delegation to the Council of Europe Parliamentary Assembly). Only prime minister Tansu Çiller was unable to attend.
[62] *Turkish Daily News*, 17 December 1994.
[63] See, for example, Engin Güner (ANAP, Istanbul) in December 1994.

to the country's new Passports Law, which prohibited the entry of individuals whose 'motives in Turkey are proved to be detrimental to the security and public order of the country', to deprive human rights analysts entry to the country.[64] It is far from unusual for Turkish politicians, especially of Kurdish origin, to be prosecuted on the basis of statements which they have made at European political forums. In January 1999 the minister responsible for human rights under the ANAP-DSP-DTP coalition, Professor Hikmet Sami Türk, was incongruously and apparently without any sense of irony appointed as defence minister by the short-lived DSP minority government led by Bülent Ecevit.

GOOD INTERNATIONAL CITIZENSHIP

If Turkey's human rights record throughout most of the 1990s has been a disaster, at times mitigated but at times not, the situation has been less clear-cut in other areas of the new normative order. In the area of good international citizenship in particular the 1990s has seen the emergence of a new role for the Turkish armed forces, so often vilified for their intrusiveness in the domestic politics of the country. If the military's success in this regard has been fitful and little recognised across the world, it is because of the serious image problem from which the Turkish state suffers in the international community, and the failure of Ankara boldly to embrace a new role as a 'middle power'.[65]

At one level there is nothing strange about Turkey participating in international peace keeping and peace making efforts. Turkey is firmly part of NATO, which has helped to reinvent itself as a multilateral organisation by putting the emphasis on peace keeping missions. Moreover, Turkey's participation in the Korean war at brigade strength showed that Ankara was not intrinsically unwilling to deploy its forces far from home, if genuine benefit could be derived.

---

[64] A notable casualty of such a procedure was Amnesty International's Jonathan Sugden, who was refused a visa in November 1994.

[65] The term is used to describe the role which such states as Canada and Australia sought for themselves at the end of the Second World War, that is to say roles of influence based on good international citizenship. With the failure of these middle powers to acquire a specifically political role within international society, such states have increasingly concentrated on projecting their influence and boosting their status through international peace-keeping activities.

Indeed, as a state which has been prepared to play a growing role in the activities[66] and future of the UN,[67] it should not be surprising that Turkey has become willing to shoulder some of the burden in wider attempts to bolster peace and stability in the post-Cold War era.

Historically, of course, Turkey's role within the UN has been circumscribed. This is partly because the country uneasily straddles two groups of states within the UN, the Asian group and, for election purposes, WEOG, the Western Europeans and Others Group. Like Iran, Turkey has traditionally exercised little influence within the Asian group because of the Arab block of states therein; within WEOG, human rights and the Cyprus problem have invariably proved to be a major impediment. Since 1961 and the creation of the Non-Aligned Movement, which helped to organise Third World states at the UN, Turkey's opportunities to play a constructive role have been further curtailed, and it is no coincidence that Turkey has not been a non-permanent member of the Security Council since 1961.[68] Furthermore, Turkey has never presided at any session of the General Assembly or its main committees, nor has it held any of the high level elective posts at the UN,[69] though one of its retired ambassadors, İlter Türkmen, did serve as Commissioner General of the UN Relief and Works Agency (UNRWA) in the first half of the 1990s. Turkey therefore found itself in what one longstanding Western diplomat working on international organisations has called a 'double bind' as far as the UN is concerned. On

---

[66] In 1995 Ankara said it was prepared to put itself forward for Security Council membership in the year 2000.

[67] Turkey has been active in the debate surrounding the tortuous process of UN reform. In doing so, it has adopted a middle power's perspective evocative of Canada and Australia. Emphasis has repeatedly been placed on the increased transparency and democratisation of the Security Council as a way of increasing its moral authority and hence its effectiveness. In particular, Turkish representatives have been attracted by the creation of what might be called an intermediate category of membership, whereby an additional membership would rotate among a limited group of states. See, for example, İnal Batu quoted at length in *Turkish Daily News*, 15 October 1994.

[68] Turkey has been elected to serve three terms on the UN Security Council: 1951–2; 1954–5; 1961, when it shared a split term with Liberia.

[69] Üner Kirdar, 'The UN and Turkey: for a Better and Stronger System of Humane Governance', *Insight Turkey*, vol. 2, no. 1, January–March 2000, p. 35.

the one hand, Turkey is not part of a 'cosy' group of states; on the other, it has a bad track record with international civil servants.[70]

The involvement of Turkey in UN peace-oriented activities actually began, albeit in small numbers and as part of observer rather than peace keeping forces, on the Iraq border. Turkey took part in the military observer mission, Uniimog, on the Iran-Iraq border, very much a 'tester' presence. Ankara then followed this up with a slightly larger presence with the UN Iraq-Kuwait observer mission (Unikom), also on the Iraq border, beginning its personnel contributions in May 1991.

Buoyed up by this low-profile and highly successful involvement in Iraq, Turkey rather veered to the opposite extreme in its first major, high profile and complex engagement in peacemaking and peacekeeping in Somalia. In doing so, Ankara tended to ignore the very different nature of the respective missions, beguiled, no doubt, by the close involvement of the US in such operations. Turkey's initial involvement, however, was auspicious, and gave no indication as to the events that would unfold over the following months.

Turkey's participation in the Unified Task Force (Unitaf) began as a result of an approach from the United States on 4 December 1992, in the final days of the Bush presidency. The mission had been inspired by American public opinion, distressed at the human suffering and concerned that the original UN Operation in Somalia (Unosom) mission should be salvaged.[71] Its brief was country-wide enforcement with, as its source of international legitimacy—UN Security Council resolution 794—stated, the aim 'to establish a secure environment for humanitarian relief operations'. The mission itself was not to be a UN one *per se*, but an operation effectively subcontracted to a group of member states, led by the US.[72] It was designed to be an interim response to a real and immediate security and humanitarian crisis, eventually giving way to something more permanent once the situation had become stabilised.

---

[70] Non-attributable interview, 13 May 1999.

[71] The original Unosom mission, comprising some 500 Pakistani peace-keepers, had been confined to the Mogadishu port area and thus had been unable to make much impact on the situation in the country. See Peter R. Baehr and Leon Gordenker, *The United Nations and the End of the 1990s* (Macmillan, London, 1999), p. 83.

[72] See forthcoming Jane Boulden, *Peace Enforcement, The United Nations Experience in Congo, Somalia and Bosnia* (Praeger, Westport, CT, 2001), p. 73.

In order to authorise the despatch of troops abroad, approval was sought from the Turkish parliament. The relevant motion was successful by 265 votes to 44, the opposition of those deputies, notably from the Islamist Welfare Party, who were suspicious of the US leadership on Somalia being softened by its shrewd presentation together with a motion on the deployment of peace keepers to Bosnia. In the end Turkey sent some 300 troops in the form of a mechanised battalion, in an operation that also included France, Canada, Belgium, Italy and Morocco. This was to be Turkey's first overseas military mission as part of a multilateral force since the participation in the Korean war.

The Unitaf intervention was quickly deemed to have been a success, with many of the formerly warring clans adopting a low profile, and an increasing volume of humanitarian aid being distributed. However, these were successes of a superficial nature. Unitaf had not sought to disarm the Somali factions, as was the understanding of the UN Secretary-General, the US appearing content simply with the removal of weapons from sight.[73] With the US the dominant force on the ground, its conception of the mission won the day. Washington then manoeuvred the UN into taking over the peace keeping activity, but on the basis of a Chapter Seven resolution that would emphasise peace enforcement by the newly constituted Unosom-2.[74] Though it was formally now a UN operation, the US was to try to have its cake and eat it. The Americans attempted to control the operation through the UN Secretary-General's special representative, Jonathan T. Howe, a retired US admiral who had served on the Bush NSC, while keeping its crack forces on the ground separate from the UN command.

It was against this backdrop of a UN mission largely taken over by the United States that the Turks became further involved. It was agreed that Turkey should make a contribution to the Unosom-2 troop contingent, as they had done with Unitaf. However, there was to be more. At US instigation a senior Turkish army officer, Lt.-Gen. Cevik Bir, who was later promoted deputy chief of staff, was

---

[73] For a discussion of the importance of this dispute over disarmament and its ramifications see ibid., pp. 65–6.

[74] SCR 814, adopted on 26 March 1993. See Geoff Simons, *The United Nations: A Chronology of Conflict* (Macmillan, London, 1994), p. 197.

appointed to be the officer in command. In obtaining the appointment of General Bir, the United States and Turkey had to fight off a determined attempt by Italy, the former colonial power, to command the force. The circumstances surrounding Bir's appointment would remain a source of resentment on the Italian side for the duration of the mission.

For the US, the appointment of Bir was to be a reward for a loyal and valued ally. Even so, Washington was obviously not taking any chances. A senior US soldier, Major-General Thomas Montgomery, was appointed as his second in command. More importantly, the US contingent in Somalia was not to be placed at his disposal: 3,000 men in logistics reported to an American chain of command within Unosom-2, while a Quick Reaction Force of up to 1,300, which was available to support UN activities, reported direct to Joint Special Operations in Tampa, Florida. In short, Bir was denied operational control. It speaks volumes for the awe in which the Turkish military held the world's one remaining superpower that it was willing to stomach such an obvious indignity. Nevertheless, it was with a rousing sense of gravity that President Özal sent his contingent off with the message: 'Your duty is a difficult one but it is important for the international prestige of Turkey.'

Bir arrived at the end of February, and Unosom-2 officially took control on 4 May 1993. Its fortunes began to go awry from the outset, notably as a result of the swift and unexpected withdrawal of the American contingent with Unitaf, a precipitate act that exposed the disorganisation of its successor and jeopardised the veneer of security that had been established in the country. The disintegration of the UN effort in Somalia cannot be seen as primarily the fault of Ankara, the Turkish contingent or General Bir, who hardly enjoyed sufficient authority to make a critical difference.[75] A combination of American naïveté about Somali politics, the ambitious nature of the UN mandate, the existence of what were effectively three chains

---

[75] It is a measure of the nominal nature of General Bir's command that the published works on UNOSOM-2 hardly mention him. For example, the account by the UN Secretary-General, Boutros Boutros-Ghali, only mentions him once, and then only to say that he was 'a strong and silent representative of the Turkish military tradition'. See *Unvanquished: a US-UN Saga* (I. B. Tauris, London, 1999), p. 93.

of command, the difficulty of a 33-state force delivering effective co-operation,[76] and the tenacity of the supporters of Somali warlord Muhammad Farah Aideed all soon contributed to the undermining of the operation. If there was an area where Bir courted controversy it was in amending the rules of engagement as the security situation began to deteriorate in Mogadishu in May.[77] His decision to sanction the use of force on a much broader basis than had been the case with Unitaf created the context for the bloody exchanges that would punctuate the following few months. It also resurrected the dispute with the Italian contingent, which refused to carry out Bir's orders in response to the more forceful approach adopted.

The declining fortunes of the mission began to set in on 5 June, the date on which it took its first tentative steps in the direction of disarmament, when 26 Pakistani peace-keepers were killed in fighting with the supporters of Aideed. As the level of violence increased, Italians, Americans and a Malaysian peacekeeper were killed, together with many Somalis. Admiral Howe called in Delta Force. It was US army rangers from this force that comprised the 18 servicemen killed on 3 October, whose deaths resulted in the US decision to withdraw all its forces by 31 March 1994. The announcement effectively crippled the remainder of the mission.[78]

As the loss of life increased on both sides, so did the mutual recrimination, the whole affair demonstrating, in Michael Williams' words, 'what could only be called a 'Dis-United Nations'.[79] The Turkish side was certainly not immune to the soul-searching, an intense debate emerging between the Foreign Ministry and the Turkish General Staff over whether the Turkish contingent should be unilaterally withdrawn. The former won the debate, with the argument that a premature withdrawal would undermine Turkey's credibility within international forums carrying the day. Consequently, General

---

[76] Indeed, a number of country contingents would not carry out orders received from General Bir without first checking them through their own national commands at home. See Boulden, op. cit., p. 69.

[77] Bir amended the rules of engagement thus: 'organized, armed militias, technicals and other crew-served weapons are considered a threat to UNOSOM Forces and may be engaged without provocation'. See Boulden, op. cit., p. 65.

[78] Meisler, op. cit., p. 309.

[79] Michael C. Williams, *Civil-Military Relations and Peacekeeping* (IISS/Adelphi Paper 321, London, 1998), p. 47.

Bir served out his period as commander to 22 February 1994. In turn, Turkey decided to maintain its contingent in Somalia, but, as with other country contingents, only for as long as US troops remained. The military credibility and logistical capability of the force would be greatly undermined by the ending of the US commitment, while Ankara was also no doubt mindful that the diplomatic utility of the mission in boosting Turkish–US bilateral relations would only exist while the US engagement was maintained. In the end, both the American and the Turkish contingents were withdrawn at the end of March 1994.

In spite of the bureaucratic victory of the Foreign Ministry in keeping Turkey involved in the Somali mission, the negative, longer term impact of the experience could not be assuaged. The trauma of the Somalia operation certainly made the Turkish military generally more wary of sending troops on such missions, especially in sizeable numbers and where the background of the operation was little understood. While such sentiments were understandable, an opportunity was, nevertheless, being lost to bolster Turkey's reputation as a good international citizen. This new reticence caused Turkey to decline a further international commitment soon after the end of the Somali operation. In April 1994 the Turkish army blocked an initiative by the Foreign Ministry in refusing to contribute to a UN mission to Angola. The invitation was declined politely on the grounds of the insufficient availability of resources.[80]

This reversal did not, however, mark the end of Turkey's interest in multilateral peacekeeping. Turkey supported the proposal of UN Secretary-General Boutros Boutros-Ghali to establish a standing force under UN command that would be able to react swiftly to crises around the world. Ankara also said that it would be willing to commit troops to such a force. Indeed, the Turkish Foreign Ministry also came up with a variety of suggestions for the financing of such a force, to include a tax on arms sales, together with other ideas to expedite UN peacekeeping initiatives.[81]

Neither did the Somalia experience deter Turkey from actual participation in future multilateral efforts, especially in trouble spots close to Turkey's borders, although there was a tendency at first to scale

[80] *Turkish Daily News*, 12 May 1994.
[81] *Turkish Probe*, vol. 5, no. 72, 8 April 1994.

down the level of commitment to numbers more akin to the early Iraq missions. Though it was potentially more contentious for geo-political reasons, in fact both sides in the Georgian civil war and both the Israelis and the Palestinians sought Turkish participation in helping to defuse local tensions. Consequently, a handful of Turks have participated in the UN observer force in Georgia (Unomig) since October 1994, while some 16 have taken part in the multina-tional observer team in Hebron (TIPH), commencing in February 1997. Thus Turkey's participation in peacekeeping arrangements began to overlap with its commitment to managing external in-securities in the three regions to the west, north-east and south of its borders.

A further, more substantial example of Turkish involvement in regional peacekeeping was the case of Bosnia, which is dealt with in some detail in Chapter 10. Some 1,450 Turkish troops were included in the force of UN peacekeepers that began arriving in mid June 1994, as the conflict began to enter its end game. The Turkish troops were stationed at Zenica, among both Croats and Bosnian Muslims, thereby helping to underpin the Washington Agreement between the two communities, and establish a context in which the Bosnian Serbs might be pushed back on the battlefield. The Turkish troops apparently enjoyed a good reputation among both communities and there were no complaints about their presence, in contrast to some other national contingents wearing the blue beret, notably in Sarajevo. When the mandate of Unprofor ended and NATO stepped in with its IFOR mission Turkish troops were asked to stay on, with the greatly enhanced responsibility of patrolling a zone of separation some 1,850 km in length. A contingent of more than eighty Turkish police was recruited in December and March 1995 to be based at Velika Kladusa in Bosnia, where they were responsi-ble for helping Bosnian refugees in Croatia return to their homes.[82]

Furthermore, Turkey has also shown itself willing to accept com-parable missions outside a strict UN or NATO context, though re-maining clearly within a multilateral context, especially where issues of regional security in adjacent areas are concerned. Most notably Turkey took part in the Italian-led Operation Alba in Albania, in response to the breakdown in order in that country in the aftermath

---

[82] *Turkish Daily News*, 6 December 1995.

of the collapse of a pyramid savings racket. The UN Security Council authorised the OSCE to establish such a multinational force. Turkey contributed a marine battalion task force, consisting of 779 servicemen, which was engaged in Tirana and the northern part of the country from mid April 1997. The Turkish contingent returned home on 1 August 1997, the operation having been generally pronounced a success.

In systemic terms, Turkey has been a status quo power par excellence. Before the end of the Cold War, it was a loyal member of NATO that was preoccupied with containing Soviet and Communist expansionism. While its central concern remained just that, it suddenly found that between 1989 and 1991 the aims, aspirations and outlook of the rest of Europe had been transformed. Owing to force of circumstance rather than deliberate design, Turkey was a loser from such change in Europe, which saw it relegated politically to the periphery which it occupies geographically.

But the story did not end there. The Gulf crisis convinced the US, with its keen geopolitical sense, of Turkey's enduring strategic importance. A rash of regional conflicts from the former Yugoslavia to the Transcaucasus simply reaffirmed this point. As a co-operative state Turkey could continue to play a valuable role within the Western alliance; as a negative or revisionist state its ability to cause problems could be disastrous. While Ankara was far from pleased at some of the directions in which security co-operation evolved, notably the weakening of the CFE Treaty and an eastward expansion of NATO which has not included any south-eastern European states, a sufficient body of the core values of the organisation was retained to satisfy Turkey's strong Atlanticist inclinations. Thus a strong NATO, together with a firm US commitment to the future security of the European area, remains a situation of which Turkey definitely approves.

Paradoxically, however, the strong and enduring sense of a Western security orientation underpinned by the political influence of the military in Turkey has helped to darken wider European perceptions of the country. The 1980 military takeover and the persistence of harsh treatment of prisoners, together with a swathe of illiberal practices and laws, have damaged Turkey's reputation among European civil society. Moreover, Turkey's performance in a range of human rights areas has deteriorated just at a time when a new normative era has emerged in Europe, one which has more than ever before judged states according to such criteria. Of course Ankara and much of the Turkish people justify such methods on the grounds of the existential challenge posed by Kurdish ethno-nationalism and the violent insurgency of the PKK. With the issue of human rights and the Kurdish issue having become intertwined and confused, though, such protestations have been largely dismissed.

2

PLAYERS AND PROCESSES

In thinking about the making of Turkish foreign policy two starkly contrasting images predominate. The first is that of the elite diplomat, fluent in several languages and the graduate of the best *lycées* and universities in the country, who decides upon and executes foreign policy as deliberately as any ideal-type, rational actor in the academic literature on international relations, unencumbered by the messiness of the political and wider societal process. Though this image is forged most pristinely in our recollection of Ottoman times, it remains strong and enduring in Republican Turkey. The second image is of the utter chaos of the mid-1990s, epitomised say by 1995, the year of the four foreign ministers, a time when no-one seemed to be in charge and foreign diplomats struggled to know what Turkish foreign policy was, let alone who was making it.

These may be the abiding images associated with foreign policy-making in Turkey today, but how much credence should we give to them? Are they meaningless clichés that simply mask the bureaucratic, organisational, political and personality complexities of the foreign policy-making process? Are they close approximations to reality, with forgivable analytical embellishment being used to bring out the changing styles and processes in foreign policy-making? Are they two sides of the same coin, with civil servants providing the consistency and continuity for weak and distracted politicians that typifies foreign policy in most complex democracies?

This chapter sets out to address these questions. It does so first and foremost through a consideration of which elements are indeed of most importance in Turkish foreign policymaking. The chapter shows that in Turkey foreign policymaking is a dynamic interplay between three factors: overall political context; the powers and traditions of institutions; and the personalities and priorities of the leading players. In order to explore and develop this argument, and to show the fluctuating nature of these factors, this chapter is divided into two. First, to ensure that this does not become an ahistorical exercise, the chapter begins with a periodisation of Turkish foreign policy since the mid 1980s, and a discussion of the leading actors during these times. The latter part of the chapter is given over to a focus on the actors and institutions themselves, with a broad distinction being made on the grounds of their primary or secondary importance.

Three phases in Turkish foreign policy

Turkey has experienced three distinct phases in terms of foreign policymaking since the beginning of the end of the Cold War.[1] The first phase was the overriding personal approach closely associated with the figure of Turgut Özal, who dominated Turkish politics from the ebb of military power in the mid 1980s through to the ousting of his protégé Yıldırım Akbulut as premier in 1991. The second phase was the collegiate, bureaucratic approach, in which for most of the time foreign minister Hikmet Çetin worked closely with the staff of the Foreign Ministry to produce carefully crafted and well co-ordinated foreign policy. The third phase has been one of a weak, fragmented and competitive approach, with foreign policy-making since 1994 reflecting the clutter and confusion of domestic party politics.

I. OVERRIDING PERSONAL APPROACH, 1986–91

The period of the pursuit of an enhanced, personalised foreign policy is most closely identified with Turgut Özal, who was Turkish prime minister between 1983 and 1989 and president of the republic between 1989 and his death in 1993. During such a period of great upheavals in the international system, Turkey had a man of vision and quick wits as its helm. After a careful start, in the wake of rule by the generals, Özal came increasingly to dominate civilian politics. From his sweeping election victory in 1983, in which he outwitted the military, until the ousting of Yıldırım Akbulut

---

[1] Taken to correspond roughly with the rise to power of the last Soviet leader Mikhail Gorbachev.

in 1991,[2] Özal is widely regarded as having transformed the policy-making context. 'For a one-line guide to current Turkish affairs,' it was written in the *The Economist* survey of Turkey in June 1988, 'you can do worse than this: for Thatcher, read Özal.'[3]

In trying to extend his influence over foreign affairs, Özal had to circumscribe the influence of the security forces, often referred to as behaving 'like a state within a state'. Özal faced the additional constraint of the leader of the original coup, Kenan Evren, occupying the presidency from 1982 to 1989. In foreign policy, as with security and education affairs, President Evren sought to exert critical leadership. Özal was helped in his quest to re-civilianise politics by knowing the military well, both as an institution and as a set of individuals, by virtue of having worked under them as economic supremo during most of the time the generals directly wielded power. He was therefore well placed to judge when and when not to try to push back the authority of the military.[4]

Özal began his tenure as premier cautiously, and suffered reversals at the hands of President Evren, especially in terms of the composition of his cabinets. Indeed, at one stage the president even proved able to force Özal to sack his foreign minister. These reversals did not, however, intimidate Özal. When he felt strong enough he steadily pushed back the influence of the military. When, for example, he discovered that Turkey's main intelligence agency, the MİT (*Milli İstihbarat Teşkilatı*) was giving more information to President Evren than to him, he forced through a new head of his choice, making the symbolic statement of appointing someone from a civilian background. As the decade went on and Özal became more confident so he looked to assert himself and the role of the civilian

---

[2] Özal was elected president in October 1989 by a parliament still dominated by his Motherland party. He then engineered Akbulut's succession to the premiership, but continued to pull the strings of his puppet, regularly chairing cabinet meetings. In the words of one US State Department official working on Turkey, Akbulut just faded away. Interview, Washington DC, 20 April 1990.

[3] *The Economist* Survey of Turkey entitled 'Getting Ready for Europe', 18–24 June 1988, p. 4.

[4] For a discussion of the recivilianisation of politics in Turkey see Ahmet Evin, 'Demilitarization and Civilianization of the Regime' in Metin Heper and Ahmet Evin (eds), *Politics in the Third Turkish Republic* (Westview Press, Boulder, CO, 1994).

domain at the expense of the military. Consequently, he named an airport and a major monument after Adnan Menderes, the prime minister removed by the military in 1960 and executed a year later. He even inspected a formal guard of honour wearing a pair of shorts and a T-shirt, a public discourtesy to an institution which so highly prizes propriety and formalities.

Özal's decisive showdown with the army came in 1987 when he refused to allow the anointed general, Necdet Öztorun, to become chief of staff, instead appointing another senior figure, Necip Torumtay, to the top post. Though horrified by the move, the military chose not to try to oppose it. Özal was then more easily able to assert the primacy of civilian control in politics. However, even Torumtay had his tolerance threshold. He resigned as CGS in November 1990 over Özal's personalised handling of the Gulf crisis. Torumtay departed soon after Özal and his cousin the defence minister visited the chiefs of the various services without the chief of staff in the runup to an important meeting of decision-makers to discuss the UN ultimatum to Iraq.[5] The internal tensions in the armed forces caused by Özal's handling of the 1987 appointment issue helped to ensure that resignation was the only lever in the hands of Torumtay.[6]

In addition to circumscribing the military's role in policymaking, foreign affairs included, Özal also brought in and brought on a new generation of younger, educated technocrats, who were attuned to his dynamic and reformist approach. While most of these were to be found in the realm of economic policy, there was also an important cluster in the domain of foreign affairs. When Özal first became premier, diplomats like Özdem Sanberk and Cem Duna were brought into the prime minister's office to be his personal advisers, making them at a stroke more influential than even the serving under-secretary in the Ministry of Foreign Affairs.[7] When Özal became president his Foreign Ministry advisers included people like Kaya Toperi, and Nabi Şensoy, who was his *chef de cabinet*. In all cases it was the ease and regularity of access which made these figures so influential.

---

[5] *The Independent*, 4 December 1990.
[6] *The Guardian*, 4 December 1990.
[7] Interview with former Under Secretary, 25 January 1995.

However, it was in the areas of strategic thinking and the broad contours of policy, rather than in the detail or execution of that policy, that Özal's influence was most felt. From the Gorbachev accession, through the new thinking in the Kremlin and the transformation of the politics of Eastern Europe, virtually to the dismantling of the USSR itself, Özal was the key figure in charting Turkey's future direction in a turbulent and changing world. Özal's goal, in his words, was 'to make Turkey an influential country in its region and the world'.[8]

During this time, Özal was particularly adept at being able to spot good opportunities and, in moving quickly and with purpose, well able to exploit them. Cases abound of Özal's dynamism in foreign policy, especially in the field of foreign economic relations. Two examples will suffice to illustrate this.

The Soviet opening. Özal was always a keen exponent of the notion of complex inter-dependency. That is to say that he believed that the best way to stabilise difficult bilateral relations among states was to increase the levels of economic integration in order to increase the cost of, and hence reduce the likelihood of, breakdown, tension and conflict. Arguably, the best example of this strategy in action was in relation to Turkey's historic foe, the Soviet Union. Özal's economic embrace of Moscow was not, however, merely an alternative security strategy. It also came increasingly to make good commercial and macro-economic sense. At the forefront of this approach was the discovery and exploitation of Soviet gas, which was clearly a cheap and plentiful alternative to Middle Eastern oil. Thus Soviet gas offered the possibility of both a motor for bilateral trade and a diversification away from an over-reliance for a strategic commodity on an endemically unstable region.

A gas accord was first forged between Ankara and Moscow in 1984. Once a gas delivery pipeline across Bulgaria had been built the first gas began to flow in 1987. The supply of gas established the parameters for what was essentially a countertrade relationship between the two sides, with the 1984 agreement providing for a combination of Turkish manufactured goods and produce, and contracting services to be used in payment. In 1989 bilateral trade

---

[8] *Turkish Probe*, vol. 2, no. 23, 20 April 1993.

was worth $1.2 bn, triple what it had been in 1986, rising to $1.9 bn in 1990. By the time of Özal's effective political eclipse, 4.4 bn cu.m. of gas was being exported from the USSR to Turkey each year. Such was the promise of the new trading relationship that Turkey lubricated it with export credits. Turkey's Eximbank extended two credit lines to the value of $150 mn in 1989 for the purchase of Turkish consumer goods. A further $350 mn by way of investment credit was extended to help finance the foreign direct investment activities of Turkish contractors, which, by the end of 1989, were involved in 30 turnkey projects ranging from hotels to a copper wire plant to a shoe factory.[9]

The Iran-Iraq war. Relations with Iran and Iraq during their eight-year conflict must also be chalked up as a major achievement for Özal. He developed a policy of 'positive neutrality' towards the two protagonists. So successful was this approach that when the two combatants eventually severed diplomatic relations they sought representation in one another's capitals through the respective Turkish missions. The strategy also yielded secondary benefits to Turkey outside the region. In the wake of the difficult relations between the United States and both Iran and Iraq, Turkey's successful diplomacy brought it a certain cachet in both US and NATO circles.[10]

Through the adoption of the positive neutrality approach, Özal not only stabilised relations with both Iran and Iraq at a time of potentially great volatility, but also managed to exploit good ties with Baghdad and Tehran to the benefit of the Turkish exchequer. As with the Soviet Union, Özal pursued a strategy of economic inter-dependency as a way of stabilising and softening what had been difficult bilateral relationships in the recent past. Such was the effectiveness of the policy of positive neutrality and the consequently advantageous impact on Turkey's balance of payments that even opposition political leaders were happy to commend Özal for such skill.[11]

---

[9] Reuters, Ankara, in *Jordan Times*, 1 January 1990.

[10] Discussion with three State Department officials on Turkey, Washington, DC, 6 February 1989.

[11] For example, Bülent Ecevit speaking at Chatham House on 24 January 1989, while criticising other aspects of foreign policy, called Özal's Middle East policy 'balanced, realistic and successful'.

For Iran, the positive Turkish stance was a welcome relief, contrasting with the varying degrees of antipathy shown towards it by the Arab states, Syria excepted. For Iraq, Turkey offered the strategic advantage of a secure route for trade, and especially for its oil exports, its existing routes across Syria and through the Gulf having proven to be extremely vulnerable to political and military pressure respectively.

Turkey rapidly emerged as both a source of manufacturing imports for Iran and Iraq and a conduit for imports from third countries, notably European suppliers. Again, a primary commodity, in this case oil, was the motor for trade. In the 1980s Iran and Iraq dominated Turkey's Middle East import profile. Over the duration of the eight year war Turkish imports from Iran and Iraq, overwhelmingly oil, came to $7.1 bn and $9.1 bn respectively. In turn, Turkish exports to Iran and Iraq totalled $5.4 bn and $6.3 bn.[12]

The commercial benefits of this positive neutrality were not confined to trade. Iraq increased its strategic dependence on Turkey between 1976 and 1987 through the construction and expansion of two oil pipelines, with a combined capacity of 1.5 million b/d. Additional volumes of oil moved through Turkey by tanker truck in a 'moving pipeline'. As well as the indirect benefits of such traffic, Turkey also received some $250 million a year in pipeline transit fees. Such was the success of this relationship that Iraq and Turkey agreed to the integration of their electricity grids, as part of a wider creation of economic inter-dependencies also involving Syria and Jordan. Turkish companies also received lucrative contracts in construction and heavy engineering in Iraq, with some $2.5 bn worth of work being completed between 1974 and 1990, and more than $1 bn worth of work outstanding at the time of the Gulf crisis.[13] It took a contingency of the dimensions of Iraq's invasion of Kuwait and the global consensus in support of the introduction of UN economic sanctions under Chapter Seven of the Charter to undo a decade's worth of growing interdependence.

Iran's strategic integration with Turkey was less conventional. It was, nevertheless, still considerable, especially in the field of migration. Hundreds of thousands of Iranians settled in Turkey, especially

[12] IMF *Direction of Trade Statistics Yearbook*, 1989; SIS Foreign Trade Statistics.
[13] *Turkey Confidential*, no. 10, June 1990.

in parts of Istanbul, after the Iranian revolution, and much tourism and commerce between the two countries followed.

In forging ahead with these foreign economic opportunities, Özal also had to galvanise his own business sector. He did so in character-istic fashion by taking the horse to water. Most notably, wherever he travelled abroad, Özal always took several tens of Turkey's most senior and influential businessmen with him. In doing so, Özal showed an acute sense of what motivated and what would facilitate Turkey's private sector. Thus he sought to ensure that Turkey, with its newly-aligned, export-oriented economy, took advantage of every foreign opening being developed, of every high-level personal con-tact made in the sphere of political affairs.

During this period of overriding personal influence over foreign policy there were two main drawbacks. First, Özal's judgement was not perfect. His intuitive and sometimes impulsive decisions and statements, unleavened by bureaucratic checks and balances, meant that when he was wrong the consequences were often more serious than if Turkey had been pursuing a more traditionally cautious for-eign policy. One example of this was his intemperate comments to a Greek newspaper that 'The Dodecanese Islands were never Greek' and that 'if I had been Ismet Inonu I would have have gone in and taken them in 1944', a statement which he made in May 1991.[14]

Many point to the Gulf crisis of 1990/91 itself as an example of this. Özal supported the initial US effort against Iraq with a presen-tational flourish as well as substantive action.[15] In doing so, he assumed that great economic and diplomatic benefits would accrue to Turkey. While one could argue that the strategic value placed on Turkey in the United States today was in great measure predicated on Özal's prompt and forthright action, the outcome of the crisis, from the continued economic sanctions against Iraq to the creation of a

---

[14] See Selim Deringil, 'Introduction: Turkish Foreign Policy Since Atatürk' in Clement H. Dodd (ed.), *Turkish Foreign Policy, op. cit.*, p. 6.

[15] There was, for example, no doubt that the decision to close the pipelines and the way in which it was done was his and his alone. On the day of the closure deci-sion his prime minister Yıldırım Akbulut was opening a sugar factory in Kars. Interview with Western diplomat 1, Ankara, 14 November 1990.

political twilight zone in northern Iraq, have certainly not been to Turkey's advantage.

Second, Özal was bad for foreign policymaking in Turkey because of the way his *modus operandi* helped to subvert the institutionalised nature of decision-making. During his period in power Özal's personal approach to foreign relations began to undermine the rule-based system that made the bureaucracy, and especially the diplomatic service, run smoothly and effectively.[16] The unsettling effect of this period can be seen in the discontinuities of contact and in the confusion of methods and procedures for contact. Perhaps the best, certainly the most high profile, example of this was Özal's telephone diplomacy with President Bush during and immediately after the Gulf crisis, and his refusal to take officials and even his foreign minister into meetings in Washington with the Americans in 1990. In that way, Özal began to establish a style and system of foreign relations which only he could operate. His attempt to build in his own indispensability simply disadvantaged Turkey as an actor once his influence waned.

The political demise of Özal was followed by a difficult adjustment period when foreign policymaking had to be re-institutionalised. This increased the challenges for the Ministry of Foreign Affairs, coming at a time when it was increasingly stretched by the necessities of dealing with a more complex and combustible world. Ultimately, no matter how professionally Turkey's diplomats proceeded to regularise the processes of foreign policymaking after Özal, it proved impossible to return to the level of institutionalisation evident before the advent of Özal.[17] This weakening of the bureaucratic pillars

[16] The controversial impact that Özal made on existing structures and processes is of course not confined to the Foreign Ministry and foreign policy. Heath Lowry, for example, in reviewing the Özal legacy, asks whether it is a case of the Turkish economic miracle or 'the fish stinks from the head'. See Heath W. Lowry, 'Betwixt and Between: Turkey's Political Structure on the Cusp of the Twenty-First Century' in Morton Abramowitz (ed.), *Turkey's Transformation and American Policy* (Century Foundation, New York, 2000), p. 25.

[17] During the years when Özal was at the height of his powers in the late 1980s it was common for Turkish bureaucrats to complain about how he was weakening the traditional ministries and building up alternative centres of authority, either through the bolstering of the standing of state ministers or through the increased use of extra-bureaucratic advisers for the development of policy. Interview with Western diplomat 2, Ankara, 14 November 1990.

of Turkish foreign policy was to have more critical consequences in the middle of the 1990s. Lesser figures, notably Tansu Çiller, were to attempt to exploit the precedent created by Özal of a more personalised style in the execution of foreign policymaking out of motives of self-interest, invariably to the detriment of the interests of the country.

II. COLLEGIATE BUREAUCRATIC APPROACH, 1991–4

In the end, the waning of Özal's power came rapidly. In April 1991 he was still supreme, in this instance in driving Western policy for the protection of the Iraqi Kurds, leading to the creation of the safe haven and Operation Provide Comfort 2. By June 1991, the stewardship of the government by Özal's 'dull witted' successor Yıldırım Akbulut[18] could be sustained no longer. Akbulut's successor, the former foreign minister Mesut Yılmaz, bridled against such a degree of presidential interference in a way reminiscent of Özal's struggles with Evren in earlier days. In the end, the degree to which Özal's wings had been clipped was rendered academic by ANAP's defeat in the October 1991 general election, which brought a coalition of the DYP and the Sosyal Demokrat Halkçı Parti (SHP) to office. With Özal's great rival Süleyman Demirel back as prime minister, Özal was to suffer the frustrations of a political marginalisation from which he would not recover.

The accession to power of the DYP-SHP coalition may not, at face value, have looked very promising. There was deep division between presidency and government; the government itself comprised a two-party coalition drawn from different ideological hues; many of those participating in government were inexperienced, and even Demirel himself, nothing if not a political old stager, had been out of office for some 11 years, during which time the world had changed profoundly.

In spite of the apparently inauspicious circumstances, the period between 1991 and 1994 was to prove to be an island of ordered foreign policy management between two periods of relative chaos. In this phase, Turkey emerged as a weighty force for stability and continuity during the most turbulent phase of the post-Cold War

---

[18] To quote Hugh and Nicole Pope in their *Turkey Unveiled* (John Murray, London, 1997), p. 265.

systemic transition. During this time, Turkey managed to harness the caution of the Kemalist era, but without succumbing to the blinkers of Kemalism, for example in its contempt for engagement in such regions as the Middle East. Increasingly, continuity and co-ordination came to typify government, as the system rowed back from the highly personalised approach of the Özal era through the partial re-institutionalisation of the conduct of foreign affairs. Turk-ish foreign policy may have been low key and unadventurous dur-ing this period, and certainly eschewed the grand initiatives of the Özal period, but, with instability and even conflict all around, this 'softly softly' approach was the perfect antidote to the tumultuous conditions of the day.

Demirel returned to the premiership having shown little inclina-tion for foreign affairs in the past. His contribution was, however, important in laying down some general guidelines for foreign pol-icy, notably that Turkey should not act alone but jointly with other countries, and preferably its allies, under proper international aus-pices.[19] Beyond such parameters, he was content to give consider-able leeway to his foreign minister, Hikmet Çetin, on the condition that he was kept regularly briefed. This was a generous decision in view of the fact that Çetin was a member of the junior SHP. In turn, the leader of the SHP, Erdal İnönü, who was somewhat of a gentle-man politician, was also content to give his man considerable author-ity, not least perhaps because Çetin had a reputation for reliability, being a bit of a party apparatchik.

Demirel also showed wisdom in his decision to continue to work with the incumbent under secretary of the Foreign Ministry, Özdem Sanberk. His first inclination was to appoint a new man, because of Sanberk's close association with Özal. Demirel was persuaded to retain Sanberk on the grounds that he was in fact non-partisan, extremely able and capable of working professionally with which-ever government might be in power. Thus was formed the Çetin-Sanberk team which was to serve Turkey so very well in managing the destabilising events that were to unfurl all around over the next three years.

From the establishment of the coalition in November 1991 through to Demirel's election to the presidency on 16 May 1993, Çetin and

[19] *Turkey Confidential*, no. 34, December 1992, p. 12.

Sanberk, backed up by a relatively small group of senior diplomats, presided over policy-making. In general, this foreign policy management team continued to hold sway through the twin political successions, when Tansu Çiller replaced Demirel as DYP party leader and hence as premier in June 1993, and when Murat Karayalçin succeeded Inonu as leader of the SHP three months later.

Çiller was certainly different to Demirel. Erratic, inexperienced and politically extremely insecure, she was more prepared to intervene in foreign affairs than her predecessor. Indeed, she began ominously by appointing a senior diplomat, Volkan Vural, to be her personal adviser; shades, she might have believed, of Charles Powell to her Margaret Thatcher. Such thoughts, however, were illusory. Her interventions in foreign affairs were to remain limited owing to the necessities of constant manoeuvring at the domestic political level just to retain power, her grasp on office appearing precarious from June 1993 through to as late as September 1995.[20] When Mrs Çiller did dally with foreign affairs it was principally with the old Kemalist preoccupations of Europe and the US, in which her interests became increasingly those of form rather than substance. For most of the time, then, the Çetin-Sanberk team prevailed.

Çetin retained the foreign ministry until he was removed in a reallocation of the SHP portfolios in the coalition government on 27 July 1994. As has become the way in Turkish domestic politics, the reasons for his removal had little to do with the direction of Turkish foreign policy, or indeed his performance as foreign minister. Karayalçin was somewhat reluctantly pushed into a reshuffle by the growing pressures from within his parliamentary party for a redivision of the patronage spoils of office. The fact that Çetin learned of his imminent replacement through the national press, while on an official visit to Paris, simply added to the indignity of the episode.[21] President Demirel was known to be unhappy about the removal of Çetin, the two men having continued their 'special relationship' under the Çiller premiership.[22] In the face of the parochial demands of party politics, however, affairs of state were shown to be

---

[20] It is ironic that Çiller's downfall as prime minister came so soon after she had finally consolidated her hold on her own party.

[21] *Turkish Probe*, 2 December 1994.

[22] *Turkish Probe*, 29 July 1994.

of subordinate importance, a harbinger, it was to turn out, of things to come.

III. WEAK, FRAGMENTED, COMPETITIVE APPROACH, 1994–9[23]

The removal of Çetin and the banality of the prevailing circumstances ushered in a third period in Turkish foreign policymaking, that of fragmentation and competition. Overall, this period has been characterised by intensive competition among largely insecure leaders at the head of weak political parties, divided, with the exception of the Islamist right, on a binary basis.[24] Far from proving a political clearing of the air, the December 1995 general election failed to result in a clear-cut victory for any one party. The intensified ideological clash between the old Kemalist forces, led by the military, and political Islam had exacerbated systemic instability.

More specifically in the foreign policy domain, the personality struggles, especially among the left of centre parties, together with the short lived coalition governments of the 1995–9 parliament, resulted in a large turnover in foreign ministers. It is worth noting that Turkey had nine foreign ministers between July 1994 and June 1997. Moreover, the unstable personal and party competition for power resulted in the Foreign Ministry being captured, admittedly for rather brief periods, by some decidedly hard-line and undiplomatic personalities, notably Mümtaz Soysal and Coşkun Kırca. At other times, the Foreign Ministry has simply represented a status symbol to bolster politicians in their pursuit of overall power, most particularly in the case of Tansu Çiller.

TURKISH FOREIGN MINISTERS, 1991–

Nov. 1991–July 1994	Hikmet Çetin
July 1994–Nov. 1994	Mümtaz Soysal
Nov. 1994–March 1995	Murat Karayalçın

---

[23] It is too early to come to firm conclusions about the Ecevit-led coalition that came to power in spring 1999. However, the ideological span of the three party coalition, which consists of the left of centre DSP, the right of centre ANAP and the ultra-nationalist MHP, together with the division of foreign affairs responsibilities, suggests that this period of weak and fragmented coalition government is continuing.

[24] Two main parties are competing for virtually every inch of Turkish ideological territory: for the nationalist right, BBP and MHP; for the secular right, ANAP and DYP; for the left of centre, CHP and DSP.

March 1995–Sept. 1995	Erdal İnönü
Sept.–Oct. 1995	Coşkun Kırca
Oct. 1995–Feb. 1996	Deniz Baykal
March 1996–June 1996	Emre Gönensay
June 1996–June 1997	Tansu Çiller
June 1997–	İsmail Cem

This treatment of the foreign affairs portfolio ultimately had a demoralising effect on the ministry itself. Career diplomats were able to furnish continuity in foreign policy, but only up to a point. Sanberk soldiered on at the helm of the ministry until May 1995. But the absence for long periods of a policy lead at a political level, punctuated by short bursts of overly robust leadership, such as Soysal's pursuit of an 'honourable foreign policy', helped to drain some of the authority from Turkish foreign policy. Once again, it was the Republic of Turkey which suffered as a result of these aggregated upheavals.

The lack of political leadership at the Foreign Ministry was not, it should be pointed out, merely a function of the high turnover in ministers and the differing styles and priorities of some of their number. Even a relatively lengthy incumbency was no guarantee of serious and consistent policy engagement. Tansu Çiller was foreign minister between June 1996 and June 1997, yet this 12-month 'presence' did little to remedy the weaknesses of the previous couple of years. During this period Çiller also held the position of deputy prime minister, and looked forward once again to assuming the premiership upon the coalition's agreed rotation of office in June 1998. From 28 February 1997 onwards the military was actively engaged in trying to bring down the coalition and in attempting to precipitate a collapse of Çiller's party, and hence the government, through the encouragement of wholesale defections. Consequently, for much of this 12-month period, Çiller was distracted by national political, rather than foreign policy issues.

During this time Çiller rarely visited the Foreign Ministry building in Balgat, Ankara. She kept in touch with developments in foreign affairs through briefings given to her by senior diplomatic staff. Having ensured that her nominee for secretary-general, Onur Öymen, had replaced Sanberk, she let him preside over foreign affairs. Çiller became famous among increasingly cynical Turkish diplomats for only turning up to the Foreign Ministry when there was a photo opportunity in the offing; in other words she was a foreign

minister more interested in style than substance. Even the important area of relations with the West only proved to be a limited
exception. Earlier, when prime minister, Çiller had allotted little
time for the negotiation of the Customs Union, in spite of its
pivotal importance to closer ties with the EU, and this led to delays
and bottlenecks in the system.[25]

Neither was the confusion surrounding the political direction of
foreign policy so straightforward as to be confined to a distracted
foreign minister and a professional foreign service. The foreign policy of the 12-month Welfare-True Path government, the so-called
Refahyol coalition, was additionally more complicated because of
ideological and personal uncertainties. With the RP the dominant
party in the government, Turkish foreign policy was subject to a
constant and microscopic monitoring by all manner of observers
and commentators to see if the new government was subjecting
policy to an Islamist treatment. In fact, scrutiny of the period of the
Refahyol government shows that Turkey's traditional foreign policy
orientation was not adulterated; indeed, if anything, the secular,
pro-Western nature of it was actually strengthened, certainly in
contrast to the Ecevit-influenced Yılmaz-led coalition that was to
follow between June 1997 and January 1999.

Judging the nature and content of the Refahyol foreign policy
was, however, rendered more difficult because of what became an
increasing division of labour on foreign policy. While Çiller concerned herself with traditional Kemalist policy preoccupations, the
RP increasingly took on the hitherto largely neglected task of improving relations with the Islamic world. Indeed, the controversial
creation of a Development-Eight (D-8) group of countries, most of
which had large Muslim populations, in imitation of the G-8, was a
foreign relations initiative worthy of Özal. Lines of responsibility
with regard to foreign policy were further obscured by the emergence of an RP Minister of State, Abdullah Gül, as the man who
gave the political lead on such relationships. Though the description given to him in parts of the press as being a 'shadow foreign
minister' was technically inaccurate, and there were perhaps surprisingly few turf conflicts between Çiller and Gül, he certainly quali-
fied as a *de facto* junior minister with functional and geographical
responsibilities.

[25] Interview with former Foreign Ministry under secretary, 25 January 1995.

The collapse of the Refahyol government in June 1997, under intense and sustained pressure behind the scenes from the military, was thought by many to represent the final failure of viable government in the 1995–9 parliament. This did not prove to be the case. However, in order to put into place a government that was not dependent on the Welfare Party or the discredited Çiller, the Kemalist establishment had to go through political contortions. A three party coalition government of the secular right ANAP, the left of centre DSP and the small Democratic Turkey Party, consisting of the old Demirel supporters from DYP who had defected in an attempt to bring down Çiller, came to power under the ANAP leader Mesut Yılmaz. It was a minority government, which made it internally weak and vulnerable, and was dependent for its survival in parliament on the support of the smaller left of centre party, the CHP. In fact, with the military increasingly impatient at its unwillingness to push through anti-Islamist reform and the CHP leader Deniz Baykal increasingly threatening to scupper the coalition from the spring of 1998 onwards, the shortcomings of this ramshackle coalition were increasingly evident. Eventually it passed in January 1999, to be replaced by a DSP minority government which steered Turkey through to early elections in April 1999.

Though there was greater continuity in foreign policy at a presentational level, through the presence of İsmail Cem as foreign minister, in fact the weakness and brevity of the two governments prevented the development of clear and coherent policy. While Cem began to emerge as an effective spokesman on foreign affairs, especially towards the West, he was ineffective as a policy initiator. In fact, as in the preceding two years, policymaking was a fragmented affair. Yılmaz took a close interest in relations with the EU, only to be unable to contain his vitriol after perceiving a personal slight when the Luxembourg summit refused to give Turkey candidacy status. Ecevit, who was Yılmaz's deputy premier before leading the minority DSP government, maintained a weighty input into Cyprus policy and relations with Greece through his protégé, the equally uncompromising state minister Şükrü Sina Gürel.[26] Ecevit

[26] As one of Turkey's leading foreign policy commentators in the media, Mehmet Ali Birand, put it in a Reuters interview on 9 March 1998: 'Yılmaz turns a blind eye to Ecevit's Cyprus passion in order to keep the coalition running smoothly.'

also continued to take a close interest in Iraq policy, helping through skillful manoeuvring to make a looming US-led confrontation with Baghdad over weapons inspections in February 1998 ultimately unsustainable.

Arguably the best evidence of weak civilian government and the shifting responsibilities for policymaking came between late 1997 and autumn 1998, especially with the emergence of the diplomacy of the military. By this stage the Chief of Staff, İsmail Hakki Karadayı, was in any case the dominant actor in Turkish politics, having been the decisive figure in the fall of the Refahyol government. In December 1997 Karadayı visited Cairo to signal the fact that the Turkish military was not ignoring the Arabs and there was still some balance in Turkish policy. In April 1998 Karadayı flew to Georgia and Azerbaijan to boost ties with both states, and attended a WEU meeting in Athens, which was used to explore the possibility of a thaw in bilateral relations with Greece. In May he made a five day trip to Moscow to address a raft of issues of concern to Turkey, from Russia's sale of S-300 missiles to Cyprus and its toleration of the political activities of the PKK on its soil to its assistance to Iran for the development of missiles and nuclear technology and the growing Greek-Russian military co-operation. When combined with the regular forays abroad of Karadayı's deputy, General Çevik Bir, who enjoyed a platform and took pleasure in trenchant comment, there was increasingly little doubt as to which institution Turkey's friends and adversaries alike were obliged to take most seriously.

Primary players

THE GOVERNMENT

Nominally, the government, as the political expression of the democratic will, has responsibility for policy, including foreign policy. Notionally at least, therefore, the foreign minister, as the principal minister responsible for foreign affairs, has responsibility for the day-to-day political oversight of foreign relations within the policy parameters laid down by the cabinet. And on occasion in Turkey, most recently under the guidance of Hikmet Çetin, that is how the system has actually functioned.

Often, perhaps more often than not, the system works differently. It firstly works differently in terms of the messiness of governance in Turkey. The proliferation of cabinet positions, as a way of creating more senior patronage for party leaders when in office, has often meant that there is more than one figure responsible for any one area of foreign policy. Abdullah Gül and Şükrü Sina Gürel are but two examples of state ministers who have exercised considerable influence in foreign affairs even when not holding the portfolio.

Secondly, the system works differently because of the spasmodic emasculation of government. This has been the case where cabinet government has effectively broken down or been suspended for extended periods. This has proved to be a recurring characteristic of Turkish government with the fragmentation of political parties and the necessity since 1991 of coalition government. The growing incompatibility of leaders and parties within coalition governments from 1994 onwards has increased the temptation for party leaders to by pass the cabinet as the expression of the collective will of government in favour of government by cabals, cliques and committees. In the mid-1990s it almost became a pastime of political commentators to measure the time gap between successive meetings of the council of ministers, with a gap of 56 days being chalked up in 1994 under Çiller and well over two months during the last weeks of the Refahyol government in 1997.

Thirdly, the system also works differently in terms of the democratic deficit in Turkey. It is not the case that the democratically-elected government lays down policy, the implementation of which is then managed by the foreign and other related ministers. In Turkey, the guidelines of grand strategy, of high politics belong not to the government of the day as an expression of the popular will, but to the high priests of Kemalism, as an expression of the ideals of Atatürk. These guardians of the sacred will consist first and foremost of the senior officer corps of the military, supplemented at a secondary level by parts of the bureaucracy, and the top diplomats in the case of the Foreign Ministry. In other words, as members of the bureaucratic elite are often proud to point out, in Turkey one has to distinguish between 'state policy' and 'government policy'.

THE PRESIDENCY

Though the detail of its form has often changed, Turkey has, since the beginning of the emergence of multi-party democracy in 1946, always had a parliamentary as opposed to a presidential system. Under such a system, the prerogatives of the president are necessarily limited and contingent. However, in Turkey the president's role is more than merely titular. As Alan Makovsky has noted the power of the presidency 'increases proportionately to the weakness and passivity of the popularly elected government'.[27] Indeed, under the 1982 Constitution, drafted under the auspices of the military, a somewhat stronger presidency was created than had existed in the past.[28]

In the field of foreign affairs, the constitution has little specific to say beyond the obvious. The president is responsible for the promulgation and ratification of treaties, and for the accreditation of Turkey's representatives abroad and for receiving in Ankara the representatives of foreign states. On paper, at least, the post has considerable powers of appointment and discretion, including the ability to appoint the chief of the general staff and to call and preside over the NSC. With personality and context being so central to politics in Turkey, it is as easy to remember an iconoclast like Özal asserting his authority over the military in a context of the re-civilianisation of politics as it is to witness the timidity of Demirel, a man fearful of being removed a third time from office by the armed forces, in a context, since February 1997, of de-democratisation and the re-assertion of the military in Turkish politics.

In reality, that has meant that the presidency has often been a marginal force in Turkey's foreign affairs. Even Özal cut a pitiful figure as president in 1992 and early 1993 as he sought a route back to the political hub. To compensate for relative idleness, President Özal took to the air on foreign visits, notably to the Balkans and the former Soviet south in early 1993. Though such trips were generally well co-ordinated with the Foreign Ministry, they nevertheless caused some uncertainties in the regions concerned, and provided some black propaganda value for Greece and Serbia.[29] Ultimately, they simply drew attention to Özal's political frustrations as he languished outside the mainstream of Turkish party politics.

---

[27] Alan Makovsky, *Turkey's Presidential Jitters* (WINEP, Policywatch #451, 10 April 2000), p. 3.

[28] C.H. Dodd, 'Kenan Evren as President: From Conflict to Compromise' in Heper and Evin (eds), *Politics in the Third Turkish Republic, op. cit.*, p. 177.

[29] For example, the Yugoslav Federal Foreign Ministry accused Özal just after his Balkan tour of wanting to create an Islamic state in Bosnia.

For Demirel, who has never claimed any special expertise or even interest in foreign policy, the temptation of foreign affairs did not at first prove strong, especially as long as the domain was being well looked after by a coherent government and state bureaucracy. From 1994 onwards Demirel began to assume more of a profile in foreign affairs, with the areas of Central Asia, Azerbaijan and the CIS and then the Balkans and parts of the Arab World forming his personal priorities in descending order. Under the Refahyol government in particular, the first two of these areas were to become his favoured foreign affairs niches. According to one of Demirel's Foreign Ministry advisers, Demirel favoured Central Asia in particular because it was popular at home, he believed that he could make an impact, and no clear institutional framework existed for the development of such ties.[30] He could have added that consistently since 1993 no one else among Turkey's political leadership had considered it to be a priority area. Consequently, Demirel was filling a diplomatic vacuum. What is beyond doubt is that the leaders of these newly independent states warmed to his interest. In Demirel, the newly repackaged patriarchs of the former Soviet southern republics had at last found a kindred spirit.

In August 2000 the former constitutional court judge Ahmet Necdet Sezer was elected to succeed Demirel as president. During his first year in office he proved to be an aloof figure who, in keeping with his philosophy of a pared down presidency, was less active and interventionist than his predecessor, though he soon carved out a reputation for integrity and rectitude. However, foreign affairs appeared not to be a priority for Sezer, who stuck closely to the formalities of office. In April 2001 he paid a rare presidential overseas visit, somewhat surprisingly selecting the Netherlands as his first European destination.

THE FOREIGN MINISTRY

The bureaucracy has historically been the object of awe and deference in Turkey.[31] Within the Ottoman bureaucracy, the Foreign

---

[30] Interview, Ankara, 8 February 1995.

[31] For a discussion of the bureaucracy in the Ottoman and Turkish states see Metin Heper, *The State Tradition in Turkey* (Eothen Press, Beverley, 1985).

Ministry was an elite within an elite. This ethos of the Foreign Ministry as a centre of bureaucratic excellence persists in contemporary Turkey. It persists in the way that the diplomatic corps regards itself, and it persists in the deference accorded to the Foreign Ministry by ordinary Turks. After all, the ministry is famous for having the most difficult entry exam of all Turkey's ministries. In short, high status and prestige are firmly associated with recruitment to the Foreign Ministry.

The standing of the Foreign Ministry in Turkish society is further buttressed by the social and normative homogeneity of the service. New recruits tend to be drawn from a relatively small number of schools and universities, notably Ankara University and more recently Bosphorus University and Middle East Technical University, thereby reinforcing the exclusive networks at the top of Turkish society. Furthermore, new recruits tend to subscribe to the prevailing values of the Kemalist regime. It is, for instance, unusual to say the least to find a member of the Foreign Ministry staff who is a publicly observant Muslim, let alone one who either socially or ideologically stands outside the mainstream.

That is not to say that the Foreign Ministry is either a static or monolithic body. It is subject to change, as is the case with any other part of Turkish society. For instance, the ministry is no longer the only obvious professional choice for bright, well born and well educated young men; increasingly in the 1990s a well paid career in private business was likely to prove to be more attractive. It may be the case that the ministry is not quite as homogeneous as it has been in the past, with, most noticeably, a larger number of women now being recruited to diplomatic ranks. Such changes are, however, on the whole slow and incremental.

If the Foreign Ministry is regarded as part of the social elite in Turkey, it is also regarded as firmly part of the bureaucratic elite. Though only consisting of some 400 professional diplomats, the Foreign Ministry is razor sharp in its handling of certain portfolios and its performance in certain capitals and at certain forums. On issues relating to the EU, NATO, Cyprus, the WEU and the UN, and relations with the main European powers, the US and Russia, the ministry attains a level of activity well in excess of the often quite modest size of the genuinely diplomatic staff in its relevant

missions would tend to suggest. In contrast, postings to other geographical areas and multilateral institutions, notably for example to
the Middle East, have tended to be under-valued or even scorned
by those in the ministry. Even Turkey's relations with the states of
the former Soviet south have often suffered because of the nominal
diplomatic presence in these countries and the preference of top
flight diplomats for Western postings. If in developing countries in
general the collective memory of government tends to be short,
this is not the case in Turkey as far as foreign affairs is concerned. In
Turkey the collective memory tends to be much, sometimes very
much longer because of the relative institutionalisation of the Foreign Ministry.

The continuity and enduring professionalism of the Foreign Ministry have been aided by its immunisation from political patronage.
The 1970s, 1980s and 1990s have seen political parties increasingly
quick to exploit bureaucratic appointments as a way of rewarding
supporters. Even important and sensitive ministries, such as interior,
education and finance, have been subject to repeated attempts at
political colonisation by successive parties. Özal was a notable offender
against the principle of a professional and impartial civil service
during his two ANAP administrations.

If it had increasingly become the norm to make large-scale political appointments to the bureaucracy, the ambassadorial appointments would have been regarded as a particular prize to be shared
out to senior party supporters, as is the case in much of the US foreign service. In Turkey, this has not happened, as the Foreign Ministry is protected from such practice by law. Frustrated at not getting
his own way, this helps to explain why Özal came to take quite such
a personal interest in foreign policy. He was suspicious that some of
his bolder initiatives might not be implemented rapidly and in full if
left to the Foreign Ministry. Therefore, he tended to break the mould
of existing policies through often extravagant personal actions, in
order to rob the Foreign Ministry of its ability to moderate such
initiative through a process of bureaucratic incrementalism.

Özal, however, often went further than this. He had a penchant
for personalised diplomacy, because of the opportunities which it
afforded him in terms of high level connections and publicity. This,
in turn, helped to bolster his reputation as a statesman of international

repute at home, which further buttressed his larger than life image and hence, it was hoped at least, would translate into the valuable resource of votes come polling day. His personal telephone diplomacy with President Bush during and immediately after the Gulf crisis is legendary. Moreover, Özal often gloried in an ostentatious style, perhaps mischievously because he knew that it would offend and affront the diplomats in the MFA. The Turkish Foreign Ministry felt frustration at Özal's substantive initiatives undertaken without reference to them, such as his decision in 1992 to meet with the Iraqi Kurdish opposition groups. The ministry also had to repair bilateral relations damaged when Özal let off steam. His public aside during the 1990–1 Gulf crisis that the Germans were 'too fat and too rich to fight' was a case in point.[32]

The legally enforced professionialism of the Foreign Ministry has, nevertheless, not altogether preserved it from becoming tainted with domestic party politics. The appointment of the ministry undersecretary and of key ambassadorial and Ankara-based positions has certainly become both more political and more subject to public controversy since 1994 than was the case in the past. The most notorious example of this was the appointment of a successor to Özdem Sanberk as under secretary. Premier Çiller began by insisting that her former adviser Volkan Vural, then serving as ambassador to Moscow, should receive the appointment. Though his appointment was assumed to be cut and dried in the first half of 1994, and Vural had actually been recalled home, the newly installed foreign minister, Mümtaz Soysal, came to resist the promotion as his working relationship with Çiller deteriorated. Çiller, in turn, blocked ministerial promotions and postings in a bid to get her own way.[33] The name of Ambassador Candemir Önhon, then in London, subsequently came into the frame, apparently at the instigation of Soysal. When Çiller failed to get her way, and Vural's desire for the position waned, she turned her patronage to Onur Öymen, eventually winning out only after the departure from office of the quixotic Soysal. A further negative side effect of this unseemly and extended wrangle was that Foreign Ministry appointments were held up pending

[32] *Turkish Daily News*, 8 September 1992.
[33] *Turkish Daily News*, 29 November 1994.

the resolution of the stand-off.[34] Diplomats were, in the words of one anonymous commentator, 'packed up with nowhere to go'.[35] When the new foreign minister, Murat Karayalçin, came to approve the new postings, there were some 35 diplomats caught up in the human logjam.

This unseemly in fighting helped to weaken Turkey by politicising senior appointments, and creating a sense of grievance and demoralisation within the Foreign Ministry cadre. The damage to Turkey was not confined just to the period surrounding the appointment of the new Under Secretary, nor was it confined to the domestic domain. So closely associated with Çiller was Öymen that on becoming prime minister in February 1996 Mesut Yılmaz orchestrated a campaign to weaken and eventually oust the Under Secretary. In order to accomplish this, sensitive information on the Graeco-Turkish dispute over the island of Imia/Kardak was leaked to the press, in turn helping to damage Turkey's international position.[36] Again personal and party loyalties had eclipsed the wider interests of the country.

THE SECURITY ESTABLISHMENT

The military has always had a close relationship with politics in the modern state of Turkey.[37] For example, six out of Turkey's first seven heads of state were retired senior military officers, spanning the period from 1923 to 1989, the exception being the period of 1950–60 and the presidency of Celal Bayar, who was eventually ousted in the first military coup. The military also played a decisive role in the establishment of the state in the early 1920s. The centrality of the military as a feature of Turkish political life has its precursor in Ottoman times, when the military was central to the wielding and

---

[34] The situation in London was particularly embarrassing. Ambassador Önhon, Sanberk's predecessor in London, took his leave of Queen Elizabeth II in January, but then had to remain in post until the senior promotions were eventually resolved in late April. It was said that Önhon was obliged to stay away from major events for fear that he would meet the Queen and create a crisis of protocol.

[35] *Turkish Probe* No. 128, 19 May 1995.

[36] *Turkish Daily News*, 22 April 1996.

[37] For an up-to-date commentary on the Turkish military see Gareth Jenkins, *Context and Circumstance: The Turkish Military and Politics* (IISS Adelphi Paper 337, London, 2001).

retention of political power. For the first twenty-seven years of the republic the impact of the military was considerable, though usually rendered through informal contacts. Since the 1960 coup, the armed forces have played a more overt role in Turkish politics. In the last four decades the military has intervened four times to bring about governmental change: twice directly in 1960 and 1980; twice indirectly in 1971 and 1997.

Since 1961 the military has given constitutional propriety to its impact on government and policymaking through the development of the National Security Council.[38] The NSC is formally an advisory body which is chaired by the president of the republic and was, until the constitutional amendments package of October 2001 prescribed a civilian majority, made up equally of civilian and military figures.[39] Its brief is to submit its views on 'the formulation, establishment and implementation of the national security policy of the State'.[40] In practice, its impact on government is much more important than is stated. In spite of its split membership, it exists as a conduit through which the military can give their views on a range of policy matters, and the secretary-general of the organisation, though he does not enjoy voting rights, is a senior officer. It may dispense 'advice', but in practice it is virtually unheard of for cabinets and parliaments publicly to question its views, and it is a proud claim made by the NSC secretariat that there are no examples of recommendations in the realm of foreign policy that have remained unimplemented. The NSC is also responsible for coordinating the drafting and then the approval of the National Security Policy Document, a highly confidential document which establishes priorities

[38] According to the secretary-general of the NSC, the body was first established in 1933 on a statutory basis, it being the 1961 Constitution which gave the institution the full weight of constitutional authority. Interview with Gen. Cumhur Asparuk, NSC headquarters, Ankara, 7 December 1999.

[39] In addition to the president, the NSC has traditionally consisted of the prime minister; the defence, foreign and interior ministers; the chief of staff; and the heads of the four branches of the military, the fourth being the Gendarmerie. Though there is no legal provision for it, it has become a convention of the current administration to have the leaders of all three coalition parties take part in NSC meetings, Ecevit, as prime minister, with full rights, his two partners with speaking but not voting rights. In addition, other relevant figures can be invited to attend NSC meetings. Ibid.

[40] Article 118 of The Constitution of the Republic of Turkey, p. 60.

in national security threats and elaborates guidelines for responses. The November 1997 document made prominent mention of relations with Greece, Syria, the EU and the Turkic republics. It was updated in January 1999 and then again in May 2001, when the preoccupations were more internal.

In keeping with its concern with internal and external manifestations of security, the Turkish military keeps a close track of a number of issues in both domains. It does this, for instance, through the existence of the Turkish General Staff think tank, which was created in 1983 and extended in scope and authority by General Çevik Bir in 1996. It also does so through the 43 working groups within the military, the first of which was created in 1981 and whose number has been growing rapidly since 1996. Of this number there are said to be seven dealing with Greece alone, together with further groups dealing with single countries, like the United States, Britain, Iran, Iraq, Israel and Armenia, or regions such as the Balkans, the Turkic states and the EU or key issues like water, terrorism and fundamentalist movements.

Most obviously, the armed forces have dominated policy towards the Kurdish insurgency in the south-east since 1993, and hence have also had a major impact on Turkey's relations with Iraq, Syria and the EU. Since 1997 the military has spearheaded attempts to bring about educational reform as a way of undermining the attractiveness of the religious secondary schools. The General Staff has also established its own unit, the West Working Group (*Batı Çalışma Grubu*), to monitor anti-secular activities.

In the area of foreign policy the military has tended to be less overtly involved, especially during the first two periods under review. This has, however, changed quite markedly under the phase of weak, disorganised leadership. It was, for example, the army which drove forward the emerging strategic relationship with Israel, the pivotal moment of which was the conclusion of the secret training agreement in February 1996. In autumn 1998 it was the military that created the conditions under which Syria felt obliged to expel the leader of the Kurdish insurgency organisation, the PKK, Abdullah Öcalan.

The military is not, however, the only component of the security establishment that has a bearing on foreign relations. The MIT combines responsibility for both counter-intelligence and foreign espionage. It has widely been suspected that other security agencies in Turkey, notably the Gendarmerie, have their own covert operations. The Susurluk affair, a chance road crash which resulted in the revelation of links between organised crime, politicians and state functionaries in the security services, confirmed this to be the case, revealing the extent to which such agencies operate independently and even in competition with one another.

While most of the activity of such agencies takes place within Turkey, and hence is strictly speaking beyond the scope of this work, involvement does also exist beyond the borders of the country. That activity appeared to intensify from the 1970s onwards; it also became increasingly confused with the underworld of Turkish mafia gangs and the activities of the ultra-nationalists, notably those with a background in the Idealist Hearths (*ülkü ocakları*). As with much of the state's covert activity, the actions of its opponents, many of than involving the use of violence and assassination, provided a strong motivation for its expansion.

Much of this activity was developed in response to the PKK insurgency and the growing political activities of the Kurdish nationalist movement in Europe. Predating even that, the activities of the Armenian Secret Army for the Liberation of Armenia (ASALA) appear to have provided the initial impetus for the use of underworld gangs by the state. A raid on an ASALA base in the Beqaa Valley in 1984, for instance, was carried out by an *ülkücü* gang led by Alaatin Çakıcı, who went on to become a notorious mafia boss and who has recently been sentenced to an extended jail term in Turkey. The assassination of the ASALA leader Agop Agopyan in April 1988 is also alleged to have had an *ülkücü* connection.

The activities of the Turkish security and intelligence services and their associates have not been confined to the Armenian and Kurdish issues. One clear example of the foreign operations of such agencies or rogue elements within them came with the aborted coup attempt against the Azerbaijani president, Haydar Aliyev, between 15–17 March 1995, led by the former deputy interior minister Ruşen Cevadov. Following its failure, in part due to a tip-off from President Demirel, President Aliyev immediately accused official Turkish circles of involvement. Shortly afterwards, on a visit to Baku, prime minister Tansu Çiller apologised for the involvement of 'an uncontrollable

Turkish right-wing group' in the coup attempt.[41] It was subsequently revealed that a Turk serving in his country's embassy in Baku had been spirited out of Azerbaijan immediately after the coup attempt.

Secondary players

PARLIAMENT

The overwhelming focus of the Turkish Grand National Assembly (TGNA), Turkey's unicameral parliament, is with domestic political issues. Foreign affairs, consequently, are of a much more limited and spasmodic focus. Moreover, in Turkish politics the political parties are the dominant mode of political organisation, and, in turn, the leader dominates the party. In what Kamran İnan has called the 'political feudalism' in Turkish party politics,[42] parties are highly centralised and subject to the tyrannical control of the leader. The *quid pro quo* for MPs and party members is the access to power and resources which the leader's patronage can deliver provided he or she and their party are successful either electorally or during the process of coalition building. Of course, there are limitations to party discipline, and the frequent and sometimes mass defections which have punctuated the life of parliaments in the 1990s are testimony to this. However, these defections tend to be the product of individual calculation, born often of frustration at the limited advancement under the prevailing party leader; where such defections are more ideologically inspired, they rarely relate to the domain of foreign affairs.

At the political margins, the TGNA is involved in foreign affairs. There is, for example, a Foreign Affairs Commission of the Turkish parliament, which discusses new bills relating to foreign affairs, receives visiting dignitaries and undertakes a variety of trips abroad. The committee has tended to have only a very limited impact on the field in the past, and does not enjoy much of a public or media profile in Turkey. It also seems to be seen as a political backwater by the country's leading actors. In 1997, for example, Murat Karayalçin somewhat reluctantly accepted the offer of the chair of the commission, the suspicion being that this was an attempt by the Cum-

---

[41] *Turkish Probe*, 14 April 1995.
[42] Interview with the author, Ankara, 26 September 1996.

huriyet Halk Partisi (CHP) party leadership to distract him from the continuing internal party struggles.[43] The TGNA has also occasionally taken an interest in specific issues in foreign affairs, and established an ad hoc Bosnia Committee during the civil war in Bosnia-Herzegovina.

Parliament's utility lies less in terms of the activities of its individual members and more in terms of the forum for debate and policy which it offers, usually to the benefit of the government. From June 1992 onwards the Turkish government transferred responsibility for the extension of the six-monthly mandate for Operation Provide Comfort 2 (OPC 2) to the TGNA. OPC 2, since January 1997 retitled Operation Northern Watch, was the mechanism by which a handful of coalition powers enforced the no-fly zone north of the 36th parallel in northern Iraq from June 1991 onwards. The policy had met sustained criticism from the opposition, while many officials too had misgivings about it. Offloading responsibility for the six-monthly renewal of the operation's mandate onto parliament was an efficient and effective way of taking the pressure off a new coalition government.

An area of policy debate which permitted the opposition a forum for criticism was policy towards Israel. Islamist parliamentarians in Turkey have periodically criticised different aspects of the opening up. For example, Abdullah Gül roundly criticised Tansu Çiller's visit to Israel in November 1994, at a time when virtually all of the Occupied Territories was still under Israeli control. He also attacked the idea to sell water from the Manavgat river to Israel, and objected to the principle that Turkey help facilitate openings for Israel to the 'Turkic' republics.[44] RP deputies would frequently attack the pro-Israel leanings of such adversaries as Coşkun Kırca during parliamentary debate.

THE MEDIA

There has been an explosion in the amount and range of private media activity in Turkey since 1989. This has been particularly marked in the field of broadcasting. In 1989 the state still enjoyed an effective monopoly in this field. Suddenly, private television and radio stations mushroomed. The state's first inclination was to try to

[43] Interview with Murat Karayalçın, Berlin, 8 June 1998.
[44] TRT TV 3 November in BBC/SWB/EE, 5 November 1994.

suppress such activity. However, this simply resulted in private channels moving off-shore and beaming their transmissions into Turkey, notably from Germany. The state consequently and reluctantly relented, and Turkey today enjoys a broad pluralism in terms of television and radio broadcasting, as indeed it does in magazine and book publishing, though the daily Turkish press is increasingly tainted by the direct influence of media barons and the leverage exerted over them by government.

This general atmosphere of pluralism does have its shortcomings. Ankara continues to prevent any television station from broadcasting in the Kurdish languages from its territory. Kurdish television can be received in Turkey in the form of Med TV, and its successor Medya-TV, the Kurdish channel which broadcasts from Brussels under license from London, and which is widely regarded as being close to the PKK. The Turkish authorities were profoundly unhappy with this state of affairs, though its response softened with the advent of Medya-TV, but are powerless directly to prevent the transmissions. State efforts have concentrated on preventing its Kurdish population from receiving the station, and discouraging foreign countries from assisting Med TV, with some success.[45] Such persuasion and pressure eventually helped to bring about Med TV being banned from the airwaves by the London-based Independent Television Commission. The fact that Med TV continued to broadcast for so long become a major issue in bilateral relations between Turkey and both Belgium and Britain.[46] Indeed, in an otherwise cordial relationship, Med TV was the single most serious problem in relations between Ankara and London over much of the 1990s.

The media are also important in terms of external relations with respect to the so-called 'Turkic republics' of the former Soviet south. Ankara established the Avrasya television network specifically to broadcast to these emerging states. The aim was to solidify a

---

[45] The Turkish government was successful in pressuring French and Portuguese companies into cancelling contracts on pain of economic sanctions, while a satellite transmission contract with the Polish PTT was apparently cancelled following the intervention of Ankara. See *Turkish Daily News*, 5 July 1996.

[46] For example, during the visit to Turkey of the British foreign secretary, Malcolm Rifkind, in September 1995, the issue of Med TV was the biggest source of Turkish unhappiness with Britain.

broader set of political and economic relationships through cultural, and in this case, informational ties. The station aimed to acquaint the Turkic peoples of these societies with Turkish culture, politics and society, and to try to develop a common set of values and identity. As with the attempt to forge economic and political relations, the Avrasya channel has been a disappointment. The regimes in power in these new republics were wary of ceding their monopoly over information, even to an apparently friendly state like Turkey. Political obstruction therefore helped to compound technical problems, especially in the difficulties surrounding the terrestrial rebroadcasting of transmissions. This problem was further exacerbated by under-resourcing and some indifferent programming, which meant that there was generally little demand from the countries concerned to be able to receive the broadcasts.

Inside Turkey the media have already had a big impact. A range of perspectives, from the Islamist and nationalist right through the secular right to social democracy and the soft left, are nightly on offer in the form of various discussion programmes. A wider selection of radio stations, many of them locally oriented and unlicensed, offer an even broader set of ideological perspectives. Such networks and stations do include foreign affairs in their coverage, though this tends to be much less prominent in comparison with domestic issues.

Arguably of greater importance in terms of the foreign affairs debate is the press, and particularly the many foreign affairs columnists who write for the main national circulation newspapers. The Turkish press includes a much larger number of regular columnists than the British or North American press. These columnists reflect a range of expertise, being drawn from among academic experts and retired diplomats, as well as professional journalists. A handful of the best known columnists are particularly influential. In turn, they are cultivated by a range of different actors, both domestic and foreign, in the hope of influencing the wider debate in Turkey.

It is, of course, extremely difficult to measure the impact of such columnists. Much research needs to be done on the sources of information on which articles are based and their influence on the primary foreign policy actors. Suffice it to say that the esteem in which foreign affairs columnists like Sami Kohen of *Milliyet*, described by one senior Turkish diplomat as the 'dean of columnists',[47] are held can be glimpsed at in the prominence which they enjoy in their newspapers, and the attempts which are made to cultivate them.

Cyprus One of the best illustrations of the potential influence of columnists was witnessed over the Cyprus issue in the second half of 1992. The UN Secretary-General, Boutros Boutros-Ghali, was in the midst of a major diplomatic push, based on a 'set of ideas' and a 'non-map'. President Özal was keen to see the Cyprus problem solved, because of the negative impact which he felt it was having on Turkey's international standing. Foreign minister Çetin was co-operating with the US-backed UN diplomacy. The leader of the Turkish Cypriots, Rauf Denktaş, was manoeuvring for all he was worth to try to dissipate the international pressure. Prime minister Demirel was trying to avoid being drawn on the issue, mindful of its emotive force in Turkey.

With Denktaş on the defensive, he was assisted by the Turkish Cypriot lobby in Turkey, and notably Mümtaz Soysal. Soysal was then a high profile and respected academic, who was also a long standing adviser to Denktaş; he also happened to be a columnist on one of the three Turkish mass circulation dailies *Hürriyet*. He vigorously attacked the international effort to corner Denktaş, and stoutly defended the uncooperative attitude of his ally. Soysal employed a range of populist arguments to raise the alarm among Turks as to the nature of the solution being offered in northern Cyprus. For example, he wrote at the height of the diplomatic efforts that the Turkish Cypriots were being told: 'Either cede lots of land or agree to have lots of Greek Cypriots settled amongst you.'[48] He also sought to rally Turkish public opinion through historical references which played on Turkish insecurities and latent xenophobia. He wrote that if Turkey gave in on Cyprus, other demands, the West's 'bagful of Orient problems', such as the Aegean, the Armenian issue and the Kurdish issue, would follow; the 'spirit of Sèvres', he wrote, 'can come back to haunt us and the turning point is the Cyprus issue'.[49]

---

[47] Unattributable interview with author, 8 December 1999.
[48] *Hürriyet*, 24 July 1992.
[49] *Hürriyet*, 27 November 1992.

While a range of other leading columnists, such as Hasan Cemal, Mehmet Ali Birand and Sedat Ergin, were writing regularly on the Cyprus issue at that time, it was Cengiz Çandar who emerged as the chief adversary of Soysal. Known to be close to Özal, and presumed to be on occasions a mouthpiece for the president, Çandar vigorously defended the desirability of a successful outcome to the UN initiative from the perspective of Turkish national interest. He asserted the need to deal with the political reality of the dominant position of Greek Cyprus in the international community.[50] He also attacked those who were trying to move the goalposts just when the UN was close to a workable accord on the basis of a bi-zonal, bi-communal, federal settlement, the principles for which Turkey had long been arguing. Furthermore, he criticised Denktaş for trying to manoeuvre in such a way as to suggest that it was Turkey that was making territorial concessions on the island.[51]

With Turks always likely to be more swayed by the florid arguments advanced by Soysal, Demirel eventually withdrew his lukewarm support from the UN initiative. Denktaş, with the help of a handful of Turkish columnists and the sympathetic leanings of public opinion, had succeeded in manipulating Turkish domestic politics to his benefit internationally.

INTEREST GROUPS

The 1980s, and the development of a new economic strategy, saw the emergence of business groups with a direct interest in foreign economic policy. Before 1980, the business community was overwhelmingly inward focused and dependent on the state. This cosy and safe relationship began to break down with the introduction by Turgut Özal of an export-oriented economic strategy. Increasingly, companies began to look for new opportunities abroad and to become more self-reliant and entrepreneurial. While hidden barriers to imports and the rentierist practices of the Turkish economy have perpetuated some of these old practices, much of the Turkish private sector is now dynamic and innovative.

Turgut Özal's contribution did not remain purely at the level of the reform of the business environment. As we have seen, he was

[50] *Sabah*, 22 July 1992.
[51] *Sabah*, 4 August 1992.

determined that Turkish businessmen should actively profit from the new relationships which he was establishing and nurturing abroad; hence Özal's practice of taking businessmen with him on his trips abroad, together with officials and journalists. His aim was to orient business culture towards investment, trade and contracting abroad, and to ensure that business benefited from the goodwill and introductions which came in the wake of such visits. Soon leading businessmen competed with one another to be included, eager to improve their access to the prime minister. Özal cleverly exploited this understandable trait to imbue the business sector with the new values of export-oriented trade. Those leading businessmen who were alert to the opportunities being presented in turn rallied to defend Özal in the early days, when, as the generals' economic guru, he was vulnerable to outside criticism. They drew the attention of European critics, concerned that Özal's authority had been acquired under a military regime, to the positive substance of his policies.[52]

By the late 1980s parts of the Turkish private business sector had begun to establish extensive commercial ties abroad. In turn, such businessmen began to develop tangible interests in foreign policy. An increasingly central business interest was that political problems with neighbours, which have in Turkey's case always been considerable, should not be allowed to interfere with commercial operations. More specifically, this perspective took the view that economic sanctions should not be taken in pursuit of political objectives. It was, for instance, of some note that a Turkish business leader, İshak Alaton of the Alarko corporation, attempted to use his business contacts with American-based Armenians to try to promote economic interaction between Turkey and Armenia.[53] A second example was seen during the Chechen conflict in the Russian Federation. Turkish businessmen lobbied behind the scenes to persuade Ankara not to introduce economic sanctions against Russia for its crackdown on the Chechens for fear that this would damage growing commercial

[52] Interview with leading Turkish businessman, Berlin, 8 June 1998.

[53] For example, he arranged a meeting between Hirair Hovannian, whom he accompanied, and Turkish foreign minister Hikmet Çetin, at which Hovannian argued for the opening of a border gate for trade to enable Armenia to benefit from transit traffic via the Black Sea port of Trabzon. See *Sabah*, cited in Turkish Press Review, 19 February 1992.

interaction with the federation. A third significant response from the business community came in reply to the Luxembourg summit of December 1997. Though disappointed by the final communiqué, mainstream businessmen generally exerted a sobering influence, cautioning against an over-reaction against the EU and pointing out that the outcome of the summit was not entirely unexpected. In so doing, Turkish businessmen helped to temper premier Yılmaz's somewhat intemperate reaction to the Luxembourg summit.[54]

Of course, it would be misleading to view the business community in Turkey in the 1990s as being monolithic. Foreign policy interests divide the business community along sectoral, ideological and organisational lines. When Ankara was seriously negotiating the detail of the Customs Union (CU) with the EU, the textile and related sectors were enthusiastic advocates because of their relative strength at home and within the European market. Other sectors, such as the automobile industry, were much more sceptical, fearing the impact of a flood of cheaper, better quality, named vehicles. It was no coincidence that it was the Koç company, with its major interest in the co-production of cars with Fiat, that was one of the more ambivalent of Turkish companies towards the CU. Small and medium-sized Turkish industries also feared the consequences of the dismantling of *de facto* protectionist barriers against the EU.

To some extent, ideological interests overlapped with sectoral interests. Hence it was the Association of Independent Industrialists and Businessmen (*Müstakil Sanayiciler ve İşadamları*) or Müsiad, a business organisation representing mostly small and medium sized commercial interests whose owners are self-consciously practicing Muslims,[55] that was the businessmen's organisation most sceptical about the CU. Ideologically, Müsiad had none of the instinctive attachment to closer integration with the EU that Tüsiad, the employers' organisation representing the country's big firms, and mainly Kemalist in nature, has always appeared to display. The fact that Müsiad's constituency feared for its material interests in a CU gave focus to the organisation's demands for a renegotiation of the terms

---

[54] *Turkish Daily News*, 16 December 1997.
[55] For background on Müsiad see Oxford Analytica Daily Brief on 'TURKEY: Islamic Business', 3 April 1996; Ayşe Buğra, *Islam in Economic Organisations* (TESEV/Friedrich Ebert Stiftung, Istanbul, 1999).

and conditions of the CU. Müsiad's membership and activity have been accelerating rapidly since its establishment in 1990. In the case of CU renegotiation, however, Müsiad failed to persuade the Refahyol government actively to seek such a renegotiation during its 12-month tenure of office.

Müsiad may well have been marginally more successful in persuading the Refahyol coalition to expand existing and build new economic ties with the Muslim world, although this was a priority already shared by the RP when it came to power. Certainly, members of the Müsiad secretariat were happy to join Erbakan's delegation on both his Asia and his Africa tours in the autumn of 1996. In turn Müsiad, though active in many countries, appears to have made a special effort to follow-up on the Erbakan visits to Malaysia and Iran.

ETHNIC PRESSURE GROUPS

Turkey is in great part a state made up of immigrants. Successive waves of migrants have arrived over hundreds of years. More important, Turkey has received new waves of migrants, principally from the Balkans and the Caucasus, since the 1870s. Many of these people were Balkan Turks and Muslims who fled to the Anatolian core of the state as the Ottoman Empire spasmodically but inexorably shrank in south-east Europe. With natural growth, these peoples now represent formidable proportions of the total Turkish population.[56] Other waves of migrants have arrived more recently, culminating with the arrival of Bulgarian Turks fleeing the Zhivkov assimilationist policies of the mid- to late-1980s. Furthermore, Turkey has always provided a home for Turkic dissidents and émigré politicians, from Chinese Uighurs to Uzbekistani dissidents to Afghan political figures.[57]

---

[56] For instance, with intermarriage inflating the numbers, by 1994 it was estimated that up to 10 mn Turks had ethnic roots in the Caucasus.

[57] Around 20,000–25,000 east Turkistanis were estimated to have emigrated to Turkey in the early 1950s. Uzbekistani dissident Muhammad Salih spent some time in Turkey in 1994 and 1995, before leaving against a backdrop of increasing dissatisfaction from Tashkent. It was to Turkey that the Afghan warlord Rashid Dostum (also an ethnic Uzbek) fled after his temporary ousting from the north of the country in May 1997.

Many of the more self-conscious activists belonging to such waves have kept their political focus by establishing émigré political and support networks. The great majority of such arrivals have, however, been content to assimilate on the basis of the majority ideology of the state. They have taken seriously Atatürk's nationalist dictum to set aside their parochial identities and give a voluntary allegiance to the notion of being Turks: the ethnicity, identity and geographical origins of the people in the past thereby becoming unimportant. The emergence of a collective curiosity by Turks about their origins since the end of the 1980s has partly reversed this process, though only with Turkey's Kurdish communities has it taken on a strident ethno-nationalist form. For most of the rest of the population all that has taken place is a kind of cultural curiosity.

Where the voyage of self discovery has been more pronounced has been among groups of Turks who hail from areas that have encountered political change and even conflict since the end of the Cold War. These groups have been active in the assistance of new refugee arrivals; examples include the Yugoslav Emigrants Social Assistance and Solidarity Association in the case of the Bosnian refugees who began to come to Turkey in April 1992, and the Caucasia Chechen Solidarity Committee (CCSC) assisting wounded Chechen refugees in January 1995. They have also been particularly active in the provision of humanitarian aid to conflict areas, such as the CCSC which received Turkish government authorisation to launch a nation-wide appeal for Chechenya.

These and other groups have also taken on an overtly political role. Much of this effort has concentrated on advocacy work, especially within Turkish domestic politics. The Rumelian Turks Association illustrated the access which such groups could achieve in April 1992, when it met Çetin and İnönü to urge Turkey to take 'stronger measures' in support of the Bosnian Muslims.[58] In April 1993 the Azerbaijani Cultural Association urged Ankara to take 'more effective and lasting measures' in the face of the growing conflict between Armenia and Azerbaijan.[59] Such groups have also played a behind-the-scenes role in ensuring a widespread and high-level hearing for visiting politicians from the relevant conflict area. An excellent

[58] *Turkish Daily News*, 27 April 1992.
[59] BBC/SWB/EE, 5 April 1993.

example of this was the role played by the CCSC in the visit of the Chechen former Speaker of the Duma, Ruslan Khasbulatov in May 1995.[60] Such organisations have also sought to influence the position of Turkish political parties.[61] Some groups are suspected of playing an even more active role on behalf of their fellow strugglers, from supplying personnel and materials for military training,[62] through facilitating the despatch of volunteer fighters, especially in Azerbaijan, to even becoming involved in arms smuggling.

On the whole, such groups have met with only very limited success. They have tended to succeed in publicising their causes, notably in parliament and among the media. But they have usually failed to make any inroads into Turkish policy, especially when confronted by a consistent policy line backed by diplomats and military men. The nature of such groupings has often been that they would try to persuade the Turkish state to intervene more directly on behalf of their fellow strugglers. For the institutions of the state, which are historically and strategically highly attuned to the potential risks of such adventures abroad, the inclination was always to resist such pressures. In the end, the ability of such groupings to muster real, sustained political pressure has invariably been extremely limited. A combination of organisational fragmentation and personal rivalry, together with an instinctive first loyalty to the Turkish state and its interests on the part of the broader communities, rather than to their fellow strugglers, goes a long way towards explaining the relative ineffectiveness of these ethnic lobbies.

PUBLIC OPINION

The state tradition in Turkey is that the people exist to serve the state rather than the state existing to serve the people. This is a tradition that has prevailed for hundreds of years, and which characterised the Ottoman Empire. Only since 1950 has the Turkish state

---

[60] *Turkish Daily News,* 25 May 1995.

[61] For example, a representative of the Bosnian Solidarity Association addressed members of the Welfare Party in Ankara. See Yeşim Arat, *Political Islam in Turkey and Women's Organizations* (TESEV/Friedrich Ebert Stiftung, Istanbul, 1999), p. 27.

[62] In early 1994 there were estimated to be around 160 former Turkish officers in Azerbaijan in a training capacity.

adopted the formalities of democracy on a sustained basis. Beneath the structures and processes of democracy, the assimilation of democratic culture has been much more limited. Clientelist ties have typified the relationship between at least some of the political parties and their supporters, especially in the more rural, tribal and underdeveloped parts of the country.[63]

These attributes of Turkey's political culture tend to make policymaking in general and foreign policymaking in particular a predominantly elite-oriented affair. Public opinion polls of varying degrees of reliability indicate that Turks do have views on external affairs and attitudes towards other states. Nevertheless, these views rarely appear to have an impact on either policymakers or the policymaking process. It is as if the elite does not expect to take such views into account, while the mass of the population does not expect its views to be taken on board. Even on emotive issues such as Bosnia, it appeared as if the foreign policy elite in Turkey did not come under any sustained, mass pressure to adopt a more assertive approach. Attempts to convene mass rallies on such popular issues have tended not to attract demonstrators beyond the ranks of the highly politicised. Perhaps the best example of this was the February 1993 rally for Bosnia in Taksim Square in Istanbul. Under the slogan of 'Turks to Bosnia', the rally only succeeded in attracting 20,000 people, mostly drawn from those with ultra-nationalist and Islamist backgrounds.[64]

There is, however, one major exception in terms of public opinion. That exception is Cyprus, the one foreign policy issue which is able to have a major impact on domestic politics, as has already been shown in the war of the columnists in 1992. Even the issue of Cyprus is difficult to evaluate or quantify in terms of its impact on public opinion. Senior Turkish diplomats claim that Cyprus is the one issue on which a national consensus exists across Turkish society. The decision in the late 1990s by the board of the Turkish Economic and

---

[63] For an impassioned statement on the undemocratic practices which often flow from Turkey's democratic forms see Ersin Kalaycıoğlu, 'Turkish Politics: Central and local governance in Turkey', unpublished paper, p. 14, presented to a conference on 'Turkey and the European Union: A Question of Image or Governance?' at Bosphorus University, Istanbul, 3 December 1999.

[64] *Turkish Probe*, 16 February 1993.

Social Studies Foundation (TESEV),[65] arguably Turkey's leading think tank, that while it was prepared to undertake research into the extremely delicate question of Islam in Turkey it was unwilling to initiate a debate on Cyprus, points to the emotive nature of the issue.

While most commentators and analysts would probably agree that public opinion has not been very important with respect to foreign affairs in the past, there is an increasing assumption that public sentiment is of growing importance in the 1990s. This may, to a degree, be the case. Turkey is clearly a country in transition, economically, socially and in terms of state–society relations. Far fewer Turks are now dependent on the state for a living; civil society is growing, especially in the major cities; some of the Islamist mayors have, since their successes in the local elections of March 1994, largely repeated in April 1999, begun to inculcate a new value of service in the provision of local government; the media are pluralist, with a broad range of views and ideas laid out nightly by the country's main television channels. From the perspective of a Western liberal tradition, all of these trends are to be applauded and welcomed. Extrapolating normatively one might expect such developments to result in the eventual production of a population of citizens, roughly akin to a Western European model, and ergo with a greater impact on foreign affairs. Leaving aside the questionable assumptions of unilinear development implicit in such a view, one suspects that the reason why these developments have made such an impact is not their direct influence on public policy *per se* but their almost complete absence until relatively recently.

For most of the last two decades the process of Turkish foreign policymaking has been somewhat chaotic. The personal intervention of Turgut Özal, together with his strong character, resulted in a period of strategic vision and bold initiatives between 1986 and 1991. This individual approach helped Turkey to benefit from an international system increasingly in transition, although Turkey was vulnerable when Özal miscalculated. Since 1994, the chaos of Turkish

---

[65] The acronym is derived from the Turkish name of the foundation, Türkiye Ekonomik ve Sosyal Etüdler Vakfı. The think tank was located at Bosphorus University, but is now at Sabanci University.

foreign policymaking has been much more disastrous in its effects. As a result of party political weakness and the self-serving nature of politicians, foreign policy has been characterised by political discontinuity and confusion; often the state of Turkey has lost out as politicians have focused on their own short term, tactical calculations. An increasingly demoralised bureaucracy has found it hard to mitigate the problems at the political core. Amidst such confusion, the military has re-emerged as an assertive foreign policy actor.

Sandwiched between these two periods was the 1991–4 era of a collegiate, bureaucratic approach to foreign policy, where a small number of professional diplomats worked in close association with the leading politicians of the day. Together, they produced careful, solid, unspectacular foreign policy, firmly located within a Western, multilateral context of international legality. Turkey and indeed its friends were fortunate that this era corresponded with the worst of the conflict and instability of the post-Cold War period.

It is fashionable among the students of civil society to look for new, non-state players in the area of public policy. Thus, there has been a growing interest in such players as the media, public opinion and the ethnic lobbies in Turkey. To be sure, these do exist and have sporadically attempted to exert some effect upon the foreign policy-making process. Perhaps in the long term they may indeed emerge as being of primary importance. In reality, however, the leading players in the domain of Turkish foreign policy in the 1990s look much the same as those which have dominated in the past. The Foreign Ministry remains an elite institution which attracts well trained minds, and which expects to preside certainly over the day to day execution of policy. In the late 1990s, the military has emerged more publicly than at any time for the last decade and a half as the most important institution, at least in charting the strategic direction of foreign policy. Of increasingly fleeting importance in all of this are the politicians, acting through the institutions of the government and the presidency. With short attention spans, low policy horizons and a preoccupation with the vicissitudes of domestic party politics, they appear increasingly unable to give Turkey the clear and democratic lead which its foreign policymaking requires.

Part II
DOMESTIC MOTIVATORS OF TURKISH FOREIGN POLICY

3

HISTORY AND FOREIGN POLICY

As in so many recently created states, history in Turkey is so much more than simply the disparate, collected views of the past. History helps to legitimise the creation and existence of the state; it helps ideologically to orientate the state; it tells a story which embodies the myths, ideas and values which give meaning to political life within the state. Consequently, it is of little surprise that historical orthodoxies are so prized, and are often treated as being inviolable. Indeed, Ataturk himself said: 'Writing history is as important as making history.'[1] As befits a society where education is often crude, and rote learning the dominant pedagogical tool, the orthodoxies of the elite in Turkey have provided some, though not all, of the foundation stones of the world view of the masses.

The need to invoke, interpret and, where necessary, invent the past was extremely important during the first decades of independence, when projects as fundamental as state, nation and ideology building were in full flood.[2] The Ottoman Empire was eschewed as a discredited rival, and the ancient civilisations of the Hittites and Sumerians were plundered as an alternative source of greatness and inspiration. The importance of such undertakings could be seen in

---

[1] Quote following the preface of Mustafa Kemal Atatürk, *The Speech*, translated and abridged by Önder Renkliyıldırım (Metro, Istanbul, 1985), p. 4.

[2] For a discussion of the importance of the interpretation of history in the new republic's secular Kemalist nationalism, see Hugh Poulton, *Top Hat, Grey Wolf and Crescent: Turkish Nationalism and the Turkish Republic* (Hurst, London, 1997), esp, pp. 101–14.

the establishment of well funded research associations dealing with both history and language.[3]

In turn, it is little wonder that those who seek to challenge the political dogmas of the age choose to do so by attacking the historical assumptions that underpin them. An obvious and emotive case in point is the issue of the Armenian 'genocide' of 1915. Armenian organisations, especially those in the diaspora, have hounded the modern state of Turkey for what they believe was an organised act of genocide during the First World War. Such campaigns have taken contemporary political forms, most clearly in the failed attempts to pass motions accusing Turkey of genocide in the US Congress in 1989 and 2000, and in the successful effort to get the French National Assembly to pass a similar motion in 1998 and 2001. Though the trauma of the massacres and the long stateless limbo experienced by the Armenians since then may help to explain the Armenian fixation with the issue, the fact that Ankara has allowed the issue to affect its bilateral relations with France is testimony to the sanctity of a particular historical narrative in Turkey.

As has already been implied, history in Turkey is important for foreign affairs. This is obviously in the sense that the past provides the backdrop for the political relationships of the present. No Turk, and no Russian either, can conduct bilateral business today without being aware of the fact that their two countries, in their various predecessor guises, have fought thirteen wars with one another. As one Turkish journalist has whimsically observed, the Turks and Russians really are blood brothers.

However, history is also important in other more subtle ways. History is a key determinant of perception in that it helps to form an identikit picture as to the make-up of others. It is these cognitive maps which are used to make sense of the actions and statements of other states, peoples and non-governmental associations, and hence to drive the policies and strategies of the state actor in response.

The Arabs: orientalism without the sentimentality

As is the case with most former imperial powers, among the Turkish elite there is an enduring sense of superiority towards those forefathers

---

[3] Taner Timur, 'The Ottoman Heritage' in Irvin C. Schick and Ertugrul Ahmet Tonak (eds), *Turkey in Transition* (Oxford University Press, 1987), p. 6.

who were once subjects of the Ottoman Empire. This disdain tends to be stronger towards the Middle Eastern rather than the Balkan and European former provinces of the Empire, and is particularly strong in the case of Turkish views of the Arabs, or, to be more precise, those Arabs who were latterly subject to the Ottoman yoke.[4] Even at the height of Arab economic power in the late 1970s and early 1980s, when Turkish companies were chasing Arab commercial ties and Turkish diplomats were in pursuit of Arab votes on Cyprus, there was always a sense of distaste for such peoples. At best, the Turkish view of the Arab world was lukewarm. There is on the part of the Turkish intelligentsia a deep-seated lack of respect for the Arab world.

To some extent this elite view of the Arabs reflects a wider set of perceptions whereby Turks regard the Arabs as being inferior.[5] One has only to look at the Turkish language to see that a deeply pejorative view of the Arabs exists in the very structures of Turkish society. Examples abound. In Turkish the word Arab is translated as 'nigger' as well as 'Arab'.[6]

Similarly, a whole raft of phrases and sayings exist in Turkish which reflect negatively on the Arabs. The term *Çol Arabi*, or desert Arab, is often used as a throwaway reference to the simple and unsophisticated nature of the Arabs, of whom little can be expected, and is readily cited to describe Libyan leader Muammar al-Qadhafi. Indeed the term *deli adam*, or madman, is another term regularly applied to Qadhafi. In addition, the Arabs are often the object of Turkish humour, taking the role of the Poles in America, the Belgians in France and the Irish in England.

It must, however, be pointed out that this distaste is far from being one-sided. The Arabic language too is peppered with phrases

---

[4] Turks have tended to enjoy rather better relations with the Arabs of North Africa, either because of the looser or less recent encounters with the Ottoman Empire, or because the resentment engendered by subjugation is more firmly directed at the French.

[5] Richard Robinson, for example, writes of ordinary Turks looking down on Arabs as a people who are unable to conduct their affairs 'in a civilized fashion'. See *The First Turkish Republic: A Case Study in National Development* (Harvard University Press, Cambridge, MA, 1963), p. 171.

[6] A.D. Alderson and Fahir İz (eds), *The Concise Oxford Turkish Dictionary* (Oxford University Press, 1985), p. 15.

and saying which decry the Turks. Arab historiography of the Ottoman Empire too is shot through with the pejorative; as L. Carl Brown has written, 'Arabs...have interpreted the Ottoman era in Arab nationalist terms', dismissing anything that frustrates the development of the notion of an Arab political community as alien.[7] Arabic and Ottoman literature also offer examples of the mutual hostility that has existed.[8] Though not everything associated with the Arabs is regarded negatively in Turkish society, Arabesque music for example being very popular among certain social strata in Turkey (though frowned upon by polite society), such images help to enforce stereotypes rather than drawing attention to the diversity of the 'other'.

It is important to underline the fact that this pejorative view of Arabs and the Arab World is not confined to the Kemalist elite. It also extends, for instance, to the counter elite, especially those for whom Islam prescribes an all-embracing world view. Islamists in Turkey, it is true, are better disposed towards the Muslim east than their Kemalist counterparts, and are more likely to visit the region and have social and political contacts there. However, they tend not to view other Muslims and especially not Arab Muslims as being equal. The vision that is repeatedly articulated by many mainstream Turkish Islamists is of a unified Muslim world, *with Turkey at its head*. In other words, Turkey's Islamists also make the same assumptions of superiority as do their secular fellow citizens, though based upon the Turkish nationalist notion that the Ottoman Empire was a Turkish state which spiritually and politically dominated the Islamic world.

THE ARAB REVOLT

It is against this backdrop of ingrained cultural attitudes that recent historical experience should be set. The Turks' historical experience of Arabs, in living memory roughly equated with the span of the twentieth century, though spasmodic has certainly been raw and even on occasions traumatic. The defining issue for Turks was the

[7] See 'The Setting: An Introduction' in L. Carl Brown (ed.), *Imperial Legacy. The Ottoman Imprint on the Balkans and the Middle East* (Columbia University Press, New York, 1996), p. 11.
[8] Norman Itzkowitz, 'The Problem of Perceptions' in Brown, *Imperial Legacy*, op. cit., p. 35.

so-called 'Great Arab Revolt' of Sharif Hussain of Mecca, the late King Hussein of Jordan's great grandfather. The uprising followed the Hussain-McMahon correspondence between Britain and the Hashemites, the British intention being to weaken the Ottoman war effort by opening a new area of fighting at its rear. Sherif Hussain, though charged with the governance of the holiest city in Islam, eschewed the Islamic solidarity of the Ottoman Empire in favour of dynastic ambition. Though the revolt was hardly a critical factor in the defeat of the Ottomans in the First World War, it did indeed divert resources to the southern extremity of their territory, and the Ottomans sustained a string of military reverses.

Today, the recollection of the Arab revolt is still intense. It is deeply resented by Turks. It has become a recurrent illustration of the duplicity of the Arabs. *Araplar geldi bizi sırtımızdan hançerlediler,* roughly equivalent to 'the Arabs stabbed us in the back', is how Turks routinely express their views on the matter. In turn, this image is still regularly invoked prescriptively, as a sharp reminder of the inadvisability of the Turks placing too much faith in Arab support.

It is almost unnecessary to add that, as with most popular histories, recollection and reality are not entirely synonymous. The received wisdom of the Arab revolt ignores the fact that no Arab units of the Ottoman Empire defected to Sharif Hussain, nor did any political or military figures of stature join him; support for the revolt was confined to the Hijaz and some adjacent tribal areas; his supporters consisted of a few thousand tribesmen, subsidised by the British exchequer, and a handful of non-Hijazi officers, who were either Allied prisoners of war or émigrés residing in British controlled territory.[9] Thus, comparatively few Arabs did actually support what was widely viewed as a movement for dynastic ambition rather than a genuinely broadly-based nationalist effort. And, in a tribally fractured society, it is unlikely that there would have been a broad-based mobilisation even if its nationalist credentials had been less dubious. What is beyond doubt is that inestimably more Arabs continued to fight for the Ottoman side in the Imperial army than ever joined Sharif Hussain. Ironically, then, the bulk of the Arabs did indeed remain true to the ideological foundation of the Ottoman Empire, namely loyalty to the centre in the name of Islam.

[9] David Fromkin, *A Peace to End All Peace* (Avon Books, New York, 1989), p. 219.

If there exists an inevitable gap between historical perception and the facts of the past, periodic experience has nevertheless served to reinforce these enduring images of the Arabs as duplicitous. For Turkey and the Turks, this contemporary reinforcement is most regularly and intensely felt in the dealings with their immediate Arab neighbours. In 1987 the then Turkish prime minister, Turgut Özal, left Damascus following a high level visit convinced that he had a deal whereby Turkey would guarantee an annual average flow of Euphrates water across the border in return for Syria ending its practical support for the Kurdish insurgency movement, the Kurdistan Workers Party (PKK). For some weeks the Syrians appeared to keep to their side of the bargain. Before the year was out, however, it became clear to the Turks that this had only been a tactical lowering of the public profile of support and nothing more substantive. Whatever the truth of the matter, Damascus has hardly attempted to contest this conventional view in Turkey. Subsequent Turkish initiatives towards Syria up to 1998, aimed at the same elusive outcome, further confirmed the Turkish perception of the mendacity of its neighbour.

Though history has provided an important underpinning to current views and policies, one must of course resist the temptation of historical determinism. While it may indeed be the case that Turkey has at best indifferent relations with all of the Arab countries, there has been one exception, namely Jordan.[10] More precisely, relations with the Hashemite leadership of Jordan, up to February 1999, were arguably the only inter-leadership relations with the Arab world that could be viewed as cordial. Both the late King Hussein and the former crown prince, Al Hasan bin Talal, were regular visitors to Turkey and enjoyed good relations with a number of senior Turkish figures. Moreover, security cooperation between Jordan and Turkey has advanced apace since 1996, in part as a function of the emerging Israeli-Turkish relationship. The irony in all of this is that it was precisely the Hashemite dynasty that was responsible for the revolt in 1916. If there is one set of leaders in the Arab world with whom Turkey ought for visceral reasons not to have good relations it is those of the Hashemite Kingdom of Jordan. The fact that this is not the case is testimony both to the enduring importance of personal

---

[10] Writing in the early 1970s Ferenc Vali described Turkey's contacts with Jordan as 'characterized by cordiality and sincerity'. *Op. cit.*, p. 309.

chemistry in international relations and the ability, in spite of its historical and ideological baggage, of the Turkish elite on occasion to act pragmatically.

THE BAGHDAD PACT

The Arab revolt has not been the sole traumatic event for Turkey with regard to the Arab world this century. More recently, the experience of the Baghdad Pact has exposed the vastly differing political culture prevalent on the two sides. For Menderes' Turkey, the Baghdad Pact was a straightforward strategic exercise aimed at joining up the North Atlantic (NATO) and Central (Cento) treaty organisation areas with a view to preventing the spread of Communism and Soviet power. Turkey, Britain, Iran, Iraq and Pakistan formed the membership of the pact and Ankara pushed very hard for Jordan to join. For other Arab states, notably Egypt and its leader Gamal Abdul Nasser, the core aim of the pact was regarded as relatively unimportant, especially when compared with the competing agenda of national independence, and Egyptian and personal aggrandisement masquerading as Arab unity. If Turkey and Egypt found each other increasingly on different sides, it became more and more clear that the former was ill equipped to pursue its objectives in the Middle East. Ankara misjudged the aspirations of Arabs from Algeria to Egypt, and failed to realise that its alliance with Britain appeared likely to prolong colonial rule in the region, while neglecting to take into account domestic ferment in Jordan and ultimately Iraq, where bloody revolution in July 1958 did for the Baghdad in the Baghdad Pact. Furthermore, Turkey's heavy-handedness was directly counter-productive in that it drove a weak and unstable Syria, a country already with an acute 'Turcophobia',[11] into closer relations with Moscow.[12] To this day the Baghdad Pact saga remains the greatest foreign policy debacle of republican Turkey.

Dazed and disoriented by its experiences in the 1950s, Ankara reacted by affirming that it would disengage from intra-Middle Eastern disputes, while seeking correct rather than cordial relations with all states in the region. Such an approach has broadly speaking

---

[11] Ferenc Vali, op. cit., p. 299.
[12] See, Philip Robins, *Turkey and the Middle East* (Pinter/RIIA, London, 1991), p. 26.

served Turkey well, the ultimate example of this disinterestedness being the successful and profitable even-handedness pursued towards the protagonists in the Iran-Iraq war. Nevertheless, it is important to appreciate that this was a strategy born of weakness, uncertainty and dwindling self-confidence. It betrayed a perception of the Arab world as complex, unstable, impenetrable and unintelligible. It reinforced the notion of the Arab World as being different from Turkey. Because the new political values of Turkey were ones predicated on rationalism, progress and a European identity, those of the Arab world were seen as being diametrically opposed and hence as intrinsically inferior. For Turkey, the view of the Arab world was an Orientalist one, but without the sentimentality which has traditionally characterised the approach of Western Europeans. If the latter's view of the region was often patronising and indulgent, the Turkish view was more likely to be contemptuous and antipathetic.

West Europeans: friends not to be trusted

Turkey's relations with Western Europe[13] in the 1990s rested on a paradox. On the one hand Turkey is earnest, desperate almost, in its commitment to being a European state; this has been most manifest in its dogged determination to join the institutions and structures forged and developed by the West Europeans over the past half-century. At the same time, Turkey is also profoundly suspicious of Western Europe and what it regards as the political agenda of neo-Imperialists, Christian Democrats and liberal humanists alike,[14] which it fears will risk if not result in the weakening and even the dismantling of the Turkish state.[15] Thus, ironically, in demanding swift

---

[13] For a considered Turkish perspective on the relationship see Meltem Müftüler-Bac, *Europe in Change. Turkey's Relations with a Changing Europe* (Manchester University Press, 1997).

[14] For example see Şahin Alpay's quotation from a book published in 1995 by the General Staff of the Turkish Armed Forces in an article headlined 'Islamists not alone in suspicions of Europe' in a special report on Turkey and Europe in the *Independent*, 22 May 1996.

[15] For a vivid illustration of this dual attitude one only has to look at the front cover of the latest book by the respected economist from Istanbul University, Professor Erol Manisalı. It shows a man in a pinstripe suit holding out his right hand as if to shake hands, while holding a wide-blade kitchen knife in his left hand with

membership of the EU, with the far-reaching loss of sovereignty that this implies, the Kemalist elite of Turkey risks emphasising and exacerbating the centrifugal forces at home which it is so desperately anxious to stamp out.

Of course, the post-Second World War period is not the origin of either end of the paradox. Indeed, one can argue that the period from the late 1940s through the late 1980s actually softened these tendencies. During this time the overwhelming threat to Turkey and Western Europe alike was the military and ideological threat posed by the Soviet Union. Consequently, both Turkey and the Western Europeans had a strong over-arching motivation for working closely in a common alliance. Both sides had a strong vested interest in managing and even sublimating issues which potentially divided them, from human rights through the treatment of Turkish guest workers to integration beyond the specifically security field. This situation worked well enough until the collapse of Communism and the reduction of Soviet and then Russian military power. Since the late 1980s the glue that had kept Turkey and Western Europe so very close together has weakened. Once again it is the European history of the early part of the century rather than the middle to late period that most graphically informs Euro-Turkish ties.

THE IMPERIAL LEGACY

The experience of the Imperial age also provides a legacy of ambivalence. During that period the Ottoman Empire was certainly part of the European system. It featured in the inter-state politics of the continent for more than four centuries. However, it did not do so on the basis of equality. During the early engagement with the European system the agenda was one of an Ottoman bid for hegemony, an attempt fundamentally to subvert and bring down the political and ideological edifices of the continent. Once it had critically failed at the gates of Vienna, the Ottomans' European enterprise slid into a protracted period of decline. If Britain and France artificially bolstered Ottoman power during the long years of decline

---

the blade pointing upwards, which is hidden behind his back. See *Avrupa Çıkmazı. Türkiye-Avrupa Birliği İlişkileri. İçyüzü ve Perde Arkasıyla* (Europe Deadlock: Turkey-EU relations: the real truth behind the Curtain) (Otopsi, Istanbul, 2001).

in the nineteenth century, it was only as a convenient bulwark against the rise of Russian power. The strategic goal continued to be the independence of the former Ottoman provinces in the Balkans and the eradication of the oriental and Islamic empire in continental Europe. In short, the Ottoman Empire was certainly part of the evolving systemic kaleidoscope of European inter-state relations between the fourteenth and nineteenth centuries; in this sense there can be no doubt as to the status of the Ottoman Empire as a European actor. However, to infer from this that the Ottoman Empire and the successor state of Turkey is somehow intrinsically European as a result of such an experience is simply the ill informed product of wishful thinking.

If the engagements of empires form an extended historical backdrop to contemporary Euro-Turkish relations, undoubtedly the period of the post-First World War settlement provides a shorter, but also a much more intense and traumatic experience. For the West Europeans, the Ottoman Empire was a defeated power as well as a long spent force. With Britain and France left in occupation of so much of its former domains it was hardly surprising that the visionaries of London and Paris should set to work on imagining its future. In doing so, the two victorious European powers were aided by minor states which, through luck or calculation, had found themselves on the winning side in 1918 and hence were well placed to embark upon special pleading. These included, most significantly, Greece and Italy. With Britain and France distracted by a long agenda, with the classical and religious values of a small number of largely well born men informing the new vision, and with the US contribution centring on the Wilsonian ideas of self-determination, the scene was set for the indulgence of the minor states and the romantically perceived peoples of the remaining Ottoman lands. However, the Turks, to their great disadvantage, fell into neither category.

TREATY OF SÈVRES

Reflecting this constellation of influences, there then followed the Treaty of Sèvres, signed on 10 August 1920,[16] which Gün Kut has

---

[16] See *Treaty of Peace with Turkey* (HMSO, London, 1920) and *Tripartite Agreement between the British Empire, France and Italy respecting Anatolia* (HMSO, London, 1920).

called a 'crucial reference point' for Turkish foreign policy,[17] and a bold but ill fated attempt by Greece to realise its 'Great Idea'.[18] The Turks, in so far as such a people existed at this time, had by implication been marked out by the victors of the First World War to be the leading casualty of this particular passage of history. Sèvres did prescribe territory for an Ottoman successor entity in northern Anatolia with Istanbul as its capital, but this area was to be small, impoverished and dominated by larger adjacent actors. Otherwise, much of the lands included in the National Pact were to be given in a variety of forms to the control of existing states like Greece, Italy and France or set aside for nations soon to graduate as states, such as the Armenians and possibly the Kurds. In the words of Bernard Lewis, Sèvres would have left Turkey 'helpless and mutilated, a shadow state'.[19]

It is often pointed out that among much of the Turkish elite today a 'Sèvres mentality' prevails. This is undoubtedly true.[20] This mentality forms a prism through which external ties with a range of different countries, most obviously with those in the West, are perceived and distorted, hence complicating relations.[21] Most important, the Sèvres mentality is based on an erroneous misreading of the dynamics of the post First World War settlement. The attempt to foist such an unfavourable settlement on the Turkish heartlands of

---

[17] Presentation to a seminar on Turkey and its neighbours, Rome, 12 September 1995.

[18] This was the aspiration to unite all the Greek speaking areas into one central state, with its capital in Constantinople. With the large Greek populations in that city, along the Aegean coastline, in parts of the interior of Anatolia (notably Cappadocia) and on the Black Sea coast, the proponents of this 'Greater Greece' looked to Anatolia *with* covetous eyes. For further discussion of the Great Idea see Richard Clogg, *A Concise History of Greece* (Cambridge University Press, 1992).

[19] Bernard Lewis, *The Emergence of Modern Turkey* (RIIA/Oxford University Press, London, 1967), p. 247.

[20] One can see this in the regularity with which references are made to Sèvres in the analysis of commentators and the public discourse of politicians. For example: Mümtaz Soysal has referred to a 1992 proposed Cyprus settlement as a turning point in the return of the 'spirit of Sèvres' (*Hürriyet*, 27 November 1992); Necmettin Erbakan called Operation Provide Comfort 2 in northern Iraq an occupation force and a second Sèvres (TRT TV 28 December, in BBC/SWB/ EE, 30 December 1994).

[21] As one Turkish ambassador to an EU country stated at a seminar on 11 November 1997: the Western powers were 'at the gates of Ankara after the First World War'; hence Turkey smells conspiracies whenever Europeans insist on conditionalities.

the Ottoman Empire did not represent the culmination of a widely based historical conspiracy to do down the Turkish nation and rob it of its chance of greatness. Rather, it was a historically specific plan that was ill thought out and poorly executed, and reflected, to say the least, an unusual confluence of different forces. That it failed so lamely between 1920 and 1922, and that with the failure of Sèvres the great powers were so prepared to have another but very different go in the shape of the Treaty of Lausanne, is to expose the poverty of this notion of conspiracy.

In spite of this detached appraisal, it is not however difficult to understand the nature and the profundity of the Turkish national trauma. Defeat in a world war, with the death, destruction and impoverishment that came with it, was followed by a seemingly unstoppable international coalition aimed at its division, subjugation and humiliation. The Imperial capital was occupied by foreign troops and the old political and spiritual leadership of the empire humbled. Greek armies arrived in Anatolia with the aim of replacing the Ottoman Empire with their own. The whole enterprise had the legitimacy of international treaty, and the moral underpinning of being part of a new world order. Turkey was only saved through the leadership of Mustafa Kemal and a few other important, though less lauded, figures like Kazım Karabekir, together with the determined resistance of their followers. It is, on reflection, not so very surprising that many of the people of Turkey, with their penchant for Sufi mystical Islam and their long tradition of shamanism, have gone on to beatify Atatürk.

Given the trauma of the 1918–23 period, the importance of self-reliance in the birth of the modern state and the routine nature of the eulogising of Atatürk and those who fought for national independence, it is little wonder that the past and its rigid historical interpretations so intrude upon the present. Many Turks, apparently from all walks of life, regard Sèvres as a moment of clarity and insight into the real attitudes and intentions of the Western Europeans. Such a view would regard the everyday nature of inter-state intercourse as but an extended exercise in dissembling aimed at making a tactical use of Turkey in, for example, limiting Soviet power or, in the context of the Customs Union with the EU, aimed at exploiting the opportunities of a large and increasingly important domestic market.

This brooding suspicion of the Western Europeans has been periodically reinforced by Turkish experience since, again often interpreted as fleeting glimpses of the real European agenda for Turkey. The decision of Western European governments to give political asylum to a range of Turkish émigré political activists in the 1980s and 1990s, especially those of Kurdish ethnicity linked to the PKK and its front organisations, is perceived as showing a fundamental sympathy for those groups who would impose the Sèvres blueprint by stealth and from within. The difficulty which many Western European governments have in curtailing the activities of such groups is interpreted as evidence of malign intent. Turks adopting this mode of analysis fail to see that it is the democratic and human rights shortcomings in their own country since 1980 that have made it so extremely difficult for Western European governments to fend off asylum applications by political activists, or those claiming to be the victims of political persecution, from Turkey who are on the run. In short, it is the policies of Ankara and the practices of the Turkish state which have foisted large Turkish and Kurdish asylum communities on the Western Europeans and created the anti-Turkish lobby within.

THE ANKARA AGREEMENT

If Sèvres has cast a shadow across the relationship between Turks and Europeans, a shadow of which the vast majority of the latter are now really rather ignorant, it is the 1963 Ankara Agreement, which established an association agreement between Turkey and the EEC, that is the other main point of orientation in the relationship. For the government and similarly minded Turks, ever preoccupied with the formalities of institutional integration, the agreement is of pivotal significance.[22] The agreement provides the framework within which all contemporary discussions about the relationship between Turkey and the EU are couched. For the association agreement provided a road map for future structural integration, most obviously in the case of moving towards the conclusion of a customs union, and also

[22] For a recent and broadly representative example, see Ebru Loewendahl, *"Promises to Keep": The Reality of Turkey-EU Relations* (Action Centre for Europe, Chorley, Lancs, 1998).

formally conceded the notion of Turkish eligibility for member-ship of the emerging European body.

In all manner of meetings, discussions and dialogues between Euro-peans and members of the Turkish establishment the association agreement is rarely absent from Turkish contributions. However, the agreement does not act as a mutual reference point permitting both sides to address outstanding problems from a common point of departure. Rather it is a document that is far more often cited by Turks than Europeans. It is cited like a piece of scripture, setting out the principles of the relationship and the (for implied read categori-cal) promises ultimately of full membership,[23] even as Turks go on to express their fears of being left outside emerging European structures. It is frequently cited by Turks who then proceed to hec-tor Europeans for a betrayal of their obligations as outlined in the 1963 document. In short, the Ankara Agreement does not function as an important milestone for both sides in a partnership founded on reciprocity, but as a debating point to be scored again and again by legalistically inclined Turks, rather than as partners concerned together to overcome outstanding obstacles.

If for Turks dialogue with Europeans is treated more as a court-room exercise than as a fireside chat among friends or a collegiate diplomatic exercise in problem management, it says much for the distrust with which Turks approach Western Europeans. There can be little doubt that some of Ankara's sense of grievance with the EU is understandable enough, though this tends to be more the product of oversight, ignorance or weakness on the part of Western Europeans rather than deliberate design. Take three examples. First, the tetchy and insensitive handling of the December 1997 Luxem-bourg summit by the Luxembourg presidency is a recent instance of poor presentation born of the vanity, inexperience and modest capacity of a small state insistent on having its turn in a big role at a crucial moment; it is not then a function of malice aforethought.[24]

---

[23] For an example of this see Minister of State responsible for Europe and Cyprus, Şükrü Gürel: 'To become a full member of the EU is in fact a right of Turkey emanating from the Ankara Agreement of 1963' — 'A General Appraisal of Current Turkish Foreign Policy' in Mustafa Aydın (ed.), *Turkey at the Threshold of the 21st Century* (International Relations Foundation, Ankara, 1998), p. 12.

[24] As an example of this tetchiness, the prime minister of Luxembourg, Jean-Claude Juncker, was quoted as saying: 'The Luxembourg Summit is not about

Second, Brussels' protestations at an earlier Luxembourg summit, in 1975, that the EC's admission of Greece to full membership would not be allowed to impair its relations with Turkey have been exposed as pious and empty. Third, Brussels has failed to overcome the Greek veto of its contractual obligations to disburse funds to ameliorate the adjustment effects of the CU on the Turkish economy since 1996, resulting in those funds subsequently being lost, again a development in bilateral relations which is hardly Ankara's fault.

But not all of the reverses sustained by Turkey at the hands of Europe can be attributed to the EU and member states. Some were the responsibility of Turkey. For instance, if the EC did not begin to disburse, the Ecu 600 million allocated to Turkey under the Fourth Financial Protocol, that was due to the actions of the military in seizing and maintaining power in the early 1980s. Later in the decade Turkey was informally beseeched not to lodge a formal request for membership of the EC, both because it was clearly not ready for membership, and because completing the preparations for 1992 and the advent of the single market was the overriding priority for the EU, rather than further enlargements. Nevertheless, Turkey, in the form of premier Özal, persisted, the EC parrying the application through the Commission *avis* in 1989.[25]

Of course some of the injustices done to Turkey during this period were simply due to force of circumstance. When Ankara made its application to join the EC in 1987 the countries of Eastern Europe were still the sworn enemies of the West and dedicated to

---

Turkey. I will not have it that this historical moment is simply taken as a debate on Turkey.' See *Turkish Probe*, no. 258, 21 December 1997.

[25] The response from the European Commission is invariably presented in highly negative terms from a Turkish perspective. A considered and informed view from the European Commission was that the reason for this was the Turkish public's unpreparedness for the 'shock' of not being given a date on which accession negotiations would commence. See Michael Cendrowicz, 'The European Community and Turkey. Looking Backwards, Looking Forwards' in Clement H. Dodd (ed.), *Turkish Foreign Policy: New Prospects* (Eothen Press, Huntingdon, 1992), p. 19. In contrast to the pessimism from Turkey, William Hale's conclusion in *Turkish Foreign Policy, 1774–2000* (Frank Cass, London, 2000) that the *avis* was a 'polite rebuff' (p. 178) or a 'measured rebuff' (p. 234) is a more judicious assessment.

an alternative vision and organisation of humanity. If a decade later the Czech Republic, Hungary and Poland are envisaged as full members of the EU, in all likelihood some years before the earliest moment that accession can be practically envisaged for Turkey, it owes rather more to the unforeseen configurations of history, of which Sèvres many decades ago and then only fleetingly was another example, than to any grand design or strategic objective of the European states inexorably pursued through Brussels.

HELSINKI OR LUXEMBOURG?

It must, at very least, remain a moot point whether the Luxembourg summit referred to above, which David Barchard has called 'the Luxembourg debacle',[26] or the Helsinki summit some two years latter will emerge as the dominant historical reference point in EU-Turkish relations. Whichever it is, it is likely in time to acquire the historical stature of the Ankara Agreement or the Treaty of Sèvres in Euro-Turkish relations. Whatever the final fate of Helsinki, a preliminary judgement, however, suggests that Luxembourg will not easily disappear from the collective consciousness of Turks concerned with the future relationship with Europe, and that when it is cited, it will be darkly and as a by word for accumulated bitterness.

The Turkish charge against Luxembourg is twofold. First, that in agreeing to Cypriot accession negotiations the EU once again capitulated to a political agenda developed and driven by Athens.[27] The charge is technically erroneous, though politically convenient, as the decision simply codified the reciprocal part of a trade-off agreed in March 1996, whereby Greece accepted not to block the implementation of the Customs Union with Turkey in return for a commitment to the commencement of accession talks with Cyprus.

The second charge, however, was far more momentous in the psychology of Euro-Turkish relations. Turkey had been omitted from two groups of countries: the first group of six, including

---

[26] David Barchard, *A European Turkey?* (Centre for European Policy Reform, London, 1998), p. 1.

[27] For a succinct description of the Turkish view see Atila Eralp, 'Turkey and the European Union in the Post-Cold War Era' in Alan Makovsky and Sabri Sayarı (eds), *Turkey's New World: Changing Dynamics in Turkish Foreign Policy* (WINEP, Washington, DC, 2000), pp. 181–2.

Cyprus, with which the EU had agreed to commence accession negotiations in April 1998; and the second group of five countries which would have to wait for accession talks, but which would benefit from converging relations through 'accession partnerships'. Turkey was mentioned as being 'eligible' for membership, but without being formally assigned an accession partnership. By implication it was alone, the lone, friendless wolf of Turkish mythology once again confirmed, in a third category of one. Moreover, by placing Turkey beneath second group countries like Bulgaria and Rumania, former Communist states, where elite change had not been as clear-cut as in the Visegrad states and economies were only partly reformed, the EU had imposed more than national dignity could stomach.

The official Turkish government reaction to Luxembourg was one of defiant outrage, and a determination to find itself the victim of dark skulduggery.[28] Its candidacy for full membership was considered to be 'a right' under the Ankara Agreement. Turkey considered that it had not been subject to 'the same well-intentioned approach' or the same 'objective criteria' as the others. 'Partial, prejudiced and exaggerated assessments' had been made both about its domestic affairs and foreign policy, especially towards Cyprus. Ominously, the statement referred to attempts having been made 'to impose unacceptable political conditions' which have '*concealed intentions*' (emphasis added). Consequently, the government decided to suspend political dialogue with the EU.

As the weeks and months passed, so Luxembourg began to harden in the minds of Turks. Luxembourg had become a synonym for double standards, as the Europeans refused to judge Turkey according to the criteria of others, refusing to acknowledge attempts to raise the standards of democracy. In the words of one Turkish minister the EU had applied 'artificial and subjective criteria', the effect of which had been that the EU had 'lost most of its credibility in Turkish eyes'.[29] Luxembourg had also become a symbol of the EU's

---

[28] Statement by Turkish government in response to Luxembourg summit, 14 December 1997.
[29] The minister was speaking at an off-the-record round table meeting in Europe 8 June 1998.

rejection of Turkey, one that had come to be viewed with clarity by Turkish public opinion. Finally, Turks seized upon Luxembourg with a special relish because for them it constituted, like Sèvres, 'a moment of truth': a moment when the EU had eschewed the ambiguity or, for preference, the hypocrisy of its past approach to Turkey.[30] Many elite Turks were almost gleeful at what they considered to be proof of what they had suspected all along, that the EU had no intention of admitting them as full members.

Luxembourg 1997 threw a shadow over Turkey-EU relations, which prevailed for the following two years, during which the political dialogue with the EU remained suspended. The legacy of Luxembourg was eclipsed, at least temporarily, by the December 1999 Helsinki summit, at which Turkey was formally given candidate status. The change within the EU was brought about by three main factors. First, a growing appreciation on the part of European leaders, with Britain's Tony Blair to the fore, that Luxembourg had been a disaster, and a new attempt must be made to manage the question of Turkey.[31] Second, a change at the domestic level in critical member countries, notably Germany and Greece, over how best to handle Turkey the replacement of Helmut Kohl's Christian Democrats in government and a new inclusive spirit in Athens were of decisive importance in making the difference. Third, an outpouring of popular sympathy among public opinion across Europe, Greece included, for Turkey in the wake of the earthquake in August 1999 and the consequent terrible loss of life.

With Turkish elite opinion ever volatile on the European issue, Helsinki triggered a moment of euphoria. The Turkish press was packed with detailed news reporting and analysis for days to come

[30] These are phrases and sentiments taken from the notes prepared for the 8 June 1998 meeting.

[31] There is a debate about the extent to which such a change in attitude took place as a result of American advocacy on Turkey's behalf. Paul Taylor, the Reuters diplomatic correspondent, who has taken a special interest in topics like Turkey's relations with the EU and Cyprus, argues that this was a key factor (conversation with the author, 24 May 2001). This view is supported by Ulrike Guerot, head of EU research at the German Council on Foreign Relations, who was cited in 'A Survey of European Union Enlargement' in *The Economist*, 19 May 2001, as saying that in granting candidate status to Turkey the EU was 'caving in to American pressure'.

after the summit. Pictures of the European 'family photograph' taken at Helsinki, now including prime minister Bülent Ecevit and foreign minister İsmail Cem, adorned the front page of just about every mainstream daily paper. What had been quickly forgotten during this period of celebration, however, was that Ecevit was initially sceptical and suspicious of the Helsinki deal. Even Cem, who as foreign minister might have been regarded as having a bureaucratic vested interest in Helsinki, was also initially reluctant. To his credit, President Demirel's instant reaction was that the offer was decisively in Turkey's interest, and he set about giving a positive lead. Turkey's acceptance of Helsinki was sealed by a clever piece of public diplomacy by the EU's foreign and defence policy guru, Javier Solana, who ostentatiously flew to Ankara to help persuade Ecevit and returned to Helsinki with the Turkish prime minister on board his plane. Finally a senior European political figure had emulated what the Americans had been doing since the mid 1990s, that is to learn how to play the Turks.

If Helsinki was an important threshold passed for Turkey, the nature of the reaction was, ironically, likely to be problematic in terms of future relations. First, the Turkish side was unable or unwilling to appreciate that Helsinki was much more about managing Turkey in the short to medium term than the taking of a strategic decision to have Turkey as a full member of the EU.[32] Second, the euphoric reaction to Helsinki ignored the fact that Turkey was only at the beginning of a process that would require the uphill slog of considerable political changes at home, rather than at the beginning of a downhill descent towards membership. More specifically, Turkey would have to satisfy the political conditions enshrined in the Copenhagen Criteria[33] in order for pre-accession negotiations

---

[32] The French strategic commentator, Prof. François Heisbourg, while unsure whether Helsinki was an example of EU decision-making at its best (that is, building towards Turkey's eventual membership) or at its worst (that is, an example of simple expediency), makes the point that it is in Turkey's interest to act as though the former were true and hence capitalise upon the opportunity that Helsinki offers. Address made at a workshop on Turkey, Geneva, 26 April 2001.

[33] This refers to the accession criteria contained in the Copenhagen European Council in June 1993, which, on the political side, states that: 'Membership requires that the candidate country has achieved stability of institutions guaranteeing

even to begin.[34] Even in the midst of the Helsinki euphoria, Turkey-based diplomats speculated on how long it would be before the party ended and the hang over began. Third, Turkey's self-serving political class immediately began to speculate on a wholly unrealistically short timeframe for membership, keen to turn the Helsinki celebration into short-term political capital. Thus a new set of unrealistic expectations was hatched, with disappointment and disillusion inevitably to come.

The best hope for Helsinki on the European side had been that some real momentum for reform in Turkey had been generated, and that this would help create a common sense of purpose that would carry the relationship through future periods of turbulence. In fact the goodwill of Helsinki was quickly dissipated. In part this was due to some unhelpful visits by prominent EU figures, such as the Swedish foreign minister Anna Lindh, who, though well intentioned, needlessly antagonised even moderate Turkish sentiment. In part it was due to the resurrection of an old debate about how far Turkey should go in terms of domestic reform, notably over the Kurdish issue and the role of the military in politics, in order to appease the EU. By the end of 2000 a series of wrangles over European defence and the specificities of a draft accession partnership agreement had brought all parties back down to earth. In turn, the hearts of Europe's Turcophiles sank at the emergence of Mesut Yılmaz, the man who had accused Germany of a new *lebensraum* strategy just two years before, as the Ecevit coalition's lead minister in relations with the EU. With the euphoria of a year before well and truly dissipated, the question of which would become the reference point for Turkey-EU relations, 'Luxembourg or Helsinki?', was once again a moot point.

---

democracy, the rule of law, human rights and respect for and protection of minorities'.

[34] For a discussion of the Copenhagen Criteria and how they affect Turkey see David Barchard, *Building a Partnership, Turkey and the European Union* (Turkish Economic and Social Studies Foundation, Istanbul, 2000), especially Chapter 4; and Bertil Duner and Edward Deverell, *Too Bumpy a Road? Turkey, the European Union and Human Rights* (Swedish Institute for International Affairs, Stockholm, 2000).

Greece and Cyprus: the perennial preoccupations
THE MERCURIAL RELATIONSHIP WITH GREECE

Greek-Turkish relations have invariably been uneasy since the emergence of an independent Greek state in the late 1820s and early 1830s. In the nineteenth century this tension was engendered by the rising tide of Greek nationalism, sharpened by the resentment of centuries experienced under the Ottoman yoke. These ideational factors were in turn exacerbated by the rapidly shifting power and territorial configurations of the Balkans and the expectation that the Ottoman rollback could continue indefinitely. The contested nature of state, territory and order reached its apotheosis with Greece's pursuit of the *Megali Idea* and what Richard Clogg has called the 'ill-fated Anatolian entanglement' of 1919–22.[35] This ensured that, as Martin Walker has put it, 'the histories of modern Greece and modern Turkey were each born in war against the other.'[36] This second bloody conflict, with its existential dimension, together with the painful exchange of populations that ensued, has proved to be a traumatic backdrop to bilateral relations over the ensuing eight decades: for Turkey, the Greeks were the executors of the Sèvres conspiracy; for Greece, the Turks defiantly delineated the boundaries of their political and cultural resurgence at the expense of the Greeks.

If conflict, tension and resentment have come to be regarded as the chief characteristics of Greek-Turkish relations there is also enough in the bilateral history of the two states to show that this does not inevitably have to be the case. Ironically, the most important period of reconciliation came soon after the end of the Greek-Turkish war. Of even greater irony was the fact that it was the two main protagonists of the historic struggle in the early 1920s, Mustafa Kemal Atatürk and Eleftherios Venizelos, who presided over the rapprochement, which was secured through the Ankara Convention of 1930. It is to the model of the Atatürk-Venizelos reconciliation, and the legitimacy bestowed on such a course by the two leaders, to which more recent attempts at bilateral improvements have looked.

[35] *A Concise History of Greece* (Cambridge University Press, 1992), p. 96.
[36] See his special report on 'Europe's Turkish Question', *Prospect*, February 2001, p. 48.

But if Atatürk and Venizelos showed that Greek-Turkish relations did not have of necessity to be adversarial and conflictual, the 1930 reconciliation has proved to be more the exception that the rule. Since the mid 1950s relations have tended to towards the mercurial:[37] periods of fluctuating unease punctuated by fleeting but ultimately forlorn attempts to emulate 1930, but equally punctuated by moments of crisis and impending conflict. Two main reasons have tended to be cited for this. First, there is a raft of substantive bilateral problems, a handful of which, such as sovereignty over the Continental Shelf (especially in the event of the discovery and exploitation of seabed resources), some disputed island outcrops, control of air space and the militarisation of the Dodecanese, relate to the Aegean Sea. Arguably the most important of these substantive issues is Cyprus.[38] Second, there is a psychological fixation on the part of Greeks with Turkey, which results from the latter's size, proximity and superior overall power and the recent legacy of conflict and defeat; in short a Greek security preoccupation,[39] which the arrival of Turkish troops in Cyprus in 1974 and their continued presence have exacerbated.

In the 1990s a third factor has come to join and complicate the other two: a Turkish perception that Greece's foreign policy has been systematically aimed at undermining Turkish national interest. This view from Ankara has been most prevalent as far as Turkish-European relations have been concerned, but has also been evident elsewhere, notably in Turkish-American ties. Here a double asymmetry has been at work. Because of the power imbalance in favour

---

[37] For example the good bilateral relations which prevailed in the late 1940s, with the common perception of the Communist threat, and which carried through Greece and Turkey's accession in the first NATO enlargement of 1952 and the creation of a Balkan Pact, had by the mid 1950s subsided into crisis, with the riots in 1955 against the Greek minority in Istanbul.

[38] For example, the long time US envoy on Cyprus, Nelson Ledsky, used to argue that Cyprus is the issue whose resolution is a *sine qua non* for an improvement in Greek-Turkish relations, rather than the Aegean.

[39] For example, a recent study of Greece begins its discussion of Greek-Turkish relations by observing that: 'The perception of a threat from Turkey has traditionally dominated Greek thinking about the strategic environment, including defense planning'. See Ian O. Lesser, F. Stephen Larrabee, Michele Zanini and Katia Vlachos-Dengler, *Greece's New Geopolitics* (RAND, Santa Monica, 2001), p. 20.

of Turkey, Greece has devoted a disproportionate amount of diplomatic and advocacy resources towards undermining Turkey's fortunes with both Brussels and Washington. In the absence of a comparable institutional or lobby group standing within the EU and the US respectively, this in turn has affected Turkey disproportionately, as the EU has withheld the transfer of financial resources, while different areas of Turkish-US relations, especially in the area of weapons sales, have been affected.

By the mid 1990s, Turkish frustrations had gathered to such an extent that a new war was only a hair trigger away. The absence of systemic bipolarity in the wake of the collapse of the Soviet Union had removed some of the remaining impediments to a deterioration in relations between these two NATO 'allies'. On at least two occasions conflict has, as a result, come close. First, the Çiller government declared in 1994 that should Greece implement the Law of the Sea Convention[40] on a 12 mile territorial limit it would be taken as a *casus belli* by Turkey;[41] to date Athens has prudently avoided making such a declaration. Second, in January 1996 only last minute crisis diplomacy by the US averted a conflict over a barren and uninhabited outcrop in the Aegean, called Imia and Kardak by the Greeks and Turks respectively. In this second case it should be pointed out that neither the military nor the foreign policy establishments on either side had actively sought such a confrontation; a combination of media irresponsibility, populist political figures and a public opinion socialised into a mutual antipathy had nevertheless brought both sides close to war.

[40] The Convention, which was drawn up in 1982, formally came into operation on 16 November 1994. If Greece were to take up its rights under the Convention then an estimated 71.5% of the Aegean Sea would become Greek territorial waters, with just 8.8% remaining in the hands of Turkey. This in turn would have major implications for jurisdiction over the Continental Shelf. Consequently, Ankara has argued that the Aegean is *sui generis*. Even the relatively mild mannered speaker of the Turkish parliament, Hüsamettin Cindoruk, was quoted as saying that 'The Aegean Sea cannot be a Greek Sea'; an extension of the territorial waters to 12 miles would be followed by military action; Turkey is not bluffing. See TRT TV report in BBC/SWB/EE, 6 October 1994.

[41] This specific warning was accompanied by other similarly bellicose statements, such as Çiller's statement to the Metal-İş congress in Ankara on the matter of the use of the Greek veto against Turkey in EU fora. Çiller stated that: 'One can trust our friendship, but one should also beware of our enmity. I tell them to beware of our enmity'. See TRT TV report in BBC/SWB/EE, 20 December 1994.

If a rapid downward spiral towards war has been a growing risk in the 1990s, efforts aimed at stabilising and improving relations have never entirely disappeared from the bilateral agenda. A notable example of an eventually unsuccessful attempt at rapprochement came in January 1988 with a bilateral agreement in Davos. However, what became known as the 'spirit of Davos', between the aspirant latter-day Atatürk and Venizelos, Turgut Özal and Andreas Papandreou, was to last barely a year. Lesser experiments in reconciliation have also punctuated the years following.

In another of those ironies that typify Greek-Turkish relations the greatest chance for a re-run of the 1930s came in 1999, when ties appeared set to plumb the depths. The PKK leader Abdullah Öcalan, whose whereabouts were unknown after a three-month stay in Rome, had been located as enjoying the protection of the Greek ambassador in Nairobi. Though Athens had acted promptly and responsibly in making sure that Öcalan was unsuccessful in his attempt to repeat his Italian visit on Greek soil, Greece was severely embarrassed within the EU and the wider Western world, not to mention in its relations with Turkey, once the Kenyan connection was revealed. Fortunately for the fortunes of Greek-Turkish relations, the successful capture and repatriation of Öcalan ameliorated the impact of the Greek dimension in his African exile and bought some time for bilateral relations.[42] Eager to atone over the issue of support for terrorism, and increasingly irritated that other European states hostile towards Turkish membership of the EU were hiding behind the Greek veto, Athens embarked upon a path of determined reconciliation. The tragedy of the August 1999 earthquake provided a context in which this strategy could be accelerated and in which Turks more widely felt able to respond, not least to a subsequent though less devastating earthquake in Greece soon afterwards.

This process of what has become known as 'earthquake diplomacy' is now over two years old. It has been taken up by both governments, with the respective foreign ministers, George Papandreou and İsmail Cem, personally identified as being at its forefront. Its most significant success has been Turkey's candidacy status at Helsinki,

---

[42] For the circumstances surrounding the capture and repatriation of Öcalan see Tuncay Özkan, *Operasyon* (DK, Istanbul, 2000).

adopted in the face of the ostentatious absence of a Greek veto. An array of confidence building measures has followed. There has been much activity in the area of track two diplomacy, especially relating towards the various Aegean disputes. To date, however, there has been a failure to convert the new atmospherics into tangible positive outcomes as far as the agenda of bilateral problem issues is concerned. Without further substantive successes, bilateral relations will remain vulnerable to the fate suffered by the spirit of Davos. Many of those involved in trying to build a stable relationship between the two sides are agreed that Cyprus will remain the critical issue on which the future fortune of relations will be balanced.

CYPRUS:[43] 'CLASH OF INTERESTS AND EMOTIONS'[44]

Lying at the centre of the Cyprus dispute are the twin notions of security and sovereign entity. Initially, these two elements were the major preserve of Turks and Greeks respectively. Turkish Cypriots, supported by the state of Turkey, wanted to ensure that their security was not compromised by the political independence of the island from Britain. The 1959 London and Zurich Agreements were, for them, an exercise in consociational institution-building to ensure precisely that this did not happen.[45] The collapse of the power-sharing arrangement in 1963 and the ensuing bouts of blood-letting and population movement confirmed the worst fears of the Turkish side.[46] This position of enduring insecurity was addressed in the aftermath of the coup launched by the military regime in Athens, and the installation of Nicos Sampson as president in July 1974.

---

[43] For some recent perspectives on the Cyprus problem see Heinz Kramer, 'The Cyprus Problem and European Security', *Survival*, vol. 39, no. 3, Autumn 1997; Carol Migdalovitz, *Cyprus: Status of UN Negotiations* (Congressional Research Service Issue Brief, Washington DC, 26 June 1998); Clement H. Dodd, 'Turkey and the Cyprus Question' in Alan Makovsky and Sabri Sayarı (eds), *Turkey's New World* (WINEP, Washington DC, 2000).

[44] To quote William Hale. See *Turkish Foreign Policy*, op. cit., p. 252.

[45] As Keith Kyle has put it, the consociational form of government is one which 'gives the preservation of the ethnic balance higher priority than majority rule'. See *Cyprus* (Minority Rights Group Report 30, London, 1984), p. 8.

[46] The more trenchant advocates of the Turkish Cypriot position see these bouts of violence as nothing less than 'a systematic attempt at genocide'. See Michael Stephen, 'How the International Community Made a Cyprus Settlement Impossible', *Perceptions*, vol. VI, no. 1, March–May 2001, p. 62.

It was only with the arrival of a large military force from Turkey on 20 July, justified by Ankara on the basis of the 1960 Treaty of Guarantee,[47] that this position of endemic insecurity for the Turkish Cypriots was alleviated. In the words of one senior Turkish diplomat long involved in the Cyprus issue, 1974 brought to an end 'a dark decade' for Turkish Cypriots. Consequently, for many Turks in Turkey and northern Cyprus the Cyprus problem as they define it, that is to say in its essence a security problem, was solved in 1974.

The security dimension of the Cyprus dispute has not, however, remained static. It has taken two further forms since the pre-1974 era. Here again the notion of a double power asymmetry is useful in understanding dynamics. First, the arrival of Turkish forces and the permanent stationing of some 30,000 troops on the island have created a security imbalance for Greek Cypriots. Alarmed by the Turkish military presence and the proven willingness of Ankara to use such forces, Nicosia has searched for ways to balance such a presence or deter its use. Though such a strategy may be futile and even potentially counter-productive, successive Greek Cypriot administrations have nevertheless pursued it, through such policies as the acquisition of modern military hardware, the development of a defence relationship with Greece and the construction of a major air base at Paphos.[48] This multi-stranded defence strategy has in turn increased the particular power disparity between the Greek Cypriots and the

---

[47] The riposte to this justification is that at best the Turkish side had the right to re-establish the 1960 constitutional settlement and neither to expand the territory that it controlled, which it did in a subsequent military operation in 1974, nor to remain in permanent occupation of part of Cyprus. Ankara in turn contends that the restoration of the 1960 status quo was neither possible nor desirable, as it was this constitutional arrangement that had led to the attacks on the Turkish Cypriots in 1963 and 1964. Subsequent events also have a bearing on the Cyprus situation by way of analogy. The 1999 Kosovo intervention by NATO enabled the Turkish ambassador in London, Özdem Sanberk, to argue in a speech marking the 25th anniversary of the 1974 intervention/invasion that 'even if the Treaty of Guarantee has not existed, Turkey would have had at least as much right as NATO did in Kosovo to land a force on Cyprus to protect the Turkish Cypriots and', in anticipation of a long NATO involvement in Kosovo, 'keep it there for as long as they were at risk': 'Remarks' delivered at a meeting at House of Commons, 13 July 1999.

[48] The Paphos air base became operational in January 1998 in line with the joint defence doctrine between Greece and the Greek Cypriots.

Turkish Cypriots of the north, who have consequently become potentially more dependent on Turkey for their security and survival, hence making a complete withdrawal of Turkish forces even less likely.

The second way in which the security issue has moved on since 1974 is in terms of the new description of Cyprus' importance for Turkey's security in the wider context of the eastern Mediterranean, bearing in mind that Cyprus is located just 40 miles from the Turkish mainland.[49] The formal inclusion of a Turkish security dimension into the Cyprus question took place in July 1997, coinciding with the return to government as deputy premier of Bülent Ecevit, the man who presided over the July 1974 intervention/invasion,[50] and the man whose reputation more than any other stands or falls on the Cyprus issue.[51] The change took place in the context of the Cyprus government's ill-fated attempts to acquire S-300 missiles from Russia in 1997–8,[52] as part of the balancing strategy described above. The leading argument deployed by Ankara against such an acquisition was that with minor modifications such weapons could be turned into offensive medium range missiles, capable of hitting targets in southern or even central Turkey. Furthermore, it was argued that the acquisition of such missiles could not be divorced from the overall issue of the military balance between Greece and Turkey, with such missiles potentially offering cover for Greek

[49] Cyprus is some 250 miles from the nearest Greek island, Rhodes, and 460 miles from the Greek mainland.

[50] Ecevit returned to government as the leader of one of the parties comprising a three party coalition under the overall leadership of Mesut Yılmaz, though Ecevit, who assumed the position of deputy prime minister, was to take a close interest in Cyprus policy in conjunction with his close political associate Şükrü Sina Gürel, who became responsible for Cyprus affairs in the new cabinet. See *Turkish Daily News*, 4 July 1997, *Turkish Probe*, 4 July 1997.

[51] One leading expert on Turkey, protected from attribution by Chatham House rules, has stated that Ecevit's entire career as a politician was only saved from abject failure by the successful Cyprus strategy in 1974. It is for this reason that he is so unwilling personally to entertain flexibility on the subject. Seminar on contemporary Turkey, 27 April 2001.

[52] Having taken the decision in January 1997, the Clerides government abandoned the plan under concerted Western pressure in December 1998. In order to save face the Greek government agreed to install the missiles on the island of Crete.

naval and air access to Cyprus or for a Greek move across the Aegean.[53] Indeed, it has even been suggested that Turkey has both energy and economic security arguments for retaining a military presence on Cyprus.[54] What was beyond doubt was that the growth of a set of broader security interests, which have continued to be articulated since the end of the S-300s saga, suggests that the issue of security is not necessarily confined to a particular focus on the island of Cyprus.

To illustrate the depth of its feelings on the subject representatives of the Turkish state dropped periodic hints that Turkey would not stand for the missile deployment and reserved the right to intercept such missiles en route, or, in the event of their delivery, to 'hit' them once deployed.[55] In the end, under growing international pressure, the Clerides government in Nicosia dropped the purchase of the missiles. However, the emergence of a broader argument about regional security did raise the question of whether Turkey perceived an interest in retaining its military deployment on the island beyond the specific issue of the security of the Turkish Cypriots; whether it would, in other words, insist like Britain after independence on the retention of sovereign bases.

The other key issue in the Cyprus imbroglio has been that of the island as a sovereign entity. When Cyprus received independence it did so in its entirety, with the single exception of the British sovereign

---

[53] Indeed, it is argued from the Turkish side that Cyprus (and the threat of a possible invasion of southern Cyprus) continues to have 'big value' for Turkey as a deterrent to potentially unwelcome Greek actions in the Aegean, such as the extension of the territorial limit.

[54] No less a person than the former head of the Turkish navy and then adviser to the prime minister, Admiral Güven Erkaya, has argued this point in the context of the Cyprus issue, underscoring the fact that 45 per cent of Turkey's energy needs flow through the Aegean and the eastern Mediterranean, as well as a large volume of its general trade. Seminar on Cyprus organised by Turkish embassy, London, 28 November 1997. Presumably this Turkish interest would increase in the event of the construction of the long awaited Baku-Ceyhan oil pipeline.

[55] A range of threats relating to the deployment of the S-300s was made around this time, differing only in terms of the extent to which they were veiled. Some examples include a cabinet minister, who spoke of Turkey having recourse to 'extra military means' in the event of their deployment (seminar, 8 June 1998), and a senior Turkish ambassador stating candidly that Cyprus 'should not call our bluff' on the missiles (ibid.).

bases. That is to say it did so as a complete political community, even though it had only been the Greek Cypriots who eagerly campaigned for decolonisation. At the point of independence Cyprus was in any case demographically mixed, so the concept of physical division and demographic separation simply did not apply. Unrest in the early 1960s in the context of constitutional breakdown began the process of ethnic separation, a spasmodic trend that by the aftermath of the Turkish invasion/intervention was a process complete.

The fall of the military regime in Athens and the failure of the Sampson coup opened the way for the eventual convening of intercommunal talks on the future of the island. These resulted in an agreement in principle in 1977 on the formation of a bi-communal federation on the island of Cyprus.[56] Such an objective was designed to address the ultimate core objectives of both communities: to reassure Turkish Cypriots that their security would be ensured through a combination of continued ethnic consolidation, self-administration, and the continuation of a Turkish guarantee; and to reassure Greek Cypriots that the commitment to the political indivisibility of the island would be retained. However, since this overall big picture agreement the devil has truly been in the detail. Attempts either to define what exactly would be meant by 'federation',[57] or to chart a course to the implementation of these overall goals through such milestones as confidence building measures, have proved to be unsuccessful.

Though the final aim of a bi-zonal, bi-communal federation on Cyprus has become a mantra of political discussions relating to the island, evidence has begun to snowball to suggest that Turkey has become equivocal on the subject. The first major example of Turkish ambivalence concerned a key development on the issue of sovereign entity in November 1983, when the Turkish Cypriot government formally declared the 'Turkish Republic of Northern Cyprus'. This new, apparently separate entity was recognised by Ankara, but no other state has yet followed suit. The additional Turkish policy

[56] This was the outcome of a meeting between President Makarios and the Turkish Cypriot leader Rauf Denktaş.

[57] For a discussion of federation and confederation in the Cyprus context see Clement Dodd, 'Confederation, Federation and Sovereignty', *Perceptions*, vol. IV, no. 3, Sep.–Nov. 1999.

of settling peasant emigrants from Anatolia in northern Cyprus has further helped to consolidate the Turkish ethnic nature of the north, though this has, in part at least, only compensated for Turkish Cypriot emigration.[58]

Since the mid 1990s there has been a growing perspective away from a federal outcome, and in this the growing profile of EU-Cyprus relations has been pivotal.[59] Ankara remains ever sensitive to the EU membership issue, in this case irked by the prospect that Brussels might seriously contemplate the admission of a divided Cyprus while remaining so equivocal towards Turkey's own long term membership aspirations. Rauf Denktaş has been able to exploit this sense of injured dignity on the Turkish side to bolster the north's increasing political detachment.[60] In doing so, the Turkish side was

[58] Precise numbers are inevitably disputed. The TRNC side estimates that 30,000 out of an overall population of 200,000 Turkish Cypriots have arrived from Turkey (see speech by Hakkı Müftüzade, London representative of TRNC, at Chatham House, 9 December 1998). Independent Turkish sources have indicated that the figure could be as high as 80,000, or some 40 per cent of the total. By contrast, some Greek Cypriot estimates place the number of settlers as high as 100,000, with the balance of the 200,000 or more population made up by 70,000 Turkish Cypriots and 30–40,000 Turkish troops (*Cyprus News*, 27 November 1997, cited in Stelios Stavridis, 'Double Standards: Ethics and Democratic Principles in Foreign Policy: The European Union and the Cyprus Problem', in *Mediterranean Politics*, vol. 4, no. 1, spring 1999, Fn 29, p. 109).

[59] For background on the relationship between Cyprus and the EU and the former's membership aspirations see Neill Nugent, 'Cyprus and the European Union: A Particularly Difficult Membership Application', *Mediterranean Politics*, vol. 2, no. 3, winter 1997.

[60] A few of the more courageous voices in Turkey have spoken out against Denktaş' influence over Turkey's Cyprus policy and the direction that it has been taking in the 1990s. A leading example has been Cengiz Çandar (*Yeni Şafak*, 31 May 2001, reprinted in *Turkish Daily News*, 1 June 2001), who has periodically adopted a trenchant line on the matter. He described the situation thus: 'For about a decade it has been as if no Turk lives in the Turkish Republic of Northern Cyprus (KKTC) other than [KKTC President] Rauf Denktaş. Whatever position he takes becomes Turkey's position as well. Turkey does not have a Cyprus policy of its own. It is Denktaş who determines Turkey's Cyprus policy. It is as if anybody who opposes that policy will be considered a traitor.' Though Çandar's statement seems to ignore the existence of pockets of elite support for Denktaş in the military, in the Foreign Ministry and among some politicians in Turkey, his words convey both the extensive influence of Denktaş in Turkey and the almost eery absence of any serious public debate on the Cyprus issue.

determined to prove wrong the collective hope from the EU that the prospect of Cyprus' accession would provide a strong incentive for the reunification of the island.[61]

The key moment of departure came in December 1996, when, following the EU's formal decision to begin accession talks with the Nicosia government on behalf of a divided Cyprus, Denktaş pronounced that inter-communal talks had ended (though the lesser formula of proximity talks through the UN was to take place three years later), and that future direct talks would only occur between states having equal status; the Yılmaz government soon afterwards stated that Turkey would accelerate the integration process with the TRNC. Here, though, lay a contradictory strategy as far as the Turkish Cypriots were concerned.[62] On the one hand, they were effectively stepping up their demand for the acknowledgement of a separate existence; on the other, they were moving in the direction of a *de facto* union with Turkey.[63] Subsequent developments have confirmed these apparently incompatible trends. The following January, Denktaş and President Demirel issued a five page joint declaration, which Denktaş described as 'going beyond a joint defence doctrine'.[64] In August 1998 the Turkish and Turkish Cypriot

[61] Voices sympathetic to the Turkish Cypriot cause underline this. See, for example, Michael Stephen, who writes that 'Poor as the prospects were for a Cyprus settlement in the international environment... those prospects were completely wrecked when the EU held out to the Greek Cypriots the prospect of membership for Cyprus as a whole without requiring them first to reach a settlement with the Turkish Cypriots', *Perceptions*, op. cit., p. 72.

[62] David Buchan and Kerin Hope bring out this point well in the *Financial Times* Survey on Cyprus, 6 April 1998.

[63] Relations between Turkey and the TRNC were already, in the words of the Turkish columnist Sami Kohen, 'somewhat meshed' (*Milliyet*, 28 August 1996). Not only did the TRNC rely upon Turkey for its defence but it also received substantial annual budget assistance from Ankara, in addition to further aid on an ad hoc basis. The extent of the economic dependency of northern Cyprus can be seen in the comparable rate of inflation it sustains, and the fact that financial crises in Turkey, such as that experienced in spring 1994, also plunge it into recession. See Reuters on trends in the economy of the TRNC, 16 January 1997.

[64] The declaration, which was strongly defence oriented, included: a commitment to provide comparable air and naval facilities in the TRNC to those being developed in southern Cyprus by Greece; the elaboration of a 'joint military concept', which would facilitate military planning and cooperation; and the

sides formally ditched the idea of federation, with the announcement that Cyprus should eventually become a confederation of two sovereign and equal peoples and states.[65]

If Turkey and the TRNC have been edging towards a closer organic relationship, what one Ankara-based diplomat has even called 'Hatay in slow motion',[66] the prospect of a formal decision on the accession of Cyprus to the EU in late 2002 or 2003 may be expected to accelerate such a trend. Leading figures inside the EU had hoped that the prospect of EU membership would have a 'catalytic effect' as far as the Cyprus problem was concerned; they seem set to be proven correct, though not necessarily in the positive way they might have imagined. If that is indeed the case, it is likely to have a deleterious effect on both Turkish-EU relations and Turkish-Greek relations. With the Turkish Cypriots 'Turkey's leading national cause',[67] once again much of Turkey's foreign policy is mortgaged to the fate of Cyprus.

The minorities question: strength through homogeneity

The minorities issue is a combustible subject in Turkey today, as it has been since before the creation of the modern state. A series of accumulated experiences during the latter stages of the Ottoman Empire and the birth of modern Turkey helps to explain this.

During this former period the issue of ethnic-nationalist minorities was used by Europeans to justify the dismantling of the remainder of the Ottoman Empire in Europe. In turn, the issue of religious minorities was used to justify the repeated interference in what would otherwise have been deemed to be the internal affairs of the Ottoman state. The French most notoriously used the existence of a Catholic Arab population in the Middle East, notably the Maronites,

---

expansion of presidential cooperation to include defence matters. *Turkish Daily News*, 21 January 1997.

[65] For the text of Denktaş' 31 August proposal see Rauf R. Denktaş, 'The Crux of the Cyprus Problem', *Perceptions*, op. cit. p. 22.

[66] Confidential conversation, 7 February 2001. Hatay is the name given by Turkey to the Sanjak of Alexandretta, a territory it acquired in 1939 from Syria, then colonially administered by France.

[67] To quote Alan Makovsky in 'Turkey and the Bush Administration: The Question Marks' (WINEP Policywatch 527, 30 March 2001).

to legitimise their expanding presence in the region, and their disregard for Ottoman sovereignty. The existence of ethnic and religious minorities therefore acted as a corral of Trojan horses in the steady undermining of the coherence of the Ottoman state.

The issue became even more sharply focused with the post-First World War settlement. At Sèvres, the minorities issue emerged as being at the very heart of the existential challenge to the aspirations of the new Turkish nationalist movement. As we have already seen, Sèvres was a further indulgence of some of the main minorities of the Empire and their external patrons. The failure of the Sèvres project represented a success for that other minority nationalist idea, Turkish nationalism.

Once it had won a crucial victory on the battlefield, this new nationalism had to address the implications of its own minority status. Anatolia and eastern Thrace was at the time a territory populated by a whole collection of ethnic minorities, bound together only by a shared Muslim faith, many of which had fled to the territorial core as the spatial dimensions of the Ottoman Empire had contracted. These communities from the Balkans found a heartland without a strong sense of ethnic nationalism. The fact that Islam had provided the ideological cement of the Ottoman Empire had removed any need for the ethnic or cultural assimilation of its populations. And besides, assimilation to what? The Ottoman Empire was a multi-cultural empire within the parameters of Islam.

Turkish nationalism had rather then to start from scratch in ideological terms, if not in terms of political power. The fact that it was the Turkish nationalist movement which had defeated the Greeks and seen off the great powers invested it with both initiative and moral force. The recently victorious nationalists then set about addressing two agendas: a domestic agenda to incorporate the political periphery and invent a new subjective national identity based on agency rather than ethnicity; and an external agenda aimed at formally overturning Sèvres and having the new state recognised by the international community, as a way of both securing the legitimacy of the state and its sovereign exercise of power and reducing the likelihood of external intervention. The result of this latter effort was the treaty of Lausanne.

THE TREATY OF LAUSANNE

If Sèvres had ignored Turkish interests, the Lausanne treaty signed on 24 July 1923,[68] 'the founding document of the modern Turkish state',[69] addressed them almost in full. Turkey came away from Lausanne with the precious political commodities of recognition, independence and sovereignty.[70] The convening of the peace conference resulted in the final demise of the Ottoman government as a rival to Ankara. The treaty itself then duly recognised Turkey as an independent state, with full sovereignty over the territory under its control; with the fate of Mosul set aside pending its incorporation into northern Iraq, Turkey was otherwise (with the subsequent incorporation of the Sanjak of Alexandretta) to realise control over all the territories that it claimed. The successor state had finally shrugged off the humiliating curbs on the sovereignty of its predecessor, securing complete control over its domestic affairs, responsibility for its own finances (save the residual international obligations on the outstanding Ottoman debt) and complete jurisdiction over foreign nationals. The one exception was control of the Straits which would remain under international supervision, although this was only to be so for a matter of time, with Turkish control coming with the Montreux Convention of 1936.

In addition to the recognition which it bestowed upon Turkey, Lausanne was also significant for its conclusions over the issue of minorities. The treaty only recognised the existence of religious minorities in the new state of Turkey, section three on the 'Protection of Minorities' being sprinkled with exclusive references to the 'Non-Muslim minorities'.[71] Only in insisting that 'No restrictions

---

[68] *Treaty of Peace with Turkey and other Instruments* (HMSO, London, 1923).

[69] To quote the under-secretary of the Turkish Ministry of Foreign Affairs, Faruk Loğoğlu, in a supplement entitled 'Turks of the World' in the *Turkish Daily News*, 10 April 2000.

[70] It is almost impossible to exaggerate the importance of sovereignty for the Turks both then and now. Indeed, the premium which the Turkish delegation placed on sovereignty and their pursuit of it nearly drove the British foreign secretary and leading figure at the conference, Lord Curzon, to distraction. 'The same old tune, sovereignty, sovereignty, sovereignty', he was memorably quoted, 'Yours is not the only sovereignty in the world'. See Selim Deringil, *Turkish Foreign Policy during the Second World War* (Cambridge University Press, 1989), p. 68.

[71] See *Treaty of Peace with Turkey*, op. cit. pp. 29–35 (esp. pp. 30, 32 and 34).

shall be imposed on the free use by any Turkish national of any language...', an entry subsequently largely forgotten, did the text implicitly apportion safeguards for ethnic minorities.[72] This limited definition of what constituted a minority came in contrast to the tripartite agreement in respect of Anatolia at Sèvres, which, in its brief preamble, had boldly referred to the 'religious, racial and linguistic minorities'.

Under Lausanne, then, ethnic minorities among the Muslim population of Turkey, notably the Kurds and Arabs, were left without any special status or recognition. To have given that would have been to risk the ideological hegemony which the Turkish nationalist movement foresaw for the vast majority of the population of the new state. Hence, for the government of Turkey, the ethnic minority communities were solely subject to the freedoms bestowed upon the majority Muslim population as a whole. The nearest these communities got to any specific provisions was in Article 39, which related to language. It stated:

No restrictions shall be imposed on the free use by any Turkish national of any language in private intercourse, in commerce, religion, in the press, or in publications of any kind or at public meetings. Notwithstanding the existence of the official language, adequate facilities shall be given to Turkish nationals of non-Turkish speech for oral use of their own language before the courts.

It is almost impossible to underestimate the continuing significance of Lausanne in the ideology and mythology of the Turkish state. Indeed, it is a modern incongruity, though not by any means a surprising one to those who know the Turkish Foreign Ministry well, that the 75th anniversary of Lausanne should have emerged as the cause of a diplomatic incident between Switzerland and Turkey in 1998. In June, Ankara went so far as to withdraw its ambassador from Berne for consultations after the Swiss government refused to allow Turkey access to the Rumine Palace, the venue for the signing of the treaty, as part of its celebrations of the Lausanne agreement.[73]

---

[72] ibid., p. 31.
[73] See *Hürriyet* cited in *Turkish Press Review*, 21 July 1998.

More generally, the Turkish state and its spokesmen have found a continuous refuge in Lausanne in fending off international criticism of its conduct of internal affairs, especially in relation to the Kurdish issue. Whenever foreign NGOs, officials and politicians criticise Ankara's treatment of the Kurdish minority, they are told that Lausanne lays down that non-religious minorities do not exist in Turkey. Even since 1989, when a degree of relaxation has made it possible to mention 'the Kurds' and discuss related issues as a matter of public policy, Lausanne is still implicitly invoked with such oft repeated statements as that all Turkish citizens have equal rights and opportunities regardless of their origins.

Nor is the minorities question purely a residual Turkish fixation, an anachronistic hangover from the past. Members of those minorities continue to be active in trying to confront or embarrass the modern state of Turkey. In pursuing such a campaign, these minorities have found ready allies in Western Europe and the US. No longer do these allies tend to be drawn, like Lloyd George and Curzon, from among the narrow stratum of the political elite. Today, they are more likely to be found within civil society, and among the liberal intelligentsia. At a national level, organisations like human rights associations, liberal and leftist political parties and trade unions have taken up the plight of the Kurds. At a supranational level it is institutions like the European Parliament, which have settled upon human rights issues as a way of carving out a raison d'être, which have emerged as the most active campaigners for the Kurds.

The United States: the unreliable ally

The United States has been a close political ally of Turkey since the mid 1940s.[74] This enduring friendship resulted from a mutual perception of threat from the USSR. Stalin had expansionist designs on the Straits and parts of Anatolia since before the end of the Second World War.[75] By 1946 Washington had come to appreciate as

---

[74] For a comprehensive discussion of Turkey's emerging security relations with the US at this time see Ekavi Athanassopoulou, *Turkey: Anglo-American Security Interests, 1945–1952* (Frank Cass, London, 1999).

[75] In March 1945 the Soviet Union informed Turkey that it did not want an extension of the Turco-Soviet treaty of 1925; in July Moscow laid a territorial claim against Turkey.

much. Turkey was eager to benefit from the Americans' growing anti-Soviet stance. Indeed, the US administration used a proposal to Congress for funds for Greece and Turkey as an occasion to announce the Truman Doctrine to 'support free people'. With the strategic basis of the relationship laid, an economic co-operation agreement followed in 1948, and Turkey supported its new ally by contributing some 4,500 troops to the Korean conflict in July 1950, the third largest contingent after Americans and Koreans. If it was not until 15 February 1952 that Turkey became a full member of NATO, this owed more to the doubts of smaller states like Denmark and Norway than to the equivocation of the US. Turkey then became what Erik Zurcher has called a 'a solid-albeit peripheral' member of the Western political and strategic alliance.[76]

Yet, looking back on five decades of what George Harris famously labelled 'a troubled alliance',[77] the United States is perceived as having been an unreliable or, in Kemal Kirişci's view,[78] an 'ambivalent' ally for Turkey in spite of these auspicious beginnings. This is because, at certain critical times for Turkey, the US has either failed to deliver or has shown itself willing to trade its Turkish assets in favour of some greater reward. This lingering impression of unreliability continued to be spasmodically reinforced in the 1990s. Moreover, this perception of the United States as an ally that waxes and wanes overlays what for many in Turkey is an instinctive anti-Americanism. Built upon American neo-Imperialism, this ambivalence towards the United States has been nurtured by the ideological radicalism of the period from the 1960s to the 1980s, much of which has rubbed off onto mainstream views and ideas. Anti-Americanism, whether in the form of left wing or Islamist extremism, and complemented by the xenophobia of ultra nationalism, is an enduring undercurrent in Turkish politics.

THE JOHNSON LETTER, 1964

Turkish-US relations at the security level were close and co-operative throughout the 1950s, with President Eisenhower regarded as a good

---

[76] Erik J. Zurcher, *Turkey: A Modern History* (I.B. Tauris, London, 1993), p. 245.

[77] George S. Harris, *Troubled Alliance: Turkish-American Problems in Historical Perspective, 1945–1971* (American Enterprise Institute, Washington, DC, 1971).

[78] See his 'Turkey and the United States: Ambivalent Allies' in B. Rubin and T. Keaney (eds), *US Allies in a Changing World* (Frank Cass, London, 2000).

friend of Turkey's, in spite of such differences as the American refusal to become a full member of the Baghdad Pact. However, the
experience of the Cuban missile crisis should have been sufficient
to show the Turks that on matters of global strategic importance
their interests were expendable. Şükrü Elekdağ has drawn attention
to the fact that during the crisis Turkey was not aware of the bargaining taking place between the two superpowers at its own
expense. In October 1962, as a result of the final compromise that
ended the crisis, the United States, without consultation with Ankara,
agreed to withdraw the Jupiter nuclear missiles which had been
based in Turkey since 1957.[79] In the words of William Hale, there
was 'more than a hint of a Turkey-for-Cuba trade' in the outcome
of the Cuban missile crisis.[80] Though they would have been super-
seded by the submarine-based Polaris missiles in any case, the Jupiter missiles experience was a salutary reminder of the asymmetrical
nature of the Turkish-US alliance, and has not been forgotten by
Turkey's foreign policy and security elites. As Elekdağ has porten-
tiously written, there are many lessons to be drawn from the Cuban
crisis, experienced 35 years ago.[81]

If the Turkish reaction was one of mild concern in 1962, less than
two years later it was to be one of widespread national shock in
response to the Johnson letter,[82] a document that was to make 'a
lasting imprint' on Turkish-US relations.[83] The controversy was
sparked by political ructions on Cyprus, less than four years after the
island state had received its independence. The government of
Archbishop Makarios moved in December 1963 to subvert the
constitutional provisions of the original settlement to accrue more
power for the dominant Greek community, a move which was
accompanied by attacks on the Turkish Cypriot minority and an

[79] For a discussion of the Jupiter missiles, and their 'psychological value', see Bruce
R. Kuniholm, 'Turkey and the West Since World War II' in Vojtech Mastny and
R. Craig Nation (eds), *Turkey Between East and West, op. cit.*, pp. 51–5.
[80] William Hale, *Turkish Foreign Policy*, op. cit., p. 135.
[81] Writing in *Milliyet*, 7 October 1997.
[82] For the full text of the letter, and the response from prime minister İnönü, see
the Document section in *Middle East Journal*, vol. XX, no. 3, summer 1966,
pp. 386–93.
[83] To quote Ferenc Vali, op. cit. pp. 132.

ethnic consolidation of territory. The reaction of Ankara, as one of the three guarantor powers, was to sabre-rattle, in the form of a threatening demonstration of air power, a device which was repeated in August 1964. Though it is widely believed that Turkey's limited naval capacity did not make an invasion a feasible option, a letter sent to prime minister İsmet İnönü from the American president, Lyndon Johnson, on 5 June 1964 aimed to deter any possible thoughts of intervention.

The letter warned that a Turkish military intervention might in turn precipitate Soviet involvement, and that Ankara should not automatically expect a NATO response in the event of such a scenario. President Johnson further warned that Turkey should not contemplate the use of US military hardware in a Cyprus operation. The stark nature of the missive, the apparent unconcern at the Turkish view of unfolding events and the seeming alacrity with which Washington contemplated the strategic sacrifice of Turkey was indeed a traumatic experience for the Turks. If the substance of the letter was bad enough there was also consternation at its tone on the Turkish side.[84] The letter was subsequently leaked to the press and therefore was widely read. It provoked an anti-American backlash in the form of demonstrations in August 1964, and helped to generate and nurture a more widespread anti-Americanism.

A measure of the disquiet in Ankara provoked by the letter was the subsequent new direction in Turkish foreign policy, precipitated in major part by the experience. Turkey opted for a more multidimensional foreign policy. In the words of Nuri Eren Turkey 'belatedly succumbed to the mystique' of the Third World, as a counterweight to the superpowers.[85] This included a more active engagement with the Non-Aligned Movement, in part also aimed at galvanising international support over Cyprus.

The most striking manifestation of this broader approach to foreign relations was a warming of relations with Moscow, which had remained cold since Stalin's day. In 1963 the two sides exchanged official delegations for the first time in almost two decades, with a

---

[84] See retired ambassador Nuri Even, writing in the *Turkish Daily News*, 15 June 1992.
[85] See *Turkey, Nato and Europe: a Deteriorating Relationship?* (Atlantic Institute for International Affairs, Paris, 1977), pp. 41.

cultural agreement concluded in November 1964. There then followed high level visits to Turkey in 1965 and 1966 by Nikolai Podgorny and Andrei Gromyko, and Alexei Kosygin respectively. In 1967 Turkey concluded an economic agreement with the USSR worth $200 million in cheap credits.[86] In 1972 Ankara and Moscow signed a Declaration of the Principles of Good Neighbourly and Friendly Co-operation, even though martial law remained in place and Turkey had yet to return to democratic rule after the 1971 military intervention in domestic politics. By and large this improvement would continue until the Soviet invasion of Afghanistan in December 1979.

1974 ARMS EMBARGO

If the Johnson letter shook the Turkish establishment, the events of 1974 confirmed that there were limits to which Turkey could rely on her superpower ally. As in 1964, the problems of a decade later also grew out of Cyprus. Turkey reacted to the July 1974 coup in a sturdier manner than before. The Turkish coalition led by Bülent Ecevit launched a military intervention, citing its guarantor status as justification. With talks on the future of the island proving fruitless, a subsequent round of fighting in August allowing Turkey to expand its territorial base, action which was much more difficult to legitimise,[87] left it in possession of one-third of the island, from Famagusta to Morphou. With a further flight of population, following that which had taken place some ten years earlier, the ethnic division of the island was complete. Turkish troops have remained ever since.

Whereas Ecevit became a national hero overnight, the conduct of Turkey was rather more frowned upon in the wider international community. Turkey was the subject of UN condemnation and subsequent resolutions demanding its withdrawal from the island. The US, with its large and well organised Greek community, was not

---

[86] Robert S. Eaton, *Soviet Relations with Greece and Turkey,* Occasional Papers no. 2 (Hellenic Foundation for Defence and Foreign Policy, Athens, 1987), pp. 8–9.

[87] It was at this point that what had hitherto been an intervention, legitimised by Turkey's guarantor status, qualitatively metamorphosed into an invasion, thereby creating the military conditions for an occupation, of indefinite length, of the northern part of the island.

immune to these pressures. With the executive and legislative branches split on a response, Congress imposed a direct arms sales embargo on Turkey against the wishes of both the Ford and Carter administrations. Though the ban was never anywhere near watertight, it did create a wider atmosphere of resentment and distrust in Turkey. As in 1962 and 1964, the decision to impose a military cost upon Turkey at a time when the Soviet threat remained real enough cast a shadow across the Turkish-US strategic relationship. It was not until 1978, against a backdrop of strong lobbying by the Pentagon,[88] that the arms embargo began gradually to be rescinded.

The events of the 1960s and the 1970s paved the way for what has been a somewhat chequered bilateral relationship. On the one hand, the US has continued to value highly Turkey's strategic importance, during both the 'Second Cold War' of the early 1980s and the post-Cold War period of the 1990s.[89] Yet, on the other hand, bilateral relations have been punctuated by developments that have tended to reconfirm the Turkish intuition that the United States cannot entirely be relied upon.

By the 1990s, this ambivalence in US policy was clearer than ever. Within the American foreign policy establishment there was a strongly held notion that Turkey was strategically important, and that this fact should outweigh all other considerations. The view from Congress, and among ambitious politicians at important times during the electoral cycle, was less coldly strategic and more swayed by domestic US considerations. Figures such as Representative John Porter have latched onto Turkey's indifferent human rights record as a way of boxing in the executive's room for manoeuvre.

With comparatively little room for policy manoeuvre, the Clinton administration opted increasingly for gesture politics as a way of managing bilateral relations against a backdrop of turbulence. From 1995 onwards, Marc Grossman, operating first as US ambassador in Ankara and then as a senior official in Washington, ensured that Turkey was the destination of a stream of senior officials and defence

---

[88] Interview with a respected member of the US defence policy community, then a young member of the Pentagon staff dealing with Turkey, Washington, DC, 21 July 1998.

[89] For an overview of bilateral relations since 1989 see Kelly Couturier, *US-Turkish Relations in The Post-Cold War Era* (Friedrich Ebert Stiftung, Istanbul, 1997).

personnel. The high water mark in bilateral relations came with the visit of President Clinton to Turkey in November 1999, when the American president's charm mesmerised the Turkish elite and public alike.[90] In addition to its public diplomacy, the US gave limited political support to Turkey in foreign policy areas that were deemed to be relatively cost free. As senior Israelis had already found out, Washington discovered that shrill support for Turkish membership of the EU, though meaningless in substantive terms, would win some appreciative words in the press and from senior figures. Washington's support for the Baku-Ceyhan energy pipeline project from 1995 onwards stands out as an area where the US was able to invest real political capital in a core Turkish foreign policy objective, with few negative side-effects.

For Turkey history is not a pastime. It is a body of critically important stories that says who the Turks are, where they come from, what their formative experiences have been, and even what their mission is in the modern world. As such, it is something to be repeated and reaffirmed, whether in the school room, in the barracks or at the seminar table, something that has far more to do with the present than the past.

In helping to make sense of the here and now, history is as important in the realm of foreign affairs and foreign policy as in any other. Turkey's sense of its own critical experiences moulds its perceptions of others, and hence helps to inform policy-making. But the lessons of history as perceived by the Turks are not joyous. History tells Turks that the nation has been subject to the unwanted attention and destructive schemes of outsiders, with the post-First World

---

[90] There was no better example of this than Clinton's address to the Turkish Grand National Assembly on 15 November 1999. With a consummate politician's skill Clinton flattered his audience ('Turkey's past is key to understanding the 20th century. But, more importantly, I believe Turkey's future will be critical to shaping the 21st century.') He fulsomely praised their positive contributions ('I thank Turkey for its support of Operation Northern Watch, which allows us to deter Saddam's aggression...'; 'Turkish forces in NATO helped to end those [Balkan] wars and thus to end this century with a powerful affirmation of human dignity and human rights'); and gently chided them for their political shortcomings in a way that they would hardly have noticed ('We must also work hard to reach a just settlement in Cyprus').

War peace settlement the trauma that eclipses all other examples. It tells Turks to be suspicious, especially of their neighbours, who covet their territory or seek to erode the greatness of the nation through devious means. Finally, the message of history for Turks is that they cannot even entirely trust their friends and allies, even NATO stalwarts like the US and the West Europeans. With these notions of grievance being periodically underlined and re-emphasised by what one might call new historical experience such as the Luxembourg summit, history will continue to provide Turkey with a rawness through which the world is regarded for some time to come.

4

IDEOLOGY AS FOREIGN POLICY

When the new state of Turkey was created in 1923, it was a *tabula rasa*. It possessed little sense of itself other than what it did not want to be. The independence war had been fought against external notions of what should succeed the Ottoman Empire; its leaders had few ideas other than clearly to depart from the *ancien régime*, with its recent record of decline, defeat and subjugation. Once a line had been drawn under Sèvres and the Porte, it was time to concentrate on what values and ideas should underpin the new state. The birth of Turkey almost invited the domination of the visionary.

Turkey did not have to look far or long to find its inspiration. The leader of the independence movement, Mustafa Kemal, was already eligible to be its spiritual guide. He was a war hero twice over, a strong personality and a charismatic figure. Moreover, he was a man who had a clear notion of what the new Turkey should be. More Lenin than Marx, however, Mustafa Kemal was not an ideologue. Though he liked to talk politics, he was much more the man of action than of reflection. Thus, he made few attempts to develop his ideas into a cogent ideology. Beyond the sloganeering of the 'Six Arrows' (*altı ok*) and many long and rambling speeches, there was never a codified Kemalism from the pen of its founder. The liturgical and ritualistic minutiae of the new dogma were therefore missing, though there were many more prosaic successors who sought to fill such gaps.

Nevertheless, Atatürk was Moses-like when it came to the adoption of central commandments. Turkey was to be a European nation-state. The state was only to span the space enshrined in the National Pact of 28 January 1920, with the residual territories of empire finally and irreversibly disavowed. The nation was to be built upon an imagined and homogenised Turkish identity, with an ethnic inclusivism born of the necessity of wartime population movements; only the remnants of the religious *millet* would be classified as minorities and hence receive special status within the state. As with the notions of state and nation, the prevailing philosophy of Turkey was to be 'modern'. 'Ignorance' would be stamped out, whether the mechanical backwardness of illiteracy and economic underdevelopment, or the cognitive backwardness of Islamic piety and the Arabic script.

In implementing his new code of ideas Mustafa Kemal was fortunate. He was aided by a conjunction of circumstances and experiences. These included the overall regional context of the age, the political traditions of the Ottoman Empire and the quiescence of most of Turkish society. From the emerging Europe of the 1920s Mustafa Kemal was helped by a climate of new nationalism, as the Austro-Hungarian and Ottoman empires splintered. He was also helped by the growth of the authoritarian ideologies of the day, notably Communism and Fascism, with their culture of a dominant and centralising elite implementing a social as well as a political blueprint for change on a passive population. These values were reinforced by the Ottoman tradition, with its legacy of political centralisation, a strong state and the subjugation of the individual to the will of the ruler. The existence of a predominantly peasant society, with its attachment to the land, poor communications and high illiteracy rates, simply cemented the power of the centre as a cultural hegemon.

Given this auspicious context, Mustafa Kemal did not require a large pool of supporters to propagate his new ideas. The new elite that fully assimilated, accepted and defended his ideas was therefore rather small relative to the overall population. The professional officer corps of the military, the senior administrative elite, a big business elite created by the state, the intelligentsia who provided an intellectual apologia and the newly emancipated women of the middle classes formed the bedrock of the Kemalist system. For such groups, Atatürk and the ideas he espoused are critical to the retention of a system which enshrines this elite's position of material and social privilege, and maintains the cultural hegemony of their value code.

The rest of society ranged from the selectively supportive through the inert to the suspicious and even antipathetic. There was, of course, opposition to this new ideology from the outset. The Shaikh Said rebellion of 1925 challenged the supremacy of the state and the displacement of Islam in favour of the new nationalism. That, together with lesser revolts, perished at the hands of the superior force of the state. It was not until the late 1940s, and the advent of democratic politics, that a more sustainable exercise in ideological revisionism emerged, with the role and nature of religion at its core. Since then, Turkey has witnessed an intensifying ideological struggle between Islamism and the Kemalist conception of secularism, with such policy areas as education the recurrent focus of competition.

The realm of foreign affairs and foreign policy making remained largely exempt from this fitful process of the re-Islamisation of society, which began in the late 1940s and grew more rapid from the early 1980s onwards. The government of Turkey was routinely in the hands of Kemalist or Kemalist-dominated political parties; the executive apparatus of the Ministry of Foreign Affairs and specialist government agencies largely epitomised the Kemalist elite; in the background, Atatürk's successors in the Turkish armed forces guaranteed, through coercive means if needs be, that the old priorities remained. It is therefore hardly surprising that, with the exception of the final years of the Menderes government,[1] Turkey has witnessed such a consensus over foreign affairs. It is thus only in the 1980s and beyond, with the iconoclasm of Özal, the extensive though subterranean influences of the *tarikats* or religious orders and the rise of the Islamist Welfare Party as a major domestic political force, that foreign policy has become a contested area between Turkey's two gravitational ideologies.

Foreign policy in the Kemalist paradigm

The strong ideological orientation given to Turkey by Atatürk contained an umbilical link between the Western value system of the Kemalist elite and the external orientation of the state.[2] Kemalism

[1] For an example of the bipartisan approach to foreign policy under attack, see letter from Chancery, British Embassy, Ankara to Southern Department, FCO, FO371/136456, 26 September 1958.

[2] As Bernard Burrows wrote when British ambassador in Ankara, for the Republican People's Party, established under Atatürk, 'a Western foreign policy is an inseparable

thus provided important parameters within which foreign policy would be framed. The best examples of the ideologically driven nature of Kemalist foreign policy was in its *Westpolitik*, embracing as it has done a variety of different issues from Turkey's membership of NATO and its relationship with the United States, to its attempts to become a member of the EU and the WEU. Here the ideological paradigm of the Kemalist elite was bolstered by other factors: in the case of the latter, a certain historical continuity in the form of the Ottoman Empire's increasing emulation of Europe during the nineteenth century; with respect to NATO, the immediacy of the perceived threat from Stalin's USSR to the north in the mid to late 1940s. Nevertheless, the relentless way in which Ankara has pursued such goals has often had the character of a fixation, born of the values and insecurities of the narrowly based Kemalist elite, rather than a more detached and comprehensive evaluation of national interest.

THE PURSUIT OF THE E.U.

Speaking in Paris at the beginning of September 1997, Turkey's latest in a long line of recent foreign ministers, İsmail Cem, asserted that Turkey's eventual membership of the EU remained a 'goal' not an 'obsession'.[3] It was a phrase which he has repeated periodically during his tenure. In speaking so frankly the minister was trying to mitigate an impression built up during the 40 years or so that Turkey has pursued the EU. Mr Cem's words were, however, ultimately unconvincing, a matter of the man protesting too much. For evidence of the Turkish elite's ideological obsession with Europe one has only to focus virtually at random on any aspect of that relationship over the preceding decades.

From the outset Turkey's ambitions in Europe have owed at least as much to the ideological orientation of the ruling elite as to more material motivations. Consider the example of the first establishment of an organic relationship between the two. The original application for an Association Agreement with the European Economic

---

part of the striving for the westernisation of Turkey'. See FO371/163832 Burrows-Earl of Home, Annual Report on Turkey for 1961, 22 January 1962, p. 12.

[3] *Milliyet* and *Cumhuriyet* cited in *Turkish Press Digest*, 4 September 1997.

Community (EEC), as it was then, was in part prompted by the need for economic aid, in response to the poor conditions prevailing in the country. The EEC was minded to supply that assistance and even to contemplate the admission of Turkey, for fear that the Soviet Union would otherwise seek to fill the gap. In the aftermath of the 1956 Suez crisis, and the diminution of both British and French prestige, the Europeans could be forgiven for this bout of over-anxiety.

Contemporary commentators were, however, in no doubt about the primary motivations of the Turkish side. The Ankara correspondent of *The Times*, writing at the time of the activation of the Association Agreement, stated that 'among Turkey's westernized leaders the overwhelming motive for joining Europe is not economic but ideological'.[4] Other commentators concurred, with, for example, a *New York Times* journalist judging Turkey's new associate status as having 'for the present, more political than economic significance'; by establishing an organic link with the EEC, Turkey was seen as having made a political choice between East and West.[5]

In this view the foreign journalists of the day were undoubtedly influenced by the language and discourse of the Turkish leadership itself. İsmet İnönü, the Turkish prime minister, had constantly emphasised in his speeches during the negotiation of the Association Agreement that Turkey is bound to the West 'not merely', he somewhat surprisingly stated, by 'a sterile military alliance, but by full political and ideological ties'.[6] Perhaps the best example of the Turkish elite's drive for an umbilical relationship with the EEC, as an expression of its own unrepresentative values, was the overblown rhetoric of the foreign minister on the activation of the agreement. For Feridun Cemal Erkin the implementation of the Association Agreement meant that the domination of the ideals of Kemalism was now irreversible as it represented 'the final consecration of Turkey's European vocation, the aims and ideals constantly pursued and repeatedly proclaimed for centuries'. For him 'Turkey's future and Turkey's welfare are closely bound up with her union with Europe and the European civilisation'.[7]

---

[4] *The Times*, 1 December 1964.
[5] *New York Times*, 10 January 1964.
[6] For an example of one of these speeches see *The Times*, 22 May 1963.
[7] Quoted in *The Times*, 1 December 1964.

Consider then the example of the belated deepening of the relationship, through the establishment of a Customs Union (CU)
which came into operation in January 1996. The most prudent and
constructive course for Ankara to have followed once it had been
formally adopted would have been to make an economic success of
the union, thereby increasing complex interdependencies with the
EU member states. Turkey could then have deployed the argument
that not only did it have a CU in advance of membership, unlike
other aspirant members from central Europe, but that it had one
that was proven to have been successful. The relative improvements
in the Turkish economy, together with a legal infrastructure increasingly harmonised with that in existence within the EU, would have
given a further boost to Ankara's goal of closer integration.

In reality, the commencement of the CU was accompanied by a
new diplomatic onslaught led by the Foreign Ministry towards the
attainment of an early, and hence totally impossible, full accession.
This renewed and ill advised effort came against a backdrop of election politics, when the outgoing Prime Minister, Tansu Çiller, had
tried to milk the CU success for all that it was worth. For instance,
immediately after the Strasbourg vote in which the European Parliament finally agreed to the CU, she crowed: 'We will enter the
European Union. We will go there with our mosques. We will make
them accept us.'[8]

Of course Kemalist ideology was never one dimensional. While a
Western orientation and European aspiration were central to it, it
had to coexist with other, potentially contradictory, features. Two
are of particular relevance. First, as we saw in Chapter Three, there
was what has been called a 'Sèvres mentality', an equally obsessive
suspicion that Turkey was the object of a continuing conspiracy by
outsiders to dismember it territorially. Second, there was a prickly
Turkish nationalism, which is swift to perceive insult and injury, and
even quicker to opt for the defiant rejoinder or gesture, regardless of
its consequences for established goals. This combination of suspicion
and thin-skinned nationalism has meant that Turkish politicians and
diplomats are, with some honourable exceptions, forever damaging
the pursuit of the strategic Kemalist goal of EU membership.

[8] *The Independent*, 14 December 1995.

Perhaps the best example of this defiant and prickly sensitivity was the reaction of prime minister Mesut Yılmaz and the Turkish government to the December 1997 Luxembourg summit, which Ankara erroneously interpreted as ending all realistic hope of full membership of the EU. The Turkish government decided to suspend political dialogue with the EU and not to participate in a European Conference, which was aimed at promoting increasing policy harmony among the member and aspirant states of the EU. In doing so, Ankara retarded its ability to work closely with the EU even though the UK, one of the leading EU states which enjoys generally good bilateral relations with Turkey, was about to assume the presidency of the Council of Ministers. Yılmaz testily resorted to empty threats, stating that Turkey would give the EU six months to put its house in order on pain of withdrawing its application for membership, a position which was subsequently quietly dropped.[9] If indulgent European ministers could overlook such an over-reaction, less forgivable were his gratuitous remarks about Germany. Yılmaz referred to Bonn's desire for *lebensraum* in its vision of a Central Europe-oriented enlargement, a crude reference to an old Nazi strategic doctrine. The remark could hardly have been less well timed from a Turkish national perspective, coming as it did as Austria joined the troika of past, current and future presidents for the first time, and as a German presidency loomed beyond that of Austria's. It is incongruous to have to note that Mesut Yılmaz's latest reincarnation in government came in July 2000, when he was appointed deputy prime minister and minister in charge of European Union affairs.[10]

A further, shabby example of this thin-skinned nationalism was state minister Ayvaz Gökdemir, from the ultra-nationalist wing of the DYP, who in June 1995 referred to three visiting female MEPs, who had been among the most outspoken critics of Turkey, as 'the three prostitutes'. In addition to being offensive, the remark was injudicious in view of the seniority of the visitors,[11] and the fact

---

[9] *Turkish Probe*, no. 262, 18 January 1998.

[10] For a discussion of Yılmaz's appointment to this newly created position see *Briefing*, no. 1301, 17 July 2000.

[11] Pauline Green was the head of the Socialist bloc in the EP, Claudia Roth was the head of the Greens, while Catherine Lalumiere is a former Secretary-General of the Council of Europe.

that the Kemalist establishment was engaged in an extensive lobbying exercise in order to try to persuade the European Parliament to
endorse the Customs Union. In spite of the context, Turkey's elite
was unable to prevail upon Gökdemir to do anything other than
issue a 'grudging apology', and then only one released through the
press.[12] He retained his cabinet position.

Examples of the intrusive nature of other aspects of Kemalist
ideology litter Ankara's recent dealings with the EU. There was, for
instance, the sentencing of the Kurdish nationalist MPs, who had
had their parliamentary immunity withdrawn. The sentences were
handed down the day before the EU's six-monthly summit in Essen
in Germany, and therefore could not have been better timed to
damage any consideration of relations with Turkey at the summit.
Furthermore, in the runup to the European Parliament's consideration of the Customs Union the Turkish state chose to indict the
country's best known author, Yaşar Kemal, for spreading separatist
propaganda. Though he was eventually acquitted, the drawn out
and high profile nature of the legal proceedings, together with the
fact that his case was being heard by a State Security Court, did
Turkey's standing no good at the centre of the EU.

THE PURSUIT OF THE W.E.U.

Turkey has pursued WEU membership with dogged determination. It has done so in spite of the fact that the organisation was the
subject of ridicule within European circles for the first three
decades of its existence, which the Oxford based expert on European contemporary history, Anne Deighton, has called its 'period of
long sleep'.[13] Even after it woke up, the activities and achievements
of the WEU have been modest. Its greatest success was arguably the
co-ordination of mine hunting activities in the Persian Gulf during
the final phase of the Iran-Iraq war, though even here the involvement of the WEU only served as a political convenience to enable
Belgium and Holland to join the effort.[14] There has invariably been

---

[12] *Turkish Daily News*, 15 June 1995.

[13] Speaking at a conference entitled 'European Security, Defence and Integration:
Western European Union, 1954–96' at St Antony's College, Oxford, 21 June 1996.

[14] Dr Trevor Taylor speaking at Anglo-Turkish Round Table organised by Chatham
House and the Foreign Policy Institute in Ankara, 16 March 1989.

widely shared scepticism about what the WEU could achieve on its own, beyond humanitarian and peace-keeping tasks.[15] The main utility of the WEU seemed to be its representation as an institutional model of European co-operation in the defence field.

Many members of the Turkish elite have remained impervious to such observations. They have pursued membership with a vigour wholly disproportionate to the profile, role and potential of the organisation. Ankara followed such a path in the late 1980s for a combination of two reasons. First, attaining membership of the WEU was probably regarded as helping to expedite Turkey's application for full membership of the EU itself. Second, at a time when the re-Islamisation of Turkish society was moving apace the acquisition of membership in yet another Western club would bolster Turkey's increasingly embattled Kemalist elite. As one of Turkey's leading political scientists, Prof. İlter Turan, remarked at the time, the importance for Turkey of WEU membership was one of 'symbolic gratification'.[16]

Ankara's quest for WEU membership was facilitated by the expansion of the organisation and the adoption of a Protocol of Accession, the so-called Petersberg Declaration, on 19 June 1992. Turkey became eligible to join as an associate member together with other NATO, non-EU members, Iceland and Norway. However, the changes made in 1992 brought further problems as far as Turkey's future relationship with the WEU was concerned. Ankara felt aggrieved over the areas where its status fell short of full membership. Moreover, Turkey felt its intermediate status particularly sharply because of Greece's full membership of the WEU. Finally, Turkey was more justifiably concerned at the implications of Article 5 of the Petersberg Declaration which promised the support of member states against third party aggression, on the grounds that it could encourage Greece into 'provocative action'.[17]

---

[15] For example, see Dr Philip Gordon, then of the IISS, speaking at the St Antony's conference (see note 13).

[16] Contribution made during a discussion, Anglo-Turkish Round Table (see note 14), 16–17 March 1989. It is worth adding that the report to the director made by his special assistant Keith Kyle on returning from the Round Table on the subject of the WEU stated: 'The Turks showed themselves to be obsessed by the issue.' Chatham House Memorandum, 25 April 1989.

[17] *Turkish Daily News*, cited in *Turkish Press Review*, 31 January 1992.

The response of the WEU and its leading members was to look for further ways to accommodate Turkish sensitivities. In July 1992 the WEU Council of Ministers declared that the organisation would not permit Article 5 to be invoked in disputes between NATO members. Turkey's associate status was subsequently enhanced at Luxembourg in May 1994 by a meeting of WEU defence ministers.[18] Rather than acknowledge the energy expended on its behalf and accept the many gestures made in its direction, Turkey remained prickly about its status in the WEU. Though Turkey subsequently played an active part in the practical areas of the WEU's work, the agreement remained unratified by the Turkish parliament. Indeed, within six months of the Luxembourg meeting Turkey was threatening to reassess its relations with its allies if the WEU opened its doors to Central and Eastern European states.[19] More than two years later, Ankara was insisting on seeking to upgrade the relationship to full membership and pressing for such a goal at every platform,[20] regardless of the prospects for success or the impact that such pleas would have on member state attitudes towards Turkey.

Foreign policy as a symbol of Islamist revisionism

Foreign affairs have been an important and potent symbol of the growing divergence in outlook and values between the Kemalist establishment and the emerging Islamist movement in Turkey. Foreign policy has not, of course, been the only difference which has helped to define the Islamists as being essentially different from the mainstream Kemalist parties. Social affairs and education are also controversial areas of policy divergence. Nevertheless, foreign policy, unlike these other, more immediately sensitive areas, was apparently perceived by Professor Erbakan and his supporters as an area where they could speak more freely, perhaps because it risked less of an electoral cost. Consequently, Erbakan, who has been the actual

[18] Consequently, Turkey was permitted to contribute military forces to the WEU and establish formal channels for liaison with the WEU Defence Planning Cell, while also being linked into the WEU communications network.
[19] Turkish Foreign Minister Mümtaz Soysal on TRT TV 13 November, cited in BBC/SWB/EE, 15 November 1994.
[20] As Defence Minister Turhan Tayan put it in November 1996.

or *de facto* leader of organised Islamism in Turkey for more than 30 years, in particular indulged his tendency towards hyperbole by regularly thinking aloud about foreign affairs without inhibition. It was also an area where a new series of transnational ties could be developed which were very different from the predictable, official level relations, predominantly with the West.

THE RHETORIC OF CHANGE

Erbakan has punctuated most of his time in active politics with the rhetoric of foreign policy change. This has been the case as much in the 1970s as in the 1990s. Favourite themes have included Europe, the United States, Zionism, building a resurgent Turkey and the need to establish stronger links with the Islamic world. The repetitive and largely consistent nature of such sentiments articulated over time, it is therefore safe to assume, gives us real insight into Erbakan's instinctive attitudes and feelings towards such subjects. His rhetoric reveals a man one who combines a mixture of pious Islamism, 1950s style Third World struggle and truculent, xenophobic Turkish nationalism.

A typical insight into Erbakan's world view can be seen by comparing his ideas over a 15-year period. In 1977 he spoke freely on the issue of membership of the forerunner of the European Union, as the issue of enlargement came to the fore. On a typical occasion he likened the EEC to a three storey house: on the top floor, he said, lived the Zionist capitalists; on the middle floor were the Europeans, officials in the service of capital; on the bottom storey were the lackeys and labourers, and it was in fulfilling such a role that he believed that the Europeans wanted to drag Turkey in.[21] Instead, Erbakan advocated the creation of an Islamic Common Market. He also spoke strongly against relations with Israel and in support of the cessation of diplomatic ties with the Jewish state.[22]

Some 17 years later, Erbakan's vision was broadly similar. His ideas on closer Islamic co-operation had been elaborated into what seemed to be an alternative and parallel international order for the Muslim world. Indeed, during an unofficial trip to the US in October 1994 Erbakan paraphrased US President George Bush in calling for the creation of a 'new Muslim world order'. This was to consist of

---

[21] Retold by Robin Laurance in *The Times*, 10 May 1977.
[22] *The Guardian*, 6 July 1977.

an Islamic United Nations embracing some 200 Muslim communities, with the geographically dispersed components of the Muslim *umma*, rather than the contemporary Westphalian state-based international order, as the basic organising principle. Erbakan also advocated the establishment of an Islamic NATO, an Islamic equivalent of UNICEF (the United Nations International Children's Emergency Fund), a common Islamic currency and, as before, an Islamic Common Market.[23] 'When we come to power', Erbakan declared with characteristic bluster, 'Turkey will start such an Islamic Union'.

Similarly, he continued to reject membership of the EU, though he appeared much more willing to focus on policy issues in order to propagate such a stance. Here, Erbakan's response may have resulted from growing misgivings within Turkish society. On the issue of negotiations, Erbakan attacked the lack of transparency in decision-making in Brussels on EU relations with Turkey, which he saw as taking place in 'a dark room', without recourse to parliaments and people.[24] However, it was the issue of the Customs Union, negotiation on the introduction of which had been taking place in earnest since 1993, that appeared most to stimulate comment. Here Erbakan repeatedly focused on the practical effects of the Customs Union, which he stated, no doubt mindful of his party's support among the *esnaf* or small businessmen and shopkeepers, would completely wipe out local tradesmen.[25]

Firmly rooted behind such practical considerations, however, lay the more deep-seated objection to an organic relationship with the EU. This opposition was founded not least on the importance Erbakan gives to the issue of sovereignty. In the same statement, Erbakan voiced his fears of Turkey losing its independence if it became more structurally linked to the EU, while one of his long standing lieutenants, Oğuzhan Asiltürk, put it most baldly when he stated that joining the Customs Union would be the equivalent of becoming a colony of Europe.[26] It would indeed be problematic for 'a great Turkey' to 'be built again', as Erbakan promised in a populist speech marking the beginning of Welfare's 1995 general election

[23] *Turkish Daily News*, 21 October 1994.
[24] Issue discussed by Sami Kohen in *Milliyet*, 17 December 1995.
[25] *Turkish Daily News*, 20 March 1995.
[26] *Turkish Daily News*, 12 April 1995.

campaign,[27] if key decisions on trade and economic organisation were being taken abroad. At the root of Welfare's objections to integration with the EU, however, lay the belief that Turkey was fundamentally different. As another senior colleague and party moderate, Abdullah Gül, has said: 'Our opposition to the European Union is based on the idea that we are from a different culture, we have a different identity and a different economic structure than European countries.'[28]

By the end of the 1990s the position of Turkey's main Islamist party had, formally at least, changed on relations with the EU. Islamists now argued that they were even in favour of EU membership for Turkey, having come to value such European norms as democracy, freedom of speech and pluralism. It may be that this policy sea-change represented, for some of Turkey's more reform minded Islamists, a genuine change of view. What is undoutedly clear is that this change of line coincided with what has come to be known as the 28 February process, and the sustained pressure of the military on the forces of Islamism, moderate, conservative and radical alike. The closure of the RP and the prophetic expectations that its successor party, the Fazilet or Virtue Party (FP), would also be shut down by the courts appeared to revalue such liberal ideas in the minds of Islamists, especially in comparison to more culturalist values. The relative suddenness and instrumental nature of the change towards the EU have understandably left some sceptical as to the sincerity of the change.[29] Even if the motivations of the leaders concerned are not questioned, it is still the case that the RP and then the FP are associated with an anti-EU stance and hence that the support base, whether at a party cadre or voter level, is likely to be suspicious of or even hostile towards the idea of EU membership.

---

[27] *Turkish Daily News*, 18 November 1995.

[28] *Turkish Daily News*, 28 November 1994.

[29] For example, an authoritative Swedish monograph on EU-Turkish relations opined as follows: 'it should be kept in mind that Virtue's U-turn on the EU was belated. What the Islamic voters really think about the EU is a more complicated question. However, one thing is certain; Virtue's 'aye' is neither affirmative nor definite. A lot of the support for the EU within the party seems to be contingent on the fact that accession would make it well nigh impossible for the state to ban Virtue or one of its successor parties'. Bertil Duner and Edward Deverell, *Too Bumpy a Road? Turkey, the European Union and Human Rights* (Swedish Institute of International Affairs, Stockholm, 2000), p. 13.

Florid though many of Erbakan's opinions might be, it is not possible simply to dismiss them all as being those of a 'religious fanatic'[30] or 'dreamer'[31], as the foreign press of the 1970s believed. Erbakan's exhortations for Turkey to have closer relations with the Islamic world, whatever the motivation, actually indicated a certain perceptiveness. His insistence that Turkey take relations with the Islamic world more seriously came at a time when rising international oil prices and rapidly growing earnings by the Middle Eastern oil producers had given such countries increased economic and diplomatic power. As a net energy importer of some size, Turkey had seen a swift deterioration in its balance of payments current account and was beginning, consequently, to experience the emergence of a burdensome foreign debt, which has handicapped the country ever since. An early engagement with the oil producers of the Islamic world would have spared Turkey some of this agony and stimulated its export industries at an earlier stage. In reality, it would be a further three years before such structural changes were addressed by a Turkish government, when Turgut Özal, economic guru under the Generals, reoriented the economy from an import substitution strategy to one of export-led growth. By that stage, however, the millstone of foreign debt, so large and requiring such handling a decade later, was already firmly secured around the country's neck.

THE NEW TRANSNATIONAL LINKS

The contrasting paradigm of foreign relations can also be seen in Turkey's Islamists' choice of friends abroad. While the Kemalist elite and parties have largely eschewed a relationship with the Islamic world, Erbakan and his supporters have few friends beyond it. This has been a function of both necessity and choice. Historically, the governments, diplomats and journalists of the West have tended to give a wide birth to Erbakan and his parties. For example, until 1995 it was US Embassy policy not to have contacts with the Welfare Party, even though it was a legally constituted entity and had a significant presence in parliament. To a limited extent this is understandable. At different times in his political career Erbakan was a marginal political figure, both ideologically and electorally, in Turkey.

[30] *Financial Times*, 16 December 1976.
[31] *Financial Times*, 6 December 1976.

In the early 1970s, for example, Erbakan was dismissed as 'the Colonel Qadhafi of Turkish politics'.[32] This lack of interest is, however, much more difficult to explain at other times. From the October 1973 election to the downfall of the National Front coalition in January 1978, Erbakan was a politician of central importance,[33] routinely holding office as one of the country's deputy prime ministers and acting somewhat as a king-maker.

The absence of contact has not, however, been unidirectional. Erbakan and his colleagues have consciously set out almost exclusively to court states, groups and networks in the Islamic world, or, in the case of Germany for example, among Islamists in the Western world. The Islamist ideology of the RP and its predecessor parties have consistently emphasised relations with the Muslim world. Links with foreign governments have been developed, most notably with Saudi Arabia, Libya and Iraq.[34] By the time he assumed the premiership in June 1996, for example, Erbakan had visited Saudi Arabia on 25 separate occasions.[35]

Indeed, these contacts appear to have been crucial in the activities and survival of Turkey's Islamist parties. There have, for instance, been persistent accusations that Erbakan's Islamists have received funding from the Islamic world dating back to the early 1970s, most notably from Libya and Saudi Arabia.[36] For example it was claimed that the Welfare Party received $500,000 in 1989 from a Libyan backed organisation called Invitation to Islam.[37] Erbakan seems to have been associated with a wider Libyan attempt to establish an Islamic international, agreeing to join the International Islamic People's Command, a body which also claimed the involvement of the leading, though controversial Arab Islamist thinkers Hasan al-Turabi and Rashid al-Ghanushi.[38] Indeed, Erbakan and his supporters seem

---

[32] *International Herald Tribune*, 9 October 1973.

[33] In (3 August) 1977 *Le Figaro* called him 'l'homme de toutes les coalitions'.

[34] See Ruşen Çakır, *Ne şeriat, ne Demokrasi* (Neither Shariah nor democracy) (Siyahbeyaz, Istanbul, 1994).

[35] *Middle East International*, 11 July 1997.

[36] See, for example, Emin Çölaşan, 'Para ve Refah' (Money and Refah) in *Hürriyet*, 13 May 1994, pp. 295–7, reprinted in Turhan Dilligil (ed.), *Erbakancılık ve Erbakan* (Erbakanism and Erbakan) (Arkadaş—Adaş, Ankara, 1996?).

[37] Sedat Ergin in *Hürriyet*, 13 October 1996.

[38] ibid., and 20 October 1996.

hardly to have bothered to deny such rumours, especially in the early years.[39] Nevertheless, in spite of the longevity of such accusations, absolute proof is difficult to come by.

Furthermore, during its long period in Turkey's political wilderness, it was with Islamists from around the world—notably the Muslim Brotherhood in Egypt and Syria and the *Front Islamique du Salut* (FIS) in Algeria—that Erbakan and his associates developed ties. Interaction with such groups and personalities did not wane when the RP came closer to power. Indeed, Welfare's control of the Istanbul city government was actively used further to foster such ties. Take for example the Islamic Communities Association, which was backed by the Welfare Party until its dissolution in 1999. In May 1996 the fifth convention of the Association was held in Istanbul and addressed by both Erbakan and the RP Mayor of Istanbul Recep Tayyip Erdoğan, then the leading contender for the party's eventual leadership succession. The gathering was attended by an eclectic mix of Islamic and Islamist figures. These included both Syrian Muslim Brotherhood leader Hasan Tal and the Mufti of Syria, Ahmad Kuftaru[40] (who was known to be close to President Asad) at a time of some improvement in the otherwise cold and suspicious relationship between the Asad regime and Islamists. Leaders of the Palestinian Islamic Resistance Movement (Hamas) then based in Jordan, in the shape of Muhammad Abu Ghanimah and Muhammad Nazzal, together with leading figures from Afghanistan, Lebanon and Pakistan also attended.[41]

This was not by any means the only example of the Welfare Party acting like a fringe opposition group when in or close to power. In February 1996 senior RP personnel shared a platform with the controversial American black Islamist activist Louis Farrakhan, when he visited Istanbul on a Middle Eastern tour which also took him to Iran, Iraq, Syria and Libya. A month earlier, Erbakan had seemed keen to keep up his old contacts in the region, meeting with the deputy leader of the Syrian Muslim Brotherhood, Hasan Huwaydi,[42] in

---

[39] *Dawn*, 4 November 1973.
[40] Who was reported at the time as having referred to Erbakan as a '*mucahed* [sic]', a fighter for a sacred cause. See *Turkish Daily News*, 31 May 1996.
[41] ibid.
[42] Economist Intelligence Unit, *Syria Country Report*, 3rd quarter 1997, p. 17.

January 1996.[43] Ironically, such links threatened to embarrass Erbakan with regimes from the Islamic world with which he sought better relations during his term as prime minister between June 1996 and June 1997. In the course of Egypt's President Mubarak's visit to Turkey in July 1996 Erbakan was warned in candid terms to end his co-operation with the Muslim Brotherhood.[44] In a characteristic display of *chutzpah*, Erbakan offered to mediate between the Egyptian government and the Muslim Brotherhood, an audacity which apparently did not entirely spoil the visit.[45]

It is, however, the ties established with Islamists in the West that have been more important even than these ties, because they have been forged either with Turkish expatriates or with groups which by dint of their host country can operate with greater freedom, such as those in the US. This was also the case with Germany. Erbakan knows Germany well, having studied in Aachen. He admires the country, especially its post-1945 economic transformation, and speaks the language. Yet, in spite of such apparently auspicious conditions, it is overwhelmingly through the Islamist networks in Germany— historically active and generous supporters of his political activities—that Erbakan has recent experience of German politics and society,[46] rather than through Germany's mainstream political parties and associations.

There are at least 1,364 associations in Germany which are Islamic in orientation.[47] The Welfare Party is closely associated with the most powerful of these, the European National View Organisation (*Avrupa Milli Görüş Teşkilatları*), which is strong all over Europe where Turkish migrant workers of rural origin are to be found. The organisation was established under another name in 1974, and was subsequently renamed the Islamic Community National View (*İslam*

[43] *Turkish Daily News*, 17 January 1996.

[44] *Hürriyet*, reprinted in *Turkish Daily News*, 13 July 1996.

[45] *Turkish Daily News*, 12 July 1996.

[46] This also seems to be the case in other European countries, such as Denmark, where the link between Welfare and the Turkish diaspora is strong. See Eva Ostergaard-Nielsen, 'The Political Participation of Turkish Immigrants in Europe and in Denmark' in *Les Annales de l'autre Islam. Turcs d'Europe...et d'ailleurs* (Institut National des Langues et Civilisations Orientales, Paris, 1995), p. 392.

[47] Ertuğrul Özkök in *Hürriyet*, 22 September 1993.

Toplumu Milli Görüş) in 1995.[48] The opaque nature of the organisation and its operations makes it difficult to estimate even such basic characteristics as the number and size of its branches. The organisation does though have a global outreach, with 'tightly structured' branches as far afield as Western Europe, North America, Australia and Central Asia.

In Europe the Milli Görüş controls around 470 mosques, each of which tends to have its own affiliated youth, women's, sports and other networks. It claims to have some 57,000 'mosque members' and around 161,000 followers, although this may be an under estimate. In Germany, the organisation probably controls some 275 mosques, and is believed to have some 26,000 members and to be an important source of funding for the Welfare Party and its successor the Virtue Party in Turkey.[49] Erbakan's German connections are important in terms of providing a pool of supporters and potential new voters. Two of the Welfare Party's successful candidates in the December 1995 general election came from the Milli Görüş in Germany, one of whom, Osman Yumakoğulları, was the leader of AMGT. During its time in office the Welfare Party was particularly interested in arranging a system whereby expatriate Turks in Germany could vote in national elections.[50] During the December 1995 general election the Milli Görüş was even known to have chartered an aircraft to fly voters home from Holland.

Perhaps the best example of Erbakan's partial and Islamist-oriented experience of the world came with his visit to the United States as the guest of the American Muslim Council in October 1994. True, a meeting was hastily arranged with a junior State Department team, though a mooted meeting with the Senate Foreign Relations Committee did not take place. However, the overwhelming majority of Erbakan's engagements were with Muslim Americans and their associations, and Muslim politicians from abroad. Meetings were held

---

[48] Dr Gülistan Gurbey, lecturer at Berlin University, interviewed in *Turkish Daily News*, 15 April 1994.

[49] Report published in January 1996 on Islamic extremism in Germany, prepared by Federal Office for the Protection of the Constitution, in Cologne, cited in *Turkish Daily News*, 23 May 1996.

[50] For example, justice minister and senior party figure Şevket Kazan visited Bonn in November 1996, where he discussed different possible procedures with his German counterpart. See *Turkish Daily News*, 27 November 1996.

that included Yemenis, Sudanese and FIS representatives, together with opposition deputies from Pakistan, Sri Lanka and Kuwait. Even a delegation from Brazil was reported as having flown to Washington to meet Erbakan.[51]

When he was appointed to the premiership in June 1996 it was from such organisations as the American Muslim Council and the United Association for Studies and Research that Erbakan received enthusiastic messages of congratulation, even as the US government agonised as to how it should react to his elevation to power.

Foreign policy as a contested domain

The end of the 1980s was pivotal in the emergence of foreign policy as a contested domain in Turkish public policy. There were two reasons for this, one at the unit or state level and the other at the systemic level. First, at the unit level, there was the increasing re-Islamisation of Turkish society in general, and its growing implications for the political domain. The most graphic example of this was the growth in electoral support for Islamist candidates. Underway since 1983, with the Islamist component in Özal's broad church Motherland Party, the electoral successes of political Islam grew with the establishment of the Welfare Party in 1987. Though Erbakan's party performed indifferently in the election in that year, its voter support grew steadily from 7.2% in 1987 to perhaps some 12% four years later.[52] In 1994 Welfare made its electoral breakthrough, winning control of some 28 major cities, including Istanbul and Ankara, in the local elections of that spring. In the December 1994 general election Welfare emerged as the largest single party, with 21.4% of the popular vote.

Second, and coincidental with the first trend, there was the changing nature of international politics, as a result of East-West détente, the rise of Gorbachev, the end of the Cold War and the collapse of Communism in Eastern Europe and the Soviet Union. During the days of Cold War friction and the perception of an imminent military

[51] *Turkish Daily News*, 21 October 1994.
[52] The Welfare Party contested the October 1991 general election in an electoral alliance with the ultra-nationalists led by Alpaslan Türkeş; it is therefore only possible to approximate the RP vote during this election.

threat it was possible to hold a broad consensus behind the idea of NATO membership and close military relations with the United States. Not everyone in Turkey favoured such a course, but those who objected tended to be on the fringes of left wing and ultra-nationalist politics. Most importantly, Kemalist and Islamist alike could agree on the strategic need to oppose the threat from Moscow. With the Soviet invasion of Afghanistan in 1979 suggesting a renewed interest on the part of the USSR in southern expansion, this common perception was reinforced. The rise of Gorbachev in 1986 and, arguably most important, the ignominious withdrawal of the USSR from Afghanistan in 1988, followed in the early 1990s by the collapse of the pro-Moscow regime of Dr Najibullah, were crucial in the emergence of diverging threat perceptions in the eyes of different parts of Turkish society.

The profound changes in domestic and international politics meant that the old consensus on foreign policy was breaking down just at a time when an ideological competition over the strategic direction the country should take was both emerging and becoming more intense. Though such areas as local government, education and social policy all came to the fore at different times, it was in the arena of foreign affairs that the tensions were to be the most sustained. From the December 1995 general election to the end of February 1997 and the military's decisive move against the Welfare-led coalition, foreign policy-making became as much an expression of this ideological high noon as it was a reflection of *raison d'état*.

The best way to illustrate the degree to which domestic ideological considerations drove external relations is to consider foreign policy in action during this time. One of the best cases is Turkey's Israel strategy, driven in 1996 in particular by the military, the self-appointed guardians of the Kemalist legacy; this is described in some detail in Chapter Seven. The second involves two key moments in the year long period when Welfare Party leader Necmettin Erbakan was prime minister, when its Islamist orientation set the agenda.

ERBAKAN'S ISLAMIC OPENING

When Professor Erbakan was finally appointed Turkish prime minister on 28 June 1996 his position was comparatively weak. Though Welfare was the largest single party in the parliament it was unable to govern alone. Erbakan was therefore obliged to enter a coalition government with the predominantly secularist True Path Party (DYP). Moreover, the new government had to contend with the power of the Kemalist state, especially in the guise of the armed forces. Consequently, Welfare's room for ideological revisionism was constrained.

Erbakan began by adopting a strategy of survival to ensure a lengthy tenure in power and to routinise Welfare as a party of government. He therefore did not question any of the basic areas of strategy under the control of the Kemalist elite. During this period such an approach pervaded foreign policy. Consequently, Erbakan chose not to contest key issues, in spite of the fact that conditions, to varying degrees in the country, were ripe for policy re-evaluation.[53] He decided this in order not to provoke the military, which thrice before had intervened to subvert civilian politics. While this quiescence was greeted with relief by Turkey's Western friends and members of the Turkish Foreign Ministry alike, members and supporters of the party soon questioned this inactivity. Mindful of Welfare's looming fifth party conference, and the almost unprecedented challenges emerging from below to the party machine,[54] Erbakan became increasingly keen to achieve some success. Given the nature of the audience, that success had to be ideological in content.

The result was the two major foreign tours of Erbakan's premiership: an Asian tour to Iran, Pakistan, Malaysia, Singapore and Indonesia, and an African tour to Egypt, Libya and Nigeria. The former was, with the exception of one lapse, an impressive success.[55] Erbakan was able to make the trip in the name of a 'multi-dimensional' foreign policy, which would build ties with significant middle powers

---

[53] See Philip Robins 'Erbakan's Foreign Policy', *Survival*, summer 1997.

[54] The most visible and celebrated case was the struggle for the chairmanship of the Ankara provincial organisation in which Mehmet Tellioğlu beat the official candidate Zeki Çelik before the election was annulled by the party's executive board. However, Ankara was far from being the only case of a grass roots rebellion against the centre, and, likewise, far from being the only case where local party elections were overturned.

[55] In Malaysia, perhaps as a result of finding a kindred spirit in premier Mahathir Muhammad, Erbakan could restrain himself no longer, making largely gratuitous comments, such as asserting that the West had made no contribution to the development of science.

to the east, without jeopardising Ankara's traditional ties with the West. During the visits themselves Erbakan was comfortably able to defend his new initiative on the grounds of *raison d'état*. In Tehran, clearly the leg of the visit that was the most difficult to finesse, Erbakan signed a gas deal aimed at partially alleviating Turkey's desperate, looming energy shortfall, while satisfying the non-party members of his team by firmly raising the issue of Iranian links to the PKK. Further eastwards, Erbakan, who travelled with a large delegation of businessmen, talked of the commercial potential of closer relations with some of the Asian tigers.

Erbakan's Asian tour succeeded in wowing much of his support base at home. His statements that Turkey wanted to be a 'Muslim Japan',[56] and that he favoured preserving its Muslim identity while promoting modernism and innovation like Indonesia and Malaysia, were well received by Islamist intellectuals already excited by the prospect of the global economic centre of gravity shifting from the north Atlantic to the Pacific Rim.[57] It also drew varying degrees of applause though not uncritical, from among the cream of the foreign policy commentators in Turkey: Mehmet Ali Birand declared that the Welfare's foreign policy was 'right in principle';[58] Sami Kohen saw it as 'a dynamic new move for Turkish foreign policy' with 'potential';[59] Cengiz Çandar wrote that it was 'important and valuable to provide the "Asian dimension", something Turkish foreign policy had lacked until now'.[60]

Erbakan's triumph was, however, to be short-lived. The Asian tour alone would probably have been sufficient to give him the boost that he required before his party's congress. Perhaps Erbakan was intoxicated to the point of hubris by the success of his first tour; perhaps he felt that he had to balance the signing of a defence agreement concluded on 28 August with the state of Israel, into which he had been manoeuvred by the military; yet again, perhaps

---

[56] Erbakan interview with İlnur Çevik in *Turkish Daily News*, 12 August 1996.
[57] This was certainly the tone of a number of contributions from the floor at a one-day conference on the D-8 held in Istanbul, 7 June 1997, in which the author took part.
[58] *Sabah*, 12 August 1996.
[59] *Milliyet*, 21 August 1996.
[60] *Sabah* 18 August 1996.

Erbakan was concerned to have a further fillip closer to the 13 October congress-whatever the reason, Erbakan decided to push ahead with his Africa tour. Such a mission would in any case have been harder to justify, Africa lacking the economic dynamism and strategic importance of Erbakan's Asian destinations. The Welfare Party leader also chose to ignore some critical warning signs. It was only through the combined efforts of Abdullah Gül and senior members of the foreign ministry that Erbakan was persuaded not to press ahead with his intention to visit Islamist Sudan.[61]

Erbakan showed rather less prudence in the midst of objections from Tansu Çiller and Abdullah Gül to the proposed Libyan leg of the trip. Gül considered such a visit 'misguided' coming, as it did, against a backdrop of Colonel Qadhafi's encouragement of Kurdish separatism.[62] If anyone would have had a feel for the context of Libyan-Turkish relations Gül would. He, together with a DYP state minister, Namık Kemal Zeybek, had been present in Erbakan's place at the 27th anniversary of Qadhafi's coming to power on 1 September; in Tripoli Gül had been snubbed for the absence of Erbakan and insulted by Qadhafi's attack on Turkey's treatment of its Kurdish minority, which turned out to be a rehearsal for the trenchant criticism made by Qadhafi when Erbakan subsequently turned up in person.[63] Yet Erbakan insisted on making the visit, mindful of a potential domestic political success if he could persuade the Libyans to honour outstanding payments due to Turkish construction companies.

The first leg of Erbakan's Africa tour in Egypt, with a visit to the Islamic university at al-Azhar included, turned out tolerably well. Indeed, the Turkish prime minister's arrival provided an opportunity for President Mubarak to decline a mini summit in Washington on the ailing Arab-Israeli peace process; providing the excuse for a snub to the Americans would, no doubt, have elicited quiet glee on the part of Erbakan. From then onwards, however, the trip was an unmitigated disaster. In spite of due warning, Erbakan was 'stunned' by Qadhafi's call for an independent Kurdish homeland in

---

[61] One source states that senior Turkish diplomats demanded that Erbakan should not visit Khartoum. *Sabah*, 27 September 1996.

[62] Editorial by İlnur Çevik, who was then close to Erbakan and his inner circle, in *Turkish Daily News*, 7 October 1996.

[63] *Turkish Daily News*, 24 September 1996.

his presence at a news conference, at which he also criticised Turkey's growing links with Israel. Rather than cutting his losses,[64] Erbakan repeatedly exacerbated the situation: first, by agreeing to a final communiqué that implied that the US was guilty of terrorism;[65] second, through a demeaningly lengthy negotiation aimed at attaining a Libyan commitment to settle the outstanding debt to Turkish contractors.[66]

At home, the secularist press and political opposition went on the rampage. *Cumhuriyet* carried the headline 'Erbakan defends Libya'; *Sabah* wrote of a 'night of shame' for Turkey; *Milliyet* wrote of how the Libyans had treated the Turks as though they were beggars. While Erbakan lamely claimed that he had wrested concessions from Libya, the press view was that the concessions had flowed in the other direction. Erbakan's rash handling of the Libya visit, today widely acknowledged as 'a mistake, a great mistake' in Islamist circles, threatened the very survival of the coalition, with ANAP leader Mesut Yılmaz calling on Erbakan to resign for damaging Turkey's honour, and Çiller ultimately opting to ignore a perfect opportunity to end the coalition in favour of wresting an enhanced status within it. In between, Erbakan was further criticised for consorting with the pariah regime in Nigeria. Ironically, however, this was arguably the most successful part of the tour, with Sani Abacha, the Nigerian leader, so thankful for the visit at a time of international ostracism that a Turkish company received two multi-million dollar contracts soon afterwards.

Ideology is at least as important as geopolitics in the formulation and pursuit of Turkish foreign policy. Throughout the 75 years of the existence of the Turkish state the Kemalist ideology has been a key factor in the definition of national interest. With its admiration for scientific rationalism and its identification with a European

---

[64] Abdullah Gül rather effectively did so by dismissing Qadhafi's remarks as 'lunatic nonsense' unworthy of further comment.

[65] The final communiqué referred to 'countries engaged in terroristic activities against Libya', provoking a candid response from Nicholas Burns on behalf of the State Department, and retaliatory remarks from the Turkish Ministry of Foreign Affairs.

[66] The talks on repayments continued for some 12 hours.

model of development, it is little wonder that for most of that time Turkish foreign policy has been skewed towards Europe and away from the Middle East. Consequently, successive Turkish elites have pursued membership of the EU with a zest which often crosses the boundaries of obsession, and have used up reserves of good will on a pursuit of membership of the WEU wholly disproportionate to the standing or effectiveness of the organisation.

The centrality of ideology to external relations is not by any means confined to the Kemalist elite in Turkey. The Islamist mainstream has for three decades used foreign policy issues as an avenue through which to articulate a religious-cum-nationalist vision, as well as a safety valve through which to let off steam. In its development of foreign ties it has proved to be just as selective as the Kemalist elite, with its Third Worldist penchant for Islamist movements, some respectable, some less so. Even in power, it has often appeared as if the Welfare Party, and in particular its leader Necmettin Erbakan, have been more comfortable with the rhetoric of opposition than with working within the policy constraints of government.

The critical months between December 1995 and February 1997 proved to be a period when the competing ideological visions of Kemalism and Islamism wrestled and at times battled with each other in the domain of foreign affairs. With the imperatives of domestic politics and the tussle for the soul of the Turkish nation-state uppermost during this period, foreign policy, whether played out as the military's feverish embrace of Israel or the Welfare govern-ment's opening to the Islamic world, had comparatively little to do with foreign affairs.

5

SECURITY AND FOREIGN POLICY

Turkey's strategic culture

The issue of security is a core component of just about every facet of public policy in Turkey. Consider its profile. The rationale of security is used to justify a large army, the second biggest in NATO; the defence component accounts for 11.4 per cent of the national budget,[1] rising to close to 20 per cent if various other allocations for military industries are taken into account; the state has sought to develop an extensive domestic arms production sector; security is invoked as the justification for an array of measures which erode liberal conceptions of freedom, from press censorship in the southeast to the laws which allow certain political parties to be closed down. At the centre of this enduring preoccupation with security are the armed forces, the Gendarmerie and a plethora of intelligence and other security services, which have proliferated in the 1990s, and whose raison d'être is to sniff out and snuff out threats to the state.

The reason for the enduring centrality of security in Turkey is the historical experience of the Turkish state, reinforced by the perceptions and experiences of the present, especially those of the security establishment. Key to the former is, as we saw in Chapter Three, the experience of the early 1920s, when the armed forces resisted attempts from great power diplomats and Greek generals to carve up the rump of the Ottoman empire, which would have reduced an emerging Turkish state to the proportions of a silver of territory in Anatolia. Though the Turkish army was successful in resisting such a goal, the impact of this existential struggle was traumatic. The legacy of this period has been to create what is now

---

[1] This was the allocation for 1995.

widely referred to as a 'Sèvres complex', whereby foreign-inspired plots are perceived to exist to implement the defunct Treaty of Sèvres, the 1920 blueprint for the division of the territory that now forms contemporary Turkey. Although, the Turkish military continues, as one former senior Turkish official has put it, to live in the 1920s, this obsession with conspiracies so beloved of the Balkans and the Middle East[2] is far from being the exclusive preserve of the uniformed.

This insecurity complex, now nearly eight decades old, has been reinforced by other experiences of outside threats and dangers during the intervening time. These have ranged from Stalin's expansionist statements in the mid 1940s, when Moscow coveted the Straits (that is the Bosphorus and the Dardanelles, which provide access to the Black Sea) through the territorial revisionism of the Syrian state aimed particularly at Hatay but also encompassing swathes of land beyond, to the unreliability of the US, which played fast and loose with Turkish security by trading elements of it during the Cuban missile crisis and, through the Johnson letter, being prepared to contemplate the compromising of the country's protection. More recent concerns, from Armenian and Syrian irredentism through bilateral military co-operation between Greece and Syria to long term anxieties about a resurgent Russia, must therefore be viewed from the perspective of an ingrained cognition of insecurity.

Going hand in hand with this enduring perception of the threat from outside is the threat from within. Historically, these threats were identified with external powers and were focused on ethnic and religious minorities among the population, as the Ottoman Empire both contracted and weakened. During the interregnum between the collapse of the Ottoman Empire and the establishment of the republic the threat came from an irredentist Greece, which sought to exploit the presence of the large Greek population in Turkey. Between the 1960s and 1980s the chief threat was seen to be ideological, with the exploitation by foreign countries of radical leftist

---

[2] For an extensive discussion of conspiracy theories in the Middle East see Daniel Pipes, *The Hidden Hand* (St Martin's Press, New York, 1996), although one might contest his conclusion about Turkey that 'Few mainstream political, intellectual or religious leaders engage in conspiratorial thinking, which exists at the fringes of polite society'.

and Islamist movements. Latterly, these attempts to exploit ethnic and ideological cleavages in Turkey have fused with the attempt by external actors to ratchet up the Marxist-cum-Kurdish ethnonationalist challenge to the integrity of the Turkish state.

The result of this fixation with security has been to give an important, and at times a pivotal, place to the military within the Turkish system. The Turkish armed forces, as the guardians of Atatürk's ideological legacy, see themselves as the ultimate guarantors of the state and its orientation; the repeated nature of external and internal security challenges necessitates that the military remain strong, vigilant and prepared to step in directly whenever required. Though external actors, from human rights agencies through many Western states to multilateral organisations like the Council of Europe, may consider this to be a gross perversion of democratic standards, to the military and indeed many Turks such interventions are absolutely essential. Indeed, for many who hold this perspective, the liberal stance of outsiders who would toy with the security of the Turkish state is but further evidence of the threat from without.

This chapter will discuss some of the key threat perceptions of the Turkish state, both lying outside and inside its territory. The second half of the chapter will focus on the capabilities of the state in facing down such threats, and the implications that such strategies have had for its bilateral relationships.

Threat perceptions and foreign relations

One might expect that as the world has changed rapidly, so Turkish threat perceptions would have changed rapidly. After all, the demise of the USSR and the Communist ideology in Europe has removed the one great existential threat to the republic, combining, as it did, the power of force with the mobilising power of a subversive set of ideas. Since 1989 Turkey has indeed seen the disappearance of Communism as a revolutionary ideology while the military capabilities of Russia have been hobbled, with the Chechen war, both Mark I (1994–6) and Mark II (1999–2000), providing proximate, visible and compelling evidence of this. With Russia's military effectiveness reduced, Turkey now has as its neighbours a number of states that are smaller, weaker or, in the case of comparable powers such as

Iran, weakening states.[3] Of course the emergence of new and unstable states has brought with it its own problems. However, these have been largely of a lesser nature than before, and certainly do not contain the existential component of the time of the Soviet Union.

Furthermore, one might have assumed that Turkey would have been receptive to the new definitions of security gaining currency in Western states. There, the notion of security has been redefined to include a range of softer threats ranging from the effects of environmental damage to illegal drugs and organised crime. In Turkey, however, this has largely not been the case. As in most developing countries, awareness of environmental matters is embryonic, largely confined to certain parts of the middle class, and hence with little impact on most areas of policy-making. This is rather short-sighted, especially in view of the rapid growth of the country's tourist industry and the tremendous potential for expansion which still exists, particularly on the Aegean and Mediterranean coasts.

The same observation might be made with respect to illicit drugs. Turkey has long been a significant country as far as international narcotics crime is concerned. Until the mid 1970s this involvement was a function of Turkey's status as an opium poppy producer and the diversion for illicit purposes of a proportion of this domestically produced crop. Since the 1980s Turkey has emerged as a significant route for the narcotics trade and an important centre for the refining of raw opium. Though it may be argued that the country's informal economy benefited from the drugs trade and associated money laundering, the advent of narcotics trafficking ultimately had a corrosive effect on the Turkish state, the extent of which was glimpsed at with the Susurluk affair of November 1996.[4] It was not

---

[3] Iran is a 'weakening state' in three senses: first, in terms of the domestic political tensions and convulsions, which have become increasingly evident since the election of President Muhammed Khatami in May 1997; second, militarily, because of the debilitating nature of the Iran-Iraq war, compounded by the difficulty of procuring modern weapons systems because of penury or of foreign and especially US embargoes; third, because of the contracting resource base of the regime, principally as a result of the oil price, which tended to be depressed for much of the 1990s.

[4] A Mercedes saloon containing a senior police officer, a politician from Tansu Çiller's DYP and a notorious ultra-nationalist hitman and drug smuggler was involved in a serious accident at Susurluk, thereby revealing what many had

until the end of 1996 that the Turkish government began to take the issue of drugs more seriously,[5] hitherto being more intent on using the issue as a propaganda tool against the PKK.[6] It was not until the aftermath of the 1999 Helsinki summit and Turkey's receipt of EU candidate status that there was concerted cooperation in the fight against narcotics.[7]

In spite of these developments, there has been little attempt to broaden the concept of security. Even in the mid to late 1990s, Turkey's view of security was still determined by traditional, hard security issues like external military threats and, in the case of the PKK led insurgency, 'terrorism'. It was not until the end of the decade that Turkish threat perceptions of Russia began to soften.[8] This situation may be explained by recourse to three different types of threat.

THE THREAT FROM NEIGHBOURS COMBINED

Turkey may indeed have little to fear in the short and medium terms from each of its neighbours individually. That, however, is not the whole story. In spite of its repeated protestations of pacific objectives, almost all of her neighbours hold fears of Turkey. Though such

---

suspected, the close relationship within the 'deep state' of organised crime, some politicians and some members of the security establishment. For more detail on the Susurluk affair see *The Susurluk Report* produced by the Office of the Public Prosecutor, Istanbul State Security Court, 30 January 1997, and reprinted in *Cumhuriyet*, 4–5 April 1997.

[5] For example, the reorganisation of the Gendarmerie as a reflection of the increased importance given to illegal drugs began in 1997. Interview with senior Gendarmerie officers, Ankara, 26 September 2001.

[6] Though the connection between the PKK and extortion and racketeering is frequently made by British and continental European law enforcement officers, Britain at least has yet to see any significant signs that the PKK is involved in drug trafficking. See, for example, the presentation by a member of Special Branch at the Pan-European Conference on Turkish Crime, London, April 1999.

[7] British officials involved in the fight against heroin are convinced that Helsinki represents a watershed in cooperation with Turkey on the issue, and draw attention to statements made to this end by Turkish law enforcers. For example, interview with British official with almost 10 years' experience of the Turkish heroin connection, London, 14 November 2000.

[8] For a review of the 'frustrating and promising' nature of Russian-Turkish bilateral relations see Duygu Bazoğlu Sezer, 'Turkish-Russian Relations: From Adversity to 'Virtual Rapprochement'' in Alan Makovsky and Sabri Sayarı (eds), *Turkey's New World: Changing Dynamics in Turkish Foreign Policy* (WINEP, Washington, DC, 2000).

views may, depending on the vantage point of the detached, appear to owe much to imagination or eccentricity, it must be acknowledged that as perceptions they are real enough. They include: concern that Turkish troops might overrun the whole of the island of Cyprus; notions of neo-Ottoman expansionism, whether in the Balkans or the Middle East; Greek concerns that islands in the Dodecanese might be overrun; Syrian anxieties that Turkey could use its control of the Euphrates to disrupt the volume of water flowing across the border.

Other threat perceptions of Turkey, notably by Armenia, Cyprus and Greece, have been rendered more vivid by the reality of neighbouring states' experience of Turkey. Armenia was subject to a complete blockade by Turkey in partnership with Azerbaijan in April 1993, a move which was partially alleviated for humanitarian purposes two years later.[9] Cyprus has been alarmed by threats made in January 1997 to 'hit' a consignment of S-300 missiles,[10] which it ordered from Russia, should they be installed. In turn, Greek fears of attack have been stoked as a result of threats made by Ankara should Athens exercise its rights under the Law of the Sea Convention to extend its territorial waters from 6 to 12 miles.

Such threat perceptions of Turkey have prompted neighbouring states to adopt a range of defence oriented strategies, from the conciliatory diplomatic engagement of Bulgaria and Romania, through the pursuit of conflict through diplomatic means as favoured by Cyprus and Greece (in the latter case up to 1999), to the mixed strategies of conciliation and confrontation pursued by Iran and Iraq. In all such cases, there has been something of the mercurial in bilateral relations with Turkey in the 1990s, which in turn has helped to foster a more generalised atmosphere of insecurity. Rarely then has there been a stable relationship between Turkey and its neighbours during this time. An exception has been visible in Turkish-Ukrainian relations.[11] Ankara's and Kiev's mutual perception of strategic

---

[9] It must be noted, however, that the blockade was imposed in reaction to Armenian gains at the expense of Azerbaijani territory in the war over Nagorno-Karabakh. Indeed, the imposition of a blockade represented a more measured response than the military intervention advocated by some Turkish politicians.

[10] *Turkish Daily News*, 11 January 1997, quoting military sources.

[11] Some Turkish commentators claim that Turkish-Georgian relations would fit into the same category. While it is true that Ankara's relations with President

convergence made for a relatively uncomplicated relationship, as both middle powers of the Black Sea have given each other succour in the difficult challenge of managing relations with Russia.[12]

An alternative option for Turkey's neighbours not fully committed to conciliatory engagement has been to look for alliances that might pool aggregate strength in a way capable of providing deterrent value or leverage against Turkey. Perhaps unsurprisingly it has been these relationships which have, in turn, alerted the strategic planners in Ankara and exercised the popular imagination more broadly in Turkey. In such cases of alliance making among neighbouring states there has been a resonance with Turkey's historic fear of encirclement, which was especially strong during the Second World War.[13]

The following three sets of relations have excited most interest.

Armenia and Russia. The continuing relationship between Armenia and Russia, which has straddled the collapse of the Soviet Union and the establishment of the Commonwealth of Independent States (CIS), is arguably the most convincing example of the pooling of security resources on the part of Turkey's neighbours. Yerevan's continuing dependence on its large neighbour to the north was confirmed in treaty form in December 1991, just as the Soviet Union was breathing its last breath. In particular, Turkey's restriction on all but food supplies in transit to Armenia has helped to foster Yerevan's dependence on Moscow.[14]

Shevardnadze have indeed been mostly cordial, and the Georgian head of state talked towards the end of the 1990s of a 'growing strategic partnership' with Turkey (quoted in *Turkish Daily News*, 16 March 1998), the periodic bouts of internal conflict in the Caucasian state, together with the vulnerability of Shevardnadze, himself suggests a precariousness to the relationship which has not existed with Ukraine.

[12] Though it should be noted that Turkey has not provided Ukraine with any aid, as it has done with many of the other newly independent republics of the former Soviet south, a shortcoming that has provoked some criticism from Kiev.

[13] Mahmut Bali Aykan, 'Ideology and National Interest in Turkish Foreign Policy Toward the Muslim World, 1960–87', unpublished doctoral thesis, University of Virginia, 1987, p. 59.

[14] Leszek Buszynski, *Russian Foreign Policy After the Cold War* (Praeger, London, 1996), p. 137.

This dependent relationship was strengthened by the outbreak of hostilities with Azerbaijan over the Armenian populated enclave of Nagorno-Karabakh. Though Ankara's policy towards Nagorno-Karabakh was generally one of caution,[15] born out of a desire to contain the conflict and crucially to ensure that its confessional nature did not entangle Turkey into a broader Christian-Muslim division,[16] the proximity of both the Karabakh war and the border with the Turkish republic some 125 miles away made Armenia's pursuit of closer relations with Russia almost inevitable. Ankara's instinctive official reserve of 1991 and 1992 did not always extend to the maverick personality of Turgut Özal, who, though by this time he enjoyed little power, still possessed a certain stature. His widely reported sentiments that Turkey should 'scare the Armenians' into abandoning their fight for Karabakh and block their export routes in March 1992 hardly helped to allay Yerevan's fears of its much larger southern neighbour.[17] Neither were opposition politicians necessarily constrained by the official line. Özal's successor as ANAP leader, Mesut Yılmaz, who had until five months earlier been Turkey's foreign minister, raised the question of sending Turkish troops to the conflict zone.[18]

Even the renewed bout of fighting in early 1993, when the Armenians went on the offensive to strengthen the access corridor linking Karabakh with the Armenian republic, and opposition

[15] Ankara's official reaction to the Karabakh war of 1991–2 was a template for the management of such conflicts in the future, whether in Bosnia or Chechnya. This included: a public diplomacy that espoused a 'responsible and careful policy'; repeated public statements in favour of a ceasefire, the maintenance of the territorial integrity and borders of the protagonists, and a process of reconciliation; close cooperation with interested multilateral institutions, in this case the CSCE; repeated attempts to persuade allies in the West to engage with the issue; the organisation and provision of humanitarian aid. See, for example, prime minister Süleyman Demirel's statement in BBC/SWB/EE, March 1992.

[16] Since Soviet troops had put down unrest in Baku with some severity in January 1990, there had been a growing tendency to perceive the issue in confessional terms. There was anger at what were perceived as double standards, the US and the Western Europeans vigorously protesting against Soviet repression in Lithuania around the same time while ignoring or even sending messages of understanding over the Baku incidents.

[17] *Financial Times*, 7 March 1992.

[18] *Turkish Daily News*, 13 March 1992.

politicians at home again clamoured for action,[19] Turkish official-dom's essential caution towards the conflict was hardly strained. There was, in short, never any serious prospect that Turkey would intervene and fight a war against Armenia.[20] In spite of this reality there was probably just sufficient equivocation on Turkey's part to confirm Armenian perceptions that a close Russian alliance was a *sine qua non* for winning and holding Karabakh. Whether by Demirel's refusal to rule out the use of force in stating that all options re-mained on the table, senior ambassador Tugay Özçeri's statement that Turkey might have to 'reassess' its neutrality, or the flying of military jets along Turkey's eastern border, government, bureau-cracy and military in Turkey had demonstrated in a coordinated fashion that they had at least to go through the motions of register-ing discontent at events on the ground.

With Nagorno-Karabakh defying attempts to find a political settlement, the strategic relationship between Armenia and Russia tightened as the 1990s wore on. A bilateral agreement in 1995 for-malised the presence of Russian forces in the republic, together with their basing facilities at Gyumri and Yerevan. In August 1997 the two states signed a comprehensive security treaty, which included the provision of a mutual assistance clause in the case of external attack.[21] This means that of all the successor states to the Soviet Union, only with Armenia and Belarus has Russia forged a close strategic partnership.[22]

For Yerevan the presence of a Russian military tripwire has helped to reduce vulnerability to the Turks. This relationship has in

---

[19] Again President Özal was at the forefront of such sentiments. Rightly convinced that it was no longer possible to solve Armenian–Azerbaijani differences through negotiation, Özal argued that Turkey must be prepared to take 'calculated risks', the expression that he had used during the Gulf crisis in supporting Turkey's participation in the war against Iraq. In turn, both foreign minister Çetin and senior Turkish diplomats were 'upset' at his 'harsh tones'. See Sami Kohen in *Milliyet*, 9 April 1993.

[20] Indeed, Turkey even baulked at Baku's request for a handful of helicopters to expedite the evacuation of refugees, for fear of how this would be perceived.

[21] Rajan Menon, 'After Empire: Russia and the Southern "Near Abroad"' in Michael Mandelbaum (ed.), *The New Russian Foreign Policy* (Council on Foreign Relations, New York, 1998), p. 130.

[22] Survey on Russia, *Financial Times*, 9 April 1997.

turn enabled Russia to maintain leverage in its 'near abroad' at a time of domestic weakness. From a Turkish perspective the Russian military presence gives bite to Armenian territorial ambitions in areas of Anatolia formerly populated by Armenians. In turn, the Russian presence reduces the efficacy of the belt of buffer states which promised in the late 1980s to reduce the proximate nature of the historic Russian threat. The planned withdrawal of Russian troops from Georgia, if and when it eventually happens,[23] will help to soften Turkish threat perceptions of the former superpower, though Ankara's concerns about resurgent Russian power are most definitely longer term ones.

Armenia, Greece and Iran. The second group of states whose increasing co-operation has irked Ankara has been Armenia, Greece and Iran. In particular a meeting of the foreign ministers of the three states in Iran in September 1998 caused great agitation in Turkey. This was in spite of the fact that the three ministers concerned were careful not to antagonise Turkey. The summit was billed as being concerned with economic matters, and the memorandum of understanding which came out of the meeting focused on how to increase economic co-operation among the three.

In spite of this the Turkish media widely interpreted the gathering as 'an omen of an emerging antagonistic alliance against Turkey'.[24] In drawing conclusions which were more strategic than economic in orientation, the Turkish side was not incorrect. That was certainly the generally held view of the meeting in Tehran shortly after it was concluded. What was perhaps harder to explain was the Turkish reaction which also followed. Though the Turkish Foreign Ministry had been circumspect about the meeting during its deliberations, İsmail Cem rushed to Tehran just a week after the summit. He used Tehran, and a joint press conference with his counterpart,

---

[23] Moscow has stated that it needs 15 years to close its remaining four military bases in Georgia (one of which, at Akhalkalaki, is located close to the Turkish border, where there is an increasingly nervous 60,000 Armenian population), though Tbilisi wants it to complete the withdrawal in three. See 'Russian Bases in Georgia: Managing Withdrawal', IISS *Strategic Comments*, vol. 7, issue 4, May 2001, www.iiss. org/stracom.

[24] *Turkish Probe*, 20 September 1998.

as the forum from which to launch a stream of invective against Greece. In an outburst of surprising ferocity in reference to the three country summit, Cem accused Athens of attempting to 're-cruit Muslim soldiers to take part in the new Crusades'.[25]

Greece and Syria. The third grouping of neighbours which has excited security interest in Turkey is that which has been perceived as emerging between Greece and Syria. A Greek-Syrian defence accord was concluded in Summer 1995, just half a year before the Imia/Kardak crisis when Greece and Turkey came the closest they have been to war since the 1974 Cyprus crisis, this time over an uninhabited rocky outcrop in the Aegean. As with the Israeli-Turkish agreement, detail about the Greek-Syrian relationship is confused and contradictory. The matter was complicated by the ill advised action of some in Greek defence circles in suggesting that the agreement included secret understandings for the use of Syrian naval and airport facilities by the Greek armed forces. Since April 1996, Athens has denied that the accord includes these provisions.[26] Nevertheless, Turkish suspicions that Greek planes would indeed be allowed to use such bases in the event of a conflict with either Turkey or the 'Turkish Republic of Northern Cyprus' have endured. Such mistrust has also been fuelled by wild talk from well known hawks, including the former Greek Defence Minister, Gerassimos Arsenis, about the desirability of Athens forming an anti-Turkish bloc to embrace Iran, Iraq, Syria, Armenia, Russia and Bulgaria.[27]

Although one might well be sceptical as to the nature and worth of a Greek-Syrian military accord, the seriousness with which it has been taken in Turkey is best illustrated by the substance given to one of the most influential strategic evaluations to enter the public domain in the 1990s: the 'two and a half wars strategy' (*ikibuçuk savaş stratejisi*), which requires that Turkey be prepared to fight on two and a half fronts simultaneously. This view was developed and propounded by the respected strategist, columnist and former Foreign Ministry under secretary, Şükrü Elekdağ. In a series of articles

---

[25] *Turkish Daily News*, 14 September 1998.
[26] *Middle East International* No. 566, 16 January 1998.
[27] *Turkish Daily News*, 4 April 1996.

in the daily newspaper *Milliyet*,[28] Elekdağ argued for a big increase in defence spending on the basis that the state needed to be ready for a contingency whereby it would find itself fighting a war on two and a half fronts. In his articles Elekdağ assumed that the Aegean would form one front, while a second front would probably be found in the Middle East, most probably involving Syria; the 'half a war' meant the Kurdish insurgency campaign in the south-east, which would be used by Turkey's two external enemies to weaken it from within.[29]

THE THREAT FROM WITHOUT AS THE THREAT
FROM WITHIN

Elekdağ's notion of a war fought on two and a half fronts points to the issue of the threat from within as an extension of threats from outside the country. This idea certainly has a long historical resonance. During the latter stages of the Ottoman Empire external actors used communities and peoples within the Empire as a way of increasing their leverage against the centre. The French did it with the Catholic Christians of the Near East, notably the Maronites; the Russians did it with their Orthodox counterparts; during the First World War the Russians used the Armenians against the Ottoman state;[30] the British encouraged an Arab revolt based upon the Hijaz as a device to weaken its Ottoman foe from within.

This view of external powers exploiting domestic cleavages to weaken or undermine the state continued after the end of the Ottoman Empire. In the early 1920s, Greece used the Greek communities in Asia Minor as a justification and a partner in its military intervention; the British were widely perceived to have incited a Kurdish uprising against Ankara in 1925, in order to weaken Turkey's

---

[28] The series ran on 2, 3 and 4 December 1994 under the headlines 'If you want peace be prepared for war!' (*Barış istersen savaşa hazır ol!*), 'The mastermind of the PKK is in Syria' (*PKK'nın beyni Suriye'de*) and 'Let's increase defence spending' (*Savunma harcamalarını artıralım*) respectively.

[29] See most notably his article in *Milliyet*, 27 November 1994.

[30] For an example of Turkish historiography that identifies the Armenians as a Russian fifth column see Kamuran Gürün, *The Armenian File: The Myth of Innocence Exposed* (Rustem & Bro., Nicosia, and Weidenfeld & Nicolson, London, 1985). The author asserts that 'we find in almost every source that the Armenians cooperated with the Russians when the [First World] war broke out', p. 191.

bargaining position over the future of the vilayet of Mosul; during the Cold War the Moscow-based Comintern sought to use Communist groups in Turkey against the state. By the end of the 1990s the challenge from political Islam, itself perceived to be the product of external encouragement, had emerged as the main threat from within as perceived by the Turkish military.[31] For a decade from the late 1980s it was the Kurdish issue that had emerged as the Achilles heel of the Kemalist state. By 1989 it was clear that the threat posed by the Kurdish nationalist movement in the form of the PKK had grown into the most serious internal challenge since the war with Greece in the early 1920s.[32]

The PKK. Throughout virtually its entire existence the PKK has been extensively involved with foreign states. This involvement began with Syria in the early 1980s, as the PKK leadership sought refuge from the security forces following the Turkish military takeover in September 1980. It then continued with Lebanon, where the PKK had training bases, and Syria, which housed the movement's leadership headquarters, during the 1980s. By the late 1980s and early 1990s, when the Kurdish insurgency in the south-east of the country was accelerating in intensity, other Middle Eastern states, notably Iran and Iraq, had also become spasmodically involved in patronising the PKK. As the organisation sought to diversify its activities more into the political realm, it began to open a number of front offices abroad, especially in Europe in the early to mid 1990s. By the mid 1990s senior and influential sources in Turkey had accused eight states of directly aiding the PKK,[33] and a further dozen or so of giving succour to its members and its front organisations.

While foreign assistance was crucial to the survival, organisation and military operations of the PKK it is important to emphasise that it was not a foreign creation without rationale or support in

---

[31] The national security policy document approved by the National Security Council in November 1997 placed Islamism alongside 'separatism', both of course essentially internal threats, as the primary threat to Turkish security. See *Turkish Daily News,* 6 November 1997.

[32] For a history of the PKK, see İsmet İmset, *The PKK, A Report on Separatist Violence, 1973–1992* (Turkish Daily News Publications, Ankara, 1992).

[33] These are: Armenia, Cyprus, Greece, Iran, Iraq, Lebanon, Russia and Syria.

Turkey itself.[34] On the contrary, the PKK could not have grown so rapidly and prospered so extensively without the co-operation of Kurdish communities in the south-east of Turkey in particular. The critical factors which facilitated this were: the increasing growth of a self-conscious Kurdish nationalism inside Turkey; the material disdain for the south-east on the part of the Turkish state, which provided few resources for economic development or social services; structural economic factors, which have helped to accelerate the sharply growing relative poverty in Turkey; and the coercive nature of the Turkish state, both in terms of forced assimilation to the values and ideology of Kemalism and in terms of the increasingly extensive activities of the security services. The very receptivity of many Kurds in Turkey to the PKK is evidence of the conditions inside the country.

The dominant view of the Turkish state, however, during most of this time, has been to reject such a description. Before 1989 and after 1993 the Turkish state has doggedly maintained that there is no Kurdish problem, other than one which relates directly to security. Given that the challenge was one of violence, so the thinking went, the only appropriate response was one which employed violence. Even between 1989 and 1993, when Turgut Özal was at his most engaged with the Kurdish issue, there were many who did not share his belief that there needed to be a cultural and even a political response to the issue. From June 1993 onwards, following the death of Özal in April 1993, the response was swiftly reduced almost exclusively to a function of national security, with consequent implications for Turkey's foreign relations. Extra-judicial killings increased and later units of special forces were introduced in order to supplement the regular military, Gendarmerie and intelligence presence in the south-east. These operated with impunity until 1997.

Those who espoused this security-first response perceived the PKK as a terror organisation, acting under the control of foreign governments, with no standing inside the country other than that

---

[34] For the best and most up to date books on Turkey's Kurdish challenge see Henri J. Barkey and Graham E. Fuller, *Turkey's Kurdish Question* (Carnegie/Rowman & Littlefield, Lanham, MO, 1998), and Kemal Kirişci and Gareth M. Winrow, *The Kurdish Question and Turkey* (Frank Cass, London, 1997). For an authoritative study of the Kurds, see David McDowell, *A Modern History of the Kurds* (I.B. Tauris, London, 1996).

which it could achieve through intimidation and extortion. The Kurdish insurgency was consequently reduced to the level of being an extension of Turkey's problematic relations with its difficult neighbours. Increasingly, as one of Turkey's leading journalists and commentators, Mehmet Ali Birand, has put it, Ankara 'indexed' its relations with key states on their stance towards the PKK,[35] thereby allowing bilateral relations increasingly to be dominated by the issue. This, in turn, gave the PKK some latitude with which to sully Turkey's bilateral relations with a number of states. As the insurgency intensified between 1989 and 1995, and a growing number of countries were perceived to have a relationship with the PKK, so Turkey's relations with a series of countries became affected.

The PKK and Turkish-Syrian relations. The relationship which has been most affected by the PKK factor has been Turkey's relationship with Syria. In 1987 Turgut Özal attempted to forge a comprehensive settlement with Syria designed to address Damascus' concerns over water in return for an end to its sponsorship of the PKK.[36] Within six months the initiative had failed, as Syria, following some brief reduction in the visibility of its contacts, was shown to have maintained its ties with the PKK. The Özal visit was to prove to be the first of what became five initiatives in six years as far as the issue of the PKK was concerned.[37] During this time Turkish policy towards

[35] Mehmet Ali Birand writing in his column in *Sabah*, 22 February 1996 about Turkish-Syrian relations (although the argument also applies, though to a lesser degree, to other bilateral relationships). It should be noted that Birand also described Syrian attitudes towards Turkey during the same period as being indexed on the water issue.

[36] This led to the conclusion on 17 July of two protocols, one on economic cooperation (including water) and one on security issues. Both were subsequently ratified by the Turkish parliament, though only the former was published in the *Official Gazette*. The former guarantees Syria an annual average throughflow of water from the River Euphrates of 500 cu metres per second; the latter stipulates that Syria should end its relationship with the PKK. The separate existence and status of the two protocols enables Ankara to argue that no direct water-security linkage was included in the agreements, though the juxtaposition of their negotiation leaves little doubt that this was the implicit intention. I am grateful to Gün Kut for important insights in clarifying the background to the two protocols.

[37] In addition to the Özal initiative in 1987, there were others by Yılmaz in 1989, Sezgin in 1992, Demirel in January 1993 and Çiller in November 1993, all security related.

Syria 'zigzagged incredibly', as different branches of the Turkish state fought for the upper hand in determining the strategy to be pursued with Syria. Similar overtures were embarked upon by different governments in Turkey, all beginning with optimistic sentiments and ending in bitterness and recrimination. Minor successes such as the closure of a Kurdish military base, the so-called Mahsum Korkmaz Academy, in the Beqaa Valley in Lebanon, apparently on Syrian instructions, in late 1992 proved to be no hindrance to the activities of the PKK.

Arguably the best example of this zigzagging came at the end of the summer 1993, with the resumption of the Kurdish insurgency after the April to June cease-fire, when the frustrations of the Turkish establishment were starting to show. Indirect threats towards Syria began to be made about the use of force. By the end of October the Turkish prime minister, Tansu Çiller, who had forged a close relationship with the military's top brass, publicly named Syria as a source of terrorism. At a meeting of the National Security Council on 25 October it was decided to change strategy towards Syria and adopt a tougher stance. An ultimatum followed when Çiller visited Damascus in November. Further evidence of a more robust approach included press reports of Turkish hot pursuit across the Syrian border, together with Turkish success in persuading President Clinton to bring up the issue of the PKK in his Geneva summit with Syrian president Hafez al-Asad in January 1994. Soon, however, this hard-line approach dissipated, softened perhaps by a further short period of diplomatic co-operation. Yet by the autumn the old Turkish frustrations had reappeared, only to be repeated the following year when small scale confidence building measures ended with mutual disappointment, suspicion and recrimination.

On this occasion, however, the cycle of hope and frustration which had previously been contained within a predominantly bilateral context was broken. This latest diplomatic dispute, coming as it did on top of such a turbulent recent history, was partly instrumental in the blossoming of an Israeli-Turkish alliance. Syria broadened both the issue focus and the arena of the diplomatic conflict by complaining about the GAP scheme to European governments and the Arab League in mid December 1995. By the end of the month, Damascus had enlisted the support of its fellow Damascus Declaration countries, that is the six members of the Gulf Co-operation

Council together with Egypt, for the first time in its water dispute with Turkey. Ankara, meanwhile, tried to maintain a central focus on security within a narrower arena by angrily rejecting the Arab League's intervention. Foreign minister Deniz Baykal accused the Syrians of wanting to wash the blood on their hands with more Euphrates water.

It was then Turkey's turn to escalate the dispute, by raising the question of the waters of the Orontes (or Asi) River at the beginning of January 1996.[38] Turkey seemed resigned to the broader regional arena within which the problem had been lodged when President Demirel, in a message to the Damascus Declaration countries, candidly called on Syria to 'give up using terror as an instrument of foreign policy'.[39] Ankara was not purely reactive in such a response. At around the same time Turkey had escalated the arena of the dispute in its own way, concluding a secret military agreement with Israel, which became public in April.

The Kurdish 'parliament-in-exile'. While Turkey's approach to bilateral relations with Syria has been dominated by the issue of security, as the 1990s progressed, so Ankara's relations with a whole collection of other countries were partly blighted by the issue of security and the PKK. Arguably the most public manifestation of this was over the convening of the so-called Kurdish parliament-in-exile, a body dominated by the PKK and its political wing, then called the National Liberation Front of Kurdistan (ERNK). The Kurdish 'parliament' is a conference of symbolic importance that has met intermittently and was part of the PKK's attempt to widen its struggle to embrace political as well as military methods. Its immediate objective seemed to be to embarrass and rile the Turkish state, and complicate its relations with a series of European countries, an aim that it has spasmodically achieved.

The inaugural session of the body took place in Holland on 12 April 1995. The Dutch maintained that they were powerless to prevent the convening of the session, as the protagonists were not

---

[38] Syria had always claimed that it was losing out as a result of the exploitation of the Euphrates water because it was a downstream state; in the case of the Orontes, Turkey established a claim against Syria on the same grounds.

[39] *Turkish Daily News*, 25 February 1996.

infringing Dutch law.[40] The US stoked the flames of anti-Dutch feeling in Turkey by implicitly criticising the action of the Netherlands. Alexander Vershbow of the US National Security Council was quoted as saying that 'we believe that concerns about fighting international terrorism should take precedence over the long-standing Dutch tradition of promoting freedom of expression'.[41] Assistant Secretary of State Richard Holbrooke, playing to his audience during a visit to Turkey with Strobe Talbott, let it be known that he had phoned the Dutch foreign minister to express the concerns of the United States at the convening of the parliament-in-exile.

The Turkish press took its cue from this criticism, using it as a springboard to attack the Netherlands. The Dutch and Belgian governments were criticised for having 'turned a blind eye' to the actions of the PKK on their territory, especially with regard to the intimidation and extortion of funds from residents of Turkish origin. The fact that the Netherlands allowed the convening of the 'parliament', it was written, 'should be regarded as an unfriendly act'.[42] In the heat of the moment, the Netherlands military assistance to Turkey during the 1991 Gulf war with Iraq, which had included a Patriot missile battery, Hawk ground to air missiles and chemical weapons protective wear, and which had far exceeded support given to Turkey by most other European states at the time, was forgotten.

Once the 'parliament' meeting had taken place Ankara withdrew its ambassador for consultations and announced that it was putting Holland on its 'red list', that is a list of countries from which Turkey would not contemplate procuring military equipment. In the end, this ban was only maintained for some eight weeks, although it was not rescinded in full, the Netherlands then being place on a 'yellow list', alongside Belgium, Germany and Luxembourg, that is countries from which stable supplies of arms could not be deemed to be assured.

---

[40] There, as one British diplomat admitted in private at the time, 'but for the grace of God go any of the rest of us'.

[41] Quoted in article by Uğur Akıncı datelined Washington in *Turkish Daily News*, 19 April 1995.

[42] The quotation being from Ilnur Cevik's editorial in the *Turkish Daily News*, 14 April 1995.

There is some reason to believe that the vigour of the Turkish reaction had a deterrent impact on other European countries, which worked harder to discourage Kurds from using their territory for subsequent meetings. But the deterrent effect only worked at the margins because further meetings of the 'parliament' there were. A second meeting of the body was convened in Vienna on 30 July, Austria evading tangible sanctions by claiming that the meeting had been organised secretly and no official permission had been given. The benign nature of the reaction from Ankara was probably expedited by a letter made public from the then Austrian foreign minister, Alois Mock, just six weeks earlier in which he called the parliament-in-exile a 'secessionist body', and stated that Austria considered the parliament of Turkey to be in Ankara.[43] Moreover, just over two years earlier, Turkey had successfully lobbied Austria on the issues of security and terrorism, Vienna responding by declaring the PKK to be a terrorist organisation, banning its activities and, perhaps more importantly, concluding a Security Co-operation Agreement with the Turkish government.[44]

Ankara was rather less charitable in dealing with the next meeting of the parliament-in-exile in Moscow on 30 October. As in the Austrian case, officials of the Russian Federation denied that official permission had been given for the assembly. However, the fact that the occasion took place in official buildings belonging to the Russian parliament made it harder to shrug off. Unlike the situation with Austria, the runup to the event was less auspicious in terms of security co-operation. Moscow had been concerned about Turkey's relations with Chechnya stretching back to the early 1990s. For the Russians, the Kurdish card was useful both in deterring Turkish assistance to the Chechen separatists and in punishing behaviour which was perceived by the Russians to be helpful to the Chechens.

Consequently, the previous 18 months had been punctuated by Russian flirtations with the Kurdish nationalist movement with these twin aims in mind. Examples abound. In mid February 1994, a three-day conference was convened in Moscow entitled the 'History of Kurdistan', though it was widely associated with the PKK, a

---

[43] *Turkish Daily News*, 21 June 1995.
[44] BBC/SWB/EE, 16 March 1993.

speech from the party's leader, Abdullah Öcalan, being read out and members of the ERNK being present at the meeting. Some seven months later the ERNK held a conference in Moscow which brought together 85 delegates, said to represent 10,000 Kurds from the old Eastern bloc. A little over a month after that, at the end of October, a further ERNK meeting was held in Moscow to discuss the political situation and ways of supporting the Kurdish independence struggle. Turkey's demands that the meeting be prevented went unheeded. Near the end of December a 'Kurdish House' was opened in Moscow, with the intention of housing a variety of Kurdish cultural and other organisations, all said to be affiliated with the PKK. Though no-one from the Yeltsin government attended the opening, the size and prominence of the event made it difficult to believe that it took place without the tacit encouragement of the Russian authorities. Once the parliament-in-exile had been inaugurated in Holland, some of its members travelled to Moscow, where they met Russian deputies in the parliament building. An ERNK delegation subsequently was invited to attend VE Day celebrations in Moscow in May, an event also attended by the Turkish prime minister Tansu Çiller.

Against such a backdrop, it is perhaps not surprising that, in the words of the veteran Turkish columnist Sami Kohen, the convening of the parliament-in-exile brought bilateral relations 'to the brink of a crisis'.[45] The Turkish Foreign Ministry summoned the Russian ambassador twice in two days to present him with letters of protest, while the US State Department also joined in by stating that the 'parliament' was funded by the PKK, and expressing concern to Moscow at the meeting. The response in Moscow was the by now traditional one that no permission had been given for the meeting to proceed. But, under additional pressure, the Russian Foreign Ministry went a step further in condemning the meeting, saying, somewhat unconvincingly, that it had been organised by a Russian parliamentary committee and billed as a scientific meeting. With overall bilateral relations between the two countries complex and sensitive and their deterioration potentially mutually costly, the incident was allowed to fizzle out without precipitate action.

[45] *Milliyet*, 3 November 1995.

THE THREAT OF DISORDER AND DISINTEGRATION
NEXT DOOR

When the Cold War came to an end, Turkey immediately found itself lying between three regions of unpredictability: the Balkans, the Middle East, and the former Soviet south. Though geopolitically marginal to each sub-system, Turkey was affected or potentially affected by the developments on its three sides for a range of different and inter-related reasons, from historical, human and cultural relations to strategic and economic interests. Consequently, since 1989 a major security challenge for Turkey has been to manage, contain and resolve the disputes, conflicts and instabilities which have manifested themselves adjacent to it in a way that minimises costs to and maximises opportunities for the Republic.

Disorder next door: Abkhazia. The Abkhazia conflict within Georgia was a case typical of the many tensions and conflicts manifest on or near Turkey's borders during the first half of the 1990s. It threatened to cause problems for Turkey on a range of different levels. At a state to state level, the case posed a problem of a secessionist movement's activities precipitating instability and conflict in Georgia, a neighbour of Turkey's. This could have exacerbated instability on Turkey's borders, in turn resulting in a range of costs for Ankara. These could most plausibly have included security headaches relating to the future use of Georgian territory for trade routes, notably the building of oil pipelines to the Caspian, and the possibility of the PKK seeking to exploit the turmoil in the country to establish a political and perhaps even an armed presence.

This was not the end of the complications. The turmoil in Georgia also presented systemic challenges for Turkey. There was the continuing fear that the Russian Federation might seek to exploit the instability in Georgia to project its influence and even its military power southwards. The growing suspicion that Moscow was behind the uprising in Abkhazia underlined this fear.

A third dimension of complexity related to Turkish domestic politics. Turkey was home to a substantial Abkhazian[46] and, it subsequently became apparent, Georgian expatriate population, which

---

[46] Senior Turkish diplomats have even exclaimed, no doubt with a mixture of exasperation and mischief, that there are more Abkhaz people in Turkey than there are in Georgia. Unattributable interview, Ankara, 8 December 1999.

had arrived in Anatolia together with other Caucasian peoples after the end of the Crimean War. The tensions and conflict in Georgia therefore threatened to sow discord among the ethnic groups involved inside Turkey, a danger which was rendered more potentially acute by the relatively recent re-emergence of particularistic self-consciousness on the part of many Turks.

The initial inclination of the Demirel government was to develop and deepen bilateral relations with Tbilisi once Eduard Shevardnadze had become president. Both Demirel and his foreign minister, Hikmet Çetin, visited Georgia between May and July 1992. Turkey promised 50,000 tonnes of wheat to assist its neighbour; emergency relief aid was sent through the Turkish Red Crescent or *Kızılay*; a Friendship and Co-operation Agreement was signed; Shevardnadze's support for Turkey's efforts at multilateral institution-building in the Black Sea area were welcomed.

By the end of the summer, however, with Abkhazia having formally declared independence in July, it was obvious that this warm relationship at the highest levels would not be left to mature unhindered. By October it was clear that increasing numbers of Turks of Abkhazian descent were going to fight as volunteers with their ethnic cousins; a rally of Abkhazians was staged in Turkey in solidarity with the movement in Georgia; a protest had even been organised outside the Foreign Ministry, demanding the recognition of Abkhaz independence and the resignation of foreign minister Çetin; some of the forty-one associations of the northern Caucasian peoples had emerged as pressure groups on behalf of their kin; Demirel had felt it politic to receive a delegation of Turkey's Abkhazians. The decision in Tbilisi to send Georgian troops into Abkhazia in September gave an additional urgency to such lobbying.

Such activity was not, however, confined to the level of 'outsider' pressure groups. A debate took place in the parliament, the Turkish Grand National Assembly, at which a cross party initiative led by Vehbi Dinçerler of ANAP and Oğuzhan Asiltürk of the RP argued for active support for the Abkhazian people. On its own this could have generated formidable insider pressure on the government. By this time, however, non-Abkhazian Turks of Georgian descent had also begun to mobilise. They too had their supporters in parliament, notably Hasan Ekinci of the DYP. The government was clearly concerned at the growing earnestness with which organisations representing the two communities argued their case. Hikmet Çetin warned both sides against 'allowing the ethnic disputes in the region to spill over into Turkey'.

Against a backdrop of growing emotion, but with both sides increasingly cancelling out each other's influence, Turkey, with the tight coordination between the foreign minister and senior ministry officials coming into its own, sure-footedly steered a careful, measured diplomatic course. On the one hand, Ankara sought to respond in a humanitarian fashion in order to allay domestic concerns about the suffering of the peoples concerned. Thus *Kızılay* joined forces with the Committee for Solidarity with Abkhazia in organising a campaign for emergency blood donations; food aid in the form of 16 mn tonnes of wheat was also sent to Abkhazia. Moreover, Ankara urged that the parties come to a peaceful resolution of their problems. Meanwhile Ankara, conscious of the analogy with its own Kurdish population, continued to focus on the strategic aim of respecting the integrity of the Georgian state. Hence Ankara expressed concern at the plight of the Abkhazian people, but without giving weight to their political objectives. The Turkish government further urged that the conflict be settled peacefully and within the norms of democracy, but while maintaining that the integrity of Georgia must be respected.

By the end of November, Turkey had weathered the storm. Ankara was able to welcome Shevardnadze's election and to express complete trust in him. It was, however, to be January 1994 before the atmosphere had sufficiently recovered to permit the Georgian leader to pay a first official visit to Turkey. The delay in the visit appeared to be prudent as, once it did come, it formed a firm platform on which to begin to develop bilateral relations addressing mutual interests. These included: the provision of $50 mn in Eximbank credits to Georgia; rising levels of bilateral trade; a refusal on the part of Tbilisi to countenance PKK political activity on its territory; and Turkish backing for the construction of a pipeline between Baku and Supsa to carry Azerbaijan's 'early' oil. As the relationship between Shevardnadze's Georgia and Turkey deepened as the decade went on other forms of cooperation were initiated, with Ankara the senior party. These included: military training for Georgia's young officers and international peace keepers alike; the provision of a range of military equipment from communications equipment to patrol boats; the construction of military housing and training centres.[47]

The best evidence of Ankara's deft diplomacy during a difficult and complex period was the request which came from both sides in the Abkhazian war for Turkey to contribute observers to Unomig, the UN Observer Mission in Georgia, which was charged with monitoring the cease-fire in Abkhazia.[48] This enabled the Turkish state to reassure its respective partisan constituencies that it was indeed taking a 'balanced' approach towards the Abkhaz problem.[49]

Disorder next door: Chechnya, 1994–6. If the Abkhaz issue had ultimately ended rather tidily from a Turkish perspective, the case of Chechnya was more problematic. The Chechen issue involved many of the same issues–an ethnic group struggling for independence, a military response from the centre, a strong expatriate interest inside Turkey–but to a much greater magnitude. For a start, a former superpower, Russia, rather than a small state, Georgia, was the dominant power involved in the Chechen case; thus the state power which could be employed in this case was considerably greater than over Abkhazia. Second, Russian-Turkish relations had a largely conflictual historical backdrop, and were, in addition, loaded with some heavy contemporary baggage from the Bosnian Muslim-Serb conflict in the Balkans, through the issue of access for oil tankers through the Turkish Straits, to the future transport routes for Caspian oil; in short, the bilateral stakes were much higher. Third, the outcome of the Chechen-Russian struggle would provide a model for other peoples in the north Caucasus; more particularly an expanded space of instability could have led to tens of thousands of refugees finding their way to Turkey, the recent experience of both Iraqi Kurdish and Bulgarian Turkish migrant inflows providing recent negative experiences. Fourth, while both sides in the Abkhaz-Georgian case had their expatriate supporters in Turkey, in the

[47] Robin Bhatty and Rachel Bronson, 'NATO's Mixed Signals in the Caucasus and Central Asia', *Survival*, vol. 42, no. 3, autumn 2000, p. 135.

[48] TRT TV, 7 September in BBC/SWB/EE, 10 September 1994.

[49] Presentation by Foreign Ministry representative at seminar on Turkey and Central Asia at Bosphorus University, 27 January 1995.

Chechen case there was no ethnic lobby to campaign in favour of the Russians; domestically, all the advocacy flowed in one direction.

The autonomous republic of Chechnya, under the leadership of Dzhokhar Dudayev, formally declared independence from the Russian Federation in 1991. Though Dudayev and his associates were frequent visitors to Turkey over the subsequent four years,[50] and Dudayev himself even cultivated contacts with Turkish officials and in particular ultra-nationalist politicians,[51] Ankara remained strictly attached to its status quo strategy of not prematurely recognising new states, an approach which it also adopted in the southern Caucasus and towards the former Yugoslavia. Indeed, by 1994 Turkey had, if anything, further distanced itself from Chechnya, which had increasingly acquired a reputation for being 'a bandit state'.[52] By this time, however, the damage had already been done in terms of rising Russian suspicions of perceived attempts by Turkey to exploit the Chechen issue in order to weaken the federation, and fears that an independent Chechnya would create for Turkey 'a base behind our lines'.[53]

When the political situation deteriorated in Chechnya towards the end of 1994, with Russian troops entering the republic on 11 December, Ankara maintained its conservative line. With Demirel, Karayalçın (apart from the occasional diplomatic lapse)[54] and Sanberk,

---

[50] During this time Dudayev visited Turkey both as an important political destination in itself, for instance in 1992 as part of a Middle East tour that also took him to Sudan, Jordan, Saudi Arabia and Kuwait, and also as a staging post to the wider world, such as when he visited Istanbul en route to France in June 1993. Carlotta Gall and Thomas de Waal, *Chechnya, Calamity in the Caucasus* (New York University Press, 1998), p. 109. Gall and de Waal also draw attention to Dudayev's use of Istanbul and its banking sector for financial transactions. See for example the efforts of his central bank's head to cash a cheque in Istanbul that had been refused elsewhere, ibid., p. 135.

[51] Dudayev was infamous for coming to Istanbul with nationalist cronies from the Transcaucasus and throwing lavish parties at which ultra-nationalist Turkish politicians were regular guests.

[52] The reasons for this were essentially fourfold: the increasingly obvious nature of Dudayev's own dubious character; an upsurge in hostage taking; the increasing reputation of the Chechen mafia for ruthlessness; and the apparent freedom of movement in Chechnya of wanted criminals.

[53] Anatol Lieven, *Chechnya, Tombstone of Russian Power* (Yale University Press, New Haven, 1998), p. 85.

[54] Most notably, his brief attempt to involve the ICO in the Chechen issue.

Turkey's president, foreign minister and top diplomat respectively, singing from the same hymn sheet the message was clear. Turkey wanted the Chechen situation to be resolved peacefully through negotiation; the protection of the territorial integrity of the Russian Federation; the restoration of regional peace and security.[55] Initially, Moscow welcomed this Turkish response, appreciating that it was a measured and responsible reaction, in spite of the fact that the public mood in Turkey displayed varying degrees of hostility towards Russia over the use of military force.[56]

As the conflict persisted and the intensity of it increased, so did the pressures on Turkey to depart from its line. With Dudayev writing to Demirel asking him to intercede to stop the fighting,[57] the Turkish leadership found itself drawn into the diplomatic entanglement. Unable to ignore Dudayev's message, Demirel wrote to Yeltsin urging an immediate cease-fire and the resolution of the conflict using peaceful means,[58] a sentiment further backed up by a simultaneous message from prime minister Çiller to her opposite number in Moscow.[59] Meanwhile, Karayalçın busied himself with efforts to deliver humanitarian aid to the Chechens, the first supplies going in on 5 January 1995 and being distributed through the Russians, to allay fears about the nature of the cargo.[60]

With the resumption of the Russian bombing of Grozny at the end of 1994 and the increasing international criticism of the Russians, and the Islamist Welfare Party making domestic political capital by calling for the immediate recognition of Chechnya,[61] the strains

[55] See Sanberk after meeting the Russian ambassador, Vadim Kuznetsov, for Turkey's three key concerns in TRT TV, 12 December in BBC/SWB/EE, 14 December 1994. See also President Demirel's statement in ibid.

[56] *Turkish Daily News*, 13 December 1994. The Turkish language press was also emotive and hostile in its criticism of the Russian authorities, with *Sabah* of 11 December likening the conflict to Hungary 1956, Czechoslovakia 1968, and Afghanistan 1979. The headline in *Cumhuriyet* read '*Çeçenya'da Rus çizmesi*' (Chechnya under Russian boot).

[57] TRT TV, 18 December 1994 in BBC/SWB/EE, 20 December 1994.

[58] ibid.

[59] Separate TRT TV report, 18 December 1994 in BBC/SWB/EE, 20 December 1994.

[60] Itar-Tass, 5 January in BBC/SWB/EE, 6 January 1995.

[61] For example, Abdüllatif Şener, soon to be the Refahyol finance minister, on TRT TV, 10 January in BBC/SWB/EE, 12 January 1995.

intensified for the principal actors in Turkey. More importantly Ankara became uncomfortable at the strategic implications of the Russian military action. Discomfort increased, first, at the apparent alacrity with which Moscow appeared willing to use force to settle political conflict in the Caucasus, and, second, at the prospect that this might create a precedent for the projection of Russian power in the southern Caucasus, hence close to Turkey. By the turn of the year, the tone of Turkish public diplomacy had become noticeably more robust.[62]

The preface to this change came during a visit to Azerbaijan by the normally mild-mannered Speaker of the Turkish parliament, Hüsamettin Cindoruk. He hardly missed an opportunity to describe Russia's operations in Chechnya as an inhuman attack and attributed expansionist motives to the Russian actions, seeing them as part of a general objective of intervening in the Caucasus; in a pointed sound-bite suggesting how the interests of the two countries were increasingly at odds, Cindoruk said that: 'If the Caucasus is Russia's back garden it is also Turkey's front garden'.[63] Taking its lead from Cindoruk's trenchant words, the discourse of the Turkish Foreign Ministry became noticeably more combative early in the new year.[64] By 10 January it was clear that the policy had indeed changed, with Çiller stating candidly that Chechnya was no longer an internal affair for Russia, and Demirel, in more diplomatic language, insisting on the right to speak out against such bloodshed. Karayalçın pointed to the existence of transnational links as a reason for such a change: 'We have family relations with Chechnya', he stated. 'For this reason we cannot see this problem as the internal problem of another country'.[65]

Fortunately for Russo-Turkish relations, the eventual fall of Grozny and the evolution of the fighting into a low intensity conflict managed to reduce the pressure on bilateral ties. Official Turkish

---

[62] See, for example, foreign ministry spokesman Ferhat Ataman in TRT TV, 4 January in BBC/SWB/EE, 6 January 1995.

[63] Kanal-6 TV, 30 December 1994 in BBC/SWB/EE, 3 January 1995.

[64] For example, speaking on 4 January 1995 the ministry's spokesman, Ferhat Ataman, expressed 'great regret' at the continued clashes, stated that 'we strongly condemn' the clashes in Chechnya, and said that it was 'imperative' that a cease-fire be established. See BBC/SWB/EE, 6 January 1995.

[65] Reuters, Ankara, 11 January 1995.

statements reverted to protestations of respect for Russian sovereignty and of the importance of negotiations as a means to end the conflict, although Ankara did also continue to condemn Russian operations against Chechen villages.[66]

Nevertheless, with no political arrangement emerging until Alexander Lebed's conciliatory diplomacy with the Chechen leadership in the summer of 1996, the conflict in Chechnya did spasmodically re-emerge as a fleeting source of strain between the two countries. Examples included: Russian accusations in late February 1995 that Turkey was supplying weapons to the rebels;[67] the June 1995 capture by Russian security of two Turks alleged to be working for the Turkish intelligence service, MİT;[68] unclarity as to whether Turkey would be willing to offer Dudayev political asylum, as asserted by President Yeltsin in June 1995;[69] the March 1996 hijacking of a Turkish Cypriot aircraft en route to Istanbul and its diversion to Munich by a Turk seeking to publicise the plight of Chechnya.[70] Perhaps surprisingly, the death of Dudayev in a rare moment of military precision by the Russians caused little tension in bilateral relations. Only a week before, President Demirel had played down a suggestion from Dudayev that Turkey help broker a peace accord on Chechnya; Demirel confined his reaction to Dudayev's death to an expression of sadness.[71]

Arguably, the greatest source of strain between the two countries after the mayhem in Grozny and before the second Chechen war in 1999–2000 came with the hijacking of a Russia-bound ferry, the *Avrasya*, in the Turkish Black Sea port of Trabzon by six Turks, two Chechens and an Abkhaz in January 1996. The Turkish authorities in fact handled the incident well, shadowing the ferry for four days as it sailed as far as the Bosphorus, but refusing to let it enter the Turkish Straits. With Russians, including President Yeltsin,[72] expressing increasing dissatisfaction at the Turkish response, the hi-jackers were persuaded to surrender, with none of their hostages harmed.

---

[66] See, for example, Reuters, Ankara, 8 March 1995.
[67] TRT TV, 24 February 1995 in BBC/SWB/EE, 27 February 1995.
[68] See Anatolia and Interfax, 1 June 1995 in BBC/SWB/EE, 3 June 1995.
[69] Reuters, Nova Scotia, 17 June 1995.
[70] Reuters, Istanbul, 9 March 1996.
[71] Reuters, Ankara, 24 April 1996.
[72] Cited in Reuters, Ankara, 19 January 1996.

The successful outcome to the affair did not prevent the Chechens trying to maximise its propaganda value. The self-styled Chechen foreign minister, Şemsettin Yusuf, secretly travelled to Istanbul at the start of the crisis. To the disgust of the Russian authorities, the Turkish media increasingly treated the hijackers not as terrorists but as heroes.[73]

The subsequent escape from jail of five of the hijackers, including their leader Muhammed Tokcan,[74] in three separate incidents during the month of October 1997, without adequate explanation, reflected rather less well on the Turkish authorities. Tokcan and his armed associates briefly re-emerged in April 2001 when they stormed the luxury Swissotel in Istanbul as a publicity stunt for the plight of Chechnya, much to the international embarrassment of Turkey.

Capabilities and foreign relations

The nature of threats, both as perceived from a state and as perceived by other states regarding that state, is a key variable in the development and evolution of foreign relations. Of equal importance is the issue of capabilities, both the actual capabilities of a state in pursuing its foreign policy and the capabilities which are attributed to it by other states. Moreover, the expansion and upgrading of capabilities also have foreign policy implications, especially if such an improvement is reliant upon hardware procurement.

CONVENTIONAL CAPABILITIES

Up to the 1990s the Turkish armed forces had a reputation for being large in number, but relatively ineffective as a modern fighting force.

---

[73] Reuters, Istanbul, 19 January 1996.

[74] Tokcan had actually fought for the radical Chechen leader Shamil Baseyev in his 'Abkhaz Battalion', which was responsible for the Abkhaz defeat of the Georgians (see Brian Williams, 'Shamil Baseyev, Chechen Field Commander: Russia's Most Wanted Man', *Turkistan Newsletter*, vol. 4, no. 153, 7 August 2000). By leading the hijacking Tokcan emulated his mentor, who had with two associates hijacked a Russian aircraft in 1991 and flown it to Ankara in order to publicise the situation in Chechnya. On that occasion the Turkish authorities managed to persuade Basayev to give up, but refused to hand the men over to the Russian authorities. They subsequently returned to Chechnya as heroes. See John B. Dunlop, *Russia Confronts Chechnya, Roots of a Separatist Conflict* (Cambridge University Press, 1998), p. 121, and Gall and de Waal, op. cit., p. 262.

This has helped to bolster Turkey's deterrent position, as most states would be chary of being drawn into a conventional military conflict, especially on Turkish soil. Ironically, this perception of massive but unwieldy force has probably helped to allay the fears of Turkey among her neighbours. Turkey's relative inability to project military force rapidly and effectively has retarded the practical possibility of aggressive intent.

This perception of Turkey as possessing a large but relatively ineffectual fighting force anchored to its own territory has been buttressed by Turkish national ideology, which has put a premium on Atatürk's old aphorism of 'peace at home, peace abroad'. Atatürk was firmly of the view that Turkey should abandon all claims of sovereignty over the former provinces of the Ottoman Empire. Instead, he opted for the consolidation of the nation-state of Turkey, imagined and founded on a territorial base ideologically enshrined within the 1920 National Pact. In this way Atatürk was a visionary in seeing that increasingly the new resources of state power would be modernisation and cohesion rather than the continuous acquisition of territory. Not for Atatürk, then, the instinctive return to an irredentist foreign policy once the initial atmosphere of the post-First World War settlement had dissipated. Under their authoritarian leaders of the day, Turkey and Germany were to embark on very different strategies in the 1930s and 1940s.

The moral lead was so clear and the leader so inviolable that the Turkish elite, both political and military, have hardly considered its revision since. If this philosophy of consolidating the territorial base founded on the National Pact has been weakened at all as a guiding principle of action, it is over the Turkish state's military involvement in Cyprus. The guarantor status which Turkey enjoyed arguably gave it the right to intervene on the island in 1974. What guarantor status also required was that the intervention should be directed at the restoration of the constitution and not the creation of new political arrangements on the island. By contrast, what Turkey has done has been to remain in military occupation of northern Cyprus ever since; permit a declaration of independence, which in 1983 turned northern Cyprus into the Turkish Republic of Northern Cyprus; and organise the settlement of Anatolian peasants there. All these developments have helped to weaken Atatürk's principled strategy based on the National Pact, though not fatally.

In another sense, however, the Turkish preoccupation with Cyprus has helped to reduce the latent threat posed by Turkey towards its other neighbours. The fact that some 35,000 Turkish troops remain tied down in northern Cyprus, with all of the accompanying needs of training and force rotation and the considerable expense incurred, helps to dissipate the effect of the sheer scale of the Turkish military and its manpower resources. With Cyprus clearly the external military priority of choice, Turkish military adventurism in other directions is rendered much less likely.

But the realities of Turkey's static, defence-oriented military capability have been changing since the early 1990s. The change in the international order at the end of the 1980s prompted the Turkish military to try to enact real reform in its force structures. Notionally, a thorough going reorganisation and modernisation had been the intention of the military since the 1970s. The aim was to match the defence doctrine of other NATO members in creating a smaller, more professional military, which could move more rapidly and generate increased firepower and manoeuvrability. The desirability of creating a smaller, more flexible, more effective army was a lesson further underlined for the Turkish military during the 1990–91 Gulf war.[75] Consequently, Ankara announced its intention both to reorganise its armed forces, the army in particular, and to reequip its military with modern fighting hardware.

To date the Turkish military has a mixed record as far as the modernisation of structure and equipment is concerned. In spite of the rhetoric of modernisation, the Turkish military remains large and cumbersome. In 2000 the army, for example, consisted of 495,000 men, of whom 462,000 are conscripts, out of a total active Turkish military of 609,700 men.[76] This is in spite of a restructuring process which began in 1988. Under these plans the size of the army was supposed to drop to 350,000. Attempts have been made to move away from a conscript-oriented army, most tangibly in September 1992, when the period of national service was cut from 18 to 15 months with the promise of a further cut within a year. By 1994, however, this approach had been reversed and the period of conscription

---

[75] See Defence Minister Nevzat Ayaz in *Turkish Daily News*, 6 May 1992.
[76] *The Military Balance 2000/01* (International Institute of Strategic Studies, London, 2000), p. 78.

expanded to 20 months, as a result of the need to deploy sufficient forces in the south-east in order to stem the PKK-led insurgency.

Ankara has, however, been able to take great strides towards the modernisation of its military hardware capability during the 1990s. In the early part of the decade, Turkey initially benefited from the end of the Cold War. The redundancy of the central European theatre meant that there was lots of unwanted kit on the NATO side, even after the contingency of the 1990–1 Gulf War. Much of this equipment was given away under the Cascading scheme, in the name of helping to modernise the armed forces of the old flank states. In Turkey's case, in the view of Richard Falkenrath, Cascading brought about 'enormous qualitative improvements'.[77] Greece and Turkey were the major recipients of Cascading.[78] For example, by the end of 1992, Turkey had received 1,057 M-60 Leopard main battle tanks from the United States, Germany and the Netherlands, 72 M-110 artillery pieces and 600 M-113 armoured combat vehicles;[79] indeed, in 1992 and 1993 Turkey was the world's leading importer of tanks.

The transfer of hardware from the redundant central European theatre marked the beginning of a sustained period of arms procurement, rather than an exceptional infusion of weapons. This force upgrading has also taken place through the acquisition of specific weapons systems, notably attack helicopters, which have been purchased with the suppression of the insurgency in the south-east

[77] 'The CFE Flank Dispute, Waiting in the Wings', *International Security*, vol. 19, no. 4, spring 1995, p. 143.

[78] Though the narrow military logic of modernising less well equipped allies in southern Europe was sound, the main states of NATO had skated over the deep political difficulties which existed between Greece and Turkey. One effect of Cascading was therefore to foster an arms race between Ankara and Athens which could, as during the stand-off over Imia/Kardak island in January 1996, have exacerbated a hot conflict between the erstwhile allies. For an early statement of concern at the arms buildup in the two countries see Lyle Goldstein, Tasos Kokkinides and Daniel Plesch, *Fuelling the Balkan Fires: The West's Arming of Greece and Turkey* (The British American Security Information Council, London, 1993). The main NATO states similarly did harm in their approach to the issue of the use of such weaponry internally, taking comfort, as Ian Mather wrote at the time (*The European*, 7 April 1995), in the formal pledge that such weaponry would 'not be used for internal security purposes'.

[79] *The Guardian*, 4 December 1992.

uppermost in mind. If anything, procurement plans have become more ambitious since the early 1990s, with the Conventional Forces in Europe (CFE) treaty providing a window of opportunity for the qualitative modernisation of the military, Turkey's inventories in several categories of hardware being below the newly agreed force levels.

Ankara has sought to use its planned military purchasing power as leverage to defray diplomatic pressures from abroad. In 1995 the Turkish General Staff announced that $150 bn would be needed to fund arms purchases and operations over the next 25 years, with the army, navy and air force seeking $60 bn, $25 bn and $65 bn respectively. Enticingly, it set out its needs for major new hardware priorities during this span, as follows: 750 helicopters, more than 3,600 tanks, nearly 50,000 wheeled vehicles and nearly 2,000 artillery pieces for the ground forces; 14 frigates, nine submarines, 16 patrol ships and 15 guided assault ships for the navy; and 640 fighter jets, 160 trainer aircraft and 68 transport planes for the air force. Soon afterwards, the Turkish Defence Ministry announced that $31 bn would be spent over a 10-year period to 2007. In spite of the scepticism of some observers, the Turkish military seemed genuinely committed to an annual procurement spending of some $3 bn, making it, in a context of a world recession in armaments exports, one of the leading markets. Only with the onset of the financial crisis in Turkey in February 2001 did the top brass declare that savings would have to be made in military spending, with arms procurement to take the slack.

In spite of the potentially large military sales contracts on offer throughout the 1990s Turkey has not been without difficulties in attempting such a weapons modernisation. These have principally arisen in the form of political constraints on the procurement of military hardware abroad. Turkey's arms supply relations with parts of northern Europe were bedevilled by such problems throughout the 1990s.[80] For these European countries the issue has invariably

---

[80] Most notably, as will be seen, this has been a problem in German–Turkish relations. However, other continental European states have been involved. In April 1993, for instance, Ankara placed Austria, Norway and Switzerland on a blacklist on the grounds that Turkey's future arms procurement might be subject to political fluctuations.

been regarded as one of international ethics, with a growing hesitancy to sell hardware to Turkey which might end up being used either inside the country against members of Turkey's Kurdish population or outside the state in Cyprus or in cross-border operations in northern Iraq. For Turkey, the issue has also been seen in terms of morality, but morality of a different kind. The Turkish view is of the immorality of supposed friends who would leave the Turkish state vulnerable to armed attack from its enemies at times of greatest need.

Constraints on procurement: Germany.[81] Up to the early 1990s Turkey's main arms import relationship was with the US and Germany in that order, with both states ahead of the field in the provision of supplier grants and credits.[82] Turkey received DM6.2 bn in German military aid between 1964 and 1992.[83] The procurement relationship with Bonn helped to establish high levels of bilateral trade, with Turkey purchasing in excess of DM7 bn worth of arms. By 1992, with military sales to the fore, Germany accounted for nearly 20 per cent of all Turkish trade. It also helped to give ballast to a relationship which, because of the large numbers of Turks living and working in Germany, could otherwise have encountered severe strains. It was then a matter of diplomatic routine even as late as the early 1990s to pronounce that Germany was Turkey's closest friend in Europe.[84]

Nevertheless the arms sales relationship has been subject to periodic turbulence, mainly stemming from the issue of Turkey's human rights record. It is against such a backdrop that Germany imposed a weapons sales embargo on Turkey on three occasions during the 1990s.

---

[81] For a contextualisation of German-Turkish relations and a discussion of issues of common interest, see *Minutes of the Turkish-German Round Table Meeting* (SAM Papers 2/96, Centre for Strategic Research, Ankara, 1996).

[82] For example, Turkey received military shipments from Germany worth DM260 mn over 1991–92.

[83] *Financial Times*, 19 May 1993.

[84] The golden age of German-Turkish relations extended up to the mid 1980s, when the Kurdish issue began to put a blight on ties. Nevertheless, even in the early 1990s there was still a special closeness to the relationship, an example of this being that the German president was the only Western head of state to attend the funeral of President Özal in April 1993.

First, in November 1991, the federal parliament voted for an arms sales moratorium in protest at Turkish air raids on Iraq.[85] Second, the German government decided to suspend arms shipments to Turkey in April and May 1994 because of their alleged use in the south-east of the country, a decision which was quickly rescinded owing, somewhat embarrassingly, to the discovery that there was in fact insufficient evidence from which to make such a judgement.[86] Third, the German authorities suspended a shipment of military hardware in March 1995 in protest at further Turkish military incursions into northern Iraq.[87]

Of course, the increasingly multi-national nature of the European arms industry could also complicate arms export deals, especially when one state was trying to restrict sales to Turkey while a partner was less inhibited. The deal over the joint production of the ERYX missiles was initially held up because Belgium and Germany, two members of the five-country pan-European consortium involved, objected to such a deal with Turkey.

On each of the three occasions in the German case the pattern of the unfolding dispute was roughly the same. An arms transfer crisis was precipitated by a real or imagined security trigger in Turkey. This was invariably followed by heightening domestic political pressure in Germany, with the then perennial opposition, the SPD, adding its weight to the constant anti-Turkish refrain of smaller, fringe groups. In order to fend off such pressure the federal government would introduce temporary measures against arms sales. In turn, the Turkish response was routinely characterised by strong formal protests delivered through official channels, much Turkish press invective, and pained accusations of Germany not fulfilling its

---

[85] The apparent bureaucratic error which resulted in the delivery of fifteen Leopard-1 tanks to Turkey the following year actually cost the Defence Minister, Gerhard Stoltenberg, his job.

[86] In a confused and opaque policy context the German government apparently introduced an arms embargo in a knee-jerk reaction to allegations that its weapons had been used against the PKK inside Turkey, only to rescind the moratorium a month later on the grounds that the allegations had been proved to be false.

[87] On this occasion SPD spokesman Karsten Voigt actually called for an end to German support for the Turkish military, with funds to be redeployed to the sponsorship of reform in Eastern Europe.

NATO obligations while being prepared to allow harm to come to Turkey's territorial integrity. Having fended off the domestic political pressure, and with the worst of the storm spent, the German Foreign Ministry would tend to seek quietly to repair bilateral relations, dampening the charged atmosphere by refusing to be drawn into a diplomatic slanging match with its Turkish counterpart. In the end, the three crises all passed quickly, with arms sales being resumed a matter of weeks later. However, the reversal of such temporary measures should not be allowed to obscure the cumulative nature of such experiences. Together with other spasmodic bilateral problems, the disruption of weapons transfers has had a corrosive effect on Ankara-Bonn relations.

Constraints on procurement: the United States. Turkey's procurement problems have not been with northern Europe alone. Indeed, the arms supplies relationship between Turkey and the US has never been as stable or as cordial as in the German-Turkish case. Turkey has periodically encountered protracted problems purchasing equipment from its closest military ally and NATO partner, the US, and this has helped to reinforce the perception of the United States as an unreliable ally. These constraints have invariably existed where weapons sales have acquired a domestic political dimension, and, as in the case of the northern Europeans, where an ethical element has been introduced in the form of sales conditionality.

The most important domestic constraint on weapons sales to Turkey has come from the Greek lobby, which has been active in persuading the US Congress to constrain weapons sales to Turkey. Structurally, Washington's military aid to Turkey has been subject to a 7:10 formula with Greece, whereby Athens must receive an allocation equivalent to 70 per cent of that made to Ankara, a measure introduced in 1978 as part of the trade-off for the removal of a general arms embargo against Turkey following the 1974 Cyprus crisis.[88] Such anti-Turkish lobbying, compounded by growing misgivings in the United States about Turkey's human rights record, has proved problematic for specific arms deals. In turn, both Turkish officialdom

---

[88] In practice, successive US administrations have sought to circumvent this restriction; the transfer of old equipment and co-production agreements are just two areas where this has been tried.

and the country's press subject the US policy debate and the tortu-ous decision-making process in Washington to exhaustive report-ing and analysis, focusing, somewhat incongruously, almost with relish on any manifestation of an anti-Turkish position, no matter how temporary it may be.

Accompanying these growing difficulties have been the general down-grading of the Turkish-US military relationship as a result of the end of the Cold War and the waning of the general Western threat perception of the Soviet Union and its Russian successor state. US security assistance to Turkey fell from some $500 mn in 1991 to $175 mn in 1997; the US physical presence in Turkey waned from 20,000 personnel and dependents at 20 installations in the 1960s to 8,000 at six installations in 1997. For all its magnitude at the time, Cascading was a temporary state of affairs.

For US-Turkish relations, the low point in the military sales sector came between 1994 and 1997. After the dissolution of the Kurdish nationalist party, DEP, and the trial of some of its MPs, in particular, it became markedly more difficult for the US to sell weapons to Turkey. The arms sales relationship was subject to great disruption, regardless of the branch of the services or the nature of the hard-ware involved. The most serious examples of Turkey's thwarted attempts to acquire advanced weaponry in the 1990s were the deals over ten Super Cobra attack helicopters and three *Perry* class frig-ates and an order for Sea Hawk helicopters. A proposal to sell clus-ter bombs to Turkey was also blocked by the administration, under pressure from human rights organisations.

So extended were the hold-ups in Congress and with the execu-tive branch that eventually in 1996 it became common practice to speak of a *de facto* US arms embargo against Turkey. The Cobra gunships were particularly controversial, because of their import-ance in the fight against the PKK insurgency, both in the south-east and in northern Iraq. The Assistant Secretary of State for human rights, John Shattuck, commissioned an extensive study to see if Turkey was using weaponry received from the United States against the civilian population in south-east Turkey.

Increasingly exasperated by its treatment in Washington, and con-cerned that American uncooperativeness would play into the hands of the Islamist-led coalition, the Turkish military finally began to make an issue of the problem from late 1996 onwards. Angry and exasperated by a hold-up in excess of one year, the Turkish government cancelled the $150 million order for the ten Cobras in November 1996, awarding the contract to the Franco-German Eurocopter instead. The normally pro-US General Çevik Bir was sent to Washington in February 1997 to bring home the seriousness of the situation. He demanded that the US show 'reciprocity' for Turkish cooperation over Operation Northern Watch in northern Iraq, and threatened to make an issue out of a dispute over the cost of F-16 training if the United States did not show greater cooperation. Soon afterwards the chief executive officers of three major US defence industries wrote to President Clinton requesting that the Super Cobra deal be resolved. In the end the impasse was broken by a Greek-Turkish rapprochement at the Madrid NATO summit, which, though fleeting, had the utility of opening the way for the delivery of the three frigates in November 1997; the sale of four Sea Hawks soon followed.

It did not, however, end the problem of the imposition of human rights related conditionality on weapons sales. For example, doubts yet abound about the ability of the US to win a lucrative $4 bn order for 145 attack helicopters, a preliminary evaluation of offers for which was made in July 1998. The reason for the pessimistic prospects for a contract award to US companies was the American insistence that Turkey improve its human rights record. Though it did, after months of hesitation, grant marketing licenses to Bell Helicopters and Boeing, the State Department made it clear that such conditionality would eventually determine whether such a sale would actually be approved.[89]

Alternative strategies. The Turkish authorities have explored alternative strategies in order not to fall foul of such periodic and unforeseen disruptions in supply. These have included the development of an indigenous defence industry; the widening of defence sales within Europe and to Israel; the purchase of Russian weapons, and the use of third country front companies for the routing of arms imports.

---

[89] *Defense News*, 20–26 July 1998.

Turkey has opted to develop an indigenous defence industry in order to achieve enhanced sovereign control over the supply of weapons systems. The fact that this strategy has been directed at co-production with foreign companies, often with an offset component, has enhanced the structural interest of such companies in the development of a strong military in Turkey. It has also resulted in tenacious competition among a small number of predominantly Western companies for lucrative contracts.

Turkey began to develop a local defence production sector in 1986, with the creation of the Undersecretariat for Defence Industries (SSM), an autonomous agency within the Defence Ministry, set up to co-ordinate the strategy. The United States and France were at the head of the queue of countries interested in developing such a relationship, with both having signed defence industries security agreements with Turkey by autumn 1992. Once the framework governing technology transfer and the protection of information had been worked out, the way was open for the conclusion of individual deals. In February 1998 France and Turkey agreed in principle on the joint production of ERYX anti-tank missiles in a $450 million deal.[90] Other examples of joint production deals with European partners included a tie-up between Thompson CSF and Tekfen to produce radar systems; a contract with Giat of France for the production of guns and turrets for armoured fighting vehicles; and a joint venture involving Marconi to manufacture radios.

By the end of 1996, defence industry cooperation accords had been concluded with eighteen countries. Furthermore, of the nineteen major hardware programmes announced as part of the ten-year $31 billion defence plan, fifteen involved either local production or co-production with foreign partners. The latter included four of the five most expensive projects: $5 billion for 1,000 main battle tanks; $3 billion for 145 attack helicopters; $2.5 billion for five advanced frigates; and $1.8 billion for six submarines.[91]

In view of the bilateral problems being experienced in weapons sales from Germany and the United States, Turkey sought to expand its defence relationship with other major European manufacturers,

---

[90] *Turkish Daily News*, 6 February 1998.
[91] Table of major programmes in Turkish defence survey in *Defense News*, 22–28 September 1997.

notably Britain, France and Italy. Through the 1990s defence con-tacts increased between these three European producers and Tur-key. For example, the $1.5 billion tender for the co-production of 200 transport helicopters, which was first issued in 1990, included French (Eurocopter Aérospatiale), German (MBB), and Italian (Agusta) companies, in addition to the American firms of Bell and Sikorsky.

However, an emerging defence sales relationship with the likes of France and Italy did not give Turkey the certainty of supply that it had lacked with Germany or the US. The decision of the French National Assembly in May 1998 to pass a resolution of sympathy with the Armenians over the massacres in eastern Anatolia during the First World War provoked a hard-line response in Ankara.[92] The Turkish state immediately resorted to the arms sales sector as a means through which to retaliate against France. Similarly, problems arose with Italy as a consequence of the arrival of the PKK leader Abdullah Öcalan in Rome in November 1998. The unwillingness of the Italian government to see him extradited to Turkey and Rome's inability to deal with the issue quickly left it open to a popular and official backlash in Turkey, including, as regards the former, a spon-taneous boycott of Italian-made goods. Ankara was so trigger happy in its willingness to resort to a weapons purchase ban that at one stage in 1998 it looked as if Turkey would be hard pressed to draw up a short list for tenders for some high tech equipment.

Against a backdrop of restricted procurement opportunities with all of its traditional suppliers, Turkey increasingly turned to Israel. Ankara had started to make low key purchases of military equipment from Israel since the early 1990s. This relationship became more solid, as Turkey learnt that Israel would satisfy its needs without fuss. The military procurement relationship acquired a new order of mag-nitude, and indeed became very public, in 1996. In the aftermath of two other military agreements, Israel undertook to update Turkey's F-4s in a $570 million deal finally concluded in December 1996.

With great momentum behind the Israeli-Turkish relationship, by the new year the two countries were discussing the possibility of a whole raft of different military cooperation projects, from Turkey's purchase of Merkava tanks, to the purchase of unmanned

---

[92] See Reuters, 29 May 1998, for the National Assembly's move and the Turkish response.

aircraft and a number of different ventures in the missile sector. Contracts and agreements in defence industries subsequently flowed. A joint venture was created comprising Rafael of Israel and MIKES and Roketsan of Turkey in May 1997, with a view to the joint production of Popeye II missiles; Israel received a $100 million deal to supply Turkey with Popeye I missiles, an order which was increased at the end of 1997; Israel's Tadiran Spectralink received a contract to supply airborne rescue systems for the Turkish air force in December 1997; Israel won a contract for the upgrading of Turkey's F-5s.

The Turkish interest in buying Russian weapons, notably including the $100 million worth of combat helicopters ordered in 1994,[93] stretches back to 1992.[94] While the initiative sprang from an interest in developing bilateral trade, and specific deals have invariably been linked to the settlement of Russian debt, the wider motivation has been to demonstrate unhappiness at the disruption of Western supplies. More specifically, Turkey has hoped to prompt the Western security establishment into overriding political reservations about such arms transfers. In spite of the symbolism of seeking Russian military imports, such a move does not amount to much more than gesture diplomacy. The one-off nature of the contracts, together with their moderate value, has not bought significant influence with the Russian Federation, with Moscow, for example, proceeding undeterred with the sale of S-300 missiles to Cyprus in 1997 and 1998, although Nicosia's climbdown ensured that those missiles were never delivered to Cyprus.

Turkey has sought to use companies from third countries to expedite the export of hardware that might be prevented or at least delayed if official channels were used. In January 1997, for example, the Belgian Defence Ministry confirmed press reports that Thomson-CSF, the French defence company, was acting as a commercial conduit for the sale of Belgian and Dutch-made missiles for Turkey. The

---

[93] The order was included in an accord reached between the two states as part of an attempt to settle a $520 million outstanding trade debt. See BBC/SWB/EE, 4 August 1994.

[94] During a visit to Moscow during which he signed a security and co-operation agreement, Interior Minister İsmet Sezgin also agreed in principle to the purchase of arms, including helicopters, armoured vehicles, small arms and night vision equipment. See BBC/SWB/EE, 31 October 1992.

former was to have included the Hawk missile system, made in Belgium under license from the United States. An attempt to procure such missiles using orthodox commercial means could have resulted in a particularly lengthy delay in delivery, as both the Belgian government and the United States would have had to approve such a deal. The employment of a conduit was aimed at side-stepping such regulations and expediting the weapons transfer.

Non-conventional capabilities. As compared with conventional weapons procurement and development, Turkey has been surprisingly inattentive in the field of weapons of mass destruction (WMD). In spite of growing fears about proliferation in the Middle East in the mid to late 1980s, Ankara remained apparently unconcerned. In the words of one leading Israeli strategic commentator who has taken a special interest in Turkey, Professor Efraim Inbar, this was 'a surprisingly nonchalant attitude'.[95] This was in part because of the strategic depth enjoyed by Turkey's population and economic centres, relative to the different threats perceived to exist from the Middle East. There was also a widely held assumption on the part of members of the Turkish elite that the country, through its membership of NATO, would be protected by the US nuclear umbrella.

This overall complacency began to change with the 1991 Gulf war, when Iraq resorted to Scud missile attacks on Israel and Saudi Arabia. There were widespread concerns at the time that Turkey too might be targeted. There were even fears among the population of Turkey that Iraqi Scuds might be used to mount attacks on Ankara and even Istanbul. Though such fears were almost certainly ill founded, not least because of the distances involved, these perceptions did underline the extent to which missile technology had eroded Turkey's strategic depth in psychological if not material terms.

Turkey did respond to the use of ballistic missiles in the 1991 conflict, but only in a low key and ultimately unconvincing way. This did not suggest that WMD had become a priority area. The Chief of Staff's office did revise some of its joint projects under the Air Defence Master Plan. This included the introduction for the first

[95] See *The Turkish-Israeli Entente: The New Power Alignment in the Middle East*, unpublished paper.

time of the concept of countering medium range missiles and nuclear warheads from countries to Turkey's south and south-east. However, the package adopted only provided for the gradual implementation of such measures; a revision of procurement plans to embrace missiles and early warning aircraft alone was to be considered.[96]

By February 1993 the Turkish military was still perceived to have no missile defence strategy.[97] By August of that year the Turkish General Staff was still committed to an 'active and passive' approach to the missile threat, which combined a reliance on NATO, the enhancement of early monitoring systems and (suggesting unawareness of the imprecision of the Middle East missile threat) the increased camouflage, mobility and repair of targets; the 'basic principle', it was stated apparently without due consideration of the difficulty of destroying mobile Scud launchers in the 1991 Iraq war, was the destruction of missiles before they were launched.[98]

The fact that the strategic threat from WMD has yet to sink in is underlined by Turkish attitudes towards the UN Special Commission (Unscom) before its eventual dissolution in December 1999? and its investigation into Iraq's non-conventional weapons and delivery systems. Unscom's work had focused both on the discovery and neutralisation of Iraq's past programmes in WMD and the establishment of a verificatory framework which would prevent such a programme being resurrected in the future. In view of the unpredictability of the Iraqi regime and its own relative and increasing vulnerability to such weapons, one might have expected Turkey to be an enthusiastic supporter of the Unscom effort. Instead, the reality was very different. Turks, both at an elite and a mass level, tended to speak and act as though they were immune to Iraq's WMD capability. The implicit assumption on the Turkish side was that Iraq's WMD embodied a specific problem for the US, rather than a security threat by which they were directly and immediately affected. In that regard, the apparent indifference of the Turkish establishment has mirrored that prevalent among the far less strategically sophisticated countries of the Arab Gulf.

---

[96] *Turkish Daily News*, 11 August 1992.
[97] *Turkish Daily News*, 26 February 1992.
[98] Interview with Brig.-Gen. Hurşit Tolon, the secretary-general of the Turkish General Staff, in *Turkish Daily News*, 27 August 1993.

It has only been since 1995 that Turkish military planners have woken up to the threat from WMD proliferation in the Middle East. Ankara is now more generally aware that its problematic Middle East neighbours have all invested heavily in non-conventional weapons and medium range delivery systems. Iran and Syria both possess chemical weapons and the ability to target them at all of eastern Anatolia to just short of Ankara.[99] Iraq too has had such a capability, as well as possessing a biological weapons and nuclear programme; until its dissolution Unscom believed that Baghdad retained a capability for chemical and biological weapons.

Turkey's increased concern at proliferation in the Middle East has occurred, presumably not coincidentally, at a time when it has developed a close military relationship with Israel. Indeed, Turkey's Middle East threat perceptions have increasingly come to resemble those of Israel.[100] Attempts by Ankara to join the US-Israeli project to develop an Arrow anti-missile missile system were thwarted by the fact that the US has long included Turkey on its restricted missile control list. Undeterred by that setback, Israel and Turkey have struck out in a bilateral attempt to try to develop a 150 km. range missile with a similar function.

While Turkey appears ready to consider the acquisition of anti-missile missiles, there appear to be no plans to import or produce non-conventional weapons. Turkey is a signatory of both principal treaties on the issue of nuclear proliferation, notably the nuclear nonproliferation treaty, which it signed on 18 April 1980. Ankara has signed a further agreement with the International Atomic Energy

---

[99] See Ian O. Lesser and Ashley J. Tellis, *Strategic Exposure. Proliferation Around the Mediterranean* (RAND, Santa Monica, 1996).

[100] For example, see the presentation by the director of foreign affairs in the Defence Industry Secretariat, Dr Sıtkı Egeli, to a meeting of experts at the Turkish ambassador's residence in London on 11 March 1999. He spoke about 'Countries that are seeking to become regional superpowers, like Iraq and perhaps in the future Iran', with WMD a 'fast track to such a status'. Later he mentioned Iran, Iraq, Libya, North Korea (and Syria 'to a certain extent') as states with 'a very strong incentive' to acquire WMD to gain some kind of equilibrium with regional adversaries, and deter foreign intervention by the West. The only mention of Israel in the presentation was as a victim (of Scud attacks during the 1991 Gulf war) or as 'a justification' by such states to acquire their own WMD capability. See Proceedings Report of conference on 'Challenges for Western Security and Defence in the 21st Century and Turkey'.

Authority (IAEA) entitling the IAEA to inspect Turkey's nuclear research in accordance with the NPT. Moreover, nuclearisation would be a costly and lengthy option for a country that has, to date,[101] no indigenous civilian nuclear programme on which to build.

Security concerns lie at the heart of how Turkey views its place in the world and hence its foreign policy. The end of the Cold War and the receding of the proximate threat from the Soviet Union and its Russian successor state have done little to ease such a preoccupation. Those security concerns lie in the traditional domain of hard security. Suspicion of co-operation among some of its neighbouring states, together with the perceived exploitation of the Kurdish issue and in particular the PKK-led insurgency by a range of outside actors, helps to explain why the security issue remains so paramount even in a context of Turkey's relative increase in power. Turkey has, perhaps strangely, been slow to appreciate the increasing regional threats from non-conventional weapons, although closer defence co-operation with Israel since the mid 1990s has drawn attention to such developments.

Turkey also remains concerned at the instability that has racked the regions to which it lies adjacent. Ankara has worked hard to manage conflicts in such diverse places as Chechnya, Abkhazia, Bosnia, Kosovo and northern Iraq. It has feared a range of negative consequences, from adverse state-to-state relations to refugee inflows and an impact on its own domestic politics. In the main, and particularly during the difficult years between 1991 and 1994, Turkey has handled such cases with prudent circumspection, to the benefit of itself and the cause of stability.

It is, though, the Kurdish issue in all of its security and foreign policy dimensions which has recurred most often since the late 1980s. The need to deploy massive conventional force in the south-

---

[101] Since the mid 1960s Turkey has toyed with the construction of a nuclear energy plant at Akkuyu in the province of Mersin because of its chronic need to create new sources of electrical power. In spite of the serious pursuit of the project since the mid 1990s, Ankara has so far recoiled from the award of a main contract because of equivocation which has been exacerbated by safety concerns, given Turkey's great vulnerability to earthquakes.

east of the country has delayed the modernisation of the Turkish armed forces; concerns about the use of imported hardware against the Kurdish population have disrupted Turkey's procurement relationship with its traditional military suppliers, especially in Europe; domestic considerations regarding the Kurds have informed Turkish policy towards the break-up of the Soviet Union and the Yugoslav federation—often Turkish foreign policy has indeed appeared to be 'indexed' to the Kurdish issue.

6

ECONOMICS AS FOREIGN POLICY

Until the 1970s economic factors were relatively unimportant in the formulation and execution of Turkish foreign policy. This was in part because of the overriding importance of strategic calculation in the development of policy, together with the manner in which the economy was structured during the first years of the republic. In the 1920s there was a reaction against the weakness and dependency of the latter years of the Ottoman Empire, especially the Capitulations. There was also a need to build a new economy, both in the wake of the degradation of the First World War and the war of independence, and in view of the country's loss of its predominantly Armenian and Greek merchant class. Little wonder then that the early republican decision-makers opted for a state-driven strategy of economic self-reliance, with the new businessmen of the day protected from international competition.

The creation of private sector monopolies at home, the symbiotic relationship between these and the state, and the growing profile of the state in large-scale industrial investment helped to entrench this economic introspection.[1] The size and diversity of the Turkish agricultural sector in turn alleviated pressures from the external economy on such parochial economic organisation. Consequently, domestic economic interests had relatively little concern for external policy, as long, that is, as the protectionist barriers remained in place.

This situation proved broadly sustainable up to the 1970s. The rapid increases in the price of oil in 1973, together with subsequent rises, did the most to undermine this cosy autarky. Heavily dependent on oil imports, Turkey quickly began to run up sizeable balance of

[1] For an overview of the economic history of republican Turkey see Ziya Öniş and James Riedel, *Economic Crises and Long-Term Growth in Turkey* (World Bank, Washington, DC, 1993).

trade and hence balance of payments deficits from then onwards. For instance, Turkey's trade deficit, which had been a manageable $45 million in 1973, had multiplied to stand at $893 million just four years later.[2] In order to finance such deficits the exchequer increasingly turned to international borrowing. Against a backdrop of the accumulation of Turkey's foreign debt, it became clear that this 'legacy of insularity' could not be sustained in the long term.[3] With external structural pressures rendering the old approach untenable, reform and reorientation were only a matter of time. In the end, it came under the direction of Turgut Özal, who was left to run the economy after the military coup in September 1980.[4]

Trade liberalisation and export promotion were the two principal features of the Turkish structural reform programme.[5] The context of the suspension of civilian politics made it easier to implement rapid economic reform and absorb the pain of transition. By the early 1980s, Turkey had acquired an economy that was far more export-oriented in approach than the import substitution model of old. It was also increasingly one where the export profile was shifting from agricultural output to manufacturing. Thus the composition of exports moved from 64% agri–food products in 1980 to 71% industrial products in 1989, with textiles taking a 35% share. Foreign currency earnings from clothing exports alone, for example, increased from $300 million in 1980 to $7.1 billion in 1997.[6]

---

[2] Ali İhsan Bağış, 'The Beginning and Development of Economic Relations between Turkey and Middle Eastern Countries' in *Dış Politika*, vol. XII, nos 1–2, June 1985, p. 88.

[3] To quote a briefing on Turkey by the Economist Intelligence Unit from early 1990. See *Turkey on Trial: Political Uncertainty in Turkey and its Implications for Business and International Relations* (EIU, London, January 1990), p. 8.

[4] For a detailed examination of Özal's reforms see Mina Toksoz, *Turkey to 1992, Missing Another Chance?* (EIU Special Report no. 1136, London, 1988), esp. Chapter 5.

[5] These were initially achieved through a range of different mechanisms, including a 33% devaluation of the lira and substantial tax rebates granted to exporters. Export subsidies began to be phased out from 1984 onwards, to be replaced by the use of exchange rates to stimulate exports and the creation of a US-style Eximbank. See Ministry of Foreign Affairs *Economic Report on Turkey-EC Integration* (Prepared for the 34th Session of the Turkey-EC Joint Parliamentary Committee) (Ankara, 1991).

[6] William Chislett, *Turkey, A Market for the 21st Century* (Euromoney Publications, London, 1999), p. 64.

The outward reorientation of the economy immediately increased the importance of economic issues in the formulation of foreign policy. Özal needed no persuasion to include economic interest in the calculation of policy. Indeed, one long time observer of Turkish affairs noted that Özal viewed foreign policy 'as a branch of international trade relations'.[7] Özal's inclusion of large numbers of Turkish businessmen in his entourage on foreign visits became legendary.

Though the initial problem of the terms of trade with foreign oil suppliers had been addressed by the mid 1980s, that was not the end of the economic agenda in foreign policy. Fortuitously this period coincided with the opening up of new markets in Eastern Europe, Russia, the Balkans and the former Soviet south, the search for new primary energy suppliers and the development of the south-east for commercial agriculture and new agro-industries. It is with this increasingly full agenda of economic issues, intersecting with wider diplomatic interests, that this chapter is concerned.

Balancing the oil bill

In order to ameliorate the effects of a deteriorating balance of payments current account, Turkey was in urgent need of developing new markets. By the end of the 1970s Turkey had initiated an 'aggressive' export drive on all fronts.[8] The main regional market to respond to this effort was the Middle East. By 1988, for example, Turkey had received $2.7 billion in concessionary funding from the Islamic world, the vast majority of which was in the form of trade finance to help offset the imbalance in trade.[9]

The country markets which saw the greatest growth were Iran and Iraq,[10] where Turkey benefited from a combination of its 'active neutrality' during the 1980–8 war and the wariness of other potential

[7] Andrew Mango writing in *Turkey Confidential*, no. 13, November 1990, p. 4.
[8] *Financial Times* Survey on Turkish banking, 8 December 1988.
[9] For instance, of the $972 m. in concessionary finance extended by the Jeddah-based Islamic Development Bank, $732 m. was in the form of trade finance. See *Turkey Confidential*, no. 1, July 1989, p. 9.
[10] For a broad setting of Iraqi-Turkish relations, see Ramazan Gözen, 'The Turkish-Iraqi Relations: From Cooperation to Uncertainty' in *Dış Politika*, vol. XIX, nos. 3–4, 1995.

exporters. There was also a significant take-off in Libyan-Turkish economic relations, while trade with other Arab oil producers such as Kuwait and Saudi Arabia also grew, though at lower levels.

The geographical proximity of Turkey to Iran and Iraq meant that a mutual comparative advantage was quickly established as far as trade was concerned. The two countries routinely supplied two-thirds of Turkey's oil imports throughout the 1980s, at an over-all price that during the first half of the decade averaged some $1.13 billion a year. There was an inevitable lead time in the build-up of Turkey's exports to Iran and Iraq, as oil provided the motor for trade and Turkish businessmen had to establish contacts more or less from scratch. By 1985 the year before the oil price crash, Turk-ish visible exports to Iran and Iraq, which had been $233.7 million and $559.1 million respectively in 1981, had risen to $1.01 billion and $961.4 million.

Though 1985 proved to be the high watermark of Turkish exports to Iran and Iraq, the value of earnings remained high in the second half of the decade and much more commensurate with the value of Turkish oil imports from the two countries. In short, bilateral trade was generally close to being in balance. Moreover, there was a grow-ing inter-dependence, especially between Iraq and Turkey, with Baghdad having built two parallel oil pipelines across Turkey to a Mediterranean outlet in an effort to diversify its lines of oil exports. The presence of the two pipelines benefited the Turkish exchequer to the tune of some $250 million a year in transit fees alone. With Iraq and Turkey also being included in a project to integrate the electricity grids of several Near Eastern states (a project which would began to be practically implemented in the late 1990s), sig-nificant strides had been taken to integrate the economies of Iraq and Turkey. It would take a contingency of the enormity of the 1990 Gulf crisis to rupture these growing sinews of Iraqi-Turkish eco-nomic relations.

It was not just in the area of trade that Turkey's economic inter-action with the leading economies of the Middle East grew. Turkish contractors received large contracts especially in such countries as Libya, Saudi Arabia and Iraq. By 1990 Turkish contracting compa-nies had completed more than $3 billion worth of contracts with

Libya and $1 bn worth with Iraq. At the time of the Iraqi invasion of Kuwait Turkish firms had more than $2.5 billion worth of contracts yet to be completed, and the Turkish conglomerate ENKA Holding, in a consortium with Soviet companies, had just received a lucrative contract for the construction of a railway between Baghdad and Basra.[11]

Turkey also became a significant exporter of labour to these countries. By the end of 1980, there were an estimated 94,000 Turks working in the Arab world, a figure that rose as high as 208,000 five years later.

Though commercial relations between Turkey and the Middle East remained considerable throughout the 1980s, by the end of the decade the spell had been broken. Nominal export earning figures flattered to deceive. The second half of the 1980s was to see the relative eclipse of the Middle East market in the overall trade profile of the Turkish external economy, especially when compared with that of Europe. Furthermore, by the end of the 1980s there was the first wave of excitement about new economic opportunities in Eastern Europe and the Soviet Union, while the impression grew that the Arab world was, economically speaking, a spent force.

TURKEY'S TRADE WITH MIDDLE EAST*
AND WITH THE E.U. COMPARED (*$ bn/%*)

	1992	1993	1994	1995	1996	1997
Imports from ME	2.65	2.79	2.53	2.69	3.21	2.65
Imports from EU	10.66	13.87	10.92	16.86	23.12	24.87
ME/EU imports	24.9	20.1	23.2	16.0	13.9	10.7
Exports to ME	1.97	1.99	2.11	2.13	2.06	2.33
Exports to EU	7.93	7.60	8.64	11.01	11.55	12.25
ME/EU exports	24.8	26.2	24.4	18.7	17.8	19.0
ME imports/total	11.6	9.5	10.9	7.5	7.4	5.5
ME exports/total	13.4	13.0	11.7	9.8	8.9	8.9

Source: Statistical Yearbook of Turkey, 1998.
 * Middle East defined as Bahrain, Iran, Iraq, Israel, Jordan, Kuwait, Lebanon, Oman, Qatar, Saudi Arabia, Syria, UAE, Yemen.

[11] *Turkish Daily News*, 18 April 1990.

Even so, the impact of the period between the late 1970s and the mid 1980s should not be underestimated. It was a time which saw the rapid widening of the interaction between Turkey and the Middle East from the diplomatic into the commercial fields, and which routinised and normalised such relations. In the 1990s some of these old associations continued. For instance, Turkish companies have continued to work in Libya, employing around 10,000 Turkish workers. Meanwhile, Turkey has re-emerged as a significant conduit for Iraq's supervised export of crude oil under UN resolution 986 and its successors; the Turkish conglomerate Tekfen Holding was responsible for the restoration of Iraq's trans-Turkey Mediterranean pipelines; road tanker traffic delivering Turkish goods in return for Iraqi refined products plied across the border for much of the 1990s. Finally, though it has certainly slipped in relative terms, the Middle East continues to represent an important market for Turkey. That market is expected to grow over the next two decades,[12] when Turkey's South-Eastern Anatolia Project (GAP) begins to increase the export output of agricultural produce and agro-industries. Though the Middle East is unlikely again to rival Europe as a market for Turkish business, the combination of proximity, hydrocarbons and economic complementarities should ensure that contacts remain extensive and rewards considerable.

Trade and the European vocation

Until the 1980s Turkey's European 'vocation' was based on the identity and ideology of the Kemalist elite who held sway, bolstered at different times by the security threat from the Soviet Union. The development of a competitive, export-oriented economy added a further dimension to this Europe orientation. With the commonly held sense of threat from Moscow having receded and the Kemalist value system under increasing challenge from a more conservative,

---

[12] For many of those involved in economic generation in the south-east of the country the Middle East is the 'natural market' for output from the region, with Iran, Iraq and Syria mentioned as having the best potential, while the prospect of a more complementary economic partnership with Israel is also viewed with some hope. Interview with Yusuf Yıldız, director of the Mardin Free Zone, 29 March 2000.

religious counter elite, it can be argued that the hard, material, tangible nature of economic interest is likely to be a more stable and enduring basis for Turkey's ties with Europe in the future.

The pursuit of new export markets in the 1980s inevitably led Turkish manufacturers to Europe. The European market was a large one, which seemed to offer complementary opportunities for Turkey, with its plentiful supply of cheap yet relatively skilled labour. Selim İlkin has shown that Turkish businessmen began to develop a real familiarity with Europe from the 1950s, on the basis of government policy more sympathetic to the private sector, together with the provision of a Western-style education system in Turkey.[13] This was supplemented by the growth of Europe both as a tourist destination and as a market for the export of labour, notably to Germany, which stretched back to the early 1960s.[14] Moreover, Turgut Özal, conscious of the importance of the development of a single European market by 1992, was aware of the rapid changes taking place on the continent, as his 1987 application for membership of the EC reflects. Finally, with the exception of the Middle East, the export alternatives were as yet few.

Of course Turkish-European commercial interaction was not unheard of before the 1980s. Certainly increasing levels of trade and growing economic integration were an assumption that had underlain institutional relations between Europe and Turkey since the early 1960s. Since the 1963 Ankara Agreement, Turkey and the EEC had been committed to the introduction of a customs union, with practical transitional arrangements introduced with the Additional Protocol of 1970.[15] Around half of Turkey's trade was with Europe in the early 1970s. Turkish exports to the EEC stood at $644.6 million in 1975. Moreover, there had already been a small number of sizeable foreign direct investments (FDI) from Europe in Turkey, notably

---

[13] Selim İlkin, 'Businessmen: Democratic Stability' in Metin Heper, Ayse Öncü and Heinz Kramer (eds), *Turkey and the West, Changing Political and Cultural Identities* (I.B. Tauris, London, 1993), p. 185.

[14] For an extended discussion of this and related issues, see Ayse Kadıoğlu, 'The human tie: international labour migration' in Canan Balkır and Allan M. Williams (eds), *Turkey and Europe* (Pinter, London, 1993).

[15] The Additional Protocol, which came into effect on 1 January 1973, envisaged the implementation of a customs union over a 22-year period.

the involvement of Fiat and Renault in joint venture motor vehicle production with Koç and OYAK respectively,[16] dating from the late 1960s.

Nevertheless, it remains the case that before the late 1970s such commercial interaction was small in scale compared to what would follow, especially in the sphere of trade. Turkish exports to the EC took off as the economy became more export oriented, with Turkey jumping from fortieth to eighteenth place in the list of exporters to the EC between 1980 and 1990. By the turn of the decade, Turkish exports to the EC were worth $6.9 billion, up from $1.3 billion some ten years earlier. Much of the largest growth in exports came in the area of textiles, which have come to comprise some 40% of Turkish exports. In turn, as the Turkish economy grew and sucked in imports, so the EC's profile in Turkish imports also grew, with Turkey rising from 27th to 12th on the list of important markets for EC producers during the same period; Turkish imports from the EC had risen from $2.4 billion in 1980 to $9.3 billion in 1990.

Interestingly, this take-off in bilateral trade between the EC and Turkey occurred independently of the fortunes of political relations. Indeed, during this period political ties were far from good. Movement in the direction of the Customs Union had foundered on Turkish protectionism in the middle of the 1970s. Relations then cooled on the diplomatic front in 1978, when the Turkish prime minister Bülent Ecevit suspended institutional arrangements under the Association Agreement. The 1980 coup resulted in diplomatic relations between the two sides entering a period of 'deep freeze',[17] with an incremental attempt to rebuild relations not getting underway until 1986. Even then the Association Council, the authoritative body presiding over the Association Agreement, was only to meet once, in September 1986, over a span of some eleven years. Relations were, if anything, frostier among representatives than they were among officials and ministers, with the EC-Turkey Joint Parliamentary

---

[16] The Army Mutual Assistance Association, or OYAK, was established in 1961 in the aftermath of the military coup. By bringing the military into the sphere of business and industry, it helped to recement relations between the army and the state as a whole. See Feroz Ahmad, *The Making of Modern Turkey* (Routledge, London, 1993), pp. 130–1.

[17] To quote the EC representation in Ankara in an internal report, October 1994.

Committee, suspended in 1980 in protest against the coup, only being reconvened in 1989.

The accession of Greece to EC membership in 1980 internalised Greek-Turkish tensions in the deliberations of the Community, in spite of Brussels' policy pledges to the contrary.[18] In particular it resulted in the blocking of various economic assistance packages, notably the Fourth Financial Protocol, which as Heinz Kramer has pointed out then became 'a political symbol of all problems burdening EC-Turkey relations' for a decade.[19] It was against such an inauspicious background that Turgut Özal, with characteristic chutzpah, made what was for Brussels his unwelcome application for Turkey's full membership of the EC in 1987, a bid which was eventually politely but firmly parried by the Commission with its *avis* in December 1989. While such developments did immense harm to the atmospherics in EC-Turkish diplomatic and political relations, they largely left the world of commercial relations unaffected.

Indeed, the rapid increase in bilateral trade through the 1980s even continued in spite of formal trade restrictions introduced by the EC. The whole southern European expansion in the 1980s fostered a greater protectionist stance towards Turkey, spanning textiles and industrial and agricultural goods. A good example of this greater protectionism was the EC's response to the surge in Turkish textile exports in the late 1970s, at what the Commission considered to be 'very low or even dumping prices'.[20] The EC consequently insisted on the introduction of 'voluntary' quantitative limits on textile imports. These were later progressively relaxed, so that by 1994 textiles accounted for two-thirds of Turkish exports to the EU,[21] making it the EU's largest single supplier of textiles.[22]

---

[18] See Commission of the European Communities, *Opinion on Greek Application for Membership*, 29 January 1976, p. 7, in which it was stated that 'The European Community is not and should not become a party to the disputes between Greece and Turkey.'

[19] Untitled paper presented to a workshop on 'Europe and the Mediterranean', organised by the Centre for European Policy Studies in Brussels, 21–22 January 1993.

[20] Commission of the European Communities, D-G External Relations, *Briefing for Commissioner Matutes, EP Debate on Dury Report*, Brussels, 13 October 1992.

[21] *Financial Times* Survey on 'Turkey: The Customs Union with Europe', 22 January 1996.

[22] *Financial Times*, 12 November 1993.

While the 1990s have largely seen diplomatic relations between the EC and Turkey bump along, characterised by a bumbling inconstancy on the part of the former and the surly gracelessness of the latter, the economic sinews of integration have grown stronger. This time they have been facilitated by the successful implementation on 1 January 1996 of a Customs Union in the area of industrial goods.[23] The dismantling of much of its remaining protectionist apparatus and the adoption of the EU's common external tariff has made Turkey a more reliable and accessible market,[24] thereby increasing its commercial importance to the larger export-oriented economies of the EU. Consequently, imports from the EU rose by nearly 35% to $22.7 billion in the first year of the Customs Union alone, catapulting Turkey to seventh position in the EU's list of most valuable export markets. In turn, Turkish exports to the EU, which have risen but more modestly, are eventually expected to accelerate, all other things being equal, as a result of the 'cold shower' to which companies have been exposed. Once they have assimilated the realities of the globalised economy, their competitiveness, and hence their export potential, are expected to increase.

Of course, it would be wrong to reduce European-Turkish economic relations just to visible trade. Between 1980 and 1989 Turkey received $4 billion in FDI,[25] nine times more than that received over the previous 25 years. That expansion was due to the liberalisation of FDI regulations, including the introduction of the BOT

---

[23] There are two ways in which the Customs Union, even some five years later, had yet to be fully implemented. These were aspects of the technical legislation of the CU, which had still to be adopted; and competition aspects of the *acquis communautaire*, such as those relating to the monopolies on alcohol and tobacco that continued to apply. Work on completing these aspects of the CU was continuing. (Interview with senior member of the Secretariat-General for EU Affairs, 4 June 2001.) Neither the EU side nor Turkey considered these to be major outstanding problems, and both were happy to refer to the successful introduction of the CU.

[24] Protectionist barriers equivalent to 30–40% of the value of products were removed as a result of the implementation of the CU.

[25] For a discussion of FDI in the context of EU-Turkey relations see Canan Balkır, 'Turkey and the European Community: Foreign Trade and Direct Foreign Investment in the 1980s' in Canan Balkir and Allan M. Williams (eds), *Turkey and Europe* (Pinter, London, 1993).

(build, operate, transfer) facility in 1984.[26] By 1990, the proportion of FDI originating from the EC had increased to 70%. Indeed, there were reasonable grounds around this time for being bullish about Turkey's inward investment prospects. At the beginning of the 1990s the country ranked in the top 20 global foreign investment venues.[27]

IMPORTS FROM SELECTED E.U. COUNTRIES (*$ bn*)

	1992	*1993*	*1994*	*1995*	*1996*	*1997*
France	1.35	1.95	1.46	2.0	2.77	2.97
Germany	3.75	4.53	3.65	5.55	7.81	8.02
Italy	1.92	2.56	2.01	3.20	4.30	4.50
UK	1.19	1.55	1.17	1.83	2.51	2.76
EU total	10.7	13.9	10.9	16.9	23.1	24.9
EU/total %	46.7	47.3	46.8	47.3	53.0	51.2
Grand Total	22.9	29.4	23.3	35.7	43.6	48.6

Source: *Statistical Yearbook of Turkey, 1998.*

EXPORTS TO SELECTED E.U. COUNTRIES (*$ bn*)

	1992	*1993*	*1994*	*1995*	*1996*	*1997*
France	0.81	0.77	0.85	1.03	1.05	1.16
Germany	3.66	3.65	3.93	5.04	5.12	5.25
Italy	0.94	0.75	1.03	1.46	1.45	1.39
UK	0.80	0.83	0.89	1.14	1.26	1.51
EU total	7.9	7.6	8.6	11.1	11.5	12.2
EU/total %	53.7	49.7	47.5	51.4	49.6	46.6
Grand Total	14.7	15.3	18.1	21.6	23.2	26.2

Source: *Statistical Yearbook of Turkey, 1998.*

While the increase in FDI compared to the days of ISI and protectionism may look impressive, in absolute terms and relative to Turkey's main competitors as the 1990s progressed it has been deeply disappointing. It may be that FDI in Turkey is high compared to

---

[26] The BOT Law no. 3096 was introduced in 1984. For a description of the law and its successors see *Emerging Turkey 1999* (Oxford Business Group, London, 1998) pp. 189–90.

[27] Foreign Investors Association of Turkey (Yased), cited in survey on 'Turkey: Industry and Inward Investment', *Financial Times*, 18 April 2001.

inward investment in the Arab World; compared to the emerging economies of the old Eastern Europe Turkey is lagging behind in attracting FDI. By 1999 Turkey ranked 57th in the world FDI league, on a par with Azerbaijan and less successful than Croatia.[28] Moreover, the great majority of the FDI that has gravitated to Turkey has done so based on domestic market opportunities, rather than seeing Turkey as a regional export base.

Tourism has also been a field of rapid expansion in EU-Turkish economic relations. In 1991, nearly 50% of all tourists were from EC countries, with a similar profile for Europeans in Turkish revenue earnings from tourism. This figure dropped as a percentage of the total after the Gulf crisis, but recovered in the middle of the 1990s, indicating its potential. With the sector aiming to boost overall tourist numbers from some 10 million in 2000 to 17 million in 2005 and 25 million in 2010, and with cultural and historical tourism, together with the conference trade, earmarked as major growth areas, the number of Europeans visiting the country in the first decade of the new millennium is expected to continue to grow.[29]

In 1993 it was therefore already possible to describe Europe as having emerged as 'a centre of [economic] gravity for Turkey'.[30] The positive impact of the Customs Union has further oriented Turkish external economic relations to Europe.[31] The deepening nature of economic relations, together with the large numbers of Turks resident in the EU, some having settled for as long as three decades, underlines the extent of the *de facto* integration which has

---

[28] Hence, in terms of inward investment, Metin Münir concludes that Turkey is 'a small global player which is becoming smaller'. See ibid.

[29] Interview with the head of the Turkish Association of Travel Agents (TÜRSAB), Başaran Ulusoy, *Turkish Daily News*, 13 July 2000. Such sentiments are a response to growing concerns about the Turkish tourist industry being dependent on summer packages, with a tendency towards the 'bargain basement' syndrome. See Oxford Analytica, *Turkey: Tourism Challenges*, 29 August 2000.

[30] See Philip Robins, *Partners for Growth: New Trends in EC-Turkish Cooperation* (Forum Europe, Brussels, 1993), p. 4.

[31] All along the European Commission predicted that the implementation of a Customs Union would have a profound, though low key, impact on Turkish-EU relations through Turkey's inevitable adoption of European standards and in terms of the harmonisation of legislation, especially in the fields of transport, energy and the environment. Interview with Turkey desk officer at the Commission, Michael Cendrowicz, 13 March 1991.

already taken place. This has led some to argue that EU–Turkish relations are now inextricably intertwined.[32] Though few things may be absolutely irreversible, it must be acknowledged that the costs of trying to unpick such economic and demographic connections would be very high indeed, for both sides, albeit in different ways. Indeed, it is noteworthy that even an Islamist political party such as the Welfare Party before its closure, while deeply sceptical about institutional integration, never actually advocated or sought to realise a reduction in let alone a severing of trade relations with the EU.

FOREIGNERS VISITING FROM SELECTED E.U. COUNTRIES
(% of total)

	1990	*1991*	*1992*	*1993*	*1994*	*1995*	*1996*	*1997*
Austria	3.6	1.9	2.9	3.2	2.1	2.3	2.7	3.2
France	6.4	2.6	3.5	4.6	3.5	3.2	2.9	3.4
Germany	20.7	14.6	16.4	17.2	14.8	21.4	24.8	24.1
Greece	3.8	2.1	2.1	2.3	1.9	2.0	1.7	1.7
Italy	2.8	1.3	2.2	2.1	1.6	1.4	1.9	2.1
UK	6.0	3.5	4.5	6.7	8.5	9.5	8.4	9.4
EU total	54.1	33.0	40.6	45.1	41.1	49.0	52.2	54.1
Grand total	100	100	100	100	100	100	100	100

Source: Statistical Yearbook of Turkey, 1998.

The fact that EU–Turkish economic integration has been rapid, uninterrupted and to the benefit of both sides ought to be viewed with a sense of mutual satisfaction; indeed, it ought to have long since emerged as the leading indicator of EU–Turkish relations, and hence been seen as a badge of rude good health. In reality, however, diplomatic relations have invariably been regarded as the barometer of ties; with the exception of rare moments such as the December 1999 Helsinki summit, this aspect of the relationship has seldom moved beyond a restricted continuum spanning cool propriety and bitter recrimination. A combination of domestic factors resulting in the ideological zealotry and insecurity of the Turkey's Kemalist elite,

---

[32] See, for example, the speech by the Turkish ambassador to Britain, Özdem Sanberk, at a conference on 'A European Turkey?', organised by the Centre for European Reform in London on 27 April 1998. Ambassador Sanberk stated that 'a complete divorce between Turkey and the EU is out of the question'.

and the asymmetrical nature of EU–Turkey relations, which makes legalistic pedants out of much of the foreign policy establishment, are the primary factors in explaining this paradox. Ironically, concentrating on the extent to which Turkey relies on Europe for jobs, profits and foreign exchange earnings would do more for securing the country's European vocation than the strident insistence on the values of secularism.[33]

Russia and the energy driver

The transformation in economic growth levels from the late 1970s onwards had a series of dramatic effects on other aspects of the economy and society in Turkey. It speeded up the trend in rural to urban migration; it changed lifestyle and consumption patterns; it increased levels of prosperity, especially in the urban areas of the country: these in turn stimulated other parts of the economy, especially the production of consumer durables, demand for which has risen at an annual 8% since the late 1980s.[34] The effect of all of these activities together was dramatically to increase levels of energy demand in the country, with profound implications for public policy and, ultimately, external relations.

This rapid increase has resulted in a surge in demand for both electricity and the primary energy resources that power the turbines generating such power. Between 1980 and 1996 net per capita consumption of electricity rose by 150% (against net population growth of 40% over the same period). In addition to such high, sustained growth, there is a widely held expectation of a continuing growth in demand into the future the economic crisis of 2000 and 2001 notwithstanding. Turkey still consumes less than half the per capita rate for electric power in Greece, the EU's poorest member. Electricity consumption in Britain is five times higher than that in Turkey, and in Germany it is four times higher.

[33] For a complementary discussion see Philip Robins, 'Turkey: Europe in the Middle East, or the Middle East in Europe?' in B.A. Roberson (ed.), *The Middle East and Europe: the Power Deficit* (Routledge, London, 1998).

[34] Saloman Bros research note cited in *Financial Times* Survey 'Turkey: Energy', 31 March 1998. It should be pointed out that the rise in demand for consumer durables has outstripped the aggregate growth in GDP over the same period, which has registered an average of around 2.5 per cent per year.

Estimating the pace of growth and future magnitude of energy demand in Turkey is problematic. Much will depend on future levels of economic growth, together with the pace of lifestyle changes. Furthermore, forecasting is affected by the fog of vested interest, with ministers, state agencies and private domestic and foreign companies all having a powerful stake in influencing the prevailing conventional wisdom and hence in future policy and investment decisions. In turn, acts of God, like the devastating earthquakes of 1999, can have a sudden and unexpected impact on demand projections. Whatever the precise figures, however, there is little doubt that growth in demand will be huge. Indeed, the situation for Turkey is of even greater urgency because of the absence of slack in the system. Turkey already has a deficit in electricity generation, which stood at 3.3 bn kW hours in 1997. In order to make up the shortfall Turkey has to import electricity, since 1997 from Bulgaria and Iran.[35] In spite of a letup in strong demand growth due to lower GDP growth in 1998 and a major contraction in growth in 1999, blackouts, which had not been seen since the late 1970s, are now common.

Turkey is poorly placed to generate itself the necessary extra primary energy inputs to satisfy either the demand for electricity or the growing demand for natural gas for domestic use in the main urban areas of the country. Turkey is a producer of crude oil, but output is only able to satisfy just over 11% of its oil needs,[36] while the location of the main oil fields in the south-east of the country, the setting until recently of the Kurdish insurgency, has helped to deter foreign majors from extensive prospecting. Turkey does have considerable reserves of coal, but the sulphurous nature of its deposits, and the resulting winter smogs in Istanbul and Ankara, have increasingly deterred use for environmental and health reasons. Turkey remains equivocal and hence undecided on whether to proceed with nuclear power, bids for the first such plant having been received in 1997.[37] Turkey is increasingly exploiting its river resources to create new sources of hydro-electric power, mainly in tandem with the GAP project in the south-east, though this alone will be insufficient to meet the magnitude of the new demand levels.

[35] *Hürriyet*, cited in *Turkish Press Review*, 18 March 1997.
[36] See www.tpao.gov.tr for further information on Turkey's domestic oil production.
[37] Oxford Analytica Daily Brief, 'Turkey: Power Investment', 17 May 1999.

Consequently Turkey has had no alternative but increasingly to look abroad for new sources of energy inputs. In doing so, energy has been viewed as being of strategic importance, energy policy being a regular item on the agenda of the monthly meetings of the National Security Council. Chief among these considerations has been the diversification of energy supplies away from its dependence on the Arab world and Iran, the Kemalist establishment being perennially wary of over-reliance on the Middle East region.

Gas: the fuel of choice. If the reduction of energy dependence on the Middle East has emerged as a critical strategic aim, a second key decision was to purchase natural gas from the Soviet Union, as a result of an agreement concluded in September 1984. Part of Turgut Özal's vision, the gas deal has grown into a means through which to foster stable relations with Moscow through the establishment of economic interdependence.

The gas business in particular has taken off exponentially since the start of the first deliveries from the USSR in 1987. This is partly because Turkey has chosen natural gas to be, as John Barham in the *Financial Times* has put it, 'the fuel of choice' to power its new generation of power stations.[38] Successive mayors of the big cities of Turkey have followed the example of Murat Karayalçın, the former mayor of the capital, in implementing an ambitious programme of making piped gas available as a source of domestic energy. Turkey's imports of natural gas from Moscow, delivered via a pipeline traversing Ukraine, Moldova, Romania and Bulgaria, have progressively increased to stand at some 6 bn cu m in 1998. This represents 67% of Turkey's gas imports from abroad.

Turkey's gas imports have, in turn, proved to be the motor for significant two-way economic relations with the Soviet Union and its Russian successor state. Under the terms of the initial accord, Moscow agreed to accept payment for the gas supplies in the form of Turkish manufactured goods, contracting services and in cash. This was the mechanism that permitted Turkish contractors to enter its domestic market. Turkish contractors began by building housing for returning units of the Red Army. This relationship enabled Turkish construction

---

[38] Survey, 'Turkey: Energy' (note 34).

companies to establish close relations with members of the new, emerging post-Communist elite at a time when its potential competitors were too cautious or unimaginative in seeking complementary alliances. As the relationship thickened and became more sophisticated, the Turkish companies formed joint venture outfits with their partners in Russia. The profile of Turkish contractors increased to such an extent that by early 1994 it was claimed that Turkish companies had completed $5.5 billion worth of housing contracts in the Russian Federation out of an accumulated portfolio worth $30 billion.[39] By autumn 1998 in excess of $10 billion worth of work had been completed.[40]

'Suitcase' trade. Because of the strong counter-trade dimension in the Russian-Turkish economic relationship, official figures have never accurately reflected the extent of bilateral economic integration. A second area of commercial interaction which is even more difficult to quantify is the so-called suitcase trade, whereby individuals from Russia and other Black Sea littoral states have travelled mainly to Istanbul and Trabzon, selling whatever they have in return for Turkish-made consumer goods. At its height, total unregistered trade has been estimated in excess of $8 billion a year, with as many as 1.5 million Russians, representing nearly 18% of all foreigners visiting Turkey, arriving each year.[41] With registered exports from Turkey in 1996 generating an added $1.5 billion, Russia ought really to have been considered to be Turkey's principal export partner, almost twice as lucrative as Germany, conventionally thought of as Turkey's leading export market.

Economic crisis in Russia, together with the poor quality of much of Turkey's manufactured merchandise, resulted in a collapse of the

---

[39] Minister of State İbrahim Tez during a visit to Russia. See BBC/SWB/EE, 3 February 1994.

[40] See 'Turkish Contracting in the International Market', briefing material produced by the Union of International Contractors in Turkey, which represents Turkish contractors active abroad, October 1998. This figure of $10 billion was earned on 436 projects. Over half of the construction projects undertaken abroad by UIC members after 1990 were in Russia.

[41] At its height, according to official records, 1.51 and 1.49 million visited Turkey in 1995 and 1996 respectively. See State Institute of Statistics, Prime Ministry of Turkey, *Statistical Yearbook of Turkey, 1997*, p. 456.

suitcase trade between 1996 and 1999, with little sign of a recovery since then. The gas trade, however, has continued to go from strength to strength. In April 1997 Turkey concluded a new deal with Gazprom to raise gas exports through the existing pipeline by a further 8 billion cu. m. by the year 2002. It was at that point that Turkey's gas relationship with Russia, which had never in any case since Özal's day been exclusively a function of commerce, moved firmly into the realm of high politics.

TURKEY'S TRADE WITH RUSSIA (*$ million*)

	Exports	Imports
1992	438.4	1.040.4
1993	499.0	1,542.4
1994	820.1	1,045.4
1995	1,238.2	2,082.4
1996	1,493.7	1,900.2
1997	2,056.5	2,174.3
1998	1,347.5	2,155.0

Source: Turkiye-Rusya Iliskileri, n.d., DEIK.[42]

TURKEY'S SUITCASE TRADE WITH RUSSIA (*$ million*)

1996	8,842
1997	5,849
1998	3,060
1998 (Jan.–April)	1,489
1999 (Jan.–April)	598

Source: Turkiye-Rusya Iliskileri, n.d., DEIK.[43]

The April deal was followed by the signing of the so-called Blue Stream accord during a visit to Turkey by the then Russian prime minister, Viktor Chernomyrdin. Under the terms of the $20 billion accord, Russia was to supply Turkey with as much as 16 billion cu. m. of gas a year over a 25-year period, via a new 1,200 km. pipeline to run 2,000 metres under the Black Sea.[44] The arrival of Chernomyrdin

[42] Turkish-Russian Business Council, *Türkiye-Rusya İlişkileri* (Turkish-Russian Relations), Dış Ekonomik İlişkiler Kurulu, Istanbul, n.d., p. 13.
[43] ibid., p. 15.
[44] *International Herald Tribune*, 13–14 December 1997.

the day after Turkey's crushing disappointment at the outcome of the EU's Luxembourg summit led to a mood swing which inflated the expectation of future relations with Russia, as epitomised by a project that was later to assume the title of the 'Blue Dream' among its detractors.[45]

Increasingly, Blue Stream became the subject of controversy. Scrutiny of the project focused on four major areas, spanning the landscape of domestic politics, high strategy and foreign policy in Turkey, thereby making Blue Stream a critical issue in the future values and orientation of the country. The first area of concern, the capability of the Russians to deliver on their promises, was in many ways the least complicated. Questions were asked about whether Moscow was capable of financing and building the pipeline, and even whether it was capable of delivering up to 30 billion cu. m. of gas per year. The involvement of the Italian oil and gas major, ENI, signalled the seriousness of the proposal. From the Turkish side, the riposte to this concern was that in view of the fact that Blue Stream was almost entirely a Russian financial liability the risks for Turkey were actually not significant. With Ankara only committed to some $350 million worth of expenditure it was, in the words of one politician sympathetic to the scheme, as if gas had been discovered off the coast of Samsun, on Turkey's Black Sea shoreline.

The second area of concern related to the role of a select number of Turkish companies with strong interests in Russia and leading politicians with which they were reputedly associated in pursuing the Blue Stream deal. It was widely reported at the time that two of Turkey's biggest conglomerates, ENKA and GAMA, had been responsible for brokering the deal. GAMA in particular had very close relations with the Russian energy giant Gazprom, the two having decided to establish a joint venture in order to bring natural gas to and distribute it in Turkey. Both GAMA and Gazprom in turn appeared to enjoy a cosy relationship with Botaş,[46] the Turkish state

---

[45] *Financial Times*, 16 March 1999.

[46] Botaş was established in 1974 in order to manage the transportation of crude oil to Turkey by pipeline. In 1987 this brief was expanded to include natural gas, and its authority broadened to cover the disposal of gas. Consequently, Botaş currently has a monopoly in the import, distribution, wholesale price determination and sale of natural gas in Turkey.

energy pipeline company, which had itself been under pressure to relinquish its domestic gas monopoly. Mesut Yılmaz, who had been prime minister from February to May 1996 and from June 1997 to January 1999, and was a member of the Ecevit-led coalition government from May 1999 onwards, was repeatedly accused of having an unhealthily close relationship with such companies.

The third area of concern was, in view of Turkey's existing dependence on Russian primary energy imports, whether it was prudent to increase the profile of Russian imported gas so massively. In other words, the project obliged Ankara to stare into the eyes of its own interdependence with Russia.[47] The issue was particularly contentious because it had been an assumption of Turkish energy policy in the mid 1990s that it was seeking to reduce rather than extend dependence on Russia.[48] If Turks had misgivings about such a trend, these were overwhelmed by the necessities of the current levels of interdependence. The Russian state, then in a position of penury, was already unhappy at the commercial imbalance in the relationship. For while Turkey had contracting services, manufactured goods and tourism to export, Russia had little to offer in return other than gas. It was therefore as much to secure current levels of business as for the pursuit of stable bilateral relations that Ankara accepted the Blue Stream scheme.

Other gas options. The fourth area of concern related to Turkey's energy relations with third countries, notably gas rich Turkmenistan.[49] Ankara had enthusiastically pursued a gas deal with Ashkhabad, attracted by the large reserves in Turkmenistan, the chance to diversify away from an over-reliance on Russia and the prospect of deepening bilateral economic and political relations with a fraternal state. A provisional accord had been concluded between the two countries in February 1996, whereby Turkey would aim to purchase an increasing volume of gas, which could rise as high as 15 billion cu. m. by the year 2020. The main constraint in the Turkmen gas

[47] The Blue Stream pipeline is set to increase Turkey's dependence on Russian natural gas from 66% to around 80%. *International Herald Tribune*, 9–10 June 2001.
[48] *Turkish Probe* No. 107, 9 December 1994.
[49] For a contemporary discussion of Turkmen gas, see the Turkmenistan energy profile in the *Financial Times's Middle East Energy*, no. 12, 5 March 1998.

deal was the absence of an export outlet, a new pipeline having to be built to transport the gas to Turkey. Critics of the Blue Stream plan, such as Sedat Sertoğlu, a columnist at *Sabah* newspaper, initially insisted that it was not a serious proposal, only a spoiler by Gazprom aimed at edging out the Turkmen option and so retaining its monopoly supply of the Turkish gas market. As the Blue Stream project has forged ahead, worries have focused on whether it will supplant the Turkmen gas plan,[50] and hence lock Ashkhabad into a perpetual dependence on Russia. Whatever the eventual fate of Turkmen gas, one thing is clear: for all its common cultural heritage and protestations of brotherhood, Turkmenistan does not compare in importance with Russia in Turkey's foreign relations.

Turkmenistan was just the most obvious of the potential gas suppliers that Turkey flirted with through the 1990s in its pursuit of new energy supplies. Other states that Ankara has dallied with include Algeria, Australia, Egypt, Iran, Nigeria, Qatar and Yemen. (The proximity and past energy relationship with Iraq would also make the purchase and piping of gas from Kirkuk an attractive option, though the continuing application of UN sanctions has deterred the serious exploration of this source in the 1990s.) With all but Iran, the Turkish interest was in liquefied natural gas (LNG), to be shipped by tanker rather than by pipeline, and to be processed at the 6 bn cu m facility opened at Marmara in 1994. With most of these countries, extensive talks, declarations of intent and even bits of paper have followed, without these being followed by hard agreements.

One relationship which has been forged to mutually good effect has been with Algeria. Turkey initially agreed to take 2 bn cu. m. of LNG from Algeria, rising to 4 billion cu. m., to get the Marmara plant working. Consequently, in 1999 Algerian imports accounted for 32% of Turkey's gas needs, more or less the balance of gas imports from Russia.[51] Direct flights between Istanbul and Algiers,

[50] See for example the opening sentence in a *Wall Street Journal* article (distributed by NewsEDGE/LAN, 17 February 2000) on the subject: 'Russia has pulled ahead in the race to be first to supply a new generation of natural gas to Turkey, pushing aside a US-backed project for a trans-Caspian pipeline to bring gas from Turkmenistan, Turkish Minister of Energy Cumhur Ersümer said'.

[51] Speech made by Botaş general director Gökhan Yardım, at a conference in Ankara entitled 'Petroleum and Pipelines', and covered in detail by *Turkish Daily News*, 16 April 1999.

Constantine and Oran, a political dialogue between diplomats,[52] and the sale of military hardware then followed as the relationship began to develop.[53]

Turkey has also shown great interest in Qatari gas, agreeing to purchase 2 billion cu. m. in 1995,[54] and going on to apply for an equity share in Qatar's second gas project, Rasgas.[55] First imports of Qatari LNG made under a spot contract took place in 1998. Turkey has also agreed to buy $100 million worth of LNG from Nigeria. Otherwise, tangible activity has proved to be as illusive as in the Turkmen case. For example, Turkey's Botas signed an agreement with Amoco and the Egyptian General Petroleum Corp at the Cairo Middle East and North Africa (MENA) conference in November 1996.[56] Yet it is by no means certain that Botaş will proceed and purchase LNG by 2002, if at all.[57]

Iran is another country with which a gas trade relationship has often been discussed, but where action has been similarly scarce. Plans to supply gas to Turkey by pipeline, which date back to the mid 1970s, were shelved early on under the Islamic regime, only to be reexamined in the early 1990s. By May 1995 the gas trade scheme had hardened into an accord which foresaw a 2 billion cu. m. gas trade eventually building to 10 billion cu. m. in 2002.[58] It was this that formed the basis of the $21 billion agreement signed by the recently installed Islamist prime minister Necmettin Erbakan during his

---

[52] See interview with Algerian ambassador to Turkey, Rachid Haddad, in *Turkish Daily News*, 23 January 1995.

[53] This took the form of a $200 m. deal in which the Koç group's Otokar supplied the Algerians with Scorpion armoured scout vehicles. See *Turkish Daily News*, 2 June 1995.

[54] See TRT TV, 3 January in BBC/SWB/EE, 5 January 1995, and Reuter's report, datelined Doha in *Saudi Gazette*, 8 January 1995.

[55] The Ras Laffan Liquefied Gas Company (Rasgas) is a joint venture consisting of the Qatar General Petroleum Company and Mobil, designed to produce 10 m. tons of LNG each year.

[56] The timing of the deal suggests that it had more to do with Egypt's desire to snub Israel and its idea of regional (i.e. Israel oriented) economic integration, and a Turkish desire to play to an American gallery—Washington being the leading supporter of the four MENA summits—than a serious intention to cut and implement a deal.

[57] See *Financial Times Middle East Energy* (Egypt Profile), no. 14, 2 April 1998.

[58] *Turkish Daily News*, 6 May 1995.

controversial visit to Tehran in August 1996. The context in which the agreement was forged, coming as it did just a few days after the signing into US law of the Iran–Libya Sanctions Act (ILSA), politicised what was actually a rather prosaic issue.

GAP and cross border water issues

If the development of a gas-oriented electric power sector was the priority in the 1990s, Turkey's insatiable pursuit of new energy inputs had already seen the beginning of the exploitation of the country's underdeveloped south-east in the 1960s. Over time an ambitious programme for the exploitation of the waters of the Euphrates (and subsequently the Tigris[59]) river[60] through the construction of a series of large dams and the installation of associated hydro-electric power plants was developed. As these plans came to be implemented the strategy began to have implications for the downstream riparian states which also had economic and ecological interests in the waters: Syria and Iraq, in the case of the Euphrates river, on which the Keban Dam, the first of Turkey's major dams, was located; for the Tigris river, Iraq.

---

[59] The Tigris river is less important to Turkey, especially as far as hydro electric power is concerned, because of the elevation of the two main rivers. However, there is a dam building programme on the Tigris as well as the Euphrates, and this includes the planned Ilısu Dam, which has been the subject of considerable international controversy for environmental, social, archaeological, and inter-state reasons in the 1990s and the 2000s. For two contrasting perspectives on the Ilısu Dam see Prof. Doğan Altınbilek, 'The Ilısu Dam Project' in *Water and Development in South-East Anatolia. Essays on the Ilısu Dam and GAP* (Turkish Embassy, London, 2000) and Ann Treneman, '"Oh yes, we're going to build the dam"', *The Times*, April 17 2000.

[60] For general background on the two river basins and the overall context of the wider water issue in the Middle East see: Thomas Naff and Ruth Matson, *Water in the Middle East: Conflict or Cooperation* (Westview Press, Boulder, CO, 1984); Natasha Beschorner, *Water and Instability in the Middle East* (IISS Adelphi Paper 273, London, 1992); John R. Kolars and Wm. A. Mitchell, *The Euphrates River and The Southeast Anatolia Development Project* (Southern Illinois University Press, Carbondale, 1991); Greg Shapland, *Rivers of Discord: International Water Disputes in the Middle East* (Hurst, London, 1997).

The concerns of the downstream states increasingly related to the cross border flow of the rivers. As Gün Kut has argued, the loose arrangements that prevailed for the rivers worked well enough, but only as long as the waters were used at a minimal level.[61] This happy circumstance had come to an end by the mid 1960s, when an early version of a trilateral dialogue discovered that aggregate utilisation goals amounted to one and a half times the average flow of the river. By the mid 1970s the large scale exploitation of the Euphrates by Syria and Turkey had become a reality, with the completion of the Tabqa and Keban dams respectively, within a year of each other.[62] Almost immediately the issue erupted into a foreign policy controversy for the three states concerned, as the simultaneous impounding of the waters took place at a time of drought.[63]

Downstream concerns increased as Turkey's ideas on the development of its rivers grew, and in 1977 the strategy developed into an integrated programme packaged as the South-east Anatolian Project (*Güneydoğu Anadolu Projesi*-GAP).[64] Together with the energy strategy, the GAP also envisaged the extensive irrigation of agricultural

---

[61] Gün Kut, 'Burning Waters: The Hydropolitics of the Euphrates and Tigris', *New Perspectives on Turkey*, no. 9, fall 1993, p. 3.

[62] In Turkey's case, the preliminary surveying of the Keban dam site and the establishment of gauging stations dates back to 1936, which confirms that the exploitation of the Euphrates is not a recent idea in Turkey. I am grateful to Kerem Öktem for bringing this point to my attention and indeed for his re-evaluation of the Keban Dam in comparative perspective. See 'The Power of Dams: Great Infrastructure Projects and State Politics in the Middle East' (unpublished MST dissertation, Oxford, 2001).

[63] It should be noted that the resulting controversies were far from being exclusively Arab versus Turkish. Indeed, on this occasion the most intensive clashes were between Iraq and Syria over the filling of Lake Asad. This issue helped to contribute to a decline in bilateral relations that included not merely furious diplomatic exchanges, but also an intensified propaganda war, the massing of troops on the common border and the provision of assistance for dissident groups. However, it should be noted that many commentators are sceptical about the notion of inter-state conflict exclusively as a product of a struggle for water, as opposed to water being just one symptom of wider political hostilities. For instance, see Naff and Matson, op. cit., p. 101, and its description of the 1974–5 Iraqi-Syrian hostilities as a 'Water Crisis', p. 93.

[64] For a semi-official description of the GAP project see Ali İhsan Bağiş, *Southeastern Anatolia Project. The Cradle of Civilisation Regenerated* (Gelişim Yayınları/Interbank, Istanbul, 1989).

land in the massive Harran Plain, using the waters of the largest of its proposed dams on the Euphrates, the Atatürk Dam.[65] The completion of the Atatürk Dam in 1989 gave Turkey the ability to make a major impact on the volume of Euphrates water flowing downstream, with the expected capacity of the Urfa irrigation tunnels capable of channelling up to one-third of the river's flow. Turkey's controversial filling of the Atatürk Dam reservoir in January 1990, with its profound though temporary impact on the flow, caused consternation in Syria,[66] as it was perceived to be a demonstration of the hydropower that Turkey now enjoyed. As well as exacerbating the issue of cross border flows this also raised a further issue for the downstream riparians of the quality of the water that would flow across their borders, mass irrigation in concentrated areas of commercial agriculture routinely causing fears of degradation, especially through growing salinity.

It was against this background of the growing exploitation of the rivers and the rapid transformation of the waters from a plentiful to a scarce resource that Iraq, Syria and Turkey formally came together to discuss the issue. A Joint Technical Committee (JTC) was established in 1982 to review the situation, though meetings at both official and ministerial levels invariably ended in deadlock. There were three areas of disagreement where the three states found themselves unable to transcend their national interests: on how to define the nature of the problem (waters of the Euphrates against the combined basins of the Euphrates and Tigris); on the basic concept that should determine who gets what (sharing versus allocation); on how to judge the needs of the three riparian states (self-declaration versus objective assessment),[67] in all three cases Turkey favouring the

---

[65] The assertion has been made that Syria only began supporting the PKK as a response to the Turkish decision to begin construction of the Atatürk Dam. See for example, the lecture by Israeli PhD student Arnon Medzini, School of Oriental and African Studies, London, 16 October 1992.

[66] Turkey had compensated for the low throughput of water during the filling of the reservoir by releasing larger than usual flows in advance. This, however, did not allay the fears of the Syrians. For a brief description of the crisis see Philip Robins, *Turkey and the Middle East* (Pinter/RIIA, London, 1991), pp. 90–2.

[67] Presentation made by Turkish hydropolitics specialist Prof. İlter Turan at a seminar on the Ilısu Dam at the Turkish ambassador's residence, London, 17 February 2000.

latter approach. There were, as Greg Shapland has succinctly concluded, 'meetings, but not of minds'.[68]

Against such a backdrop, Ankara unilaterally pledged in 1987 to ensure that an annual average of 500 cubic metres per second (cusecs) of Euphrates water would flow across the border with Syria,[69] pending a final agreement on the matter. In its defence the Turkish side argued that the establishment of a network of big dams on its side would actually facilitate its ability to implement such a pledge and to minimise seasonal fluctuations for the downstream states. Ankara further argued that its pressing need for electric power meant that Turkey's interests demanded that a steady throughput of water should continue to flow in order to power the generators; the notion of restricting flows as an instrument of political leverage would therefore be costly and hence undesirable.[70]

---

[68] See Greg Shapland, op. cit., p. 118.

[69] Because of the sensitivity of the subject Turkey scrupulously calculates the flow every month, with adjustments being made the following month if the 500 cusecs average minimum is undershot. Interview with senior personnel, Birecik dam, 31 March 2000. Though Turkey remains committed to honouring this figure and the Syrian side is noticeably more relaxed about the issue than it was a decade earlier, the 1987 undertaking remains essentially a gentleman's agreement.

[70] While these points were convincing enough and sincerely made (indeed, the Turks have been as good as their word since 1990, both in not restricting the water flow as an instrument of leverage and in maintaining the 500 cusecs guarantee), they have not prevented Damascus from fearing the worst, especially when Turkish public diplomacy has strayed from a disciplined path. For example, in summer 1992 prime minister Demirel made a statement in which he referred to water as being a natural resource like oil. The subsequent reaction in the Syrian capital was described by one leading Turkish journalist as being a 'hysterical mood' (Hasan Cemal in *Sabah*, 3 August 1992), as the Turkish ambassador, Uğur Ziyal, was summoned to the Syrian Foreign Ministry on two occasions. Coming just after a semi-official visit to Istanbul by President Herzog of Israel, the Syrians feared a Turkish-Israeli-American conspiracy to use the Euphrates against them. A further example of an unfortunate public statement came in an article by Turkey's otherwise highly respected ambassador to the OECD, Orhan Güvenen. In what may have been a typo or a Freudian slip, an article published under his name in 1994 stated: 'The headwaters of the Tigris and Euphrates lie on Turkish oil [*sic*].' See his 'A Frame Approach to Economic Development and Peace in the Middle East Through Cooperation on Natural Resources, Trade and Joint Ventures', *Dış Politika*, vol. XVIII, 1994, p. 125.

In order to try to move the issue forward, the Turkish side unveiled a three stage plan in 1984,[71] which largely continues to be the basis of the Turkish position a decade and a half later.[72] The plan was a holistic attempt to address the water situation from an overall demand and supply perspective, crucially taking into account the larger economic contexts in which national aggregate demand was calculated. If from a Turkish point of view the plan represented 'a sort of concealed compromise', more typical of a supra-governmental body than a nation state,[73] for Iraq and Syria the plan was unacceptable because it was perceived to move the focus from the equitable division of a scarce resource into an evaluation of sectoral practices in the downstream states. For Baghdad and Damascus alike the three stage plan was nothing but a diversion. the plan has therefore never been seriously considered, let alone implemented.

Meanwhile, the overall trilateral consultative context was enfeebled in the aftermath of the Gulf crisis. This was partly for political reasons, the fact that Syria and Turkey had played important parts in the confrontation of Iraq jeopardising the early resumption of talks.[74] It was also partly because of the radically changed public policy agenda in Iraq resulting from the impact of coalition bombing and economic sanctions. The Euphrates water issue diminished in importance for Iraq, which was now struggling with more pressing demands such as keeping domestic power generation going, trying to maintain the quality of potable water and managing an economy in a state of near collapse. Lastly, it became more difficult to convene the JTC after 1993, when Turkey announced that it would proceed with the

---

[71] The 'Three Staged Plan for Optimum, Equitable and Reasonable Utilization of the Transboundary Water Courses of the Euphrates-Tigris Basin' was unveiled at the November 1984 meeting of the JTC. The three stages were: the exchange and verification of hydrological and meteorological data in order to establish the exact flow of the river at certain points; achievement of a consensus on the irrigable land potential in all three states; and development of a master plan on the basis of the preceding two stages to include a water budget based on agreed allocation models.

[72] Turan presentation (note 69).

[73] Kut (note 63), p. 13.

[74] There were 15 meetings of the Joint Technical Committee and two ministerial meetings prior to 1990; there was, however, no meeting of the JTC between March 1990 and September 1992 owing to the Gulf crisis.

construction of the Birecik Dam, the latest of the big dam projects on the Euphrates, the building of which was completed early in the new century. The 1990s were therefore a barren decade as far as negotiations on the water issue were concerned.

There was, however, one exception to this general context of diplomatic inaction during the 1990s. It came in January 1993, with the visit of prime minister Demirel to Damascus. It was announced at the end of the visit that the two sides would work out a 'final solution' to the Euphrates flow question, with quotas to be allocated to all sides by the end of the year.[75] With Iraq and Syria having already agreed a percentage division of their cross border flows in 1989,[76] the statement reflected the Syrian concern to extract a guaranteed flow in perpetuity from the Turks. Though the respective foreign ministries were charged with remaining seized of the matter, no further progress took place, the year ending with a crisis in bilateral relations over Syrian support for the PKK. That Damascus was disappointed by the outcome was evident in the statement of the Syrian foreign minister, Faruk al-Sharaa, at one of the Iranian, Syrian and Turkish tripartite meetings in February 1994, when he accused Turkey of changing its mind over water.[77]

The fading hopes for an accommodation between Syria and Turkey on the Euphrates waters have reflected the growing power disparities between the two countries as the post-Cold War era has extended. There may be no formal accord on water, but Turkey has forged ahead with the construction of dams and their utilisation for hydroelectric power unabated, eschewing calls for restraint on the grounds of national sovereignty. By the turn of the century 62% of planned energy generation from the GAP programme was underway, with a further 12% of capacity under construction,[78] the former figure

---

[75] BBC/SWB/ME, 22 January 1993.

[76] This took place at a JTC meeting in Baghdad in April 1989, under which Syria pledged to release to Iraq 58% of the Euphrates waters flowing across its border with Turkey.

[77] See Sharaa cited by Mehmet Ali Birand, *Sabah*, 7 February 1994, reprinted in *Turkish Daily News*, 8 February 1994.

[78] Presentation by Dr Olcay Ünver, President of the GAP Regional Development Administration, at a seminar on the Ilısu Dam at the Turkish ambassador's residence, London, 17 February 2000.

comprising 12.4% of Turkey's total energy production, hydraulic and thermal.[79] In 1995 Turkey began to use Euphrates waters for irrigation purposes, and by early 2000 some 11% of the target irrigation area (or around 201,000 hectares) was under irrigation, with a further 10% being developed.[80] Turkey has felt sufficiently sure of itself on the water issue to oppose (when it was in a minority of three with Burundi and China) and then not to ratify the 1997 Convention on the Law of the Non-navigational Uses of International Watercourses, elements of which are problematic for the Turkish position on Euphrates waters.[81] Ankara may have been as good as its word in the delivery of minimum annual flows, but the power disparities between the two states reflected in the water situation are nevertheless palpable.

However, while Turkey may hold the whip hand over the utilisation of Euphrates water, the situation is markedly less one-sided as far as other areas of the GAP's activities are concerned. By the end of the programme 1.7 million hectares of land will have been brought under irrigated agriculture, boosting the commercial output of the sector. Produce as diverse as barley, cotton, lentils and vegetables is expected to see a big increase in cultivation and production, while a range of new products like soybeans, groundnuts and oilseed will be planted as second crops. In turn, this expansion in agriculture is expected to service a greatly expanded agro-industrial sector, which would add value to the primary production in the region area.[82] Agro-industrial output as varied as frozen, dried and canned fruit

---

[79] *Latest State in [sic] Southeastern Anatolia Project* (Prime Minister's Office/GAP Regional Development Administration, Ankara, September 1999), p. 7. This was actually the figure at the end of June 1999.

[80] Ünver presentation (note 80).

[81] Ankara's objections to the Convention appear to fall into two parts: first, that the Convention moves beyond the establishment of general principles to lay down what may be considered to be specific rules regarding dispute settlement, to the disadvantage of the Turkish position; second, that the Convention does not refer to and hence entrench the notion of sovereign control over water courses, and so helps to weaken a central plank of the Turkish argument. For a discussion of the Convention and Turkey's position see Dr H. Bülent Olcay, 'The Euphrates-Tigris Watercourse Controversy and the 1997 Convention on the Law of the Non-Navigational Uses of International Watercourses', *Dış Politika* nos. 3–4, 1997.

[82] *GAP Action Plan 1995* (Prime Minister's/GAP Regional Development Administration, Ankara, 1995), p. iii.

and vegetables, vegetable oil, herbs and spices, semolina and macaroni and even wine are envisaged for the region.[83] With the infrastructural investment largely being provided by the Turkish state, two elements essential to the future success of this strategy will be project investment and the discovery of new markets, and both of these have potential to impact upon foreign relations.

With much of the infrastructure of irrigation still to be completed it is early days even to make assessments about the prospects of foreign investment in the GAP region. Turkey would very much like to attract FDI from abroad in its newly transforming region. In 1999 GAP-GIDEM, a network of entrepreneurial advice centres, reported that it had received initial approaches from some 200 companies from fifteen countries about investment opportunities. While countries concerned included Syria and Yemen, it was with approaches from Israel, as well as the US and a handful of leading European countries, that the Turkish authorities were most excited. Israel was regarded with great interest partly because of its acknowledged expertise in agriculture, agro-industries and water resource management in similar climactic circumstances, and partly because the growing bilateral relationship in the 1990s has created an upbeat atmosphere. From a practical point of view this sense of expectation was apparently not misplaced. By the turn of the century, Turkey had already received $120 million in grants from Israel for water activities related to the GAP.[84] In March 2000 an Israeli company was one of only a handful of foreign concerns negotiating in earnest on a joint venture investment in the GAP region, in this case a 20,000 hectare development in the western part of the region.[85]

---

[83] *Southeastern Anatolia Project Investment Opportunities* (Ministry of Foreign Affairs, Ankara, 2000), p. 17.

[84] Answers to questions, Ünver presentation (note 80). An insight into the place of Israel in the mindset of the GAP's senior management can be seen when Ünver stated in the main presentation: 'We also collaborate with international agencies and foreign governments that vary from Canada to Israel, from France to the United States'; in other words, with the exception of Israel, they hardly vary at all. See 'The Southeastern Anatolia Project (GAP): an Overview' in *Water and Development in Southeastern Anatolia: Essays on the Ilısu Dam and GAP* (Turkish Embassy, London, 2000), p. 20.

[85] Interview with GAP Regional Development Administration personnel, Atatürk Dam research station, 30 March 2000.

If it is still early days for the establishment of new projects, the eventual destination of the new GAP region output is even less certain. Indeed, there is still some uncertainty on the Turkish side as to how much of the increase in agricultural and agri-industrial production will be available for export,[86] in view of the large and expanding domestic market. It has, nevertheless, always been a working assumption of the GAP programme that there was a large and growing market for locally grown foodstuffs in the Middle East,[87] and one which for Turkey had been increasing irrespective of its regional irrigation plans, especially in the product areas of fresh fruit and vegetables. The fact that the GAP was expected to transform Turkey's market potential in the Middle East even for the export of cereals[88] underlines the extent to which the Middle East has tended to be regarded as the obvious market outlet for a rejuvenated south-east. Those assumptions were still being made at the turn of the century.[89] The free zone at Mardin, for example, was established with the markets of the neighbouring Middle Eastern states in mind.[90] It is as the steep growth in agricultural produce and agro-industry output from the GAP region becomes imminent, and assuming that its commercial success rests on access to neighbouring markets, that Ankara will feel the incentive growing to look again at the issue of cooperation with its downstream neighbours.

---

[86] For instance, a technical report published in August 1992 concluded that: 'Contrary to optimistic expectations, not much will be left over for a dramatic expansion of exports'. See *Agricultural Commodities Marketing Survey. Planning of Crop Pattern and Integration and Crop Patterns Studies* (Prime Minister's Office/GAP Regional Development Administration, Ankara, 1992), p. 33.

[87] See the illuminatingly entitled chapter eight, 'GAP and the Trade War Over Middle Eastern Agricultural Markets', in Bağış, *Southeast Anatolia Project*, op. cit., p. 223.

[88] ibid. p. 230.

[89] See, for example, *Financial Times*, 26 February 1999, in which the Middle East and North Africa are described as being 'prime candidates for increased food exports', or *Financial Times* Survey on 'Turkey: Banking and Investment', 20 November 2000.

[90] The sub-title on the front of the free zone brochure reads *Ortadoğu Pazarına Açılan Kapınız* ('A Gateway to the Middle East Markets' [their translation]), and it carries a map with arrows pointing to Iran, Iraq, Jordan, Kuwait, Saudi Arabia and Syria.

Before the 1970s economic and commercial factors hardly intruded at all into the forging and development of foreign policy. This situation began to change owing to external factors with the quadrupling of the oil price. The process was then greatly accelerated as a result of internal factors, notably Özal's sweeping economic policy reforms, which replaced Turkey's autarkic strategy with one of export orientation. Consequently, from the early 1980s onwards, economic issues became increasingly important in Turkish foreign policymaking.

Though Özal himself was only a momentary foreign policy player in the 1990s, the trajectory on which he set Turkey was maintained and reinforced throughout the remainder of the decade. Consequently, economic matters have had a critical impact in key areas of foreign policy. Increasingly Ankara has had to consider issues of general trade, the export of contracting services and specific areas of imports like energy imports in its foreign relations. In the future, the export of agro-industrial products from the GAP region may join this list.

This in turn has had an important impact on the geographical orientation of foreign ties. With respect to the EU, commercial relations have created a third pillar of bilateral relations, and one which looks relatively robust compared to the older pillars of security relations and identity politics. Indeed, it is important to note that EU-Turkey commercial relations began to take off at a time of extended strains in political ties. With respect to Russia, the development of a clutch of different types of economic relations, with the natural gas trade at its heart, has helped to create convergences and complementarities at a time when bilateral relations were often under periods of great political strain. The fact that the gas relationship has endured for more than fourteen years is suggestive of the value placed on it by both parties. But economic issues have also helped to exacerbate foreign policy difficulties as well as ameliorate them, the outstanding case of the Euphrates and the Tigris rivers being a case in point.

Part III
TURKISH FOREIGN POLICY IN ACTION

7

TURKEY AND ISRAEL: EMBATTLED ALLIES IN THE 'NEW MIDDLE EAST'

As recently as 1991 Israeli–Turkish relations were low key and constrained, with diplomatic representation formally confined to second secretary status, the product of Ankara's protest against Israel's declaration of a unified Jerusalem as its capital in 1980. Yet by the beginning of 1999 the relationship had been transformed.[1] An Israeli–Turkish axis had emerged, developing so far and so rapidly as to make a profound impact on the power relations and psychology of power in the region.

Many have attested to the profundity of the impact of the Israeli–Turkish relationship. From the Arab viewpoint it has been called

---

[1] So much so that commentators have struggled to find and agree on the right terminology to describe it. For Ian Lesser in *NATO Looks South*, 'The Israeli–Turkish relationship is multidimensional and evidently "strategic"' (RAND, Santa Monica, 2000), p. 17. For Efraim Inbar in his unpublished paper, *The Turkish-Israeli Entente: The New Power Alignment in the Middle East*, the relationship is an 'entente'. For Meliha Benli Altunışık in 'Turkish Policy toward Israel' in Alan Makovsky and Sabri Sayarı (eds), *Turkey's New World. Changing Dynamics in Turkish Foreign Policy*, the relationship is 'an alignment' (WINEP, Washington, DC, 2000), p. 69. For this author the relationship is still less than an alliance, with its emphasis on formally agreed mutual defence and deterrent arrangements (as illustrated by the October 1998 Syrian–Turkish crisis, when Israel distanced itself from the confrontation); but it is also more than an entente, with its exclusively diplomatic focus, lack of policy detail and emphasis on a more limited rapprochement, regardless of how cordial. Perhaps then the term 'axis' approximates to the most appropriate, with its emphasis on common values leading to defence

239

'the most important politico-strategic development [in the Middle East] since the Gulf war'.[2] From the Israeli side it is 'the most important story of the decade',[3] 'a major change in the geopolitics of the Middle East',[4] and even the most important regional realignment since Sadat went to Jerusalem.[5]

It is not just the distance travelled by Turkey between these two positions over this eight year period that is worthy of note. It can be argued that neither position actually conforms to what one would have expected Ankara's foreign policy towards Israel to be. In the wake of the regional turmoil of the mid to late 1950s, a turmoil in which Turkey not only found itself in the midst but also to which it was a significant contributor, Ankara decided largely to disengage from the politics of the Middle East. It consequently evolved a handful of key principles to guide its policies. These included non-interference in disputes between states and the development of bilateral relations with all states in the region.[6] Neither of these, however, has provided an explanatory, let alone a predictive guide to the mood swings in Turkey's relations with Israel.

Policy predicament

A leading policy dilemma for Turkey since the onset of the end of the Cold War has been in what way and at what pace to improve its relations with the state of Israel. In facing this question Turkey has

---

cooperation and the establishment of a pivot around which other states (like Jordan) might cluster.

[2] H.J. Agha and A.S. Khalidi in 'The Struggle for Iraq: Saddam and After', still unpublished report undertaken under the auspices of St Antony's College, Oxford, p. 175.

[3] Headline in the *Jerusalem Post*, 14 June 1996, referring to Israeli ties with Turkey.

[4] Former Israeli defence and foreign minister Moshe Arens, cited in 'The Demise of the "New Middle East"', a special report of the Foundation for Middle East Peace, Autumn 1998, p. 2.

[5] Professor Efraim Inbar, Director of the Begin-Sadat Center for Strategic Studies at Bar-Ilan University, speaking at Chatham House, 17 July 1998.

[6] For a Turkish perspective on the major principles governing Turkey's Middle East policy, see Seyfi Taşhan, 'Contemporary Turkish Policies in the Middle East: Prospects and Constraints', *Dış Politika* (Foreign Policy), vol. XII, nos 1–2, June 1985.

not found itself in a unique position. A raft of Arab countries, from Qatar and Oman in the Gulf to Tunisia and Morocco in North Africa, have faced a broadly similar dilemma; a number of sub-Saharan African countries which, like Turkey, severed or substantively reduced their ties with Israel in the 1970s and 1980s have also faced the same issue. Yet such comparisons simply add to the peculiar nature of the predicament: Turkey never subscribed to the practical or rhetorical hostility to Israel of the Arab World; and as a state, Turkey has enjoyed greater coherence, stability and strength than most of the new states of black Africa.

The key to understanding the Turkish predicament of how and how fast to normalise relations with Israel lies in recent historical experience. That historical experience, ironically, had little to do with bilateral relations. For the record, Turkey opposed the UN's 1947 plan to create two states in historic Palestine, thereby opposing the creation of a Jewish state, but that was based on the fear of the spread of Soviet power, in the expectation that Israel would come to be an entrée for Moscow into the region. Hence Turkey's calculation had much more to do with the emerging politics of global confrontation than with specifically regional interests.

Turkey's disinterest in the early stages of the emerging Arab-Israeli conflict, in turn, made it easy to execute a policy *volte face*. Again, global rather than regional interests prevailed. In pursuit of a strategic relationship with the West in the emerging Cold War, Turkey allowed its opposition to soften. In March 1949 Turkey formally recognised Israel, conveniently citing the changed circumstances emerging out of the first Arab-Israeli conflict. With the Arabs weak and distracted by their independence struggles, the new approach appeared virtually cost free. In 1950 Turkey's recognition was formalised with the appointment of a minister plenipotentiary to Tel Aviv; this *de jure* recognition conveniently contrasted with Greece, which limited its recognition to the *de facto* level. In 1952 Israel and Turkey upgraded relations by exchanging ambassadors.

But if Turkey's Middle Eastern policy had been relatively autonomous and cost free in the late 1940s and early 1950s, the regional context was to change profoundly after 1952, coinciding, combustibly, with a period of greater assertiveness in Turkish policy towards the region. Turkey allowed its participation in the bipolar struggle between the West and the Soviet bloc to inform its regional strategy in the 1950s. It consequently pursued a Middle East policy which was ill informed and lacked judgement. Rather than attuning itself to the national aspirations of an Arab world grappling with the last vestiges of European colonialism, Turkey insisted on seeing the new politics of the region in terms of a strictly East-West paradigm. Consequently, Ankara tried to inflict the anti-Communist Baghdad Pact on an obviously reluctant region.[7] With unrest in Jordan and later revolution in Iraq in 1958 leaving the Arab element of the strategy in tatters, Menderes' Turkey lurched towards Ben Gurion's ethnically informed strategy of an anti-Arab 'periphery' pact.[8] Though the periphery pact never appears to have been formalised, the cognitive convergence that it represents identifies it as the high water mark of Israeli-Turkish relations over their first four decades.

The downfall of Menderes and his government allowed the Turkish establishment to draw a line under the disasters of the previous five or more years. There was a grateful return to Atatürk's strategic compass, with its bias towards the West and its reticence towards all points east and south. The inevitable consequence of not being drawn into the volatile and opaque politics of the Middle East was the devaluation of relations with Israel.

This trend was accentuated by two further developments, Cyprus and petrodollars. By 1964 Cyprus had emerged as a major issue in Turkish foreign policy, following the breakdown in the power-sharing agreement two years earlier. In its pursuit of diplomatic support at the UN over Cyprus, Turkey began to take the newly emerging developing world of states more seriously. For Ankara, the numbers game began to matter, and the Arabs offered more potential votes than solitary Israel.

A decade later, Ankara found the petro-diplomacy of Saudi Arabia and the new-found wealth of the oil producing states of the Middle East in general to be an irresistable policy force. The advent of Arab

---

[7] And it was Turkey, and not Britain as the conventional wisdom would have it, that tried to inflict the alliance on the region in spite of the increasingly ominous omens. Thus it was Ankara that tried to bounce Jordan into the alliance in 1956 rather than a reluctant General Templer; similarly, it was the efforts of Turkey which did so much to persuade Iran into membership.

[8] Ben Gurion actually paid a secret visit to Ankara in August 1958 in order to try to cement this relationship. See Inbar, *The Turkish-Israeli Entente*, op. cit.

financial power was to exert a strong psychological effect upon Turkey. This was to inhibit Turkish policy towards the Middle East for the next two decades. Consequently, in January 1975 Turkey recognised the Palestine Liberation Organisation as the sole legitimate representatives of the Palestinians, and in November 1975 it voted in favour of the UN General Assembly resolution equating Zionism with racism. It was against a backdrop of oil prices again rising, and in spite of Egypt's emerging separate peace with Israel, that on 2 December 1980 Turkey 'vigorously protested' at the Israeli Knesset's decision to declare united Jerusalem its eternal capital by reducing diplomatic representation to Second Secretary level.[9]

With the period 1979–84 marking the nadir in Israeli-Turkish relations,[10] by the time of the beginning of the end of the Cold War the only way was up. The initial improvement in bilateral relations from 1986 onwards was slow and tentative, in line with the traditional caution of Turkish foreign policy. Indeed, there was some wisdom in such an approach, as a more impetuous pace might have been damaged by the onset of the Palestinian 'uprising', the *intifada*. Nevertheless, there was a palpable sense of psychological inhibition, born of the trauma of the Baghdad Pact and the linear nature of policy since the early 1960s, that appeared to reduce the Turkish policy choices towards the Middle East to that of an Oman or Tunisia.

Successive thresholds passed in the early 1990s, during the Gulf crisis and as a result of the Madrid and Oslo Arab-Israeli peacemaking, helped Turkey to disgard its inhibitions. With the Arab world weakened and divided as never before and the oil price at real pre-1973 levels, Turkish policy towards Israel was at last free of the constraints of the previous three decades. In such a context, bilateral ties thrived, and did so, in contrast to most previous exercises in interstate relationships in the region, on a wide foundation embracing diplomacy, politics, tourism, higher education, intelligence and the military.

[9] For discussion of Turkey's motives in taking this step see Mahmut Bali Aykan, 'The Palestinian Question in Turkish Foreign Policy From the 1950s to the 1990s', *International Journal of Middle Eastern Studies*, no. 25, 1993, pp. 100–2.

[10] Debra Lois Shulman, 'Periphery to Prominence: The Evolution of Turkish-Israeli Relations, 1948–1998', unpublished M. Phil. dissertation, Oxford, April 1999, p. 68.

But still there remained unaddressed the question of the final aim, or at least the prudent level of relations to be wisely enjoyed in the late 1990s. It was at that point that the Turkish military miscalculated. Ignorant or insensitive to the undulating nature of the peace process, and distracted and preoccupied by domestic ideological developments, the Turkish General Staff used the relationship with Israel as a masculine demonstration of its primacy in the strategic orientation of the Turkish state, and as a deterrent to any Islamist politicians at home who were at all inclined to change the nature of foreign relations. The result was the distortion of a broad-based bilateral relationship into what increasingly appeared to be a defence-dominated axis, and a surge in regional tension and unease born of the open secrecy and exclusive nature of the agreement.

Subterranean relations, 1986–93

In the same way that Turkey came to regard the US as taking it for granted in the early 1960s, so Turkey began to bridle at the complacency of the Arab world in the early 1980s. Both experiences helped to precipitate a change in direction. Promises of Arab financial assistance had failed to materialise. No Arab state was prepared to take the plunge and join Turkey in recognising the so-called 'Turkish Republic of Northern Cyprus', which was declared in 1983. Moreover, the Arab world seemed disinclined to take any serious interest in Turkey, its structures of power and its core foreign policy interests.[11] Such offhandedness had in the mid 1980s begun to be increasingly risky. By 1986 the oil price slippage of earlier in the decade had turned into a wholesale rout; this more than anything drew attention to the fragility of Arab power.

Simultaneously, the cost of improving ties with Israel was falling. Israel completed its withdrawal from all of Lebanon, save the so-called 'security zone' in the south, in 1985. By this stage, incremental steps were being taken to reintegrate Egypt into the Arab fold, without obliging it to relinquish its separate peace with Israel. It was

---

[11] For a comparatively rare piece of collective self-criticism see the Arab commentator Arfan Nezameddin writing on the strategic shortcomings of the Arabs in relation to Turkey in *al-Hayat*, and reproduced in *Mid-East Mirror*, 1 September 1997.

against this backdrop that Israel approached Turkey with the idea of each having a more experienced diplomat as head of its mission. Consequently, in 1985 Yehuda Millo, an Ottoman scholar turned diplomat of minister-counsellor rank, took up the position of chargé d'affaires in Ankara; in the autumn of 1986, after a suitable delay for caution, Turkey appointed Ekrem Güvendiren, a diplomat enjoying ambassadorial rank, to be its new 'Second Secretary' in Tel Aviv.

The remainder of the 1980s was a period of incremental improvement in bilateral relations between the two countries. In 1986 the Turkish national carrier, Türk Hava Yolları, began direct flights between Israel and Turkey. In the same year the Israelis added a second diplomat to their mission in Ankara. Through an adroit series of small measures[12] the Israeli side built up the status and profile of its diplomatic representation. In 1987 the two countries resumed meetings of their foreign ministers in New York at the UN General Assembly. By 1988 Turkish MPs, who had been strongly discouraged from visiting Israel two years earlier, were keen to make such trips. Access to the Turkish military, always problematic for small missions, became increasingly easy; by 1989 the Israeli representative was being received by the chief of the general staff, and the notion of military co-operation, especially in the area of joint defence industries production, had taken root. Ankara was also being helpful diplomatically in passing messages from Israel to third parties.

As Israel set itself the objective of building up an 'infrastructure of normalcy', anything became possible as long as it was low key and uncontroversial, and the Turkish side was given the time to feel its way. An excellent example of this was the political dialogue, which was initiated in 1986. The two sides built up the nature of the exchanges in terms of venue, agenda and levels of representation over a two-year period. At first, the meetings took place on neutral

---

[12] For example, both the senior and the junior Israeli diplomats in the Ankara mission were promoted during their postings in the second half of the 1980s, and the Turkish side made no objection. The former was promoted from minister-counsellor to minister rank in 1988; the latter was formally promoted twice from attaché to second secretary to first secretary, although the attaché rank was a presentational convenience in recognition of the level of diplomatic representation that prevailed. By 1990 the notion of second secretary representation had become a quaint anomaly.

territory in Geneva, were confined to bilateral issues and were limited in terms of participation to the respective Foreign Ministry research centres. Meetings then moved in stages to Istanbul and then to Ankara; participation was expanded to involve junior diplomats, then directors-general, rising finally to be headed by deputy foreign ministers. By the culmination of this process, a nucleus of a strategic dialogue had been commenced with a long agenda which ranged over the panorama of regional issues and included Russian policy towards the Middle East.

In spite of the incremental improvement in ties in the second half of the 1980s, these remained essentially subterranean. Senior Israelis realised that bilateral relations with Turkey were mortgaged to the Arab-Israeli dispute, and care was shown in ensuring that Turkey was not pressured or embarrassed. If further evidence was needed of the dangers of too high a profile in Israeli-Turkish relations it came in September 1986, with the Neve Shalom synagogue massacre in Istanbul.[13] Consequently Israel contented itself with discreetly improving bilateral ties, while enticing Turkey in the direction of better relations, notably through indicating its potential usefulness to Turkey in Washington.

Evidence of improving ties on a broad front is widespread from this time. There was the beginnings of a take-off in bilateral trade, officially worth some $65 million in 1988, but in reality probably double this amount, with Turkish businessmen preferring to use front companies in Europe, such was their residual fear of the Arab secondary boycott. Similarly, joint venture concerns were established, largely in the agricultural and high tech fields, but with few functioning openly.[14] Intelligence co-operation, especially with respect to Lebanon, flourished.[15]

In Washington, Israel came increasingly to assist Turkey between 1987 and 1989, though this was mostly performed indirectly rather than through direct advocacy. Thus, for example, the Israeli lobby

---

[13] In this attack by an Arab suicide squad, twenty-two worshippers were killed; it was described as the first such event in the five centuries that the Jewish community had lived in the city.

[14] Interview with senior Israeli official, 14 March 1989.

[15] Interview with senior US diplomat, 9 May 1990, confirmed in interview with senior Israeli diplomat, Jerusalem, 11 October 1993.

extended advice to the Turks on how to establish their own lobby activity, though this was adjudged not to be a success owing to the impatience of the Turks. Arguably, the greatest achievement in Washington for Turkey during this period was the alteration of the traditionally pro-Greek stance of the Israeli lobby to a position of neutrality between Greece and Turkey. In turn, Israel also increasingly urged Jewish groups in the United States not to support the Armenian lobby in its pursuit of Turkey for the mass deaths of Armenians in Anatolia during the First World War. The pro-Israel lobby is even said to have played a role in actively assisting Turkey in the narrow defeat of an Armenian inspired draft resolution to the Senate in 1989 denouncing the massacres,[16] although the influence of the American-Israel Public Affairs Committee in this activity should not be exaggerated.[17]

The low key nature of relations was at least partially vindicated with the outbreak of the *intifada* in December 1987. The subterranean relationship meant that little adjustment had to be made in the incremental improvements which had preceded the uprising. Thus, while some, more visible areas of cultural relations were affected,[18] trade and tourism continued as before. Moreover, the low key nature of the relationship also meant that the Turks did not feel

[16] Private discussion meeting with under secretary at Turkish Ministry of Foreign Affairs, Tugay Özçeri, at Chatham House, 19 October 1989. For this and other aspects of a relationship 'flourishing at all levels' Özçeri expressed himself to be 'very grateful'.

[17] Interview with then Turkey desk officer Carolyn Huggins, US State Department, 18 April 1990, who pointed out that some of the sponsors of the Armenian resolution were big city Democrats in other words precisely the sort of figures with which AIPAC would enjoy a close relationship. General view confirmed by then US ambassador to Turkey, Morton Abramowitz, interview, 9 June 1998.

[18] The gossamer sensitivity of the Turkish foreign policy elite extended to the area of cultural diplomacy. For example, when the Ankara-based Foreign Policy Institute decided in the spring of 1990 to invite the leading Israeli academic Itamar Rabinovich (later to be a distinguished Israeli ambassador in Washington and head of the Israeli delegation to bilateral peace talks with Syria) to speak, the first time it had ever issued such an invitation to an Israeli, it deemed it prudent to clear the invitation in advance with the Foreign Ministry. The invitation was intended to indicate displeasure with the Arabs, presumably Iraq and Syria, while also restoring a modicum of even-handedness in a set of relationships perceived to have tilted too much in favour of the Arabs. Interview with the director of the FPI, Seyfi Taşhan, 7 May 1990.

obliged to use intemperate language as a way of balancing improved relations, a point which again was noted and valued by Israel.[19]

The *intifada* made the Palestinians the central focus of the Arab-Israeli issue for Turkey.[20] In its approach towards Israel and the Palestinians, Ankara tried to retain balance, and to use its endorsement as an inducement to encourage the PLO to moderate its policy. Nevertheless, Turkey's relations with Israel essentially remained in hock to the Arabs, the Turkish line being that whatever was acceptable to the majority of Arab governments would be agreeable to Ankara.[21]

The fact that the majority of Arab governments lined up with the pro-Western coalition against the Iraqi invasion of Kuwait in 1990, and then either took part in or supported the Madrid peace conference with Israel in October 1991, helped to soften the context for Israeli-Turkish relations in the early 1990s. And indeed, relations did inch forward. Thus the two countries at last re-established full, ambassadorial relations in December 1991, Ankara using as its alibi the fact that participation in the multilateral track of the peace process, which commenced with a plenary session in Moscow in January 1992, required all non-protagonist participants to have full diplomatic ties with the central parties.

In turn, President Chaim Herzog visited Istanbul in July 1992 for the quinquennial celebrations of the Ottoman Empire's acceptance of Jewish refugees fleeing Spain; Shimon Peres subsequently visited in April 1993 to attend the funeral of President Özal. A Turkish-Israeli Business Council was established in March 1993.[22] Even as Turkish-Israeli relations began to move above ground, Ankara appeared to hold back, as both trips only took place on an unofficial basis, though Herzog's did enjoy some official trappings. In spite of the fact that Egypt, with its peace treaty with Israel, had been fully rehabilitated by the Arab League in 1989, in spite of the convening of the Madrid summit and the subsequent bilateral talks between

---

[19] Interview with Israeli official (note 14).

[20] For a wider discussion of the Palestinian issue in Turkish foreign policy see Mahmut Bali Aykan, 'The Palestinian Question in Turkish Foreign Policy from the 1950s to the 1990s', *International Journal of Middle Eastern Studies*, no. 25, 1993.

[21] Interview with senior Turkish diplomat, Ankara, 15 March 1989.

[22] DEİK Bulletin, *Turkish-Israeli Relations*, January 1996.

Israel and its Arab neighbours, and in spite of the multilateral track of the peace process, which helped to normalise relations between Israel and the outer ring of Arab states, at a diplomatic level Ankara still seemed loath to move bilateral relations too far above ground. The psychological hold which the Arab World appeared to exercise over Turkish diplomacy towards Israel had still not been totally shattered.

But increasingly this rarefied diplomatic world was divorced from the practical and material realities of the relationship, which openly thrived. There had been a rapid increase in the number of Israeli tourists visiting Turkey, topping 45,000 in 1991 and rising to 160,000 a year later as cheap packages to Turkey's Mediterranean resorts became accessible to the Israeli mass market. In 1992 those Israeli tourists were estimated to have spent $250 million. Meanwhile, a large number of Turks were now working in Israel as migrant labourers,[23] as Israel sought to diversify its casual labour needs away from the Palestinian population of the Occupied Territories. Direct, recorded bilateral trade, however, tended to shadow the diplomatic track, with only a modest increase being recorded as trade volume rose from $157 to $197 to $202 million from 1991 to 1993.[24]

From mistress to wife, 1993–6

Little is known of the relationship between Israel and Turkey in the late 1950s, during the years of the 'Periphery Pact'. Turkey's insistence on the confidential nature of this relationship is one central reason for this state of affairs. One celebrated exception is the oft repeated expression of exasperation by David Ben-Gurion that Turkey treated Israel as a mistress (its wife being the Arabs) and not as a partner in a full marriage. If that was the case in the late 1950s and, as we have just seen, during the 1986–93 period, it ceased to be so in 1993. By 1993 the two countries were engaged; by 1996 they were wed.

---

[23] The official figure was nearly 3,000. In fact the real figure was 'much higher', owing to the presence of a significant number of Turks working illegally. Comments on an earlier draft by a Turkish diplomat.

[24] State Institute of Statistics, Prime Minister's, *Türkiye İstatistik Yıllığı, 1996* (Statistical Yearbook of Turkey), p. 523.

There had been some signs that Ankara was edging forward diplomatically in its relationship with Israel before the breakthrough in the Israeli-Palestinian track of the peace process at Oslo. The Turkish Foreign Ministry's deputy under-secretary, Bilgin Unan, visited Israel in October 1992, an important trip in terms of protocol. The two states exchanged visits by their respective tourism ministers, Abdülkadir Ateş and Uzi Baram, in June 1992 and July 1993. During the former, a tourism agreement was signed, the first public bilateral accord for many years, which helped to facilitate air charter traffic.

Juxtaposed with this tentative willingness to increase diplomatic interaction was the significant hurdle of the first visit to Israel by a Turkish foreign minister. The Turkish predicament somewhat resembled that of the diplomatically timid Japanese around this time, who were also agonising about how best to improve relations with Israel without spoiling their links with the Arab world. As ever, it took some time longer for the Turks to muster the *sang froid* necessary actually to go ahead with the visit, two earlier proposed trips, both of them during Hikmet Çetin's period as foreign minister, being postponed. On the second occasion the Foreign Ministry axed the Israeli leg of a regional tour at the last minute when Çetin was already in Jordan, in response to and in protest at Israel's 'Operation Accountability' in south Lebanon. Interestingly, the Turkish press expressed impatience at this excessive diplomatic sensitivity, and criticised the government,[25] a reaction which was not lost on Israeli officials. In retrospect, Ankara was shown to have been mistaken in postponing the visit. Turkey had missed a trick by not undertaking the visit shortly before the public revelation of the Oslo process at the end of August 1993, thereby failing to associate itself with a diplomatically prestigious, historic breakthrough in the Arab-Israeli peace process.

Çetin eventually paid his first visit to Israel on 13–15 November, after the Israelis and Palestinians had signed the Declaration of

---

[25] While a few commentators were inclined to give Çetin the benefit of the doubt, such as Sami Kohen who called the third cancellation 'justified to a certain extent' (*Milliyet*, 3 August 1993), others, like Ertuğrul Özkök, were having none of it, calling it a reversion to the 'timid' foreign policy of the past, and noting resentfully that Turkey had got nothing from showing solidarity with the Arabs in the past (*Hürriyet*, in *MidEast Mirror*, 30 July 1993).

Principles on the White House lawn in September 1993. Now that the Turks had finally managed to cast aside the psychological inhibitions of publicly doing business with the Israelis, the two sides embarked upon a fast and furious diplomatic love affair. The sudden surge in cordial bilateral relations should not be viewed as a surprise. The Turkish foreign policy elite had long viewed Israel as being 'like us'.[26] Elites on both sides shared political values of secularism and democracy,[27] they shared a common identification with Europe and the West, and they shared a common set of threat perceptions, from problematic neighbours to terrorism.[28] The speed with which relations improved once the initial psychological obstacles had been overcome is testimony to the importance of the notion of identity in alliances in the Middle East.[29]

When the breakthrough eventually did take place, its effects were impressive, whether measured in terms of high level visits, in which important symbolic breakthroughs occurred with a regularity almost verging on the mundane, or new bilateral agreements. To make the point, it is worth listing the high level political traffic from this time:

President Ezer Weizman visited Turkey in January 1994, the first official visit by an Israeli head of state; Shimon Peres visited Turkey in April 1994 as foreign minister; Premier Tansu Çiller visited Israel in November 1994, the first official trip to Israel by a serving Turkish prime minister (accompanied by the ministers of foreign affairs, public works and housing, energy and natural resources, agriculture and village affairs, and transport, together with one state minister, in effect nearly a quarter of the cabinet); Yossi Beilin, Israeli deputy foreign minister and close confidant of Peres, visited Turkey in May 1995;

[26] Interview with retired Ambassador Zeki Kuneralp, Istanbul, 17 May 1989.

[27] These shared values actually prompted three younger Turkish academics to develop the notion of 'like-minded states' as an important category in the Middle East sub-system, which they then, much less plausibly, tried to apply to other regional actors, Egypt, Jordan and the Palestinian entity. See Ali Çarkoğlu, Mine Eder and Kemal Kirişci, *The Political Economy of Regional Co-operation in the Middle East* (Routledge, London, 1998), pp. 1–2.

[28] Such factors have prompted Neill Lochery to write of Turkey as 'the natural choice of ally' for Israel. See 'Israel and Turkey: Deepening Ties and Strategic Implications, 1995–98', *Israel Affairs*, vol. 5, no. 1, autumn 1998, p. 45.

[29] For a detailed discussion of the issue in general, see Michael N. Barnett, 'Identity and Alliances in the Middle East' in Peter J. Katzenstein (ed.), *The Culture of National Security* (Columbia University Press, New York, 1996), pp. 400–47.

Çiller, together with state ministers Coskun Kırca and Ali Dinçer, attended Rabin's funeral in November 1995; and President Demirel went to Israel in March 1996, the first ever trip to Israel by a serving Turkish president, the earlier date for the trip the previous November having been postponed owing to the Rabin assassination. In addition, there was considerable high level traffic among officials and technical experts.[30] There was also an attempt rapidly to deepen the relationship, with, for example, opposition politicians being invited to Israel,[31] and a rash of bilateral round table meetings and academic exchanges.[32] Included among the numerous accords and agreements signed were a cultural agreement and Memorandum of Understanding during the Weizman visit; an environmental protection agreement during the Peres trip; an accord against drug trafficking, terrorism and organised crime in early 1995; wide ranging economic agreements during the Demirel trip.

In working hard and imaginatively to solidify the emerging new relationship at the beginning of this period, Israel had three areas in mind where bilateral interests were perceived to converge.[33] First, and inevitably foremostly, was the area of strategic consultation. This was regarded in Jerusalem as being an element in the creation of a consultation forum to review common threats in the Middle East. Such a venture was driven by the perception of threats from Iran. For Israel, this was crystallised in Iranian support for Hamas; senior Israeli officials viewed Turkey as encountering similar problems in

[30] For example, the Israeli director of security, Asaf Haffetz in October 1994, Israel's naval commander, Admiral Ami Ayalon (soon to be appointed as the new head of the Shin Beth) in November 1995, and the under-secretary of the Turkish Foreign Ministry Onur Öymen in January 1996.

[31] For example, Bülent Ecevit, whose outmoded Third Worldism comes close to rivalling Mümtaz Soysal and Necmettin Erbakan, and who was identified with a soft line towards Saddam Hussein during the Gulf crisis, was invited to Israel for five days as the guest of the Israeli Foreign Ministry.

[32] To the fore on the Turkish side were the country's most prestigious universities, such as Bosphorus University in Istanbul, the Middle East Technical University and the Bilkent University in Ankara. On the Israeli side, the Moshe Dayan Center for Middle Eastern and African Studies at Tel Aviv University and the Begin-Sadat Center for Strategic Studies at Bar-Ilan University were the most active participants.

[33] Private discussion meeting with Turkey analysts in different branches of the Israeli state, Jerusalem, 11 October 1993.

its south-east, with Iranian funds being channelled to mosques, imams and religious schools in that region. Here, Israeli experts perceived a bureaucratic schism in Turkey between the military, the main intelligence agency, MİT, and the police, which broadly accepted this analysis, and on the other hand the Foreign Ministry, the Prime Minister's office and the Finance Ministry, which took a more equivocal view.

The second part of the Israeli vision for closer relations was to be economic co-operation, high level talks already having taken place on the subject in October and December 1992. In this area too there was far from being a neat fit. Ankara wanted to create a free trade zone with Israel. The latter was wary of this, fearing that the Turks simply saw it as a device with which to gain preferential access to the US market, a ploy which might cause difficulties in Israeli-US trade relations. At that time, Israel preferred to put the emphasis on economic co-operation through regional development, in turn hoping to encourage Turkey to play a more active role within the multilateral track of the Middle East peace process, and its Regional Economic Development Working Group (REDWG) in particular. Bilateral negotiations on the establishment of a free trade agreement would not begin before September 1994.

The third element in the Israeli view of closer future co-operation was water. Israel was enthusiastic about Turgut Özal's old idea of a peace pipeline one half of which would bring the Ceyhan and Seyhan river waters to the Levant and Saudi Arabia.[34] The original idea had lapsed because of security and economic difficulties. With the heady aftermath of Oslo appearing to address the former concern, Israeli officials were convinced that for a country like Saudi Arabia the idea also made economic sense, when compared to the high costs of desalination. Israel was also keen on the transportation of Manavgat waters to the Israeli coast using giant water bubbles.[35]

In seeking to deepen the emerging relationship, Israel was undoubtedly assisted by the activities of the United States. Washington had repeatedly urged its ambassador in Ankara to push the Turks for

---

[34] See Seyfi Taşhan, 'Water Problems in the Middle East and how They could be Alleviated', Erol Manisalı (ed.), *Turkey's Place in the Middle East* (Middle East Business and Banking Publications, Istanbul, 1989).

[35] For more details, see Hugh Pope, 'A 200-ton Jellyfish could Save the Day for Thirsty Millions', *Wall Street Journal*, 28 May 1990.

an upgrading of formal relations in the late 1980s through to 1991. The sense of expectation in the new relationship felt by both Israel and the United States was, as we have seen, certainly reciprocated by Ankara. However, it was not necessarily reciprocated according to the agenda mapped out by Israel and the United States. Turkey was much less interested in the fetishising of the Iranian threat as expressed by the Americans and, to a lesser degree, by the Israelis. It was a constant element in Turkish foreign policy, undisrupted even by the idiosyncrasy of the Özal years, that Iran was a large and important neighbour that had to be managed rather than contained or confronted. This approach did not necessarily lead to policy passivity. In 1989, for example, Turkey recalled its ambassador in Tehran for consultations after Iranian criticism of a Turkish court's decision to ban the wearing of the Islamic headscarf on university campuses, and a wave of anti-Turkish attacks in the Iranian media.[36] In reality, such problems quickly blew over, to be followed by a reassertion of the traditional caution of Turkish policy.[37] For Turkey, Iran was an issue to disengage from its relationship with the United States and its budding ties with Israel, rather than to use to solidify them.

If Ankara was cautious about Iran, it had fewer reservations about Syria. With regard to Syria, it was Israel's turn to opt for a more measured approach. The Israel of Rabin and Peres was concerned that its strongly emerging relations with Turkey should not be allowed to jeopardise its peace talks with Syria. While the Israeli-Syrian track of the bilateral peace talks had yielded nothing in the months immediately after the Madrid conference of October 1991, by the time of the election of a Labour-led government in June 1992 the possibility of a breakthrough was looking more promising. The strategic emphasis placed on the peace process by both Rabin and Peres meant that it was undesirable that other factors, no matter

---

[36] *Turkish Daily News*, 19 May 1989.

[37] A good example of Turkey's patient perseverance in the face of Iranian provocations could be seen in 1989. Ankara was tolerant, first, to gratuitous national insults from Tehran, such as the Iranian prime minister refusing to pay his respects to the memory of Atatürk; second, towards direct interference in domestic affairs, such as paying Turkish girls to wear headscarves; and third, towards the violent actions of Iranian agents against émigré nationals based in Turkey.

how important, should risk hindering them. In retrospect we can see that an Israeli-Syrian breakthrough was close on two occasions, in August 1993 and January 1996, and by 1997 Damascus was widely believed to have regretted not having gone that bit further to clinch a deal. But the fact is that a breakthrough did not take place, and the Labour government would be cruelly mocked by supporters of Likud leader Binyamin Netanyahu after his election for putting Asad's sensibilities before the emerging relationship with Turkey.[38] It was only with Peres' military intervention in Lebanon in April 1996, in the form of Operation Grapes of Wrath, born of misconceived electoral tactics, and the election of Netanyahu as Israeli prime minister a month later that Israel and Turkey could begin to view the Syrian threat in complementary terms.

The centrepiece of Turkey's threat perceptions, terrorism and the PKK, was equally problematic for Israel between 1993 and 1996. Israel was guarded over the issue of the Kurds, even the issue of the PKK, in spite of the fact that the US had long accepted it as a terrorist organisation. In general terms, Israel had no outstanding problems with any branch or faction of the Kurdish national movement. After all, the Kurds too were a non-Arab component of the population of the Middle East, and one which, like the Israelis, had cause to be suspicious of the Arabs. Moreover, there had actually existed at various times a very good relationship between Israel and the Kurds, especially the Kurds of northern Iraq. Indeed, Israel had periodically assisted the Iraqi Kurds, notably in the late 1960s and early 1970s, in their struggles against the centralising authoritarianism of the Iraqi state. Those in the Foreign Ministry and different branches of the military and intelligence services that had been involved in aiding the Kurds in the past had no appetite for what appeared to be a gratuitous confrontation with the Kurds now.

As far as the specific case of the PKK was concerned, Israel was, compared to most Western powers, rather light handed in its public diplomacy. Israel refused to condemn the PKK as a terrorist

---

[38] See for example the editorial in *The Jerusalem Post*, 13 June 1996, which wrote of Labour's 'obsession with avoiding anything that might irritate Assad and cause him to withdraw from the "peace process"' in the context of a general celebration of Israeli-Turkish relations.

organisation, and refused to be drawn into a publicly enunciated policy on the issue of the creation of a Kurdish state. Instead, Israel was content to regard the PKK as an essentially internal affair for the state of Turkey, therefore requiring no bilateral co-operation. Neither did Israel request direct and active assistance from Turkey in combating Hizbollah in Lebanon. On the issue of covert action, President Weizman stated that Israel was unwilling to go beyond training and the exchange of information and intelligence.[39]

Though Israel and Turkey knew that they wanted to improve bilateral relations between 1993 and 1996, such issues as Syria, the PKK and the establishment of a free trade zone prevented the relationship from firing on all cylinders. It is, nevertheless, a measure of the warm atmosphere and reserves of goodwill at this time that these policy misfits did not blight or retard the relationship.

There was one area, however, where some Turkish political leaders in particular did take on board and embrace the Israeli–US vision for the future of the region. This was in the area of what became known as 'the new Middle East' (*al-sharq al-awsatiyyah*). This view, closely identified with Shimon Peres and his published writings,[40] looked forward to a region no longer divided by the hitherto defining regional issue, the Arab–Israeli conflict, and where peace, growing prosperity and increasing integration would characterise the future.

This view of the future, and the nature of its author, feted in the West as a statesman and the recipient of a Nobel Peace Prize, especially seemed to appeal to Turkish leader Tansu Çiller, ever eager to demonstrate her closeness to Washington and perhaps fantasising about similar adulation. It also created some resonance in the Foreign Ministry. In March 1994 Çetin would say: 'We believe that a new order is emerging in the Middle East' and 'We are resolved to collaborate in the creation of a new Middle Eastern order.'[41] While a discordant note was struck by some regional strategists, who contested the notion that Turkey's geostrategic position would be improved by Israel concluding peace with its neighbours, especially Syria, such a contingency did not materialise to test the approach.

[39] *Turkish Daily News*, 26 January 1994.
[40] Shimon Peres, *The New Middle East* (Element, Shaftesbury, England, 1993).
[41] George E. Gruen citing Çetin's 'A Statement on His Visit to Israel' in his 'Dynamic Progress in Turkish-Israeli Relations', *Israel Affairs*, vol. 1, no. 4, summer 1995, p. 58.

From the deft to the clumsy, 1996–

Writing with great prescience in 1995, the American expert on Turkey, Alan Makovsky, observed:

The flowering of Turkish-Israeli relations over the past two years marks the coming of age of a relationship long desired by both parties…Their co-operation could create a powerful axis of influence in the region. Pursued deftly, it could help lay the foundation for an alliance of moderate, pro-Western states in the Middle East; though handled clumsily, it could intimidate both countries' Arab neighbors, provoking a backlash and dividing the region along Arab/non Arab lines.[42]

Though the future course of the Israeli-Turkish relationship may yet change, the suspicion exists that it moved from the deft to the clumsy in April 1996.

The rapid expansion of diplomatic and broader civilian relations between Israel and Turkey from 1993 to 1996 had been largely lost on the rest of the Middle East. It was not until the more controversial issue of co-operation in military affairs became public that alarm bells began to ring across the region. By that stage it would prove to be very difficult to retrieve the situation. The military co-operation agreements of 1996 fitted into a highly auspicious context of excellent bilateral diplomatic relations, underpinned by increasing human and economic interaction between the two countries.

Of course the impression should not be given that military ties between Israel and Turkey began in 1996. The previous five years had seen the careful cultivation of the top Turkish officers by senior Israeli defence figures, beginning with the air force and expanding to include senior figures in the Turkish army and the broader defence establishment.[43] The regular, low key interaction at the meetings

[42] 'Israeli-Turkish Relations: a Turkish "Periphery Strategy?"' in Henri J. Barkey (ed.), *Reluctant Neighbor. Turkey's Role in the Middle East* (USIP Press, Washington, DC, 1996), p. 149.

[43] Alain Gresh claims that the 'impetus for the alliance' (if Israeli-Turkish military co-operation can really be conceived of in such terms) came from the Turkish generals rather than, as is perceived in the Arab world in general and Damascus in particular, from Israel. In fact a careful reading of the build up of the relationship indicates the complexities involved. It is probably more accurate to say that it was the defence establishments of both countries which, increasingly perceiving

of the Arms Control and Regional Security (ACRS) basket of the multilateral track of the peace process between early 1992 and summer 1995 was important in fostering mutual trust and friendship. It also brought the Israeli representatives into direct, business contact with the senior diplomats of the Turkish Foreign Ministry, who are usually to be found in such important areas of policy as NATO affairs, Europe and strategic planning. Their engagement helped to cancel out the residual caution of the Turkish diplomats of the Middle East Department in Ankara, who tend to be more Arab-oriented.

It was also during this period that the Turks began to use Israel as a supplier of defence equipment. Ankara began to place small scale orders for non-high tech equipment, requests which Israel met speedily, confidentially and without fuss. This too helped create confidence, especially in view of Turkey's problems with the human rights conditionality which arms suppliers as diverse as Germany and the United States were placing on defence contracts.

In an atmosphere resonant of the subterranean nature of relations that had prevailed in the late 1980s, Israeli–Turkish military co-operation began to accelerate, but out of the public eye. A secret security agreement was signed on 13 March 1994 dealing with the diversion of military technology to third countries. This established the ground rules for future co-operation, and was followed by an unpublished accord on training exercises in 1995. A strategic dialogue between the Ministries of Defence, but with senior diplomats also involved, on political and military affairs then followed, with the first meeting taking place in September 1995. The Israeli side had expected the meetings to take place on an annual basis; the Turkish side, however, requested that they be convened on a six-monthly basis.

THE MILITARY TRAINING AGREEMENT

It was against this backdrop that the first of the three military agreements to be concluded in 1996 was signed. The military training

---

a convergence of interest, each pushed for the same end, albeit in contrasting ways. Other bureaucratic interests in both countries, notably the respective Foreign Ministries, were altogether less enthusiastic. For Gresh's argument, see 'Turkish-Israeli-Syrian Relations and their Impact on the Middle East', *Middle East Journal*, vol. 52, spring 1998.

agreement was concluded in February 1996[44] and, in accordance with the current practice of the day, remained confidential. It was signed by deputy chief of staff, General Çevik Bir, for the Turkish side, and David Ivri, at that time the director-general of the Israeli Ministry of Defence, whose background as head of the Israeli air force had helped him to forge strong personal relations with his counterparts in Turkey. That the signatories belonged to military and civilian institutions respectively is explained by the fact that the military in Turkey is not subject to the formal political control of the Defence Ministry, the chief of staff being answerable only to the prime minister. With the process of coalition building after the December 1995 general election still incomplete, there was in fact no properly functioning premier at the time, meaning that even this notional degree of accountability was, for practical purposes, missing.

Under the accord, both sides agreed to hold air exercises eight times a year, four in each state. The agreement included provision for ground staff training. It also granted Israel emergency landing rights in Turkey, thereby facilitating its ability to conduct aerial missions further afield. While Turkey would benefit from Israeli expertise and experience, Israel would have an opportunity to train in a large air space over land.[45]

Given the confidential nature of bilateral military agreements hitherto, it was as much of a shock to the Israelis as to everyone else when the Turkish side revealed the new agreement's existence in early April 1996.[46] Though circumstances surrounding the leaking of the agreement are confused, it seems clear that it took place as a result of a deliberate act by the Turkish military. The Israelis believe that the flamboyant General Bir was responsible for the decision to go public. In yet another example of confusion and uncertainty on the Turkish side, the Foreign Ministry seemed to be in the dark

[44] Inbar states that 'several additional' military agreements were also signed between the two sides in that month. An accord on intelligence, for example, formalised and expanded previous arrangements, especially with regard to electronic surveillance, with Syria and Iran the primary and secondary targets of such cooperation respectively. See Inbar, *The Turkish-Israeli Entente*, op. cit.

[45] Oxford Analytica Daily Brief, *Israel/Turkey: Military Nexus*, 15 April 1996.

[46] The initial reaction of the Israeli side was surprise at the leak. See Steve Rodan in *Jerusalem Post International Edition*, 22 June 1996.

about elements of the agreement, and when and how it would be operationalised, when its existence became public knowledge. In scenes reminiscent of the closing of the Iraqi oil pipelines in Turkey in August 1990, a foreign minister was embarrassed by having his ignorance of the arrival of Israeli military aircraft for training purposes openly exposed in front of the media. Having briefed the press on 16 April that the military agreement did not allow the Israeli air force to train in Turkish airspace or use its bases, the Foreign Ministry was obliged ignominiously to announce a day later that such exercises were indeed already taking place. It was not just the Foreign Ministry that was thus embarrassed. Even the Turkish defence minister, Oltan Sungurlu, had also initially denied such a development.[47]

It is an inescapable conclusion that the Turkish military's intention in leaking the existence of the accord was to make a strong political statement. That statement had two components, one aimed at a domestic audience and one aimed at next door. Domestically, this was an exercise in the demonstration of the virility of power, the Turkish military making it clear to all political parties, and especially the Islamist RP, that they were sufficiently powerful to control the strategic direction of Turkish foreign policy, regardless of who formed the government or occupied the premiership. To Syria the leak contained a warning that Damascus ought to desist from its unacceptable international behaviour in support of terrorism on pain of facing an alliance of superior military might operating on two fronts.

Of course, both the Israeli and Turkish Foreign Ministries subsequently insisted on the polite diplomatic fiction that the accord was not aimed at any third party. The Turkish side even claimed that the accord was no different from the twenty or more other military training agreements concluded earlier with the likes of Albania and Macedonia. Such protestations rang hollow, with well briefed Turkish commentators happy to confirm that the agreement was most definitely an attempt to intimidate Syria. Even Çevik Bir himself, in characteristically candid terms, would, soon after his retirement from the military, point to 'Syria's more responsive attitude' over the peace

---

[47] *Jerusalem Post International Edition*, 20 April 1996.

process with Israel and the reduction of support for the PKK as being proof that the Turkish-Israeli agreement 'works'.[48]

The destabilising nature of the agreement was further amplified by the refusal of either party to publish the text, the Turks on the grounds that this was not normal procedure and that Ankara was determined not to be seen to be buckling under Arab pressure.[49] Unofficial transcripts of the agreement did eventually surface in the press in Turkish in mid May and in Arabic at the end of July, presumably as a result of official action, though the texts continue to lack formal authority and may be incomplete.[50] Nevertheless, periodic revelations of further military co-operation apparently unprovided for in agreements in the public domain, such as the existence of joint Israeli-Turkish listening posts on Turkey's borders with Iran, Iraq and Syria, have continued to disconcert regional governments.

Subsequent actions by both sides appeared further to confirm the intimidatory nature of the training agreement. Turkey was equivocal in its reaction to 'Operation Grapes of Wrath', Shimon Peres' desperate and tawdry 1996 election gamble on a military operation in Lebanon. Ankara only issued a 'belated statement' on the operation, and refused to condemn it. This was diplomacy of dubious worth, a fact that swiftly became apparent with the subsequent deaths of more than eighty civilians in the UN compound at Qana in an Israeli army attack.[51] Some six weeks after the agreement's revelation, with Arab criticism still sustained, and even the Turkish prime minister Mesut Yılmaz apparently equivocal towards it, the Israeli ambassador to Ankara, Zvi Elpeleg toured a sensitive border region between Turkey and Syria. Accompanied by bodyguards and embassy officials, he toured the controversial province of Hatay, which had become part of Turkey at the expense of French controlled Syria in 1938.[52]

---

[48] General Bir addressing the Washington Institute for Near East Policy, 26 October 1999, on 'Reflections on Turkish-Israeli Relations'. See special policy forum report compiled by Levent Onar and issued as Policy Watch # 422.

[49] Interview with senior Turkish diplomat, Ankara, 26 September 1996.

[50] *Aksiyon* magazine, 18–24 May 1996 and *al-Safir*, 29 July 1996. For a translation in English see BBC/SWB/ME, 31 July 1996. A senior member of the Turkish Foreign Ministry did, however, deny in a public forum in London on 2 April 1998 that there were any secret annexes to the training agreement.

[51] *Turkish Daily News*, 15 April 1996.

[52] *The Jerusalem Post International Edition*, 1 June 1996.

REFAH AND THE FURTHER AGREEMENTS

If the first military agreement turned out to be a defiant regional statement about the closeness of Israeli–Turkish relations, the conclusion of the second delivered a powerful message about Turkish domestic politics. The second of the three military agreements to be concluded in 1996, the Defence Industry Co-operation Agreement, was signed on 28 August. It thus came only a couple of months after an Islamist-led government was installed in Ankara, and in a context where the overtures of Israeli prime minister Benyamin Netanyahu towards the new government had been spurned.[53] Of even greater significance was the fact that the accord was signed less than two weeks after the new prime minister, Prof. Necmettin Erbakan, had visited the Islamic Republic of Iran, his first foreign trip in office and the beginning of his attempts to signal a more balanced foreign policy, which took relations with the Islamic world more seriously than in the past.

With Erbakan having raised the stakes in a highly public manner, the issue of military relations between Turkey and Israel became the barometer of who would most influence policy, the Islamist-dominated government or the Kemalist-dominated state. By the end of July, the signs did not look auspicious, with Erbakan's chief foreign policy adviser, State Minister Abdullah Gül, insisting that there would be no new military accord with Israel. The last minute postponement of a signing in early August seemed to confirm the worst fears of Israelis that bilateral relations were destined for a 'lower profile' under the Islamists.[54] With Erbakan away in Asia for ten days, the situation was in a state of flux for much of August. The Israeli defence establishment seemed powerless in the face of some opaque struggles within Turkey and had little choice but to await the outcome.[55]

Once Erbakan had returned, however, the Turkish military was able to reassert its domination over the strategic contours of foreign

---

[53] *Jerusalem Report*, 19 September 1996.

[54] See for example the Israeli mass circulation newspaper *Yediot Aharonot*, 4 August 1996 in BBC/SWB/EE, 5 August 1996.

[55] One journalist even writes of David Ivri waiting in stony silence in the Defence Ministry, waiting for a sign of whether the agreement would indeed be signed. See Steve Rodan writing in the *Jerusalem Post International Edition*, 24 August 1996.

policy, and the agreement was signed before the end of the month. Quickly realising his powerlessness to prevent the new accord, Erbakan tried to minimise the extent of his defeat by embracing the accord. Sources close to the prime minister let it be known that not only did he know the full details of the agreement, but he had made certain changes to the draft. It was vehemently denied that the agreement had been signed behind Erbakan's back.[56]

The accord, which proved the culmination of two years' worth of effort, established the framework for wide-ranging co-operation over defence industry matters. The agreement's provisions extended from reciprocal visits to defence industries, through the exchange of technical expertise and technology transfer, to the active encouragement of each other's defence firms to trade with and invest in one another's activities. The accord also provided the necessary procedures for a programme by which Israel would upgrade Turkey's F-4 Phantoms, together with its F-5s. It was a contract on this particular, high cost deal which was to be the third of the 1996 military agreements, concluded on 5 December.

If Erbakan's position on the August agreement was obscured from sight, his vigorous opposition to the aircraft upgrading was plain for all to see. Perhaps it was a case of choosing his fight carefully; perhaps Erbakan's greater public activity in this case was born of the fact that as premier he would be expected to add his signature to a successful contract. It is certainly true that Erbakan had a better chance of derailing that project than the second agreement. Negotiations between the two countries had, after all, been going on since 1994. Turkish concerns over the financing of the deal, together with doubts about the cost effectiveness of the project, in view of the age of the aircraft concerned, help to explain much of the delay.[57] Erbakan argued hard against the contract at the appropriate committees, in turn eliciting hostile criticism from the Turkish General Staff. But, with his junior coalition partners prepared to proceed with the

[56] *Turkish Daily News*, 30 August 1996.
[57] The total cost of the contract to Turkey, with interest payments, is nearly $900 mn, representing $800 mn for the 54 F-4s and $75 mn for the 48 F-5s. The last of the upgraded F-4s is scheduled to be delivered to Turkey by 2008, but, owing to metal fatigue, the planes are expected to end their working life in 2010. See Amikam Nachmani, 'The Remarkable Turkish-Israeli Tie', *Middle East Quarterly*, June 1998.

contract and the military implacable, continued opposition could have resulted in the downfall of the government. Either way, there was no doubt that Erbakan was under 'extreme pressure' from the Turkish military.[58] In order to avoid a clash with the military Erbakan was obliged to execute a U-turn. He was left protesting that he would strive to ensure that Turkish firms were given priority within the upgrading programme as a way of saving face.[59]

THE PRIMACY OF MILITARY RELATIONS

By 1997 Israeli-Turkish ties had gone seriously awry. This was unfortunate, as much of the civilian interaction of earlier in the decade was still evident or indeed was intensifying. At the height of the tourist season in summer 1998 there were more daily flights by the Turkish national carrier between the two countries than there were between Ankara and Istanbul.[60] The tentative academic interactions of the early 1990s had blossomed into routine and co-operative ventures, thereby establishing the beginnings of a bilateral epistemic community.[61] Two-way trade too was flourishing in a way that had not been possible during the subterranean years, with Turkish exports to Israel up by 54% in 1997. More recently, the swift, determined and effective Israeli contribution to humanitarian relief in the immediate aftermath of the devastating August and November 1999 earthquakes has won Israel new friends in Turkey.[62] Nevertheless, this broad and flourishing relationship had been distorted by

---

[58] *Jerusalem Post International Edition*, 14 December 1996.

[59] *Turkish Daily News*, 6 December 1996.

[60] There were as many as 25 THY flights to Israel a day, flying from a range of destinations, from Istanbul to Antalya to Dalaman. The Turkish ambassador to Israel, Barlas Özener, speaking at a conference at the Royal United Services Institute (RUSI) for Defence Studies in London, 19 October 1998.

[61] See for example the establishment of the Süleyman Demirel Program for Contemporary Turkish Studies within the Moshe Dayan Center at Tel Aviv University in June 1999. During the Spring semester that preceded the establishment of the programme, the Dayan Center brought more than a dozen prominent scholars to Israel. See the centre *Bulletin*, No. 30, Fall 1999.

[62] After the first earthquake Israel sent a 385 strong team, rescuing 12 survivors from the rubble; after the second, smaller earthquake in Düzce, Israel sent 60 rescue team members from the Israeli military, together with another 100 medical personnel. See *Israeline*, the daily news bulletin of the Israeli Consulate in New York, 23 August and 18 November 1999.

the manner of the revelations about military co-operation. Examples of civilian co-operation and interaction had appeared to pale, and were increasingly disregarded by the media on both sides. Increasingly the relationship was generally perceived to have been reduced to being a function of military affairs. It is then of little surprise that the *International Herald Tribune* could carry a headline on a piece of news analysis in April 1997 entitled 'Israel finds a friend in Turkey, thanks to the generals'.[63]

The nature of the high level interaction seemed to justify such a narrow preoccupation over the months ahead. Once again, the Turkish generals' ideological defiance, aimed for both domestic and regional consumption, was critical to the public diplomacy. As Anton La Guardia, the Jerusalem correspondent of the *Daily Telegraph* noted at the time, the Turkish military establishment 'kept up its anti-Islamist policy … by signalling deeper strategic ties with Israel'.[64]

Three examples vividly illustrate the point. On 24 February 1997 the Turkish Chief of Staff, İsmail Hakkı Karadayı, paid his first visit to Israel on a three day trip,[65] returning home to go straight into the crucial 28 February National Security Council meeting which marked the beginning of the army-inspired end for Erbakan's Islamist-led coalition. The eventual collapse of the Erbakan government coincided with the visit of a five-vessel naval battle group to the Israeli port of Haifa following the Denizkurdu-97 (Sea Wolf-97) exercises.[66] On 7 January 1998 Israeli, Turkish and US vessels took part in Reliant Mermaid, a controversial airsea rescue manoeuvre in the eastern Mediterranean; by so doing, the US anointed the relationship between the two regional allies.[67]

In more substantive terms, the military interaction came increasingly to be dominated by two elements: close and detailed joint threat assessments, and attempts by the Israeli defence industries to

---

[63] *IHT,* 16 April 1997.

[64] *Daily Telegraph,* 2 May 1997.

[65] It is worth mentioning that, in addition to the country's top brass, Karadayı was received by Israeli prime minister Netanyahu and President Weizman—as Inbar points out, 'an honour surpassing the accustomary protocol' and underscoring the importance of the visit for Israel. See Inbar, *The Turkish-Israeli Entente,* op. cit.

[66] The flotilla consisted of a frigate, a submarine, two destroyers and a supply ship. See *Milliyet,* 17 June 1997.

[67] Judy Dempsey citing diplomats in Israel in the *Financial Times,* 2 January 1998.

bid for the ambitious procurement needs of the Turkish armed forces. Indeed, even those defence policy insiders who have sought to play down the nature of the post-1996 relationship have identified defence industry cooperation as an area that became 'truly deep and meaningful'.[68]

The May 1997 round of the strategic dialogue marked a major expansion of the former, with the hapless Turkish Defence Minister, Turhan Tayan, clearly outranked by Çevik Bir, or 'little Atatürk' as he had come fondly to be known within certain Israeli circles, who arrived for the meeting with a delegation of 26 officers. Two very high profile examples among many of the latter stand out. In October 1997 the Israeli chief of staff, General Amnon Lipkin-Shahak visited Turkey; during his visit, among a portfolio of weapons systems, Israel improved its positioning of the Merkava-3 tank as the solution to Turkey's aim to acquire 800 main battle tanks, at an expected cost of some $4.5 bn.[69] Two years later Israel's prime minister and Shahak's predecessor as chief of staff, Ehud Barak, went to Turkey to inaugurate a housing village in Adapazarı to shelter 312 homeless families from Turkey's August earthquake; he then went on to Ankara for a series of defence-related meetings, Israeli defence officials hoping that the visit would accelerate deals for which Israel was bidding.[70]

The cementing of closer defence relations in turn saw Turkey raise the number of its military attachés in Tel Aviv from one to three in July 1998, adding naval and army men to join the air force officer in residence. Other than in Israel, only in its embassies in the United States, Germany and France, Turkey's main defence trading partners, does Ankara have three military attachés.[71]

From the conclusion of the three defence agreements onwards, the two sides did relatively little to reassure the rest of the Middle East as to their limited and peaceful intentions. Most such activities, like dropping the '1' from the Reliant Mermaid joint exercise to

---

[68] Written correspondence from Eli Levite, 4 February 2001.

[69] *Jerusalem Post International Edition*, 25 October 1997.

[70] In particular, big contracts to upgrade Turkey's tanks and to supply advanced attack helicopters were mentioned. See *Israeline*, 25 October 1999.

[71] *Jerusalem Post*, 13 July 1998, www.jpost.co.il

imply that it was not necessarily to be the first of a series,[72] and a brief charm offensive by the Turkish Foreign Ministry towards the Arab world in spring 1998, seemed little more than gestures. Only in relation to Egypt was high level political capital invested over time in order to allay suspicions and concerns.[73] These efforts, however, never quite succeeded in convincing, not least because of Cairo's sense of itself as the leading Arab, and hence Middle Eastern regional, power.

By contrast, the Turkish side, and notably the military, seemed to glory in an assertiveness which almost bordered on truculence. In December 1997, for instance, in a piece of diplomatic defiance that even exceeded Turkey's normally high standards, the Israeli Defence Minister Yitzhak Mordechai was welcomed to Ankara, even as President Demirel led a Turkish delegation to a high profile ICO summit in Tehran, a meeting which marked the regional diplomatic rehabilitation of Iran.[74] Demirel subsequently left the conference prematurely, following sustained criticism of the direction of Turkish regional policy. In June 1998 the Turkish military leaked the attendance of a Jordanian delegation at the strategic dialogue meeting taking place in Tel Aviv,[75] in a piece of bravado that did little more than expose a weak state at a difficult time,[76] exacerbated by the onset of a protracted and uncertain succession. More substantively, Turkey also used the growing regional discomfort at its emerging military relationship with Israel to pressurise Syria into expelling the PKK insurgency leader Abdullah Öcalan in October 1998.

---

[72] This soon proved to be an exercise in dissimulation, the joint naval exercise Reliant Mermaid-3 being held in January 2001.

[73] Spasmodic efforts to manage Egypt included a visit by President Demirel in September 1997 and a trip to Cairo by Turkish chief of staff İsmail Hakkı Karadayı in December 1997.

[74] Indeed Professor Efraim Inbar, a leading strategic commentator from the Israeli right, emphasising the importance of the timing, actually described it in such terms, calling it a defiant assertion of commitment to the relationship. See Inbar addressing Chatham House, 17 July 1998.

[75] *Jane's Defence Weekly*, 10 June 1998.

[76] The Turkish side must have been well aware of Jordanian sensitivities, having first signed a military cooperation with the Kingdom in 1984. Indeed by 1998 it appeared that Jordan had acquired a reputation for being 'a silent partner' in its military ties with Turkey, fearing that the proximity of this relationship to Israeli-Turkish military cooperation might elicit criticism from other Arab countries. See *Turkish Daily News*, 15 September 1998.

There is evidence to suggest that since the summer of 1998, some Israeli opinion formers and policymakers have been growing uncomfortable with the boldness of the Turkish generals.[77] In an atmosphere more reminiscent of the 1993–5 period, there have been concerns that Israeli and Turkish interests do not directly coincide; that Israel is having to bear the consequences of unforeseen Turkish actions in a variety of different areas, from Greece and Cyprus through the Middle East peace process to the Kurdish issue. Three sets of developments have been most startling for Israelis: Ankara's bellicose reaction to Cypriot plans, since shelved, to acquire S-300 missiles from Russia; Turkey's use of military pressure against Syria over Öcalan; and the attacks on Israeli missions in Europe after the capture of Öcalan by Turkish commandos in Nairobi in February 1999.[78] In one of the foreign mission protests, Israeli security guards shot dead three Kurdish supporters of the PKK when they tried to force entry into the Consulate-General in Berlin.

By 1999 then, as a direct result of the decisions and public conduct of 1996, Israeli-Turkish relations have become dominated by military relations. The powerful defence establishments of the two countries are the bureaucratic drivers of the relationship. Both have strong vested interests in maintaining the centrality of the ties, the Turkish generals for ideological and strategic reasons, the Israelis primarily for matters of military-related commerce. The Foreign Ministries of the two countries, Israel's rather more than Turkey's it has to be said, may periodically agonise about the effect that it has had on relations with third countries, but this has seldom been channelled into anything more than presentational action, reflecting the relative bureaucratic balances at home.

Looking back over some fifty years, Turkish-Israeli relations have usually been low key and have often been of little importance. They have rarely matched their potential. For much of the 1980s there

---

[77] For a public expression of considered scepticism, see Stuart A. Cohen of Bar-Ilan University writing on the opinion page of the *Jerusalem Post*, 23 October 1998.

[78] A Kurdish spokesman in Germany was quoted as saying: 'It was decided to single out the Israeli Consulate because the Turkish Prime Minister thanked the Israeli authorities for their help in apprehending Öcalan'. See *The Times*, 18 February 1999.

was the extraordinary situation of Turkey having lower-level formal relations with Israel than Egypt, even though these two states had fought four major wars with one another over the previous four decades. The trauma of the Baghdad Pact years and the need to garner diplomatic support in international forums, together with the economic imperative of developing strong relations with the oil exporting countries of the Middle East, all help to explain this reticence.

In the early 1990s Turkish-Israeli relations became of increasing diplomatic and commercial importance, especially once the Middle East peace process began to bear fruit. By the end of 1995 the two countries might have looked forward to a broad-based relationship across state institutions and civil society, with a solid bilateral grounding. Up to this point, such developments had elicited relatively little by way of regional alarm. Instead, the year 1996 became pivotal as a time when the direction of the relationship and, equally importantly, the perception of the relationship both at home and in the region were transformed. The broad foundation to the relationship was lost sight of as the military and defence relationship came to eclipse all else. Since then relations have neither been low key nor unimportant. With domestic political considerations of paramount importance, the Turkish military not only focused on deepening the relationship but, with Çevik Bir in the role of Turgut Özal, did so with a stylistic flourish which often appeared to be of equal importance to its substance.

8

SELF-INTEREST BEFORE SENTIMENT: TURKEY'S RELATIONS WITH THE TURKIC REPUBLICS[1]

Before the end of the Cold War there were few direct links between Turkey and the southern republics of the Soviet Union.[2] This period of economic, social, cultural and political isolation stretched back over six decades, thereby, for practical purposes, surpassing living memory. During this period all lines of political communication were conducted with Moscow, as the centre of the Soviet state. Issues of potential bilateral importance between Turkey and the southern republics were subsumed under those of Ankara-Moscow relations. Relations between the two powers were largely reduced to the central strategic preoccupation of East-West bipolar confrontation. Though Turkish-Soviet relations did enjoy periods of relative warmth and trade began to grow, such interaction never transcended this bipolar enmity. Security considerations informed relations in all other domains. As Paul Henze has written, generations of Turkish diplomats operated in a tradition that required 'almost obsequious correctness toward Moscow'.[3]

---

[1] This chapter is principally concerned with Turkey's relations with the newly emerging independent republics of the south of the former Soviet Union, with particular emphasis on those which have been described as being Turkic. These are Kazakhstan, Kyrgyzstan, Turkmenistan and Uzbekistan in Central Asia and Azerbaijan in the Transcaucasus or, as the Turks prefer it, the south Caucasus.

[2] For example, a trickle of escapees continued to arrive in Turkey from Soviet Central Asia from the 1950s onwards. Paul B. Henze, *Turkey: Toward the Twenty-First Century* (RAND, Santa Monica) 1992, p. 33.

[3] Revised version of 'Turkey: Toward the Twenty-First Century' in Graham E. Fuller and Ian O. Lesser, *Turkey's New Geopolitics, From the Balkans to Western China* (Westview/RAND, Boulder, 1993), p. 28.

This distorted situation ended unexpectedly and rapidly as the process of political change swept the Soviet Union. From 1991 the governments of the Soviet republics suddenly acquired considerable breadth of independent action. In order to assert their own power and the sovereignty of the new republics, the various leaders in the southern republics looked to construct a network of external relations beyond the Soviet Union, where none had previously existed. For reasons of cultural affinity and Western economic orientation, Turkey was one of the first countries to be subjected to these attentions. After an initial delay, Turkey in turn became excited by the changes taking place in its expanded geostrategic space.[4] There was widespread inquisitiveness across Turkey about what was perceived as this new predominantly 'Turkic world' which appeared to be opening up to the east.[5]

This initial period of euphoria seemed to presage the opening up of a new regional focus to foreign policy for Turkey. Yet these early months, when sentiment ruled the day, proved to be an inaccurate gauge of the potential for short to medium term, let alone longer term relations. By the end of the 1990s ideas of Turkic solidarity from Turkey across the Caucasus to Central Asia had been devalued, to be replaced by a Caspian strategy based on much more hard-headed calculations of hydrocarbon infrastructural interests. This chapter addresses the mercurial nature of relations between Turkey and the republics of the old Soviet south. It considers how such initially high expectations were generated, how they so quickly came to be disappointed and how relations have settled since. It also focuses on energy pipelines questions, in which a panacea has promised much but delivered little like Turkic solidarity.

[4] One longstanding US government official and expert and commentator on Turkey anticipated this sense of excitement when he said that Turkey, with its self-perception of being 'isolated and friendless in the world', would welcome the emergence of new Turkic states which at very least would increase its allies at the United Nations. Interview in Washington, DC, 20 April 1990.

[5] In Turkey it is common to hear, and see references to the Turkic states and peoples to the east. In the republics of Central Asia the term 'Turkic' appears rarely to be used. Rather, the elites of the Central Asian states tend to identify themselves as being citizens of those states. The use of the term therefore says more about Turkish perceptions and aspirations than it does about the realities of Central Asia and the Caucasus.

Policy predicament

The collapse of the Soviet Union and the emergence of a belt of independent southern republics were so sudden that it took Ankara some time to develop a policy towards these new states. Initially then, especially during the second half of 1991, the Turkish reaction was 'somewhat cautious',[6] governed by what one might call a Kemalist default option approach, as members of the foreign policy elite continued to be guided by Atatürk's old injunctions against pan-Turkist adventurism in 'Turkestan'.[7] This initial passivity was soon supplanted by a period when the official Turkish reaction was characterised by a mixture of sentiment and superiority: sentiment in that many people in Turkey suddenly believed that they had at last discovered a belt of states that would be its natural friends, based on a strong resonance of cultural affinity; superiority in that Ankara automatically assumed that owing to the hegemony of the communist system these societies must *ipso facto* be developmentally retarded, afflicted for example with social services that were inferior to the republic of Turkey. Both of these factors proved to be a deeply flawed basis on which to develop a broad-based policy.

With the Turkic republics initially acting as earnest *demandeurs*,[8] and sentiment increasingly coming to drive its approach to the emerging relationship, Ankara channelled considerable early effort into establishing an infrastructure of formal relations. In doing so, Ankara was scrupulous in treating all of these republics equally, for

---

[6] Graham E. Fuller, 'Turkey's New Eastern Orientation' in Graham E. Fuller and Ian O. Lesser (eds), *Turkey's New Geopolitics: From the Balkans to Western China* (Westview Press/RAND, Boulder, CO, 1993), p. 67.

[7] For an excellent history of Pan-Turkism, see Jacob M. Landau, *Pan-Turkism in Turkey: From Irredentism to Cooperation* (Hurst, London, 1995). For an example of Atatürk's injunction against pan-Turkism (and its variant Turanism) see his speech at Eskişehir in 1921 when he said: 'Neither Islamic union nor Turanism may constitute a doctrine, or logical policy for us. Henceforth the Government policy of the new Turkey is to consist in living independently, relying on Turkey's own sovereignty within her national frontiers'. Ibid., p. 72.

[8] Anthony Hyman cites a 'typical' response in quoting Azerbaijan's foreign minister, who declared in August 1992 that 'We want Turkey's aid in establishing links with the world'. See 'Central Asia and the Middle East: The Emerging Links' in Mohiaddin Mesbahi (ed.), *Central Asia and the Caucasus after the Soviet Union: Domestic and International Dynamics* (University Press of Florida, Gainesville, 1994), p. 258.

fear of alienating those that were not placed in the first rank. In one respect this was cannily opportunistic, as the new states and their leaders quickly came to compete with each other for the favours of important states beyond their region. More generally, however, this was a course of dubious judgement. First, because it ignored the limited nature of Turkey's resources; Ankara would have had a greater impact if it had concentrated its limited aid. Second, it was unrealistic in geopolitical terms, tending to ignore the relative importance of each state to Turkey, as well as their individual interests in relation to Ankara.

This early diplomatic investment was based on the assumption that such activities would pay a quick dividend. It soon became clear that a third factor, more a product of calculation, was also important alongside sentiment and superiority in the development of Turkish policy emerged towards the republics. This was a strategically oriented approach, which placed a premium on diversifying the new republics' dependence on old Soviet relationships, now reproduced in the form of relations with the Russian successor state. Ankara adopted the strategic evaluation that Russian weakness provided a window of opportunity within which the new republics could be weaned away from a historical and structural dependence on the former dominant power, a view that came increasingly to be shared by the Americans.

While such an evaluation was clear enough it contained a number of critical imponderables. Most notable among these were: for how long would the weakness of Russia continue, would the new republics really be willing to accept the Turkish-cum-US designs for them, and how capable was Turkey of carrying off such a structural reorientation? Events were to expose the shallowness of the notion of Turkey as some sort of a strategic alternative to Russia far more quickly than perhaps even sceptics had initially assumed. For Turkey there were three key reversals in fortune. The first came with the quick unfolding of events, with Russia quickly recovering ground both through security cooperation in Central Asia and through the sweeping victories of the Russian-backed Armenians at the expense of Azerbaijan, Turkey's *de facto* closest friend in the former Soviet south. Second, the leaders of the new republics proved capable of developing an independent sense of their own interests in a way that Turkey and the US had not credited them with. They decided that they did not much like the so-called Turkish model of democracy and liberalisation,[9] as they were desperately trying to hold on to political and economic power, not share it. Moreover, they were better able than most to assess the level of Russian's power on its southern flank, and indeed its utility for them in warding off the common threat from radical Islamism. Third, the limitations of Turkey as an economic partner were soon to be exposed, in spite of the apparent relative generosity of the Turkish state through its provision of Eximbank credits. In short, disillusionment was relatively quick to emerge, while Ankara had more than enough to preoccupy it both at home, in fighting the Kurdish insurgency, and elsewhere in other adjoining regions in the early to mid 1990s.

Except for a relatively brief period, the Turkic republics, even Azerbaijan, never actually received the sort of foreign policy priority that the first three quarters of 1992 might have suggested and which the fantastic suggestions of a new 'great game' in Central Asia had supposed. After the first 'Turkic summit' of October 1992 had punctured the euphoria in policy circles, Ankara just did not devote the sort of resources that one might have expected to the region. Consequently, the newly opened embassies were left undermanned, the high level political visits decreased (only the under-employed President Demirel could be persuaded to take a continuing interest in the region), and the initial round of trade credits was left unsupplemented (and sometimes undisbursed as a result of the high rates of interest charged).[10]

---

[9] For a period of time Turkish officialdom and its supporters in civil society enthusiastically propagated the idea of Turkey as a model for the new republics. For a good example of the latter, Seyfi Taşhan wrote: 'The principal objective of Turkish foreign policy towards the Turkish republics in Central Asia should be conceived as helping these countries to become pluralist, secular democracies, respectful of the rule of law, progressing towards market economy, to adopt Turkey as a model on the basis of mutual advantage'. See 'The Caucasus and Central Asia: Strategic Implications', *Dış Politika*, vol. XVIII, no. 3–4, 1993, p. 61.

[10] Turkey had extended all of its $1.2 billion in economic assistance (humanitarian aid and Eximbank credits) by February 1993. Some two years later, about 60% of the Eximbank financing had been used up. Fazlı Keşmir, Turkish Foreign Ministry, speaking at a seminar on Turkey and Central Asia at Bosphorus University, 27 January 1995.

From the perspective of high politics, all that was left of Ankara's ambitions by 1993 was a residue of rhetoric and a growing reduction of policy towards the republics to the level of pipeline construction and energy provision. By the end of the decade there had been a geostrategic retrenchment of Turkey's interests, with, as Gareth Winrow has argued, the Caucasus the focus of its attentions rather than Central Asia.[11] Ironically, for Turkey the future course of politics in Georgia and its implications for bilateral relations had become more of a priority than relations with most of its ethnic sibling states.[12]

Period of euphoria: September 1991–October 1992

The assumption of power in the Soviet Union by Mikhail Gorbachev and the adoption of a policy of *glasnost* heralded the establishment of direct relations between Turkey and the republics of the Soviet south.[13] This consisted of small-scale interaction, mostly in the cultural, academic and economic domains. In spite of this direct contact, the parameters for interaction continued to operate 'under the surveillance of Moscow'.[14] When President Özal visited Alma Ata in March 1991, the first visit to a southern republic by a Turkish head of state since the advent of *glasnost*, it was prefaced by a visit to Moscow. The inclusion of Kiev as the second destination of the tour emphasised that the Turkic republics were not Ankara's sole concern. In Moscow, Özal signed a friendship and good neighbourliness

[11] Gareth Winrow, *Turkey and the Caucasus, Domestic Interests and Security Concerns*, Central Asian and Caucasian Prospects series (RIIA, London, 2000) p. 3.

[12] Turkish policy had from early on emphasised that all of the states of the FSS, Georgia included, should receive 'equal attention', the basis of the policy being one of 'non-discrimination'. However, the fact that Georgia was not, for example, invited to the Turkic summits, for the obvious reasons of its population being neither Turkic speaking nor Muslim, shows the discrepancies in this approach from the outset. See undated ministerial report on 'General Economic Conditions in Former Soviet Republics' (Foreign Ministry, EIGY-II, Ankara), fax dated 13 October 1992.

[13] *Newspot*, 20 June 1991.

[14] To quote Dr Şükrü Gürel paraphrasing Ambassador Bilal Şimşir in Şükrü Gürel, Şamil Ünsal and Yoshihiro Kimura, *Turkey in a Changing World—With Special Reference to Central Asia and the Caucasus* (Institute of Developing Economies, Tokyo, 1993), p. 32.

agreement in which the two parties agreed not to interfere in one another's internal affairs. Despite the visit to Kazakhstan it was clear that Turkey was still dealing directly with Moscow as the centre of power of the Soviet state.[15]

This situation soon changed, though not because of any intention or action in Ankara. The context changed because of political developments within the Soviet state. More specifically, the failed coup d'état against President Gorbachev in August 1991 strengthened the position of Boris Yeltsin as the president of the Russian Federation at the expense of the USSR. With the Soviet Union fatally wounded even the southern republics, which had previously appeared least desirous of shaking free of the centre, began to exploit their greater room for manoeuvre. In fact the crumbling of the Communist centre triggered a belatedly frenzied dash on the part of the Central Asian republics to develop rapidly a network of independent external relations.

At the forefront of this stampede was Kazakhstan. In late September 1991 President Nursultan Nazarbayev took advantage of the earlier Özal trip to become the first of the Central Asian heads of state to visit Turkey. The four-day trip was placed in the framework of enduring cultural and historical relations. A long agenda was adopted for the trip, helping to raise expectations of this new bilateral relationship. A wide range of different issues were discussed, from regional and international affairs to bilateral co-operation in transport and telecommunications to the boosting of trade and private sector involvement. The tone was therefore set for interaction between Turkey and the Central Asian republics over the next few months.[16]

So successful did the Nazarbayev visit appear to be that the heads of state of the other predominantly Turkic speaking republics seemed almost desperate to visit Turkey. During the month of December 1991 alone, Turkey received visits from Saparmurad Niyazov, Islam Karimov and Askar Akayev, the presidents of Turkmenistan, Uzbekistan and Kyrgyzystan respectively. With Turkey also having been visited by the foreign minister of Turkmenistan and the deputy premier of Uzbekistan to prepare for the presidential trips, it is perhaps little wonder that a buzz of infectious excitement began to

[15] *Newspot*, 14 March 1991.
[16] *Newspot*, 3 October 1991.

grip Ankara and Istanbul in particular at what became increasingly perceived as the discovery of long lost brother states.[17]

The climate of popular expectation engendered by such high level diplomatic traffic was further heightened by the return visits paid by senior Turkish figures. In February the Turkish Foreign Minister Hikmet Çetin visited the five Central Asian republics (that is including Tajikistan). In late April, early May it was the turn of the prime minister, Süleyman Demirel, to make the journey (although Tajikistan was dropped from the itinerary owing to internal political unrest),[18] with the reception that they got often feeding the growing Turkish misconceptions of the relationship.[19] What was at least as significant as the visits themselves was the nature of the delegations taken by both men. The Çetin entourage was 140 strong, including businessmen and journalists as well as officials.[20] The delegation accompanying Demirel was even larger, and again consisted of people with different professional perspectives on the emerging relationships.[21] The Demirel delegation included Alpaslan Türkeş, the leader of the pan-Turkist National Action Party or Milliyetçi Hareket Partisi (MHP) , with whom the prime minister had formed a parliamentary alliance; the presence of Türkeş,[22] who had established

---

[17] Hugh Poulton points out that Turkey's state-propagated nationalism strongly stressed Central Asia as the Turks' original fatherland, this resulting in the 'retention of the sense of 'kin' in Central Asia'. This may help to explain why the sense of excitement at the emergence of these republics was so palpable between late 1991 and the autumn of 1992. *Top Hat, Grey Wolf and Crescent: Turkish Nationalism and the Turkish Republic* (Hurst, London, 1997), p. 287.

[18] *Turkish Daily News,* 5 May 1992.

[19] For example, Demirel was greeted at the airport in Kyrgyzstan by President Askar Akayev in the following way: 'You have left these lands centuries ago on horseback and with slanted eyes. You came back riding in an airplane and with your eyes round'. Incident retold by former diplomat and columnist Şükrü Elekdağ during his chairmanship of a session entitled 'Central Asia: Old Ties, New Perceptions'. See proceedings of the 'Seminar on Russia and the NIS' (29–31 March 1996, Antalya, Turkey) published as SAM Papers 1/96 by MFA Centre of Strategic Research, p. 115.

[20] *Milliyet* in *Turkish Press Review,* 27 February 1992.

[21] *Turkish Daily News,* 27 April 1992.

[22] Türkeş was also consulted by the Turkish government on policy towards the Turkic republics, though the extent of his influence should not be exaggerated. It also appears that Ankara used him as a conduit through which to convey its policy preferences to the Azerbaijan of Elçibey in particular. See Dr Idris Bal and

a close relationship with the ill-fated leadership of Elçibey's Azerbaijan,[23] could not fail to excite the expectation and suspicion that Turkey harboured leadership ambitions over the belt of Turkic states, resonant of the even more ill-fated adventure of Enver Pasha in Central Asia in the wake of the demise of the Ottoman Empire. The nature and size of the Turkish delegations seemed guaranteed to give the impression that extensive co-operation was taking place on a variety of different levels, and to ensure that such an impression received maximum publicity.

The sight of such traffic, supplemented by other numerous visits and exchanges in many different spheres, helped to raise expectations on both sides. These were bolstered by a range of formal and ceremonial developments. Turkey was the first country to recognise the newly independent states of the former Soviet south, which it did together with the other states of the former Soviet Union (with the exception of Azerbaijan, which had already received recognition) on 16 December 1991. In an attempt at myth-making the timing of this move was subsequently trumpeted by the Turkish Foreign Ministry as being a brave step, although in fact it only preceded the Alma Ata agreement to dissolve the USSR by five days.[24]

Moves were then made to open embassies in the republics and to appoint ambassadors. There was some urgency in establishing joint business councils with the individual republics. The first such council established with a Turkic state, the Turkish-Uzbek business council, was set up as early as November 1991. Cultural centres were opened in different parts of Central Asia and the south Caucasus. The high level official visits in turn spawned a host of general framework agreements for bilateral co-operation. These were to be ever further refined by more specific accords as further visits took place; so

---

Dr Cengiz Basak Bal, 'Rise and Fall of Elchibey and Turkey's Central Asian Policy', *Dış Politika*, vol. 22, nos. 3–4, 1998, pp. 44–5.

[23] There were even claims that Türkeş had financed the Elçibey regime. For a discussion of the politics of the radical right and its attitudes towards pan-Turkism and the *Dış Türkler* (outside Turks) see Poulton, op. cit., esp. chapter five.

[24] Moreover, as late as the beginning of December diplomatic sources (whether Turkish or Ankara-based foreigners is unclear) were saying that such recognitions were 'unlikely in the short-term', and Ankara would rather wait 'until the new formations in the Soviet Union become clear'. *Turkish Daily News*, 3 December 1991.

much so that by February 1993 there were estimated to be around 140 bilateral accords in existence, spanning a variety of different subjects between Turkey and the five Turkic republics.[25]

In turn, an attempt was made to expand the capacity of the Turkish state to manage these new emerging relationships. Most notably the Foreign Ministry in Ankara was itself reorganised to reflect both the recent political developments and the expectation of future workload. The existing directorate-general dealing with Eastern Europe, the USSR and Asia was divided into two. One of these new departments was made responsible for the newly created Commonwealth of Independent States (excluding the south Caucasus), together with part of Asia. This directorate-general was in turn subdivided into one department dealing primarily with the Slavic republics, while the other department was mainly charged with responsibility for the Turkic republics.[26]

The new CIS directorate-general was placed under the leadership of Ambassador Bilal Şimşir, who was described soon after as 'more of a historian and a romantic than a diplomat'.[27] During the period of euphoria his public remarks appeared to match his character; one reported example quotes him as saying that Turkey would 'not [be] an intermediary [towards the Turkic republics] but a pioneer'.[28] To accompany the organisational changes in the Foreign Ministry, a new body, affiliated to the ministry and called the Turkish International Co-operation Agency (*Türk İşbirliği Kalkınma Ajansı*), was established in August 1992. Its brief was to co-ordinate the co-operation between Turkey and the republics.[29]

In the public discourse that accompanied such efforts at co-operation and the burgeoning formal relationship, Turkish officials repeatedly took pains to reassure other powers as to the limited and benign motives of the Turkish state. It was the rhetoric that accompanied what often appeared to be such proforma statements, however, that increasingly raised concerns among Turkey's neighbours. As might be expected it was President Özal, combining public indiscretion with political vision, who led the way. As early as late

[25] Interview with Emre Gönensay, political adviser to Demirel, 18 February 1993.
[26] Interview with senior member of Central Asia Department, 22 April 1993.
[27] Interview with former senior foreign policy adviser, 29 April 1993.
[28] *Turkish Daily News*, 29 September 1992.
[29] *Turkish Daily News*, 29 September 1992.

September 1991 President Özal had stated to a Japanese audience that Turkey would enter the 21st century as 'the strongest country in the region'.[30] Such a comment could not but be taken negatively in Moscow, as the implication for Russian power of such a statement was clear. After the initial tentativeness of the Turkish government had been dispelled by the visits from four Central Asian heads of state, ministers began to speak in expansive terms about Turkey's future role in the area. For instance, on his return from a visit to Central Asia in March 1992 Çetin talked of the very important and effective role Turkey could play in the region. It was during this visit that Çetin began speaking of Turkey as a model country for the former southern republics.[31]

Arguably it was the remarks of the prime minister, Süleyman Demirel, which would most have discomforted neighbouring powers such as Russia and Iran. Though a generally cautious politician without a predilection for foreign affairs, Demirel indulged in some high-flown rhetoric on the subject of Turkey and the Turkic world.

In what was to become 'an infamous speech'[32] in February 1992, Demirel had already stated that 'a gigantic Turkish world', stretching from the Adriatic to the Great Wall of China, had appeared with the collapse of the Soviet Union. Demirel's subsequent visit to the four Turkic republics of Central Asia marks the high point of this period of euphoria. He spoke of an exclusive bond, saying that Turkey and the Turkic republics 'share the same blood, religion and language'. Continued emphasis was placed on the fact that it was Turkey that had been the first to recognise these republics, and the first to dispatch ambassadors. Having lauded "the magnificence of the Turkic world", the Turkish government secured the agreement of the republics for a Turkic conference to be held in Turkey in the late autumn.[33]

Demirel stated frequently during this visit that 'no-one should be afraid' of such efforts at co-operation. Moreover, he even announced at the beginning of April that he intended to visit Moscow towards

---

[30] *Newspot*, 3 October 1991.

[31] *Newspot*, 12 March 1992.

[32] Gareth M. Winrow, 'Turkey and the Former Soviet Central Asia: A Turkic Culture Area in the Making?' in K. Warikoo (ed.), *Central Asia: Emerging New Order* (Haranand Publications, New Delhi, 1994), p. 282.

[33] *Newspot*, 7 May 1992.

the end of May, in order, as one Turkish newspaper put it, to 'balance' the forthcoming visit to Central Asia.[34] Such attempts at giving reassurance were far from a complete success. Russia's suspicions about Turkey's Turkic policy had already been aroused in relation to Tatarstan and Chechnya. Turkey's 'initiatives' were regarded by some officials in Moscow as 'encouraging' movements for independence within the Russian Federation.[35] The failure of Demirel's reassurances during his Central Asian visit were spectacularly highlighted when the commander of the CIS armed forces, Marshal Yevgeny Shaposhnikov, warned Turkey against intervention in the Armenian-Azerbaijani dispute lest it run the risk that such action 'could bring the world into the [sic] Third World War'.[36] For all the attempts to smooth over this diplomatic embarrassment, this sentiment seemed to be held by other senior officials, notably the defence minister, Pavel Grachev.[37] The growing and increasingly active concern of the Russian government over Turkey's policy towards the former southern republics during this period prefaces the tension through proxies that was to emerge in 1993.

The tendency towards rhetoric on the part of Turkish politicians and commentators was not exclusively of concern to neighbouring states. Increasingly, even the republics grew tired and irritated at some of the assumptions and presumptions of Turkish politicians and officials at the time. For instance, Turks often assumed that the republics were backward in educational and health facilities, whereas rates of literacy and scientific education often outstripped those in Anatolia. Such resentment was not purely a matter of national pride. The elites in the newly independent states increasingly perceived a personal threat in such an approach. The enunciation of a vision for the republics on the part of Turkey included the introduction of democratic politics and an open market economy. Yet for the elites in power in Central Asia this model appeared to be little more than a euphemism for the erosion of centralised control or, worse still, their replacement by a new generation of leaders espousing

---

[34] *Turkish Daily News*, 2 April 1992.
[35] Ibid.
[36] *Turkish Daily News*, 21 May 1992.
[37] Peri Pamir, p. 8. 'Turkey in its Regional Environment in the Post-Bipolar Era: Opportunities and Constraints', paper presented to IPRA conference, Kyoto, Japan, 27–31 July 1992.

democracy. The fact that opposition politicians in exile, most notably in the case of Uzbekistan, sometimes wound up using Turkey
as a base for their émigré political activities exacerbated such feelings.

Neither was this growing dissatisfaction with the Turkish approach
confined to personal self-interest. The Central Asian republics in
particular, as newly independent and sovereign entities, were keen
to build up a framework of external relations commensurate with
this new status. They increasingly wanted to develop relations directly
with the principal states of the West. The notion of foreign relations
somehow being channelled through Ankara was therefore increasingly unattractive. Yet this was persistently implicit and even explicit in Turkish statements. For instance, during a March 1992 press
conference Süleyman Demirel spoke of Turkey being 'a cultural centre and historic magnet' for the newly independent states, thereby
implying that the states themselves were to remain on the periphery, with Turkey as the emerging power centre. The openly self-
confident tone, which could so easily be perceived as self-interested
and patronising, was evident in Demirel's follow-up statement: 'We
simply believe we can help these [newly independent] republics in
their long overdue attempt to integrate with the world'.[38] Thus it is
hardly surprising that, in spite of the reassurances, Turkey came
increasingly to be perceived by the smaller Turkic republics, to be
acting like a 'big brother'.[39]

Finally, the new republics were resentful of attempts to close off
potentially productive new areas of relations because of Western priorities often shared by Turkey. Most obviously states such as Turkmenistan and Uzbekistan had a strong interest in developing relations
with Iran because of the potential utility of their southern neighbour as a communications and supply route. Crude attempts to deter
the emergence of such a relationship, notably by US Secretary of State
James Baker during a visit to Central Asia in February 1992, caused
further resentment, some of which inevitably attached itself to Ankara.

The role of some of Turkey's closest friends was far from negligible in helping to foster this atmosphere of euphoria.[40] The United

---

[38] *Newspot*, 9 April 1992.

[39] Anthony Hyman, 'Moving out of Moscow's Orbit: the Outlook for Central
Asia', *International Affairs* vol. 69, no. 2, April 1993, p. 299.

[40] For example, Shireen Hunter writes: 'The West has actively promoted Turkey's
image as the ideal model of an Islamic, yet secular and modern, state and has

States which still viewed the world with a residual bipolar mindset, but which was also largely ignorant about the newly emerging republics,[41] was quick and heavy handed in pushing the idea of a major role for Turkey in Central Asia as a way of minimising Iranian influence. During an important visit to Washington in February 1992, the Turkish prime minister, Süleyman Demirel, was told by US president George Bush: 'Turkey is a model for the countries in the region, and especially to those newly independent republics of Central Asia.'[42] In the realm of civil society, sympathetic influential commentators and opinion formers both reflected and reinforced this view. Arguably the most influential published example of the day concluded as follows:

In the Central Asian republics, Turkey's role will be critical and of significance to both Turkey and the West. The emerging states will look to Turkey as a model for their development as well as for material help. Turkey will take advantage of these newly opened markets for investment and trade and can serve as a funnel for Western investment.[43]

Such a view was not confined to the United States The European Commission too encouraged Turkey to develop an active role for itself in the new republics. One of the EC's leading commissioners, Frans Andrieesen, stated around the same time that Turkey should be regarded as a corridor to the Central Asian and Transcaucasian states.[44] Such sentiments appeared to be shared by leading member states. During his visit to Ankara in April 1992 the British Foreign Secretary,

---

urged these countries to emulate Turkey'. See *Central Asia Since Independence* (CSIS/Praeger, Gainesville, 1996), p. 137.

[41] In one of the more judicious articles on Turkey's relations with Central Asia Patricia Carley makes the important point that ignorance underlay many of the West's ideas and assumptions about both Central Asia and its relations with Turkey. See 'Turkey and Central Asia. Reality Comes Calling' in Rubinstein and Smolansky (eds), *Regional Power Rivalries in the New Century* (1995), pp. 169–97.

[42] *Newspot*, 13 February 1992.

[43] Foreword enunciating the 'principal conclusions' of the RAND study on Turkey's new geopolitics, published in 1993: Fuller and Lesser (eds), op. cit., p. ix. The work reinforced this view, among other things by describing Turkey as 'a political, economic and cultural magnet' for 'the Turkic regions' of the former Soviet south (ibid., p. xiv).

[44] *Turkish Daily News*, 1 April 1992.

Douglas Hurd, stated that Turkey had an important role to play in the former Soviet Union, mentioning, presumably as a way of emphasising the point, such a role in the same breath as Turkey's role in Iraq.[45] Indeed, foreign politicians visiting Turkey, especially those from Europe, seemed to identify Central Asia and Transcaucasia as a relatively cost free way of heaping praise on their hosts, with whom, in other policy areas, relations were often problematic. For instance, in March 1992 the deputy chairman of the foreign commission of the German federal parliament, the Social Democrat deputy Hans Koschnik, referred to Turkey as being an 'example' to the Central Asian republics, to which the latter felt very close.[46] Senior Turkish officials were soon to come to resent being pushed into such a role.

Moment of disillusionment, October 1992

This period of euphoria lasted for roughly fourteen months. While it may be a matter of debate precisely when this period began, its demise is easier to pinpoint. It was the convening of the Turkic summit in Ankara on 30–31 October 1992 that did most to puncture this sense of excitement. With the failure of the Turkic summit and the accompanying, often public show of reticence by key Central Asian leaders displayed in Turkey itself, many of the illusions held about the potential relationship were quickly shattered.

Ironically for Ankara, the Turkic summit was to have been the highpoint of the relationship hitherto. For the romantically inclined Bilal Şimşir, speaking just before the opening of the summit, it was an example of the new Turkish diplomacy, which he was quoted as describing as 'fast and bold', 'risky and dangerous'. It represented nothing less than Turkey 'racing against time' to develop relations with the so-called Muslim republics of the former Soviet Union,[47] before, presumably, Russia reasserted itself once again as a major power. Even for more sober Turkish diplomats, the summit was important because it was the first multilateral meeting of the Turkic republics, that is to say the states of former Soviet Central Asia,[48]

[45] *Newspot*, 23 April 1992.
[46] *Newspot*, 26 March 1992.
[47] *Turkish Daily News*, 28 October 1992.

Azerbaijan and Turkey. Implicit in such a view was that these states would forge closer relations among themselves, resulting over time in increasing co-operation in a variety of areas to the benefit of all. Different models were offered regarding the eventual nature of such a framework of co-operation with, for example, the Nordic Council being advanced as a suitable blueprint.[49] There also appeared to be considerable public interest in the convening of such a summit.[50]

The sense of expectation that greeted the staging of the conference was nowhere greater than in the presidential palace at Çankaya. It was clear from his opening speech that President Özal saw the summit as a major occasion, and Turkic co-operation as offering an excellent opportunity for Turkey to capitalise upon. Özal's rhetoric was characteristically colourful. He stated that 'The Turkish world now faces an opportunity that is rare in history'; he referred to 'We, the Western Turks'; having stated that their history, culture and language are one, he said that 'I think, therefore, that our business and our power can be one as well'.[51]

More concretely, Özal attempted to set the priorities for the summit. He advocated that the summit concentrate on economic co-operation as a way of promoting peace and security. He then went on to recommend a whole series of policy objectives, including: the taking down of economic walls, ultimately leading to free trade; the establishment of the necessary infrastructure to allow the free movement of people, goods and services; and the development of an integrated system of transport, telecommunications, banking and energy co-operation. To facilitate such aims, President Özal recommended the establishment of a number of summit working groups to promote such multilateral projects. He also said that issues

---

[48] Though not considered a Turkic state, Tajikistan was invited to the October summit, but did not take part because of its civil war.

[49] Looking back on the summit in an interview with a senior Turkish diplomat, 26 and 27 April 1993.

[50] One Turkish diplomat would actually argue after the event, in an effort to play down the summit's importance, that it was staged in part to assuage Turkish domestic opinion. Interview with senior Turkish diplomat, 23 November 1992.

[51] For this and other speeches and statements from the summit see BBC/SWB/ ME, 2 November 1992.

of regional and international importance would be discussed at the summit.

The content and form of the speech represented a monumental act of political misjudgement on the part of Özal. The leaders of the Central Asian republics were not ready for such an extensive agenda of co-operation, let alone for one to be pursued so rapidly. The leaders of Kazakhstan and Uzbekistan in particular, the former mindful of its large Russian minority and the latter eager to attract the help of the Russian Federation in ending the civil war in Tajikistan, were concerned at how such an agenda might be perceived in Moscow. The fact that Özal had outlined such a blueprint for action without adequate consultation simply confirmed the earlier impression that Turkey had arrogantly ascribed a leadership role for itself within the Turkic world. The Central Asian leaders responded by slamming the brakes on the vehicle of inter-Turkic co-operation. Neither was the cause of Turkic solidarity helped by President Elçibey of Azerbaijan, who sought to bolster his own position in the eyes of Turks by deriding the lukewarm attitude of his fellow leaders.[52]

The summit consequently ran into trouble from the first hour, with some participants increasingly nervous about the purely Turkic formation of the meeting. President Nazarbayev of Kazakhstan in particular felt that any joint declaration should be endorsed more widely if it was going to contain a clear policy prescription.[53] Nazarbayev went on to put a question mark against the very future of the much vaunted multilateral co-operation by stating that he was against the establishment of groupings of countries based on either religious or ethnic criteria. While he did not rule out the further development of ties with the other Turkic states, he put a powerful constraint on such co-operation by saying that he would be party to such ties as long as they did not harm Kazakhstan's commitments to other CIS members. In other words, Nazarbayev appeared to be placing his relationship with the CIS above any notions of pan-Turkic co-operation. In expressing such views, Nazarbayev was supported by President Karimov. Indeed, the Uzbek leader seemed

---

[52] For example, Elçibey stated that because Kazakhstan and Uzbekistan were members of the CIS they are unenthusiastic about joining another organisation. *Turkish Daily News*, 2 November 1992.

[53] *Turkish Daily News*, 31 October 1992.

to be clearer in expressing the limitations of his involvement in this exercise. He ruled out any desire to establish a supranational mechanism that would co-ordinate the Turkic world.[54]

With the involvement of other countries in a final declaration clearly unfeasible, Turkey ended up having no choice but to substitute one very bland communiqué for what should have been the grandly entitled Ankara Declaration on political affairs, with a second statement on economic co-operation. In drafting such a document, the leading Central Asian states were unrelenting in their insistence that no binding commitments should be adopted.[55] The sensitivity of the Central Asians and their differing interests in comparison with Turkey became even clearer over the political issues to be incorporated into the summit communiqué. Nazarbayev again led the way in refusing to adopt a strong position on a variety of issues from northern Cyprus (the omission of the 'Turkish Republic of Northern Cyprus' from the summit already having caused some surprise in the Turkish press) to the conflict in Bosnia-Herzegovina. Such was the Kazakh sensitivity towards the Russians that the communiqué even fell short of a denunciation of the Bosnian Serbs.

However, it was over the issue of Nagorno-Karabakh that the divisions among the summit participants became most apparent. Azerbaijan, as the party suffering militarily at the hands of the Armenians, wanted not only a strong statement of political support but also tangible action. Turkey appeared to support such an approach. For the leading Central Asian states the matter was a question of wider and complex intra-CIS relations, rather than the more straight forward and simplistic notion of aggression against a fellow Turkic state. Consequently, a proposal to adopt as summit policy an embargo against the Armenian Republic was dropped.[56]

With the behind-the-scenes turbulence clearly evident to the Turkish press, the difficulties of the summit did not remain hidden from the public for long. Turkey's newspaper columnists took up the subject of the summit. One leading commentator, Oktay Ekşi of *Hürriyet*, cut through the feeble attempts of the Foreign Ministry to label the summit a success. He criticised the lack of preparation

[54] *Turkish Daily News*, 1 November 1992.
[55] Ibid.
[56] Ibid.

for the summit and the failure to agree on the aims of the gathering in advance. Ekşi reserved special criticism for President Özal who had 'pressured' the visiting heads of state. He had shown a lack of patience in developing the new relationship, and had failed to consider the implications of his opening address to the summit. Ekşi concluded by saying that the summit was not a success: the only multilateral agreement arrived at during the meeting, he observed facetiously, was to hold annual summits of this kind.[57] Even in this regard, as it turned out, Ekşi was being over generous. While the summit may have decided to repeat the exercise on an annual basis, no such gathering took place in 1993 and an attempt to reconvene in Baku in January 1994 collapsed.[58]

The Turkic summit was significant because it openly portrayed the many limitations of pan-Turkic co-operation. As a result, the Turks at all levels had no choice but to re-evaluate some of their more fanciful notions as to the potential for co-operation with the other Turkic republics. The seniority, profile and venue of the gathering helped in this rather brutal process. However, the summit did nothing more than to point to some of the underlying difficulties in forging broad based co-operation. First and foremost it was clear that the process of intra-Turkic relations was not proceeding in a vacuum. Other relationships had to be taken into account, notably those involving the Russian Federation and the other members of the former Soviet Union. Second, the various Turkic states did not share the same interests and priorities. Geographical location and demographic composition, to name but two factors, helped dictate differing responses to different issues. In view of such considerations, the potential for pan- Turkic co-operation was limited. Moreover, it only stood a good chance of success if approached slowly and cautiously, with partial rather than wider multilateral co-operation more likely to yield tangible results.

---

[57] *Hürriyet*, 1 November 1992.

[58] The reasons why the Baku summit did not take place were similar to some of the reasons why the Ankara summit was a failure-namely concerns, notably on the part of the Uzbek president, over the apparent hostility of President Yeltsin to the convening of an exclusively Turkic meeting, and friction between the leading Central Asian states and Azerbaijan.

Period of despondency, November 1992-December 1993

If the Turkic summit was the moment when the Central Asian leaders made it clear that they neither desired nor envisaged an exclusive relationship with Turkey, it was not long before they developed new relations in other directions. The most important of these was the re-establishment of close relations with the Russian Federation. The Central Asian states had been founder members of the CIS, together with Russia, when it was established in December 1991. However, the organisation was widely expected to have a short life, and was, in any case, a loose outfit compared to its predecessor. The quality of the relationship between Russia and some of the Central Asian states changed markedly, however, with the onset of the crisis in Tajikistan.[59] One of the Central Asian states had been engulfed in a bloody civil war with the overthrow of the existing regime. The other Central Asian leaders were concerned at the out break of civil conflict for fear that their positions in power would consequently be weakened. Uzbekistan, preoccupied with the potential separatism of its own Tajik population, was especially keen to see an end to the fighting and the restoration of the *status quo ante.*

In order to realise its strategic objectives in Tajikistan, the leadership in Uzbekistan was the principal motor behind the forging of military co-operation with Russia, and joint action to restore peace and stability on desirable political grounds in Dushanbe. As a result, troops from Uzbekistan, Kazakhstan and Kyrgyzystan were sent to Tajikistan to fight alongside the Russian 201st Motorised Rifle Division in mid November 1992. With the possibility of renewed political challenges and violence in Tajikistan, this military co-operation was subsequently formalised into a defence agreement. This defence accord was clearly far more substantive than any relationship Turkey could reasonably offer the Central Asian states. It therefore marked the moment at which Russia re-emerged as being a state of greater importance in Central Asia than Turkey. Furthermore, it did so virtually without effort. This was not the product of an overbearing or truculent Russia eager to reassert its domination over former vassal states. Instead, the initiative for a military partnership

---

[59] For a brief discussion of these dynamics see Roland Dannreuther, 'Russia, Central Asia and the Persian Gulf', *Survival*, vol. 35, no. 4, winter 1993, pp. 99–100.

had originated from within Central Asia, from among the very states that the Turks had perceived as seeking to throw off the Russian yoke in favour of a closer relationship with Ankara.

It was not only a newly invigorated relationship between Central Asia and the Russian Federation that emerged soon after the disastrous Turkic summit. Ankara was obliged to put up with the sight of the Central Asian states improving their relations with Iran at a time when the limited potential for relations with Turkey had been so embarrassingly exposed. It should be emphasised that this did not represent Iran displacing Turkey in the priorities of the Central Asian states. Instead, it was an inevitable process which would probably have taken place earlier had it not been for the deterrent warnings by the United States that the Central Asian states might be penalised should they develop close relations with Iran. In the wake of the Baker visit to the region the newly independent states had therefore been cautious towards Iran. But as no penalty was incurred as the Central Asian states incrementally expanded interaction with Tehran, the disincentive to having full relations with a large and wealthy neighbour gradually disappeared.

Tajikistan was the first Central Asian state to cultivate closer ties with Tehran. By the autumn of 1992 relations appeared to be improving more broadly. Thus it was to Tehran that President Nazarbayev of Kazakhstan flew directly after leaving the Ankara summit,[60] in a display of balanced foreign relations for which he has become famous. For the Turks, who had been egged on in Central Asia by the West, fearful as it was of Iranian ideological expansionism, the timing of the visit must have caused particular anguish. With President Karimov following Nazarbayev to Tehran less than four weeks later, the elevation of Iran as a major player in the Central Asian arena, simultaneous with the exposure of Turkey's limitations, was demonstrable.

These events did not, however, precipitate a collapse in Turkish diplomacy, which is nothing if not resilient and persistent. In the ensuing few months Turkey further attempted to develop its relations with the new republics. In February 1993, for example, Ankara signed military training agreements with Almaty and Bishkek, to

---

[60] For a report of the visit and its extensive agenda, see *Kayhan International*, vol. XIII, no. 3424, 5 November 1992.

go with those already concluded with Ashkhabad and Tashkent.[61] If anything, Ankara increasingly saw itself as a partner with the forces attempting to maintain stability in the southern republics rather than, as had been the inevitable implication, an agent for liberal change; in short, Turkey was in retreat from propagating the Turkish model. Most notably, at the beginning of March, Turkey launched what it considered to be a serious bilateral attempt at mediation in the Armenian-Azerbaijani conflict.[62] At the centre of power it was asserted more coherently than in the past that it had never been Ankara's intention to create a sphere of influence in the Turkic republics, with the subordination or exclusion of others.

In spite of this lower key and more conciliatory tone, Turkey's position was to be further eroded as Russia's involvement in the former Soviet republics grew and spread closer to Turkey's borders. The battlefield successes of the Armenians over Azerbaijan in April 1993, the toppling of the neo-Kemalist President Elçibey in June, and the victories of the Abkhazian rebels in Georgia were all attributed to Russian involvement. Each development increased the perception of rising Russian power and obliged the south Caucasian republics to emulate what their Central Asian fellow states had already done voluntarily, namely to seek a more secure position within a Russian dominated area of influence. Turkey was not only left even more marginalised than before—the fall of Elçibey, its closest ally in the former Soviet south, further diminishing its own standing in the eyes of the Central Asian states—, but Ankara also felt obliged itself to defer to Russia,[63] in awe of its power and concerned that a more strident policy might be grist to the ultra-nationalists' anti-Turkish mill. The subsequent clash between President Yeltsin and the Russian parliament in October, which left the head of state beholden to the army, and the strong showing of the ultra-nationalist Liberal Democratic Party in the Russian elections in December further underlined the need for Turkey's careful management of a

---

[61] *Turkish Daily News*, 26 February 1993.

[62] For details of this mediation plan, see *Turkish Probe*, vol. 2, no. 17, 9 March 1993.

[63] Turkish journalist Cengiz Çandar points to the existence of a faction in the Turkish Foreign Ministry which wanted to cooperate with Russia and for which the stridently anti-Moscow and anti-Tehran policies of Elçibey simply became too hot to handle. They preferred the less trenchant if elusive style of Elçibey's eventual successor, Haydar Aliyev. See Bal and Bal, op. cit., p. 46.

volatile Russia. In turn, Turkey was further exposed as ill-equipped to challenge Russia's position in the latter's 'near abroad'.

The extent of the deflated expectations in Turkey in the wake of the Ankara summit can be seen by the fact that it only took the early reverses apparently at the hands of Russia to bring about a crisis of confidence. Once the start of the Armenian victories had become clear in the spring of 1993, opposition politicians in Turkey were quick to criticise government policy towards the former Soviet south, including Central Asia. One leading figure from the Motherland Party, who was around that time also the party's nominee for the presidency, Kamran İnan, was specific in his criticisms. He faulted the Demirel administration in particular for: not having established a ministry for the 'outside' Turks, that is for Turks abroad; understaffing the reorganised department in the Foreign Affairs Ministry; appointing second rank diplomats to staff the new embassies in the Turkic republics; excluding the Central Asian republics from membership of the newly initiated Black Sea Economic Co-operation project, and not creating a Turkic League or Commonwealth.[64] Though some of his recommendations were of course highly controversial,[65] such sentiments reflected a widespread assumption that Turkey had already failed to forge a special relationship with the Central Asian states.

While strategic reverses, notably at the hands of Russia, were the single greatest cause of Turkish demoralisation regarding the new republics, economic factors were not insignificant. These took two forms: first, the absence of virtually any international aid being channelled through Turkey to the new republics; second, the failure of Turkish companies to capitalise quickly on the initial opening up of Azerbaijan and Central Asia. The former was a particular blow, as Turkey had initially argued that it was an attractive partner for the new republics precisely because it could act as a conduit for international aid, even to the extent of playing a facilitating role in obtaining such aid. The bald reality was, however, that most Western donors placed the Russian Federation at the top of their aid priorities; little was therefore left to be made available to the non-Slavic states.

[64] Interview, 24 April 1993.
[65] Others are generally accepted as being true, such as the appointment of second rank diplomats to staff the new missions in Central Asia.

Even where significant amounts of aid were allocated for Central Asia, for example through the European Community's TACIS scheme, existing practices made it difficult to route such aid through a non-member state.[66] While some Muslim countries, notably Saudi Arabia, pledged large aid donations to the new republics with significant Muslim populations,[67] ideological differences together with *raison d'état* have placed a constraint on such aid being channelled through Turkey.

Turning to business, the emergence of the southern republics as independent states had stimulated considerable interest on the part of the Turkish private sector. Many businessmen had travelled to these countries, not least as part of the large delegations accompanying Çetin and Demirel on their swings through the area, and in the large commercial parties that followed. Though initial interest was great, many businessmen did not get beyond the question of how the new republics would pay for Turkish exports or fund Turkish-led projects. Moreover, with new markets also opening up in Eastern Europe, the Balkans, the Black Sea area and Russia itself, the potential opportunity cost of working in the former Soviet south was high for Turkish businessmen. Though payments problems were a widespread difficulty, in the case of economic interaction with Russia the massive and growing exports of Russian gas to Turkey quickly emerged as the payments motor of such bilateral activity.[68] With big business tending to be cautious towards the new republics, it was left to the less reputable businessmen from Turkey, interested only in a quick return, to make the running. The resultant bad

[66] For a brief discussion of the problems of Turkish participation within the Technical Assistance to the CIS (TACIS) programme, see Philip Robins, *Partners for Growth: New Trends in EC-Turkish Cooperation* (Forum Europe, Brussels, 1993), pp. 27–8.

[67] The Gulf Cooperation Council states, with Saudi Arabia as the major donor, had promised $3 bn in aid to the USSR for its support during the Gulf crisis. *Guardian*, 27 February 1992.

[68] By the end of 1993 Turkey was receiving 5.5 bn cubic metres of natural gas from Russia per annum, at a cost of some $400 million: *Turkish Daily News*, 19 January 1994. According to an agreement signed between the two states in November 1992, the volume of gas sales would grow to 8 billion cu. m. by 1996. These gas sales, together with Turkish Eximbank credits, were to fund Russia's merchandise imports from Turkey and to pay Turkish contractors. See BBC/SWB/ME, 17 November 1992.

feeling from disappointed business expectations in turn helped to drive the sentiment out of the emerging relationship at an early point.

Period of realistic expectations, 1994–

During the period of euphoria expectations of relations between Turkey and the Turkic republics were inflated. The period of despondency was in part a reaction to this excessive optimism. This second phase was, in turn, supplanted by what one might term a period of more realistic expectations. Gone is the high-flown rhetoric of the early months of 1992. Gone too is the crushing sense of powerlessness felt during the period of military reverses in the Transcaucasus in particular. But also gone is the sense that for Turkey Central Asia is a major foreign policy priority. Neither has Ankara tried or been able to insist upon equality in its treatment of the newly emerging states.

The emergence of a more sober and realistic set of relations has not simply been a function of interaction between Turkey and the Turkic republics. The position of Russia has been a critical variable. Dov Lynch shows how the evolution of Russian peacekeeping strategies has affected the overall context for these relations among others. He draws attention to Russia's abandonment of adventurist schemes in the CIS after 1993. Furthermore, Lynch identifies 1997, and the chastening experience of the first Chechen war, as the moment when Moscow came to pursue its interests in the former Soviet south with a greater sense of caution, 'downscaling' its approach to military cooperation,[69] a view corroborated from the vantage point of the other side.[70] The progressive easing of this strategic context provided an atmosphere in which Turkey and the republics could at last explore their potential.

---

[69] Dov Lynch, *Russian Peacekeeping Strategies in the CIS* (Macmillan/RIIA, London, 2000), p. 2.

[70] Hugh Pope, who covered the Caucasus and Central Asia extensively through the 1990s for *The Independent* and the *Wall Street Journal*, confirms such a view: 'It was the Chechen humiliation of the old Red Army in 1994–95 that gave all the countries of what we call Eurasia the breathing space with which to establish their independence, particularly in the Caucasus.' See 'The New Great Game: A Journalist's Perspective', *Insight Turkey*, vol. 2, no. 3, July–Sept. 2000.

That potential, stripped of sentiment, has almost inevitably been mixed. Consequently, a third phase in relations between Turkey and the new republics has emerged, but one which has been more patchy, spasmodic and low key. Increasingly, it appears as if the mercurial relations from 1991 to 1994 have been a deceptive guide to the prospects for long term inter-state relations. Elite relations, private business contacts and infrastructural projects have slowly begun to provide some degree of ballast to the relationship between Turkey and the region.

ELITE RELATIONS

In spite of the bad experience of the high profile 1992 Turkic summit, the opportunities for interaction among elites have grown over time. In part, this has been a reflection of a conscious policy, with the new republics sending their young diplomats to Turkey rather than Moscow for practical training. In turn, it has increasingly become apparent that significant parts of the elite of Turkey and the new republics have come to identify with one another.[71]

Nowhere has this sense of inter-personal chemistry been better witnessed than in meetings of the heads of state of Turkey and the republics. Süleyman Demirel's assumption of the presidency of Turkey in May 1993 coincided with the nadir of relations between Ankara and the new republics. Relations remained low key for sometime after then, reflecting the post-euphoria lack of interest of the respective governments. During a visit to Ankara in January 1995, for example, Turkmenistan's President Niyazov was visibly upset at the fact that prime minister Tansu Çiller and other leading ministers were absent from the delegation mobilised to welcome him.[72]

Demirel, however, was increasingly coming to take a special interest in Central Asia and the south Caucasus, partly out of concern at this lethargy of government and partly out of a desire to find a niche for himself in the realm of foreign policy. The fact that Demirel and the respective leaders had much in common, comprising as they did a

---

[71] It has, for instance, been more and more the tendency of diplomats from these countries to stick together at large gatherings, much in the way that, say, envoys from Western European or Arab countries tend to congregate together on large multilateral occasions.

[72] *Turkish Daily News*, 17 January 1995.

cabal of hardbitten male political survivors, helped to forge this personal bond. The establishment of this cordial personal chemistry helped to provide some continuity of relations both during periods of governmental turbulence in Turkey and in the face of political leaders with obviously more important priorities. It should be noted that this policy apathy did not apply solely to Çiller's premiership, but was also a characteristic of the Islamist Welfare Party-led coalition between June 1996 and June 1997, when even the forging of cultural relations was reported as having come to a standstill.[73]

Demirel's elevation to the presidency also coincided with a growing sense in Kazakhstan in particular that the steep decline in relations with Turkey was not helpful, especially as far as the maximisation of Almaty's room for diplomatic manoeuvre was concerned. While the Kazakhs did not want to antagonise Moscow, neither did they want to slip back into a position of passive dependence. Improving relations with Turkey was important if Kazakhstan was really to pursue a 'diverse' approach to foreign policy, as its leaders maintained that its geopolitics required.[74] Moreover, it was increasingly being felt in Central Asia that Russia was taking the new states for granted. With President Karimov, whose refusal to attend had torpedoed the summit scheduled for Baku in 1993, eventually relenting and President Nazarbayev having discovered at least a limited appetite for Turkic solidarity, the scene was set for the convening of a second Turkic summit almost two years after the disaster in Ankara.

The second summit of October 1994 was convened in the more cosmopolitan city of Istanbul, a sensible choice well away from the exclusively Turkish seat of government in Ankara. The summit was altogether more measured in its tone and realistic in its methods and aims,[75] with great care expended throughout on ensuring that all of the protagonists were in agreement on items of major importance. Though the suspicions of the Russian Federation were no less than at the time of the first such summit,[76] the participants felt sufficiently

---

[73] *Turkish Daily News*, 22 September 1997.

[74] President Nazarbayev in an address at Chatham House, 22 March 1994.

[75] For example, both Turkish and Russian were used as official languages of the summit.

[76] The Ministry of Foreign Affairs in Moscow was quoted as calling the Istanbul summit 'a brain-washing meeting with pan-Turkist aims'. See the Anatolian News Agency, 19 October cited in BBC/SWB/EE, 21 October 1994.

emboldened both to embrace 'institutionalized co-operation' and to adopt the 24 point 'Istanbul Declaration', which referred to bilateral and multilateral relations 'in every field'.[77] In this regard, the summit communiqué proved to be a serious declaration of intent. The summit re-established the principle of high level multi-lateral co-operation among the six, the process proving sufficiently robust to deliver a third summit, this time meeting outside Turkey in the Kyrgyz capital of Bishkek on 28 August 1995, and later a fourth summit in Tashkent in October 1996.[78]

The Bishkek summit was particularly significant, being the first such meeting to convene outside Turkey; for the Turkish press, this alone was taken to be a matter of importance.[79] The venue indicated both the growing confidence of those involved in multilateral co-operation and the growing acceptance of such meetings on the part of Moscow, perhaps in part because Russia had come to realise that it had relatively little to fear from such gatherings. Measured realism was increasingly coming to characterise the business and output of such meetings. As Turkey respectfully backed efforts to find a peaceful solution to the civil wars in Afghanistan and Tajikistan, so the Turkic republics reciprocated by agreeing to the necessity of fighting terrorism. At the end of the summit, Ferai Tınç, writing in *Hürriyet*, encapsulated the mood swing between the first and third summits. She declared that 'the "big brother" complex of Turgut Özal is being cast aside in favour of a more rational policy focusing on cultural rapprochement'.[80] Likewise, counselling realistic expec-tations,[81] a *Cumhuriyet* leader article stated that: 'We must view the steps taken to date neither as a "conquest" nor a "fiasco". These re-lationships will develop step by step in a climate of mutual trust.'

It was not just at the highest level that close elite relations were forged during this time. A range of wider elite interactions has also taken place. Almost inevitably this has had an ideological colour to it.

---

[77] For the Istanbul summit communiqué see TRT TV, 19 October, cited in BBC/SWB/EE, 21 October 1994.

[78] April 2001 saw the convening of the most recent conference, making seven in nine years altogether.

[79] See, for example, the editorial in *Cumhuriyet*, 28 August, reprinted in *Turkish Daily News*, 29 August 1995.

[80] 28 August 1995.

[81] *Cumhuriyet*, 28 August 1995

It is no coincidence that the cabinet minister taking the greatest interest in Turkic relations during the mid 1990s was Ayvaz Gökdemir,
who came from the ultra-nationalist wing of the DYP. Ultra-
nationalist parties such as the Grand Unity Party, BBP (*Büyük Birlik
Partisi*) have emphasised the potential of developing relations with
the Turkic states.[82]

Many of the big cultural gatherings of this time also drew strong
support from this end of the political spectrum. The Turkish Hearths,
an ultra-nationalist organisation established in 1912 to promote
Turkish culture, was heavily involved in the activities of the Turkish
World Youth Organisation, which had its fifth gathering, also in
Bishkek, in August 1995. The Turkic States and Communities Friendship Brotherhood and Cooperation Foundation (TUDEV) was
another organisation which was active in organising conventions of
participants from across the Turkic world, including northern Cyprus,
and which received high profile patronage. Strongly influenced by
that stalwart of pan-Turkism, Alpaslan Türkeş,[83] TÜDEV's third
gathering in Çeşme was attended by Rauf Denktaş and senior politicians from Azerbaijan and Central Asia.[84] A fifth such convention
in Istanbul in April 1997 was hosted by Türkeş' son Tuğrul, and
proved to be a meeting that attracted much interest from among his
ultra-nationalist supporters. Demirel was a frequent participant at
many such events, including those organised by the nationalist
right, as were Özal and Ciller, which led William Hale to conclude
that they seemed to have 'a semi-official status'.[85]

BUSINESS LINKS

The role of government has been central in the creation of a framework for long term interaction between Turkey and Azerbaijan and
the Central Asian states. The role of the private sector, though

---

[82] See, for example, the interview with the BBP leader Muhsin Yazıcıoğlu in the
Turkish Daily News, 30 October 1996. Though the BBP had a representative in
Erbakan's delegation on both his Asian and African tours Yazıcıoğlu continued
to place a greater importance on links with Central Asia.

[83] Heinz Kramer, *Options for Turkish Foreign Policy: Central Asia and Transcaucasus*,
unpublished paper, p. 16.

[84] *Turkish Daily News*, 3 October 1995.

[85] William Hale, *Turkish Foreign Policy, 1774–2000* (Frank Cass, London, 2000),
p. 292.

restricted because of payments difficulties, should not, however, be ignored. The presence and activity of Turkish companies are important in terms of building relationships beyond the scope of government-to-government relations. Furthermore, in the smaller republics the impact of some of the larger, well-connected Turkish companies has been profound. The best example hitherto is to be found in Turkmenistan, where Shireen Hunter has noted that the Turkish private sector has made 'significant inroads'.[86]

More than 40 major Turkish companies were operating in Turkmenistan by the end of 1993, attracted by the stability of the country and the relative absence of competition. The profile of the Turkish firms has been enhanced by the fact that Western companies appear to have been slow in seeking business opportunities in Turkmenistan, put off by its remote location and perceived backwardness. Turkish diplomats in Ashkhabad claim that the value of contracts awarded to Turkish companies, together with the investment to be undertaken by Turkish businesses, has topped the $1 bn mark. Turkish companies are certainly strong in the area of agribusiness. Turkish businesses account for nearly 70% of all contracts between Turkmenistan's Ministry of Agriculture and Western firms. By the end of 1995 30% of Turkmenistan's raw cotton was processed locally by Turkish firms. More widely, President Demirel claimed during a visit in 1997 that 49% of Turkmenistan's post-independence infrastructure had been built by Turkish businessmen. During his trip, Demirel visited a textile factory and a farm operated by Okan Holding and laid the foundation stone of a new paper complex.[87] Turkish companies are also active in a variety of other areas, including contracting, electronics, tourism and specialist services.[88]

The involvement of the Turkish private sector in the newly restructuring economies of the Turkic world was not, however, always entirely benign and positive. The newly independent republics became a magnet for operators from Turkey working in the grey and black economies. In the early months of the relationship this often consisted of sharp practice businessmen concerned to make a fast buck. Increasingly, however, because of the economic geography of the Central Asian states, lying as they do adjacent to

---

[86] Shireen T. Hunter, *Central Asia since Independence*, op.cit., p. 137.
[87] *Turkish Daily News*, 14 May 1997.
[88] Unpublished paper on Turkey-Turkmenistan relations by Laura Le Cornu.

the major sources of opium poppies, especially in Afghanistan, such activities became increasingly linked to illicit drugs and related areas.

Perhaps the most visible example of this phenomenon was the activities of a Turkish businessman, Ömer Lütfü Topal, who ran many of the casinos in Turkey in the 1990s. He quickly established a chain of casinos in Turkmenistan, and was involved in the operation of a number of five star hotels,[89] reputedly in partnership with the Turkmen government. Turkish press reports further allege that his casinos were used as a network for the transportation of Afghan opium bound for Europe, and even that some casino staff acted as couriers.[90] The clearest evidence of Topal's involvement in the Turkish underworld came in July 1996, when he was gunned down in Turkey, apparently the victim of a deliberate killing, though no direct Central Asian connection appeared to be involved in his death.

INFRASTRUCTURE

The absence of territorial contiguity between Turkey and Central Asia and even between Turkey and Azerbaijan, apart from the enclave of Nakhichevan, makes the development of the sinews of infrastructural interdependence more problematic. Turkey does not have the option Iran has to establish direct terrestrial ties. For Ankara, both road and rail connections would have to pass through third countries; with potential conduits consisting of Iran, Georgia and Armenia such lines of communication are, to say the least, open to disruption. Indeed, road transport links running through Iran have in the early days been subject to periodic delays, with the strong suspicion prevailing in Turkey that such interference has an underlying political motivation.

In order to reduce such a geographical disadvantage, Turkey has sought to develop non-terrestrially dependent infrastructure. First, Turkey has established regular flights with the leading capitals of the Central Asian states. During 1992 direct scheduled flights by the Turkish carrier, THY, were established between Turkey and the

---

[89] For example, one of the hotels in Turkmenistan operated by Topal had been built by the businessman Güven Sazak with an Eximbank loan. Sazak was an associate of the notorious right wing mafia leader Abdullah Çatlı, who was killed in the Susurluk crash of November 1996. See *Radikal* in *Turkish Daily News*, 27 January 1998.

[90] See *Yeni Yüzyıl* in *Turkish Daily News*, 5 December 1996.

capitals of Uzbekistan and Kazakhstan. A year later regular formal flights had been extended to include Ashkhabad; regular flights to Bishkek in Kyrgyzstan followed. In addition, other airlines fly between the republics and Turkey, though these have principally been charter flights.[91] In 1996 THY was the only foreign airline flying to Kyrgyzstan.[92]

Second, Turkey has sought to link itself directly with the people of Central Asia via a system of direct broadcasts. A special channel, Avrasya, was created with the sole purpose of forging such direct contacts. Turkish technicians built earth stations in the Central Asian republics to ensure that the channel could be received. The operating schedule was brought forward to enable the first broadcasts to coincide with the visit of prime minister Demirel to the republics at the end of April, 1992.[93] Although the project was initiated with great excitement, the results have been mixed. The governments of the republics have been wary of allowing neighbouring states to broadcast direct to their citizens without any direct control. By spring 1993 Turkish broadcasts were still not being received in Turkmenistan, despite the existence of a written agreement. In Kazakhstan around the same time Avrasya broadcasts were curtailed, apparently because Turkey had not provided a variety of additional technical equipment as specified under the arrangement. While Avrasya was not being broadcast in Tajikistan, it was being received both more reliably and favourably in Uzbekistan and Kyrgyzystan.[94]

Turkey's greatest success has undoubtedly come in the third area of this non-terrestrial infrastructure provision, telecommunications. Indeed, telecommunications has been referred to as the 'industrial frontiersman' of Turkey's Central Asia policy.[95] In this area Turkey had a clear comparative advantage in respect of both manpower and technology over Central Asia's other neighbouring states. PTT, Turkey's public sector telecommunications giant, was quick off the mark in providing equipment, free of charge, to the value of some

---

[91] Interview with senior official in Ministry of Foreign Affairs, Ankara, 22 April 1993.
[92] *Turkish Daily News,* 9 August 1996.
[93] *Turkish Daily News,* 27 April 1992.
[94] *Turkish Daily News,* 15 April 1993.
[95] To quote John Murray Brown of the *Financial Times,* 4 December 1992.

$25 million to the five republics. This 'loss leader' enabled Turkey to create a dependent relationship at an early stage, which made the republics reliant upon Turkey for access to international lines. Since then Turkish private and joint venture communications companies, notably Netaş, have consolidated this link, with factories being opened in Kazakhstan to manufacture related inputs.[96]

While Turkey has made significant strides in the provision of non-terrestrially based infrastructure, the absence of territorial contiguity can only be partially ameliorated. For the vast majority of Turkish visible goods exporters there has to be physical access to the Central Asian republics. Turkey has therefore declared its intention to be part of the diversification of Central Asia's land and sea transport routes away from extensive reliance on ties with the former Soviet Union. Thus, for example, Turkey has been part of the talks on the completion of the Caucasian rail network which, through the provision of train-ferry services, would improve access to Kazakhstan.[97] Attempts were further made to boost bilateral transport links between Turkey and Kazakhstan through the conclusion of land, sea and air accords during the summer of 1993.[98] However, the difficulties presented by Turkey's geographical deficit in relation to Central Asia were brought home by the realisation that transport links between Kazakhstan and Turkey were worse than those prevailing between Kazakhstan and Iran, China and Pakistan.

Waiting for the panacea: pipeline infrastructure, 1991–

The other area where Turkey has endeavoured to create terrestrially based lines of infrastructure interdependence has been the area of energy export pipelines. From the outset of the collapse of the Soviet Union it was clear that the key to future strategic relations with the new republics would be the future course of such energy routes. For a country like Turkey, located at the periphery of the former Soviet south, but potentially on an important line of supply to the European markets, crucial to establishing a relationship of

[96] ibid.
[97] *Turkish Daily News*, 29 February 1992.
[98] See the visit to Ankara by the Kazakh Transport Minister, Nizamettin Isingarin; *Turkish Daily News*, 9 July 1993.

interdependence would be the construction of energy pipeline infrastructure across Anatolia. In short, for once the worn out and misleading old sound-bite had the potential to become a literal truth: Turkey would realise its claim to be a Eurasian bridge between two continents of critical strategic importance.

At the outset there were many unrealistic expectations on the part of just about every actor in any way involved with the new energy politics of the former Soviet south, and Turkey was no exception. Confident assumptions were made about the extensive oil reserves of the Caspian, about the inevitability of the construction of a web of new pipelines, about the ability to manage relevant geopolitical tensions so that they would not hamper the energy plans of the new republics, and about the ability to raise project funding. In reality, all four issues have proved to be more complex and less straightforward than originally thought; the fact that at the turn of the century all of these issues are characterised by uncertainty and contestation is testimony to the naive over-simplifications made almost 10 years earlier.

STAGE ONE: THE FIRST 'AGREEMENT' WITH AZERBAIJAN

But back in March 1993 it looked as if Turkey's designs for the geostrategy of energy looked set to be realised. On the ninth of that month Turkey's energy minister signed a memorandum with his Azerbaijani counterpart for the construction of an oil pipeline from Baku to Midyat in south-eastern Turkey, from where it would link up with an existing line and run to the Mediterranean terminal at Ceyhan. The official Turkish news agency, Anatolia,[99] announced that construction would begin on the project in early 1994 and would take two years to complete. Financing, the report assured its readers, would be forthcoming from a combination of international institutions and foreign banks. The route of the line was kept intentionally flexible; it would probably traverse some 67 km. of Iranian territory, though foreign minister Çetin left the door open to the possibility of it crossing Armenia. The agreement was expected to put paid to the two competing alternatives for Azerbaijani oil: the expansion of the existing outlet through the Russian energy pipeline system to the Black Sea port of Novorossiisk, and an alternative

---

[99] Report reproduced in BBC/SWB/EE, 16 March 1993.

pipeline to the Georgian port of Poti, from where the oil would be transported by tanker through the Turkish Straits.

In fact the whole arrangement had been an exercise in self-delusion. What had actually happened was that the oil companies competing for concessions in Azerbaijan had come together to establish four working groups to address different aspects of future operations, with each group chaired by a different company. The Azeri State Oil Company (Socar) had chaired the group on onshore pipelines, and had brought in the Turkish pipeline company, Botaş, to participate in the group, thereby, as far as the foreign majors involved were concerned, instantly prejudicing its outcome. The motive of Socar, operating in the newly independent state now run by the nationalists of the Popular Front, was as rapidly as possible to throw off all vestiges of the Russian yoke and forge close relations with Turkey. Though the working group predictably concluded that Baku-Ceyhan should be the route for the pipeline, the findings had no credibility with the foreign majors in the consortium, and hence were rendered meaningless.[100] The Azerbaijan of Elçibey and the Popular Front, in their enthusiasm to establish closer ties with Turkey, had, not for the first time, ignored complex realities in favour of naive and unworkable solutions.

This was not the only mistake that was made by the supporters of the Baku-Ceyhan proposal at this time. Decision makers in Ankara appeared to focus on pipeline questions as predominantly technical matters. In doing so, they failed to associate such decisions with the wider geopolitics of the region. No sooner had the memorandum been signed than the Armenians, backed by the Russians in terms of hardware supplies, stepped up their military campaign against Azerbaijan, notably seizing Kelbajar, and consolidating their position in control of the disputed territory of Nagorno-Karabakh. With Azerbaijan in disarray, and support for the Popular Front rapidly ebbing away, the scene was set for the ousting of Elçibey in June, and his replacement with the old Soviet leader, Haydar Aliyev, a man of altogether greater political savvy. No longer would Baku push the Baku-Ceyhan scheme with such alacrity, to the detriment of wider complex competing calculations.

---

[100] Interview with two members of BP Exploration, 5 April 1993, BP being one of the three big foreign players in the consortium at that time.

The difficulties surrounding the whole question of Azerbaijani energy was illustrated by the fact that it was not until September 1994 that Baku finally concluded an agreement with a consortium of eight companies for the exploitation of its oil reserves. Turkey was modestly represented in the group in the form of a 1.75 per cent stake taken by the Turkish Petroleum Company (TPAO). Even then, Russia was deeply ambivalent about the development, the Foreign Ministry in Moscow refusing to recognise the deal, even though ironically it also included Russia's state-owned Lukoil.[101] The TPAO stake rose by a further 5% in April of the following year, with Socar consequently reducing its share. Turkish complicity in the Cevadov coup attempt[102] against Aliyev the previous month enabled the Azerbaijani president to drive a harder bargain on the deal, with TPAO paying $70 million in cash for the increased stake.[103] With hard, protracted negotiations having focused on the allocation of oil prospecting concessions, it is little wonder that the debate about pipeline routes remained on the back burner after the fall of Elçibey.

STAGE TWO: AZERBAIJAN'S 'EARLY OIL'

Ankara scored a major success in early 1995 when it succeeded in mobilising US support for its pursuit of the Baku–Ceyhan line. Hitherto, the US had appeared somewhat agnostic on the subject, in spite of the fact that it shared many of Turkey's views on the strategic diversification of the new states of the FSS away from dependence on Russia. At the Clinton–Yeltsin summit in the autumn of 1994, for example, the American president appeared to defer to Moscow's strategic notion of its 'near abroad', a position that was interpreted as giving a yellow light to Russian intervention in what it regarded as its sphere of influence. The situation changed with the cooling of American-Russian relations, a development which the newly appointed American ambassador, Marc Grossman, was able adroitly to exploit, not least over the diplomacy of energy.[104]

---

[101] *Turkish Probe*, no. 96, 23 September 1994.
[102] Ruşen Cevadov was a former deputy interior minister of Azerbaijan and head of the 700-strong OMON, or elite police force. He was killed in the coup attempt.
[103] *Turkish Daily News*, 14 April 1995.
[104] An excellent example of Grossman in action came in late January 1995 at his first press conference in Ankara after his appointment as ambassador. To a

Encouraged by US support, Turkey increased its efforts on the energy front in general,[105] and, as an increasingly more pressing focus, concentrated its attentions on the route for so-called 'early oil' from Azerbaijan in particular.[106] In doing so, Turkey controversially switched the emphasis of its lobbying, in a move associated with Emre Gonensay, prime minister Ciller's economic adviser. Under the new policy Turkey now supported the construction of a limited oil pipeline between Baku and Supsa on the Black Sea coast. This formed part of the core of a proposed compromise with the Russians, whereby half the early oil would flow through this route and the balance through the existing system to Novorossiisk, Ankara having toned down its concerns about increased levels of oil tanker traffic through the Turkish Straits in this connection alone. With Moscow experiencing increasing problems in Chechnya, on the route of its pipeline system, it appeared by February 1995 to be resigned to accepting the compromise.[107]

Sensing a strengthening position, the Turkish side sought to press its advantage. Ankara tried to speed up the decision-making by offering to finance the $250 mn construction of the Supsa line, the offer being conditional on the capacity of the line being limited to 6 million tonnes a year. Turkey also insisted on purchasing all the oil

---

packed gathering hanging on his every breath, he announced that the US government was now behind the idea of transporting Caspian oil via a pipeline to Turkey; banner headlines of approval virtually throughout the mainstream Turkish press duly appeared the next day. One description of the press conference wrote of the journalists 'reeling in paroxysms of pleasure' at the announcement. See *Turkish Probe*, no. 115, 3 February 1995.

[105] For instance, in March 1995 Turkey signed a protocol with Kazakhstan for the export of Kazakh oil through a pipeline to Ceyhan. While the accord was non-binding, and the two sides continued to disagree about the direction of such a pipeline (Almaty favouring a route through Turkmenistan, Iran and Azerbaijan; Turkey wanting a line under the Caspian Sea and via Azerbaijan), the Turkish energy minister, Ahmet Gokcen, was quoted as saying: 'The protocol at least shows that Kazakhstan prefers the Turkish route over other alternatives.' For coverage of the signing, see the *Turkish Daily News*, 22 March 1995.

[106] 'Early oil' refers to the limited amount of crude oil to be extracted at first from Azerbaijan's three Caspian oilfields. The volumes concerned would run to a maximum of 5 million tonnes per year, with the early oil period spanning up to eight years.

[107] *Turkish Probe*, No. 119, 10 March 1995.

using the route, which would be shipped to Trabzon for use in a new oil refinery, thereby guaranteeing the market for the oil using the route. Turkey added one further crucial condition to the deal.[108] Ankara required that an explicit reference be made in the Supsa accord to a commitment to build the Baku-Ceyhan pipeline. In trying to persuade a sceptical home audience, Gonensay argued that: 'The realization of the Baku-Georgia route is the starting point for the Georgia-Ceyhan route'. Briefings from the Turkish Foreign Ministry also drew attention to the underlying strategic motivation of Turkish calculations in giving further insight into the decision to push the Supsa option. Emphasis was given to the fact that acceptance of the Georgian route would create 'the first system independent of the Russian pipeline network for transporting the region's oil to Western markets', a reference to the old aim of diversifying the reliance of the Former Soviet South away from Moscow.[109]

But, in spite of such an apparent focus, all was not going well for the Turkish side. Such was the preoccupation of Ankara that one foreign affairs commentator wrote of Turkish foreign policy towards the Transcaucasus as being 'indexed' on Baku; President Aliyev was seen as manoeuvring 'skillfully' over the oil route issue, maintaining Turkey's interest but without ever actually taking an irreversible decision.[110] Moreover, the consortium of oil companies operating in Azerbaijan, the Azerbaijan International Operating Company (AIOC), which had apparently been won round to the Supsa early oil proposal, bridled at the attempt to bounce it into a more costly commitment on Baku-Ceyhan.

Though Ankara continued to pursue the Azerbaijani oil issue, its ability to realise its objectives was greatly hampered by the divisions and uncertainties in its own domestic politics. The appointment of Emre Gonensay as foreign minister in February 1996, as part of the ANAP-DYP coalition, should have been a boon for Turkey, because of his accumulated expertise in the matter and his political access to

---

[108] In fact the deal had five conditions imposed by the Turkish side. In addition to the three mentioned in the text, the other two were: Turkish companies or a consortium dominated by Turkish firms must build the pipeline, and a guarantee of the regular throughput of oil must be given for eight years.

[109] *Turkish Probe*, no. 167, 16 February 1996.

[110] Cengiz Çandar writing in *Sabah*, 16 April, reprinted in the *Turkish Daily News*, 17 April 1996.

both Çiller, now installed as deputy premier, and his old mentor, President Demirel. In fact Gonensay's period of less than four months in office was a sad affair, with the minister unable to exercise much authority, even in his own ministry. With the leaders of the two coalition parties unable to work with one another, the ANAP-DYP government collapsed in June, to be followed by the Islamist led RP-DYP government. The new coalition proceeded to take responsibility for Azerbaijani early oil away from the Foreign Ministry and to give it to the Energy Ministry. With Gonensay's influence gone, the Energy Ministry, which had always opposed the Supsa route as a waste of time and money, immediately dropped it as an objective of Turkish foreign policy,[111] reverting to an exclusive emphasis on Baku-Ceyhan.

But by then the change of tack was too late. Azerbaijani early oil was split between a new pipeline to Supsa and the Novorossiisk option, the former without Turkish financing, Turkey as a monopoly consumer or, crucially, with any Baku-Ceyhan conditionality included. Ankara had unwittingly helped the cause of the Georgians without furthering its own strategic objective. The first supplies of Azerbaijani early oil duly came on stream in early 1999.

STAGE THREE: BAKU-CEYHAN REVISITED

With the early oil diversion out of the way, the focus then returned to the long term issue of how best to transport Azerbaijani oil for export. Consequently, Turkey began anew to pursue the Baku-Ceyhan pipeline scheme. Once again, the Turks received a fillip from the Americans. Indeed, with bilateral relations suffering at one level because of the existence of a *de facto* embargo on certain military exports, it was pipeline diplomacy that helped to keep relations solid.

Washington remained wedded to strategies for the former Soviet south that would lessen Russian dominance, but without substituting dependence on Iran; however, it now stiffened it by a rhetoric and public diplomacy that displayed greater conviction than in the past.[112]

---

[111] Mehmet Ali Birand writing in *Sabah*, 19 July, reprinted in *Turkish Daily News*, 20 July 1996.

[112] For example, Ambassador Morningstar has gone on record as saying that 'the US government has a duty and an obligation to play a major role' in the commercial decision-making process connected with the Baku-Ceyhan pipeline. See *Turkish Daily News*, 26 October 1998.

This resulted in the development of the 'Eurasian transport corridor' strategy,[113] whereby lateral lines of communication and supply would be created for the hydrocarbons producers of Central Asia and the south Caucasus. The most important of these were three pipeline projects, all close to the interests of Ankara: first, the original Baku–Ceyhan route; second, a feeder line under the Caspian to Baku which would collect oil from both Kazakhstan and Turkmenistan in order to aggregate volumes with Azerbaijan; third, a natural gas pipeline from Turkmenistan, the Trans-Caspian Gas Pipeline, also to run under the Caspian, going on to Turkey via Azerbaijan and Georgia.[114] Very soon the AIOC was to come under 'fierce US pressure' to agree to the Baku–Ceyhan project as soon as possible.[115]

Together with Russian spoiling tactics, a central problem with the Baku–Ceyhan proposal has always been its cost. While Turkey insisted the line could be built for as little as $2.4 billion, other estimates covered a range as high as $4 billion. In any case, even the official Turkish figure was substantially higher than the estimated cost of Baku–Ceyhan's principal rivals: $2 billion for Baku–Novorossiisk; $1.5 billion for an upgraded Baku–Supsa.[116] With the price of crude oil falling precipitously in 1998, and the whole Caspian energy programme suddenly in doubt, concerns about cost and viability redoubled, in turn more than mitigating US pressure.

Turkey had also encountered problems in its attempt to organise a concerted lobbying effort in the region. For example, Ankara succeeded in assembling foreign ministers and other officials from Azerbaijan, Georgia, Kazakhstan and Turkmenistan in Istanbul in March 1998, but, frustratingly, failed to elicit from the meeting a clear endorsement for Baku–Ceyhan. Turkey had better luck in the rhetorical stakes with a meeting in Ankara on 29 October 1998, timed to coincide with celebrations for the 75th anniversary of the establishment of the republic, when the presidents of Azerbaijan,

---

[113] An attempt to complement and operationalise this came with the adoption of a 'Caspian Sea' strategy, launched at a prestige conference in Istanbul in May 1998, featuring a 65 project menu for areas of future action.

[114] See Hugh Pope, 'US Shows Support for Caspian Sea Oil Projects', 28 May 1998, and 'US Pledges Caspian Sea Oil Funds', 1 June 1998, *Wall Street Journal* via Dow Jones.

[115] *Financial Times* Survey on Turkey, 15 June 1999.

[116] *Financial Times*, Turkey Energy Survey.

Georgia, Kazakhstan, Turkey and Uzbekistan added their signa-
tures to the Ankara Declaration in support of a lateral energy corridor for the transportation of Caspian energy to Western markets.[117]

The Turkish position was further strengthened through two developments in 1999. First, AIOC softened its long running scepticism
over Baku-Ceyhan, driven by BP-Amoco's wish to improve its relations with the US government at a time of its attempt to acquire the
American company Arco. Second, the Clinton visit and the OSCE
summit in November provided an occasion for the signing of six
'framework' agreements relating to Baku-Ceyhan. In spite of the
apparent fecundity of the occasion, like the Clinton visit as a whole
the signings were at least as much about presentation as substance.[118]
While such moves undoubtedly gave further momentum to the
cause of Baku-Ceyhan, much had still to be done. Outstanding
problems to be resolved remain much as before, including: general
doubts about Caspian reserves; uncertainties about cost and capacity; securing the minimum 1 mn b/d throughput of oil, which will
be needed to ensure commercial viability; establishing a uniform
legal regime to apply across the transit countries.[119] Even after a
decade or so of expectation, Baku-Ceyhan is still, at best, no more
than 'a job half done'.[120]

Turkey's relations with the so-called Turkic states of Central Asia
were at first mercurial. This is best explained by the lack of ballast,
whether economic, political or human, in the relationships. Initially,
expectations on both sides were exaggerated. Disillusionment was
inevitable. Expectations were, however, dashed in a particularly embarrassing and visible way during the Turkic summit in Ankara at
the end of October 1992. A period of despondency then set in, accentuated by the re-emergence of Russian power in the Transcaucasus.

---

[117] *Turkish Probe*, 10 January 1999.
[118] David Ignatius of the *Washington Post* has labelled the outcome of the Istanbul
summit 'polite but empty promises'. See *International Herald Tribune*, 28 August
2000.
[119] For a detailed report on the Istanbul signings, see *Middle East Energy*, no. 52,
18 November 1999.
[120] Simon Henderson, 'Caspian Energy Accords: A Job Half Done', *Policywatch 424*
(Washington Institute, Washington, DC, 1999).

The emotions and attitudes evoked during this period were almost as exaggerated as those which prevailed during the early period of euphoria.

Since the mid 1990s a third phase in relations has begun to emerge. Less exciting, more low key and often patchy and spasmodic, this third phase has been born of a more practical approach to relations. The sinews of this relationship have been the non-terrestrial infra-structure that has been put in place, notably in the areas of air transport and communications; the motor for the relationship has been private sector commercial activity, especially in textiles; the relationship has been cemented by low key elite interaction, which has helped to forge a mutual sense of identification. As the ballast in the relationships between Turkey and new republics has grown, the formerly mercurial relations have, to some extent at least, become stabilised.

Ultimately, however, the long term fortunes of Turkey's relations with the new states in the former Soviet south will depend on the future of the energy sector, and more specifically on the routes of future pipelines. The construction of a series of oil and gas pipelines across Anatolia would reorient the hydrocarbons producers among the southern republics away from their old dependency on the territory controlled by Moscow to the north. More importantly for Ankara, the construction of the likes of the Baku-Ceyhan line would forge real strategic dependency on Turkey, for both the producer countries to the east and the consuming countries to the west. Such has been the dream of Turkish politicians and officials for a decade now. The elusive nature of the vision so far is testimony to what lies at stake for all of the countries in the region.

9

TURKEY AND NORTHERN IRAQ: LEARNING TO LIVE WITH CONTRADICTIONS[1]

Northern Iraq was one of the thorniest and most intractable of all Turkey's foreign policy challenges through the 1990s. It was clearly not an area which Ankara would have chosen as a priority area. Northern Iraq was located adjacent to an area of Turkey which had seen negligible economic development. The Middle East region in general was not a normative priority for Turkey's Kemalist elite, preoocupied as it is with Turkey's 'European vocation'. Yet northern Iraq quickly forced itself on policymakers as an area of priority because of its geopolitics, located adjacent to the epicentre of a violent, secessionist insurgency. If existential survival was the highest of strategic priorities for Turkey's leadership in the 1990s, northern Iraq was a vortex which could not be ignored.

For Turkey this was not a new problem. The Iraqi state had effectively abandoned parts of Iraqi Kurdistan during the 1980–8 Iran-Iraq war, when it consolidated its resources in an attempt to hold off successive Iranian military attacks. That left a political vacuum in northern Iraq. From 1984 onwards the PKK began to exploit this vacuum as a springboard for their insurgency. In response, the Iraqi and Turkish states forged an agreement that would allow hot pursuit of Kurdish insurgents by Turkish forces across the border. In 1988,

---

[1] Much of the information in this chapter is based on extended interviews with those from different sides intimately involved in the issue. These include American, British and Turkish diplomats, and authoritative figures from the various Kurdish factions. Citations of individual interviews have not been made in an effort to protect the anonymity of those interviewed.

Ankara was relieved to see Baghdad re-establish its writ across the whole territory of the state.

What was crucially different between the 1980s and the 1990s was the issue of scale. In 1984 PKK armed operations had only just begun. They acquired a serious intensity after about 1989, by which time the Iran-Iraq war had come to an end. By the 1990s, however, the PKK had developed into a formidable force capable of causing extensive disruption and loss of life in south-east Turkey. Even after 1995, when the insurgency was waning, the PKK still posed considerable military challenges for Turkey. It was only in 1999, with the capture of PKK leader Abdullah Öcalan in February and his announcement of the cessation of hostilities the following summer, that the insurgency seemed as if it might be close to ending.

This chapter will focus on the challenge which the absence of Iraqi state power in northern Iraq posed for Turkey. It will begin by exploring the strategic contradictions faced by Ankara and the consequent difficulty of developing a coherent and consistent policy. In the analytical periodisation that follows such issues will be illustrated in detail, as will Turkey's attempts to wrestle with such contradictions. It is a complex story involving many actors, from disparate Kurdish factions through regional powers and the leading players in the international community to different personalities and institutions within foreign and security policymaking in Turkey. However, it is one which has illuminated foreign policymaking in Ankara over a sustained period especially well.

Policy predicament

The legacy of the 1990–1 Gulf crisis in northern Iraq posed a complex series of challenges for Turkey. These could be sub divided into three. First, Turkey wanted to ensure that the Kurds of northern Iraq remained at home, for fear of a repetition of the 1987 refugee crisis writ large. In that year between 40,000 and 50,000 Iraqi Kurds had crossed the Turkish border, with some 35,000 becoming permanent refugees. Second, Turkey did not want to see the emergence of a separate Kurdish entity in northern Iraq, for fear that this would form the basis of a Kurdish state which could, in turn, act as both a model and a source of inspiration for Turkey's own Kurds.

Third, Ankara did not want to see the political vacuum which emerged in the north as a result of the retreat of the Iraqi state exploited by the PKK as a springboard for insurgency operations across the border in south-east Turkey, as had happened during the Iran-Iraq war after 1984.

Of more general interest in terms of policy towards Iraq, though also affecting the north, were three further goals. First, to maintain the integrity and unity of the state of Iraq, for fear that an implosion of Iraq might draw the regional powers into a Lebanese-style conflict. Second, to bring about an end to the damage caused to the Turkish economy through the rigorous application of international sanctions. Third, to maintain good relations with the United States; this aim was driven both by the undisputed fact that it was the single superpower in the global system and by its centrality as the mainstay of NATO, the Western club of greatest importance of which Turkey was a member, at a time when the future of the organisation and indeed of US commitment to European security were far from assured. Perhaps curiously, Turkey did not seem particularly concerned about Iraq's residual weapons of mass destruction (WMD) capability, not at least before 1997. Ankara appeared chary of publicly acknowledging the interest that it had in the activities of the UN Special Commission (Unscom) in this area, as a benefit to help balance the economic cost sustained as a result of the sanctions.

Though otherwise such aims, specific and general, were clear enough, Turkey found great difficulty in developing a set of complementary policies capable of working towards the attainment of all six objectives simultaneously. Indeed, worse than that, such objectives were to prove to be so incompatible that Turkey often found that policies developed with one aim in mind were actually counterproductive as far as others were concerned. As successive Turkish leaders wrestled with such difficulties, they increasingly became the target of charges of policy incoherence or, worse still, of having had no policy at all towards Iraq.

Instances abound. Turkey participated in Operation Provide Comfort 2 (OPC 2), which aimed to keep Iraqi coercive power out of the north of the country and hence protect the Iraqi Kurds through the enforcement of a 'no-fly' zone north of the 36th Parallel. The specific aim of this policy was to keep the Iraqi Kurds on their land

and away from the Turkish border. However, there were three by-products of this policy that threatened to impair Turkey's pursuit of its other objectives. A first consequence of OPC 2 was that the authority of the Iraqi state was further diminished in northern Iraq, which allowed the Iraqi Kurds sufficient *de facto* sovereignty to be able to establish an autonomous administration between 1992 and 1994. This, together with other exercises in institution-building, notably elections in 1992 and the convening of a representative assembly, began to resemble an independent entity in embryonic form.

Moreover, the retreat of Iraqi state authority from the north and its replacement with what proved to be a weak and vulnerable administration in turn drew the regional powers into taking a heightened interest in the area. This they did through the patronage of the Kurdish groups most vulnerable to their influence: in the case of Iran, the Patriotic Union of Kurdistan (PUK) and the Kurdish Islamists, the Islamic Movement of Kurdistan (IMK); in the case of Syria, the PKK; in the case of Turkey, increasingly the Kurdistan Democratic Party (KDP). Thus was created the sort of unstable regional competition that Ankara had initially feared. Yet a further consequence of the weak Kurdish administration in northern Iraq was that it proved insufficient to police the territory nominally under its control. This in turn made the area more attractive for the PKK as a base of operations against Turkey. This helps to explain the persistence of the conspiracy theory in Turkey that OPC 2 was a Western plot to intensify the PKK insurgency and so keep the Turkish state weak.

A second area of policy contradictions relates to the plight of the Turkish economy as a result of the international sanctions against Iraq. By 1994 the Turks claimed that the cost of implementing the sanctions regime had reached $20 billion, the equivalent of an estimated $5 billion each year.[2] While the exact accuracy of such a figure is disputed, the economic cost had certainly been great. Turkey had, in turn, sustained an important security cost, as the deep recession caused in the economically under developed south-east as a result of the loss of border trade with Iraq increased dissatisfaction with the Turkish state to the benefit of the PKK. Ankara should therefore have emerged as an enthusiastic supporter of the rehabilitation of

[2] Foreign Minister Hikmet Çetin quoted in *Turkish Daily News*, 29 April 1994.

Iraq, in order to recommence its commercial relationship with Baghdad. However, this would have brought Turkey into diplomatic conflict with the US, which was vigorously pursuing a strategy of containment towards Saddam Hussein.

The irreconcilable nature of Turkey's goals and policies in northern Iraq left Ankara discontented and frustrated, and with the tactics and detail of policy the subject of protracted contestation. Thus the six-monthly renewal of the mandate for OPC 2 was routinely the subject of heated discussion, which explains why the Demirel government chose in 1992 to share responsibility for its perpetuation by placing ultimate authority for its extension in a vote in parliament. In the parliamentary debates that took place opposition deputies regularly abstained or voted against the measure, though only to reverse their position, as in the cases of ANAP, the DYP and even the RP, when in government, no doubt on the 'advice' of the military.

As the 1990s progressed, aided by the indulgence of her allies, Turkey gradually settled on particular approaches towards the situation in northern Iraq, being increasingly resigned to the unpalatable by-products of such policies. Broadly speaking there were three constants to this approach. First, a strategic commitment to OPC 2, in spite of periodic misgivings. Though every six months there was a vigorous debate in parliament about the wisdom of renewing the mandate, these debates increasingly took on a quality of theatre.[3] With the NSC decisively indicating that the military favoured renewal,[4] and successive cabinets endorsing such a view, it might be argued that in reality there was never a real prospect of the vote being lost. The Turkish authorities were not, however, beyond using the public re-examination of the operation to wring further

---

[3] For a discussion of why the routine retention of PC2 might well have been 'the result of a rational calculation by Turkish statesmen', see Mahmut Bali Aykan, 'Turkey's Policy in Northern Iraq, 1991–95', *Middle Eastern Studies*, vol. 32, no. 4, October 1996, pp. 354–7.

[4] The Turkish military were convinced of the importance of renewing OPC2 because the top generals believed that its existence gave them a freer hand in northern Iraq. Interview with senior Turkish diplomat, 26 February 1998. This would presumably have been for two reasons: it justified frequent cross border military activity, and it helped to deter US criticism of Turkish armed operations in northern Iraq against the PKK.

concessions from their US, British and French partners. Consequently, the provisions of OPC 2 evolved over time. At the end of 1996, OPC 2 was re-packaged, though without French participation, as Operation Northern Watch, since when the renewal of the mandate has become politically far less contentious.

Second, the Turkish approach towards northern Iraq increasingly followed the Israeli model towards south Lebanon prior to the final withdrawal of the Israeli Defence Force in May 2000. Northern Iraq was regarded as consisting of a political vacuum, which had partially at least been filled by the terrorist activities of the PKK. In the absence of state authority, Turkey took upon itself the right to undertake periodic cross border operations. Such operations met with 'understanding' in Washington. These were highly reminiscent of Israeli operations in southern Lebanon, both in terms of short raids by military aircraft on suspected guerrilla camps and the more protracted cross border operations involving ground troops as well as the air force,[5] such as Operation Accountability in 1993 and Operation Grapes of Wrath in 1996.

Increasingly Ankara co-operated with the KDP to keep the border areas clear of PKK operatives. This has been described as Turkey's security zone 'by proxy'.[6] This was again reminiscent of, though not entirely analogous to, Israel's co-operation with the South Lebanese Army (SLA), the KDP being a more formidable organisation with a greater base of support than that enjoyed by the SLA, if also less politically reliable as an ally. Ankara even spasmodically debated whether Turkey should go the whole way in imitating Israel and formally establish its own semi-permanent 'security zone' in northern Iraq.[7] Bülent Ecevit was the party leader who most earnestly advocated such a course of action, before, that is, he assumed the premiership in 1998. In the end, after very careful consideration and some apparent vacillation, Turkey formally decided against this, principally on practical grounds. However, the practical effect of

---

[5] Such protracted operations took place in August 1991, October 1992, March 1995 and November 1997.

[6] Interview with senior Turkish diplomat, 26 February 1998 (note 4).

[7] The idea of the creation of a 'buffer zone' was the subject of debate on at least four occasions, in October–November 1992, April 1994, March 1995 and September 1996.

Turkey's involvement in northern Iraq, where at the end of the 1990s it had between 1,000 and 10,000 men at any one time, together with its close co-operation with the KDP, amounts to the creation of a *de facto* security zone in the north.

The third permanent plank of Turkish policy towards northern Iraq has been solidarity with the US-led consensus on Iraq at the UN. This involved the substantive retention of the international economic sanctions against Iraq, in spite of the negative impact that they were having on Turkey. The Turkish position ultimately remained solid because of the priority given to this foreign policy goal by the United States. The impact of these sanctions has, however, been partially ameliorated. The United States was willing to turn a blind eye to the small scale cross-border trade between Turkey and Iraq via the Kurdish safe haven. Moreover, Turkey also benefited at the margins when the US and British governments came to realise that in order to maintain support, both at home and abroad, for their sanctions strategy they had to allow the Iraqi government limited oil exports to help pay for humanitarian supplies. Thus, their response, in the form of UN SCR 986, stated that 'the larger share' of petroleum and petroleum products from Iraq should be shipped via the Kirkuk-Yumurtalık pipeline through Turkey.[8]

Analytical chronology
PROVIDE COMFORT: SHORT TERM CRISIS MANAGEMENT AS LONG-TERM STRATEGY, FEBRUARY 1991–JULY 1991 AND BEYOND

Once Ankara permitted the US-led multinational coalition to use the Incirlik air base to initiate an air campaign against Saddam Hussain's Iraq on 16 January 1991, a series of events was triggered over which Turkey was to have little or no control. The 38 day aerial campaign was followed by the 100 hour land war, which drove Iraq's forces from Kuwait in disarray. This in turn was followed by a spontaneous uprising of Iraqis in the south of the country, which was then joined, possibly reluctantly, by the Iraqi Kurds in the north. A moment of

---

[8] Paragraph 6, Resolution 986, adopted 14 April 1995, though not implemented, owing to Iraqi procrastination, until December 1996.

euphoria at the initial, rapid success of the uprising was followed by a steady reassertion of the armed force of the state. Faced with the imminent prospect of the arrival of the Iraqi military, and mindful of Saddam's vengeful wrath in the recent past, the Kurdish uprising collapsed in panic and flight.

Turkey, which had been little more than a bystander in these events, was suddenly faced with its own Gulf crisis. More than 400,000 Iraqi Kurds streamed towards the Turkish border, obviously intent on escaping from the expected retribution at home. Ankara's first reaction, remembering the experiences of a similar flight on a smaller scale in 1987, was not to let the Iraqi Kurdish refugees enter Turkey. Instead the Turkish military was given instructions to keep the Kurds in the mountainous border areas. However, this option became increasingly untenable because of the humanitarian suffering of the displaced, scenes that were increasingly captured by foreign camera crews and journalists who had originally decamped to Turkey to cover the war. Faced with two deeply unpalatable alternatives, President Özal in his characteristic way conjured up a third option, whereby the Iraqi Kurds could return home under international guarantees.

Özal was fortunate in not being the only world leader under increasing pressure to act. In Europe, in particular, public opinion was proving to be a growing force for action. Britain's prime minister John Major took up the challenge, developing the idea of a Kurdish safe haven, which he then easily persuaded his fellow EU leaders to adopt as a common position on 8 April. With Turkish and European thinking converging, American support was subsequently enlisted. The resolution of the Turkish parliament the previous January allowing the presence of foreign troops on Turkish soil meant that the partners could act quickly. Operation Provide Comfort (OPC) then followed, with foreign and Turkish troops combining to help feed and sustain the Iraqi Kurds, pending their return home to northern Iraq. With coalition aircraft giving teeth to the protection of the safe haven, in the form of OPC 2,[9] the possibility of

---

[9] For a Turkish perspective on OPC2 see Kemal Kirişci, '*Huzur Mu Huzursuzluk Mu: Çekiç Güç ve Türk Dış Politikası*' (Comfort or Without Comfort? Hammer Force and Turkish Foreign Policy) in Faruk Sönmezoğlu (ed.), *Türk Dış Politikasının Analizi* (Analysis of Turkish Foreign Policy) (Der Yayınları, Istanbul, 1994), pp. 273–89.

security from attack began to gain credibility; the way was open for the refugees to return.

Though there were the inevitable anecdotes about friction involving a few foreign journalists and troops, in fact OPC had worked swiftly, smoothly and effectively. It had been a complex and difficult mission, involving many thousands of people in conditions of tremendous hardship, yet it brought about its principal goals more quickly and efficaciously than most had predicted. It was only with the immediate humanitarian goals secure that it became apparent that the widely expected collapse of Saddam Hussain and his Ba'thist regime, which had been taken for granted in Western policy circles as a consequence of his humiliating defeat in the war, was showing no imminent signs of taking place. Moreover, in rallying Sunni Arab support against the Shia-led uprising, Saddam Hussain was, if anything, getting stronger. Against this backdrop, it increasingly became clear that the creation of the safe haven, which had been conceived of as a short term measure in response to a short term problem, had in fact become contingent on Saddam Hussain's fall. In the absence of his demise, this short term response had begun to take on the trappings of a long term policy, one that has to date endured for more than ten years.

In such a context of a short term policy made long, doubts and suspicions began to fester within Turkish circles. Many Turks refused to accept OPC 2 (which they insisted on referring to by its initial, more florid, name of 'Operation Poised Hammer') on its own terms. They failed to accept that Saddam Hussain might have survived in spite of the efforts of the US-led coalition. This proved to be fertile ground for complicated conspiracy theories, a favourite of which was to explain the evolution of circumstances as a US plot to create a Kurdish state in northern Iraq as a precursor to the territorial division of Turkey itself. Thus Turks tended to lose sight of Turgut Özal's original plan to deal with the challenge of March 1991, which was as bold and as imaginative as any of his many other forays into foreign affairs. With his loss of government authority in June 1991,[10]

[10] On 15 June Özal's tenure as what Hugh Pope called 'sole ruler' of Turkey came to end with the replacement of his proxy premier, Yıldırım Akbulut, as both ANAP leader and prime minister by the Foreign Minister Mesut Yılmaz. See *Middle East International*, no. 403, 28 June 1991.

it was one of Özal's final great initiatives, yet, perversely, it is re-membered today by many as a foreign-inspired scheme to do Turkey down.

TURKEY AND THE IRAQI KURDS: A PARTNERSHIP NOT
FORGED, FEBRUARY 1991–JUNE 1993

OPC 2 was not quite the last of Özal's legacy to Turkey as far as the situation in northern Iraq was concerned. In fact Özal had estab-lished direct contact with the leadership of the Iraqi Kurds as early as February 1991, sending an invitation on the 20th of the month to their two principal leaders, Masoud Barzani of the KDP and Jalal Talabani of the PUK, to hold general discussions. In doing so, Özal acted without prior consultation with either the Turkish military or the intelligence service, the MİT. Özal's motives were aimed at addressing Turkey's Kurdish question at home, while also boosting his country's influence in a neighbouring territory. It was then a re-markable event when on 8 March the first ever formal contact between the two sides took place in the form of a meeting between the Turkish Ministry of Foreign Affairs' under-secretary, Tugay Özçeri, and Talabani himself, together with a senior Barzani senior aide, Muhsin Dizayi. Virtually in an instant, Özal had broken the taboo of Turkey not having contact with the Kurds of neighbouring states.[11]

Yet, in spite of this auspicious beginning, the period between 1991 and the summer of 1993 was one when a partnership between Ankara and the Iraqi Kurds was never quite forged. Though Özal's mind was made up, there was always a lingering doubt during this period on the part of significant groups of Turks as to the extent to which the Iraqi Kurds could be trusted. This ambivalence is best illustrated by the divisions within the Turkish state, and notably in the Foreign Ministry. Dovish diplomats, many of whom had been close to Özal in the past, agreed with the president that Turkey should engage as much as possible with northern Iraq. In particular, Özal argued, Turkey should bring the impoverished northern Iraqi economy into its orbit, as a way of maximising Turkish influence in the terri-tory. Özal believed that for as little as $30–40 million Turkey could create a relationship of dependence. The more hawkish members of

---

[11] For a detailed discussion of events, see İsmet İmset, 'Turkey and the Middle East: Hostages to the PKK', a fourth report of six in *Turkish Probe*, 3 March 1994.

the ministry, however, tended to agree with the Turkish military that any strengthening of the economy of Iraqi Kurdistan would make it more independent from the Iraqi state and hence facilitate secessionism. They argued that a weak and impoverished northern Iraq was better for Turkish interests.[12] Faced with this stand-off, the policy output during the 1991–4 period was often a half-hearted compromise. So, for example, when the Iraqi Kurdistan Front (IKF) asked Ankara for 130 mW of electricity per day to help power the safe haven Turkey offered just 30 mW a day, and often failed to deliver even on that.[13]

The ambivalence of the Turkish state towards umbilical ties with northern Iraq was arguably best illustrated by the debate about whether to extend the lira zone to the territory in early summer 1993. The issue arose suddenly after Baghdad cancelled the validity of the Iraqi dinar (ID) 25 note as legal tender. A significant bloc in the Foreign Ministry favoured the substitution of the Turkish lira, for fear that the Iraqi Kurds might instead choose to create their own currency. The Turkish Central Bank appeared to signal its approval of the move. However, Turkey's prime minister, Tansu Çiller, who was to emerge as a politician generally unsympathetic to the Iraqi Kurds, opposed the move, together with the Turkish Treasury. With Ankara equivocating, feeling among Iraqi Kurdish retailers and merchants hardened against the use of the lira because of Turkey's 'unstable and unreliable' position on the dinar crisis.[14]

Though such divisions of view continued to exist on the Turkish side, there was for the moment a more powerful factor that helped to forge co-operation between the Turkish state and the Iraqi Kurds. This was the common preoccupation with the PKK. The PKK insurgency in Turkey had been building in intensity since 1989. The organisation had used the political vacuum in northern Iraq during the Iran-Iraq war from 1984 to 1988 to boost its organisational capability and step up its attacks on Turkish territory. It sought to repeat the exercise from a more advantageous position in 1991, exploiting the confusion and foreign intervention on behalf of the Iraqi Kurds

[12] For example, see *Turkish Daily News*, 11 and 15 July 1992.

[13] In November 1993, for instance, northern Iraq was receiving 10 mW by day and 20 mW at night.

[14] Cited in *Turkish Daily News*, 24 August 1993.

in the spring of that year. Consequently, by the end of 1991, according to Turkish estimates, the PKK had set up ten bases in northern Iraq.

This first year after the Gulf war was to establish many of the features of the Turkish-KDP-PUK-PKK dynamic that were to repeat themselves as the cycles of interaction, negotiation and confrontation of the following years were to unfold. In the summer of 1991 the KDP and the PKK had virtually no contact, being sworn enemies competing for control of the same part of Iraqi Kurdistan adjacent to the Turkish border. At the same time, the PUK and the PKK, which invariably enjoyed better relations, were in regular contact with one another, but with Jalal Talabani trying to dissuade the PKK leader Abdullah Öcalan from prosecuting his attacks on Turkey from northern Iraq for fear of the consequences for that still fragile territory. Öcalan, for whom relations with Baghdad were blossoming, was in no mood to relinquish his quickening advantage. Consequently, Turkish suspicions and frustrations grew steadily, culminating in the first of at least four major cross border military campaigns against the PKK during the 1990s; as Sarah Graham-Brown has described it, this marked 'the progressive encroachment of Turkey's battle with its own Kurdish population into Iraqi Kurdistan, further complicating the political and humanitarian situation'.[15]

On 5 August some 40,000 Turkish troops crossed the border in pursuit of the PKK, backed by strike aircraft and helicopter gunships. This was followed by further secondary attacks in October. Ankara, as has since become a matter of routine, made extravagant claims about the casualties inflicted on the PKK. In reality, the cross border campaign was far from the success that was declared, with the PKK emerging relatively unscathed. Furthermore, politically the raid came close to being a disaster. Lacking good intelligence and knowledge of the political geography of northern Iraq, and without being sensitised to the intra-Kurdish political balances of the moment, the Turkish military, whether by accident or design, attacked villages loyal to the KDP, its potential ally against the PKK. To the evident embarrassment of those who cared, even the village of Barzan came under attack from Turkish forces. The potential

---

[15] Sarah Graham-Brown, *Sanctioning Saddam: The Politics of Intervention in Iraq* (I.B. Tauris, London, 1999), p. 45.

damage caused by these attacks to the Turkish cause was seen in the intemperate language used in the autumn by Masoud Barzani against Turkey, and his threats to retaliate in the future. The awkwardness that ensued would remain until the runup to Barzani's first ever official visit to Turkey in February 1992.

In view of the problems surrounding the August and October 1991 raids, both Turkey and the two main factions of the Iraqi Kurds decided that it was in their mutual interest to cooperate against the PKK. Co-operation was further expedited by the alliance between the KDP and the PUK, which saw the creation of the IKF. The Barzani visit to Ankara was consequently a resounding success. Perhaps realising the recent damage done, the Turks feted the KDP leader like an unofficial head of state.[16] He met the new Turkish prime minister Süleyman Demirel, who had hitherto not shared Özal's enthusiasm for working with the Iraqi Kurds. Ankara seemed to accept that Turkey and the KDP faced a common challenge in the PKK, but that Barzani alone was not strong enough to police the border.[17] During the visit, Barzani sought to demonstrate his worth to the Turkish state, trying, for example, to convince the deputies of the Kurdish nationalist People's Labour Party (HEP), with some success, that they ought to distance themselves from the PKK.[18] It was during this visit that the seeds of joint military co-operation between Turkey and the Iraqi Kurds were sown.

From that moment onwards the IKF adopted a more robust attitude towards the PKK, with the KDP in the vanguard. The PKK was told that it could stay in northern Iraq, but as a political organisation only. It was announced that the IKF had taken steps to prevent cross border infiltration, and Hoshyar Zebari, a close aide and relative of Barzani, did not rule out the use of force. Indeed, in April Reuters confirmed that the PKK was braced for an attack from the KDP.

Nevertheless, it has to be acknowledged that the public diplomacy of co-operation by the Kurds of Iraq towards Turkey had its other uses for the former. For 1992 was the year when the Iraqi Kurds

[16] To cite the influential columnist Ertuğrul Özkök in *Hürriyet*, 19 February 1992.
[17] *Turkish Daily News*, 22 February 1992.
[18] İlnur Çevik, who was very close to Demirel at the time, writing in the *Turkish Daily News*, 2 March 1992.

made their greatest strides towards institution-building in the absence of state control from Baghdad. On 19 May direct elections were held, the outcome of which Barzani and Talabani subsequently decided to call a draw,[19] and which led to the convening of an Iraqi Kurdistan National Assembly, with the seats divided equally between the two main factions. A single administration was formed, with ministries established and portfolios shared.

The Turkish reaction to these ambitious exercises in institution-building was characteristically suspicious and jumpy. Turkish officials bridled at the new lexicon of Iraqi Kurdish politics, with its 'Iraqi Kurdistan citizens' and its labelling of Iraqi Turcomans as an ethnic minority. Moreover, Ankara was concerned that many of the new provisions adopted went beyond the terms of the 1974 autonomy agreement with Baghdad, such as the assembly's 'right of legislation' and right to ratify agreements. Finally, Turkey refused to recognise the establishment of a Kurdish government in northern Iraq, which it dismissed as 'legally baseless and invalid'. Instead, Turkey argued its preference for a search for democracy that would benefit the whole of Iraq within the legal framework of the state.[20] Disingenuous protestations by the likes of Talabani that a Kurdish administration would enable a strong police force to emerge, capable of more effectively controlling the border, simply did not wash in Ankara.

Despite Ankara's considerable reservations, the Turkish state did little to try to undermine the embryonic Iraqi Kurdish project. This is testament to Özal's success in creating an extended moment when Kurdish politics was not anathema in Ankara; it is improbable that the Turks would have played such a passive role after 1993. It also reflects the trust that existed between parts of the Turkish state and the IKF in their common approach to the PKK. That trust was to produce a tangible output with the military operation of October 1992 against the PKK.

There was an intensification of contacts between Turkish officials and the IKF during the summer, though increasingly military figures came to predominate in the developing contacts. This partly reflected the contrast in styles between the idiosyncratic Özal and

---

[19] For the forging of a viable agreement after three days of tension, see *Middle East International*, no. 426, 29 May 1992.

[20] *Turkish Daily News*, 9 July 1992.

the more collegiate Demirel; it also reflected a greater caution and even scepticism on the part of the new prime minister towards the Iraqi Kurds. The figure who emerged as the principal pointman on northern Iraq for Turkey was General Eşref Bitlis, the commander of the Gendarmerie, the paramilitary force responsible for security in rural Turkey, and himself of Kurdish origin.

The result of heightened contact between Talabani and the Gendarmerie, supported by occasional high level political meetings, was a 'gentlemen's agreement' in July to curb the activities of the PKK. Under the so-called 'sandwich operation', the IKF was to encircle PKK forces concentrated at Hakurk and oblige them to capitulate. Meanwhile, Turkish forces would move to the border and ensure that the PKK fighters did not escape by retreating to the north.

Once the operation had begun, things were inevitably somewhat confused. The Turkish military grew frustrated at what it rightly regarded as the unwillingness of the IKF to inflict real casualties on the PKK. Moreover, the Iraqi Kurds had somewhat crudely moved to exploit the positive political atmosphere in their relations with Turkey, initially heightened in the runup to their military operations against the PKK. They did so by choosing the first day of fighting, 4 October, as the date on which their National Assembly unilaterally voted for Iraqi Kurdistan to be part of a federated state of Iraq. While to the Iraqi Kurds it may have looked as though they were reaffirming their commitment to a reformed Iraqi state, to the Turks, with their abiding identification of federal government with the diminution of the standing of the state, it looked significantly more sinister. Indeed even Özal, sidelined and frustrated in the presidential palace at Çankaya, seemed aghast at the move.

When it came, the Turkish military campaign of mid October was as robust as the previous year's. It was met with similarly resentful cries on the part of the Iraqi Kurds both at the scale of the operations and at its 'high-handed' manner.[21] The Iraqi Kurds were also concerned for the first time that the Turkish forces might not actually withdraw at the end of their operations, the possible establishment of a buffer zone proving, for a while at least, to be a tempting

[21] Two high ranking officials from the Turkish Foreign Ministry were quickly despatched to northern Iraq to allay the fears of the IKF leadership about the nature of the campaign. *Guardian*, 5 November 1992.

proposition. IKF faith in the reassurances of an imminent with-drawal was not helped by some loose rhetoric for the benefit of a domestic audience in Turkey; Demirel was the chief culprit, with his analogy of the PKK fighters as mosquitoes and description of the pressing need to 'dry up the swamp' in northern Iraq.[22]

In reality, the PKK units quickly surrendered to the PUK *pesh-merga*, in order to avoid the brunt of the onslaught and a military engagement with either the less indulgent fighters of the KDP or the Turkish military. Under the terms of the surrender,[23] the PKK forces were moved well away from the Turkish border, being taken en masse to a camp at Zaleh, deep in PUK-controlled territory, near the Iranian border. The PKK had certainly suffered a reversal of for-tunes; it had lost its camps within easy reach of the Turkish border, and it had been exposed as too weak to resist the combined forces of the IKF and Turkey in northern Iraq. However, with the PUK failing to disarm the PKK, as promised, and Iranian territory giving access back into Turkey for Öcalan's men, in fact the defeat was not nearly the setback that it at first had seemed. More importantly, the perceived ambivalence of the PUK and Talabani towards the PKK, together with their failure to implement the joint plan in full, was to begin to poison the Turkish state's view of both, a view which was to worsen over time and from which the PUK would never fully recover.

On a wider canvass, Turkey appeared altogether more at home. Ankara moved deftly to allay the fears of others at the direction which the situation in Iraqi Kurdistan was taking. Most importantly, Ankara was the prime mover in the convening of a meeting of the foreign ministers of Iran, Syria and Turkey to discuss the situation in north-ern Iraq; Saudi Arabia was also invited to take part but, apparently under pressure from Washington, declined. The first such meeting was convened in Ankara on 14–15 November, and marked the

[22] Quoted in *Turkish Daily News*, 24 October 1992.
[23] The end of the inter-Kurdish part of the fighting came with the Irbil Agreement of 30 October 1992. Under its terms, the PKK agreed to: relinquish its heavy weapons; withdraw its fighters from the provinces of Irbil and Dohuk; relocate its fighters in the PUK controlled province of Suleymaniyah; and retain its small arms for defence purposes only, when in Suleymaniyah. See BBC/SWB/ME, November 1992.

beginning of a series of informal, ad hoc consultations which were to last well into 1995.

Initially, the US was hostile to such a gathering, while metaphors involving devils and long spoons sprang to the lips of British officials;[24] others, not least the PUK, criticised the initiative for being a meeting about Iraq without any direct input from Iraq.[25] While the foreign ministers' meetings appeared to accomplish little in tangible terms, they provided an invaluable forum for the exchange of mutual reassurances about their collective lack of territorial ambition in Iraq. They also provided a platform from which the leading regional powers could reiterate their commitment to the territorial integrity of Iraq. Subsequent summits holding to much the same formula followed in Damascus in February 1993 and Tehran in June 1993.

Turkey and the IKF spent the winter trying to put into effect collaborative security systems to prevent the recurrence of PKK activity. With operational matters to the fore, General Bitlis again took the lead. An agreement was signed between Turkey and the IKF in December, confirming that Turkey would undertake a full withdrawal, while the Iraqi Kurds would assume responsibility for security.[26] An anti-terrorist control system extending across Turkey's border with Iraq was slated for implementation under 'joint control'.[27] Furthermore, Turkish liaison officers ranked at the level of colonel or above, together with their aides, were attached to each governorate, in order to boost coordination with the IKF. With the PKK at Zaleh through the winter and then Öcalan announcing a unilateral PKK cease-fire at the end of March 1993, it would be a little time yet before the inadequacies of such security co-operation would be exposed.

TURKEY AND THE IRAQI KURDS: DISENGAGEMENT
AND RECRIMINATION, JUNE 1993–OCTOBER 1994

The relationship between Turkey and the Iraqi Kurds changed markedly during the summer of 1993. During this season ties were

[24] Interview with British diplomat, London, 25 November 1992.
[25] For the PUK statement on the summit, see BBC/SWB/ME, 17 November 1992.
[26] Interview with Iraqi Kurdish parliamentary delegation, led by the president of the Assembly, Jawhar Namiq Salim, Chatham House, 10 December 1991.
[27] General Bitlis quoted in BBC/SWB/EE?, 23 November 1992.

transformed from intimacy tinged with uneasiness to coldness and distance. Quickly, those who had been the leading exponents of interaction and co-operation disappeared from the scene, to be replaced by weaker and harsher figures. Moreover, the suspicions of Turks towards the Iraqi Kurds and the PUK in particular, which had long been lingering, came to the foreground with a harmful impact on mutual trust.

The critical development in this change of attitude in Ankara was the Faustian pact between the newly installed prime minister, Tansu Çiller, and the chief of the general staff, Doğan Güreş. In order to consolidate her grip on government, Çiller believed that she needed to neutralise the military as a political force. She did so extremely successfully by ceding to the armed forces virtually complete control over policy towards the Kurdish issue, while she concentrated on the rest of the national policy agenda. Çiller consequently proved to be even less willing than her reticent predecessor Demirel to meet the Iraqi Kurdish leadership, effective political consultations coming to an end with Barzani's visit to Ankara in June 1993.

Of course the onset of the Çiller days did not take place in a vacuum. Talabani, who had played the role of midwife to the PKK cease-fire, had become ever more closely identified with Öcalan, a relationship that was to backfire on him once the cease-fire had collapsed. That collapse came on 10 June, following the provocative killing at the end of the previous month of more than 35 army recruits in civilian clothes in Bingöl by elements within the PKK who had opposed Öcalan's cease-fire extensions. By this time the only men who could have saved the relationship, Turgut Özal and Eşref Bitlis, were both dead: Özal of a heart attack on 17 April and Bitlis in a plane crash on 17 February. That the Turkish state was deeply troubled over the nature and conduct of policy towards the Kurds on both sides of the border was clear, with rumours persisting since then that Bitlis and even Özal died as a result of deliberate acts. It also became visible with the grisly and unsolved killing in October 1993 of Bitlis' right hand man, Major Cem Ersever of Gendarmerie intelligence, also known as Turkey's 'Lawrence of Kurdistan', arguably the man who knew the Iraqi Kurds the best.[28]

---

[28] For an exploration of the enigma of the Ersever killing, see İsmet İmset in *Turkish Probe*, 18 November 1993.

Whatever the forces at work in Turkey's 'deep state', by June 1993 it was clear that relations between Ankara and the IKF were on the slide. The PKK, increasingly brazen, returned to armed activities in July. The Turkish military showed their frustration by resuming cross border air and artillery operations for the first time in 1993 at the beginning of October. The IKF vainly tried to stem the growing confrontation by closing all PKK offices in northern Iraq, but to no avail.[29] The conflict now continued to ratchet up in seriousness. Less effort seemed to be spent on ensuring that the increasing Turkish cross-border air raids left KDP villages free from damage. Hot pursuit raids followed. The murder of a Turkish liaison official, Can Cemal, in northern Iraq in January resulted in a sustained air strike on the Zaleh camp. A major attack by Turkish commandos with air support in April 1994 once again offered the prospect of a prolonged Turkish military presence in northern Iraq and resurrected the debate about the establishment of a buffer zone. It was against such a backdrop of rising pressure from the Turkish state and the PKK alike that the increasingly fraught relationship between the KDP and the PUK collapsed into armed conflict on 1 May 1994,[30] with serious bouts of fighting following in August and December.

One might have expected the Turkish response to the collapse of the IKF to have been one of relief. All hopes, no matter how forlorn, that the 1992 institution-building process might contain the seeds of an embryonic Kurdish state in northern Iraq were dashed with the outbreak of the fighting. The Iraqi Kurdish administration collapsed, the National Assembly ceased to function, and the armed forces, which had in any case never been integrated, separated into warring militias. Iraqi Kurdistan divided once again into two personal fiefdoms. It is true that Turkey was in no rush to mediate between the two factions. But any relief in Ankara at the course of recent events was short-lived. The Turks soon began to fear that the outbreak of KDP-PUK feuding would give the PKK a free hand in northern Iraq, and that one or other of the Iraqi Kurdish factions would seek an alliance with Öcalan in order to tip the balance in

---

[29] Reuters, 15 October 1993.

[30] For the background to the eruption in fighting see Michael Gunter, *The Kurdish Predicament in Iraq: A Political Analysis* (Macmillan, London, 1999), pp. 74–7, and 79–80.

their conflict. Ankara was therefore prompted to issue grave warnings that it would not remain neutral in the event of either side cooperating with the PKK. It was against this backdrop of deteriorating relations that Turkey was not invited to attend a Kurdish attempt to broker peace which resulted in the ill fated Paris Accords in July 1994.

This backdrop of disillusionment and disengagement from contacts with the Kurds of northern Iraq provided an auspicious context for 'a marked warming of relations' between Ankara and Baghdad between 1993 and 1995.[31] This move was predicated on the correct assessment that there was no immediate threat to the regime of Iraqi leader Saddam Hussain, either at home or from abroad. Ankara had begun to position itself for such an eventuality as early as March 1993, when it reactivated its Baghdad embassy under a chargé d'affaires, making it the first NATO country so to do. A further normalisation in the form of high level visits to the Iraqi capital also predated the outbreak of the KDP-PUK feuding, with the visit of Özdem Sanberk, the Foreign Ministry's top civil servant, in April 1994. The collapse of the IKF made the re-establishment of Iraqi state power in the north even more desirable for Turkey. The belief in Ankara began to harden that more and more steps should be taken to normalise relations with Baghdad. The challenge for Turkey was to achieve this objective without undermining a cornerstone of its strategy towards Iraq, namely desisting from unilateral steps that would damage relations with Iraq's principal foe, the United States.

By the end of April Ankara believed that it had the ability to finesse the situation. The issue it chose was the fate of the twin oil pipelines between Kirkuk and Yumurtalık. The 985 km. pipelines were estimated to contain as much as 12 million barrels of oil, which had been lying there since they were closed as a result of the UN's anti-Iraq Chapter Seven resolutions in August 1990. The Turks feared that the double pipeline was corroding as a result of the effects of the trapped oil, and that the line would be useless if its clearance was to wait upon the full rescinding of international sanctions. Moreover, the Turks coveted the oil stuck in the line for domestic use, which they argued could be set against part of the $700 million

[31] Sarah Graham-Brown, op. cit., p. 68.

bilateral debt owed by Baghdad. Ankara therefore began to try to convince both Iraq and the United States of the desirability of flushing the pipelines.

The latter, increasingly conscious of the economic cost to Turkey of the embargo, soon agreed to the flushing. However, Washington's conditions did not make it easy for Turkey to sell the plan in Baghdad. It was made clear that UN provisions for future Iraqi oil exports would have to be enforced, with 30 per cent of the income to be set aside for a UN compensation fund for victims of the invasion of Kuwait, while the remaining income would be paid into a UN supervised escrow account, which would permit control of future Iraqi spending patterns. The Turks then turned their attention to convincing the Iraqis of the desirability of the plan. If Baghdad was hoping that the carrot of flushing the line would weaken Turkey's existing commitments to the UN and the United States alike, it was disabused by the Turkish parliament's decision at the end of June to reconfirm the mandate of OPC 2. Shortly after that, Ambassador Sanberk returned to Baghdad to calm tempers in the Iraqi capital.

The diplomatic minuet between Iraq and Turkey continued into October. The Turks played up the possible availability of funds resulting from the flushing for humanitarian imports into Iraq, on the mistaken assumption that this might sway the Baghdad regime. For their part, the Iraqis teasingly maintained Turkish interest, through such devices as giving the red carpet treatment to a party of Turkish businessmen who visited Iraq in early September. With doubts about Iraq's seriousness multiplying on the Turkish side, it was nevertheless with some acute embarrassment that the flushing proposal was swept aside, as Saddam Hussain suddenly moved his troops southwards in an operation widely perceived to threaten the Kuwaiti border in early October.

In the face of such a quick turn of events, and the disappointment of a policy being dashed, Turkey adopted a low profile during the brief stand-off. It was with evident irritation that Turkey's newly installed foreign minister, the one-time apostle of non-alignment, Mümtaz Soysal, was obliged to fall into line. Soysal, with his strong streak of anti-Americanism, would have liked nothing better than to preside over a process leading to the rehabilitation of the Iraqi leader. With Soysal resigning from the post in a short time as a result of intra-party tensions, Saddam Hussain's caprice on the Kuwait border had cost him a rare chance to make mischief between Turkey and the United States.

TURKEY AND NORTHERN IRAQ: AN INFLUENCE DIMINISHED, OCTOBER 1994–SEPTEMBER 1996

Bruised by Baghdad's cynical calculation and outpaced by the course of events in the northern Gulf, Turkish policy entered a period of introspection on Iraq, a hiatus that was to last to January 1995. This period of withdrawal born of diplomatic trauma fittingly character-ises a period when Turkish influence over the course of events in northern Iraq was at its lowest ebb. Increasingly this growing cau-tion was exacerbated by political turmoil at home, with the high turnover in foreign ministers in 1995, the general election of Decem-ber 1995 and the problems of forging a viable coalition in 1996 all contributing to the undermining of Turkey's influence, even in its near abroad.

Of course, Ankara's four-month disengagement from Iraq never looked likely to be tenable in the long term. Firstly, the conflict between the KDP and PUK, which continued through the first quarter, showed no sign of healing itself. Indeed, Turkey had con-tributed to these worsening relations.[32] Ankara's decision in Sep-tember 1994 to reopen the Habur gate crossing point into Iraqi Kurdistan, primarily to facilitate the cross-border trade in diesel, had raised the stakes for the two factions. Some 2,000 trucks a day plied across the border, the 'tax' levied on the trade reportedly being worth up to 60% of the funds of the regional administration. The KDP, which controlled the Habur point, refused to share the result-ing income, thereby exacerbating the deteriorating relations with the PUK. Secondly, the extended and bare-knuckled struggle between the KDP and the PUK presented the PKK with new op-portunities for operations from the Iraqi side of the border. Ankara

---

[32] PUK sources are convinced that the Turkish decision to open the Habur gate was a deliberate act aimed at tilting the balance of power within the Iraqi Kurdish community in favour of the KDP. Whether this was the intention or not it was certainly the outcome, with the tax 'levied' on cross-border deliveries of product being estimated at between $200,000 and $1 million a day, depending on the source.

had been particularly concerned at the KDP's predictable decision to switch its militia forces from the border area to the regional capital of Irbil, the focus of much of the fighting in December, a move which seemed certain to favour PKK operations into Turkey.

Faced with such an unpalatable prospect, and encouraged by the concern of its own allies in the West, Turkey, somewhat self-consciously, embarked upon its first effort at mediation between the KDP and the PUK. The Ministry of Foreign Affairs held meetings with the two sides in mid January. It was even announced that Ankara would be making available some $13.5 million in aid, presumably as a sweetener for the two sides.[33] Turkey also agreed to assign a representative to a State Department delegation, led by David Litt, the official in charge of northern Gulf affairs, bound for northern Iraq towards the end of the month.

By this time, however, Turkey's equivocation over policy towards northern Iraq had already begun to reassert itself. The Litt tour should have been a powerful symbolic statement of Turkish and US interest in ending the fighting. Instead, Ankara and Washington soon found themselves arguing at cross-purposes, and hence diminishing the likelihood of attaining their core goals. For the Litt mission, though its objective was a cessation of the fighting, was committed to achieving such an end by supporting a peace initiative by the Iraqi National Congress (INC), an umbrella Iraqi opposition grouping, which included the KDP and the PUK. By contrast, Turkey distrusted the INC, and feared that any strengthening of the group would increase the chances of the emergence of a federal Iraq. Consequently, while the American and Turkish initiatives both called for the end to fratricidal fighting, Ankara urged the Iraqi Kurds to enter a political dialogue with Iraq, a call that Washington clearly could not endorse.

One might have expected the US to have registered anger at Ankara, given both its role in subverting the initiative from within, and the importance of Iraq policy to US global interests. However, that was not to be the case a pattern which was to become established and would apply to the next three and a half years of US attempts to bring stability to northern Iraq. The reason for Washington's indulgence towards Turkey in this matter relates both to the centrality of Turkey in helping to contain Saddam Hussain and to the broader importance of the country to the United States. Washington realised that, in spite of Ankara's subversion of northern Iraqi peace-making from within, Turkey was still critical both in enforcing international sanctions against Iraq and in providing a home base for PC2. More generally, the Americans wanted to retain their joint basing privileges at Incirlik in the south-east of the country, the importance of which transcended the shorter term goals of peace and stability in northern Iraq.

With the US and Turkish versions of the Litt peace initiative and indeed others increasingly cutting across one another, hopes of diplomatic progress faded. With no alternative strategy, Turkey in turn reverted to type, launching a 'massive push' against the PKK in northern Iraq on 20 March 1995. Though Operation Steel, as the March attack came to be known, began as if history was repeating itself, it quickly became clear that the operation represented a watershed in such cross border campaigns. The PKK had learned the lesson of the 1992 attack, organising its forces into smaller, more mobile units and basing them in smaller camps that it could afford to abandon without a costly defence.[34] The depth of the anger of Iraqi Kurds at the heavyhandedness of the cross border operation was poignantly illustrated by the gruesome killing and mutilation of three employees of the Turkish Red Crescent near Dohuk, thereby bringing the full horror of the violence to a home audience. The intensity of the international criticism of Turkey reached new levels, eliciting, in the runup to the European Parliament's crucial vote on the Customs Union, a defensive mobilisation of Turkey's diplomatic and political resources. It was almost with a sense of relief that the Çiller government and her establishment allies allowed Washington, displaying firmness within friendship, to manoeuvre Turkey into an early withdrawal of forces.[35]

No sooner had Turkish forces withdrawn from northern Iraq in late spring than Ankara's influence there was even further restricted. The reason was the unexpected defection of Hussain and Saddam Kamel Hasan al-Majid, Saddam Hussain's two sons-in-law (and also

---

[34] *Turkish Probe*, 24 March 1995.
[35] Mehmet Ali Birand writing in *Sabah*, 23 May 1995 noted how abruptly the military operation had been brought to an end.

his cousins), together with their wives, his daughters, in early August. With Saddam's wayward kin ensconced in Amman, attention increasingly switched to Jordan, where King Hussein began a brief patronage of the Iraqi opposition. Scenting that Saddam had sustained a grave and perhaps fatal wound, the United States stepped up its mediation, in the hope that Kurdish opposition to the Iraqi regime might be maximised. Both the KDP and the PUK responded positively to the US initiative, now being spearheaded by Robert Deutsch, Litt's successor, with two rounds of negotiations being held in the Irish Republic at Drogheda on 9–11 August and Dublin on 12–15 September. Turkey, however, was ambivalent.

In spite of its waning influence, the United States, at the urging of its ambassador in Ankara, Marc Grossman, ensured that Turkey was still invited to both meetings. At Drogheda, Turkey's approach was parochial. However, on that occasion Ankara's insistence on having its 'legitimate security concerns' acknowledged by all sides did not prove to be incompatible with the meeting's main outcome, the establishment of a cease-fire. However, Ankara's lukewarm response to the idea of regime change in Iraq became even more evident at the Dublin meeting. Acting as though oblivious to the wider context, the Turkish side insisted that there should be two detailed references to Turkey's security concerns, in the preamble and the articles of the agreement. As in the face of Ankara's disruption of the Litt mission, the Americans' response was to sit on their hands. Turkey then proceeded to respond coolly to King Hussein's proposal for a federal solution to the Iraq question. Meanwhile, a vigorous PKK offensive against the KDP, encouraged by Syria, had sought to thwart the possibility of a US-imposed settlement for Iraq, with Iran further assisting by tightening its influence over Talabani and the PUK. Ironically, it was as much Turkey's uncooperativeness in Dublin as Iran's or Syria's on the ground that scuppered these chances.

With Dublin failing to capitalise on Drogheda, and the limitations of Hussain Kamel's putative leadership of the Iraqi opposition increasingly exposed, any hopes for regime change in Baghdad began to ebb away. The ill-judged return of Hussain and Saddam Kamel to a swift death in Iraq in February 1996 confirmed that Saddam Hussein had survived a difficult period of pressure. Turkey's domestic political problems from September 1995 onwards virtually removed

Ankara as a player in northern Iraq for the best part of the next 12 months. Its chief involvement during this time was a residual commercial interest as it looked forward to the implementation of SCR 986, the new 'oil for food' resolution. It would, though, be a long wait, as the resolution, though originally adopted on 14 April 1995, was not actually implemented until December 1996. With Turkey largely absent as a diplomatic player, and America losing impetus in trying to conclude an intra-Kurdish rapprochement, the Iraqi leader emerged even better placed to launch his joint strike with KDP forces into the safe haven on 31 August 1996.

TURKEY AND THE IRAQI KURDS: PARTISAN PEACE-MAKING, SEPTEMBER 1996–SEPTEMBER 1998

The failure of the Americans to bring the KDP-PUK feuding decisively to an end always left open the possibility that, in their search for powerful regional allies, the Iraqi Kurds would seek help in Baghdad. That involvement came swiftly and decisively, with the Iraqi state making common cause with the KDP to defeat the PUK on the battlefield, a situation which subsequently was only partially redressed by a PUK counter-attack. The outcome of the brief return of Baghdad was: the military balance in northern Iraq, which the KDP feared was tilting against it, was restored in its favour; the PUK was ejected from the regional capital, Irbil; the controversial military coordination centre (MCC) in Zakho, which was part of OPC 2, was overrun; and the CIA operation in the safe haven was smashed, with the loss of over 100 operatives. Together with the suppression of the uprisings in spring 1991 and the withdrawal of Unscom in December 1998, the attack represented one of the three debacles of America's Iraq policy in the 1990s.

Once the United States had fired a token salvo of Tomahawk missiles at Iraqi targets to assuage its anger, and Turkey had helped it evacuate its remaining 'human assets', the issue of what to do next then arose. The Americans were left to pick up from where they had left off in searching for a new settlement among the Kurds. This time they did so under the initial auspices of the more senior assistant secretary of state, Robert Pelletreau, with Turkey once again emerging as the focus for diplomatic activity. The incorporation of the Iraqi Turcomans, apparently recently rediscovered by Turkish policy circles, as part of what quickly became known as the Ankara Process seemed especially to appeal to Tansu Çiller, by now ensconced as deputy premier in a coalition government with the Islamist Welfare Party, and the chosen conduit for inter-governmental relations with the United States.

There was an element of the incongruous in Turkey's re-emergence as a peace-maker in Kurdish factional conflict as a result of the August/ September operation. For the truth was that Ankara, which had preempted any attempt by the United States to use its territory as a platform from which to rebuff the Iraqi advance,[36] was far from being dismayed at its outcome. Turkey, with its state-centred orientation and perennial concern at the risk of Kurdish secessionism, was not in and of itself antipathetic towards the idea of the Iraqi state re-establishing itself in the north. Moreover, the removal of the MCC ended a long-standing complaint that Ankara had had against the Americans, the centre's location suggesting that OPC 2 existed beyond Ankara's control. Finally, Baghdad's intervention in bolstering the position of the KDP at the expense of the PUK was very much to Turkey's liking.

Arguably the turning point for Turkey's perception of the Iraqi Kurds had come during its last major cross border attack into northern Iraq. By April 1995 key officials in Ankara had come to appreciate what had seemed increasingly obvious since the collapse of the PKK cease-fire in June 1993, that the greatest chance for a peaceful border would be through the forging of a close alliance with the KDP. In spring 1995 the two sides seemed set to forge such a relationship. The influential Cenk Duatepe, head of the intelligence department at the Foreign Ministry, had spoken encouragingly of Barzani as 'a reliable person'.[37] With Turkish forces beginning to withdraw from Iraq, a KDP delegation visiting Ankara in early May argued for a long term strategic relationship with Turkey. Hikmet Çetin invited Barzani himself to visit Turkey for the first time in two years at the same meeting. However, the ability to build on this auspicious springboard was impaired by Turkey's growing political introspection.

[36] Sarah Graham-Brown, op. cit., p. 118.
[37] *Turkish Daily News*, 8 April 1995.

Hand in hand with the incremental forging of ties between Turkey and the KDP was a growing perception that Ankara was at the very least ambivalent towards the PUK. Interviewed in April 1995, the PUK's Ankara representative, Shazad Saib, would trace the beginnings of serious suspicions between Turkey and the organisation to the change in the head of the Kurdish administration from Dr Fuad Massum, a technocrat, to Khosrat Rasul, a member of the PUK politburo, in March 1993. Talabani himself would complain of Turkish policy towards northern Iraq under Çiller, ruing the passing of Özal,[38] when 'Turkey was the main force in Iraqi Kurdistan'.[39] Talabani, however, always seemed eager to look for means to claw his way back to good relations with Ankara, though these attempts, such as the short-sighted praising of the ill-fated RP-DYP coalition and his complimentary remarks on premier Erbakan's position 'as a Muslim', were not always well advised.[40]

With the imperative of ensuring that the KDP had broken its ties with Baghdad giving a new vigour to the mediation, an accord between the two factions was brokered by the United States, Britain and Turkey acting together at the end of October 1996. But the Ankara Agreement was a misleading gauge of the effectiveness of the peace process. It did deliver a new cease-fire between the KDP and the PUK. More controversially, the agreement also stipulated, in a reference to Iran and Iraq, that aid from outside parties to either of the two main groups would be banned, and also, somewhat incongruously, that the Iraqi Turcomans should lead an inspection force to monitor the cease-fire. Ominously, as soon as the agreement had been signed the KDP complained about the presence of these two provisions in the peace document.

With the agreement failing to stick, a third round in the Ankara Process was held in January 1997 and yet a further round in May 1997, before the whole process finally ran into the ground with a final desperate and unsuccessful meeting in London in the autumn of 1997. Well before then, however, the US had become frustrated

---

[38] Indeed, Michael Gunter states that 'Özal was the only Turkish official that Talabani ever liked', drawing attention to the 'good chemistry' that existed between the two. See Gunter, op. cit., p. 30.

[39] *Turkish Daily News*, 10 June 1996.

[40] *Turkish Daily News*, 25 October 1996.

and disillusioned with the Iraqi Kurdish leadership and its fratricidal conflict, and seemed inclined to let Turkey increasingly make the running. In turn, perplexed by Turkish state power and eager to curry favour with Washington, the Iraqi Kurds seemed eager to appease Ankara. Playing to the Americans and Turks in the gallery, the two sides had become entirely tactically oriented, each seeking to gain a temporary advantage at the other's expense.

It was the PKK, the fortunes of which were waning on the battle-field, that bore the brunt of this drift. In the PUK-controlled areas PKK offices were closed and their cadres encouraged to relocate to Iran. Predictably, the backlash against the PKK was altogether tougher in the KDP areas. Here, PKK offices were closed and their personnel liquidated. The KDP also gave cover to Turkey's May 1997 operation, Operation Hammer, the first serious cross-border operation since March 1995. This was an attack of 'unprecedented scale',[41] with Ankara claiming that it had been 'invited' in,[42] and there were widespread reports of the undertaking of joint opera-tions. Indeed, the relative political ease of the operation resulted in its repetition in the form of Operation Dawn '97 in the autumn.

With the KDP having proved its worth to Turkey during the late spring operations in northern Iraq, Ankara virtually abandoned all pretence at even-handedness. Turkey's involvement in the KDP-PUK feud subsequently reached its zenith in the autumn, a few days after the collapse of the London meeting, when Turkey intervened robustly, at both the diplomatic and military levels, to face down an attack by the latter on the former. The Turkish military went onto a sustained military offensive to prevent the PUK from driving back its rival, with tanks and aircraft being committed.[43] At the same time, Ankara issued an unequivocal ultimatum to the PUK leader-ship to withdraw its forces. That Turkey had placed its own direct security concerns above the needs of peace-making was widely

---

[41] *Sabah*, 23 May 1997.

[42] *Middle East International*, no. 551, 30 May 1997.

[43] As with so much both in Kurdish factional politics and the fortunes of northern Iraq one must be wary of coming to firm conclusions. Nevertheless, the military involvement of the Turkish armed forces on behalf of the KDP and against the PUK seems to be clear. Michael Gunter, for example, states that 'the Turks ... intervened heavily on the side of the KDP' using both bombers and tanks. See Gunter, op. cit., p. 89.

acknowledged. The president of the executive committee of the INC, Ahmad Chalabi, drew attention to this when he urged Ankara to abandon its mediatory role in northern Iraq, on the grounds that its security interests had rendered all claims to neutrality untenable.

With the abandonment of all but Ankara's most flimsy of pretention to mediation, the whole Ankara Process as it had emerged since autumn 1996 was doomed in terms of delivering real peace and reconciliation among the Kurds of northern Iraq. The presence of Turks on the inside of the peace-making process had been exposed as a liability. Though Ankara could be persuaded that it was in its interests to see a cease-fire forged between the KDP and the PUK, Turkey was much less enthusiastic about the forging of stable government in northern Iraq, for fear of the implications it would have for both the integrity of the Iraqi state and the broader Kurdish independence movement. As one Turkish journalist famously observed, 'Turkey wants stability in northern Iraq but not too much stability'. Ankara therefore continued to subvert the process from within in the same way as it had done so during the Litt mission and at Dublin.

With Turkey effectively neutralising the PUK's military option, Talabani set about breaking the ice with the KDP during Ramadan in 1997, the two sides holding face to face meetings the following February. Scenting a new opportunity for peace-making, the US increasingly resumed its involvement, although this time alone, mindful of the failures of the Ankara Process and the unhelpfulness of Ankara. It was this initiative that was to conclude with the Washington Agreement between the KDP and the PUK in September 1998. Even then, the subordination of Kurdish factional peacemaking to the core US interests of good relations with Turkey could be seen in the subsequent trilateral US-British-Turkish statement 'clarifying' the Washington Agreement, with Ankara's sensitivities in mind.

Turkey's Kemalist political and military establishment would never have chosen northern Iraq as a foreign policy priority for the 1990s. Indeed, in a region where the view that only states count tends to predominate, Ankara would have regarded northern Iraq as the exclusive preserve of Baghdad. The Gulf crisis and its untidy denouement meant that Turkey did not have the luxury of such a perspective. International and regional events beyond its control helped to reorder the context in which Ankara would decide on its priorities. Because of its links with the Kurdish question, and the fears of the security challenge to Turkey's territorial integrity posed by ethnic politics, Ankara felt left with little choice but to engage repeatedly and extensively with the 'political limbo' which prevailed in northern Iraq from 1991 onwards.[44]

Neither was the nature or implementation of policy in Ankara often very tidy, certainly up to 1996. Until the death of Özal in April 1993 there were fundamental differences about the goals being pursued towards northern Iraq and the means to be used. Over the next two years, Ankara seemed to lose much of its leverage in northern Iraq, a situation that was then exacerbated by its own domestic political turmoil. Throughout this period Turkey struggled with contrasting and even mutually exclusive goals, individual policies almost inevitably ending up limited to the short term and with counterproductive side-effects.

Since 1996, however, Turkish policy, though hardly edifying, has acquired greater solidity towards northern Iraq. The replacement of OPC2 with Operation Northern Watch ushered in a period when policy was less contentious domestically; the growing impossibility of resolving the KDP-PUK struggle increased Turkey's manoeuvrability as the principal regional power in northern Iraq; the establishment of a *de facto* security zone helped to limit the security threat from the PKK. By late 1996 and early 1997 there was a growing sense that Turkey had become resigned to and had made the most of a situation in northern Iraq that was likely to remain intractable until the broader issue of the future of Iraq was resolved. On top of this, with the indulgence of the US, Ankara appeared to have a near permanent position on the inside of diplomatic attempts to address the future of northern Iraq. It is remarkable that for all of Turkey's unhelpfulness on the inside of four attempts at peacemaking, the US never resorted to public expressions of criticism or frustration with its close regional ally. Perhaps equally remarkable is the fact that the Turkish side never quite appreciated the advantageous position that Washington helped it to occupy during this time.

---

[44] To use Riadh Abed's phrase. See *Middle East International*, no. 631, 18 August 2000.

10

IN PURSUIT OF PEACE: TURKEY
AND THE BOSNIAN CRISIS

Up to the mid 1980s the Balkans had largely ceased to exist as a geopolitical description, for Turkey as for most states. There was Greece, with which Turkey had a number of bilateral problems; there were the southern states of the eastern bloc, which was Communist and hence part of a separate strategic grouping; and beyond that there was Western Europe, increasingly identified with the EC, membership of which was a strong Turkish aspiration. Balkan states like Yugoslavia were relatively unimportant in themselves for Turkey, their main utility being as a land transit territory to the increasingly lucrative markets of the heartland of Europe.

That situation changed in the 1980s with the ending of the Cold War and the reemergence of particularistic nationalisms, which, until then, had been sublimated beneath the generalised ideology of Communism.[1] For Turkey these trends presented risks as well as opportunities. Ankara was certainly highly conscious of the Balkans because of the Greek issue. It was therefore unsurprising that Turkey quickly became inquisitive about the Balkans.[2] Commercial ties were established with Romania,[3] a rapprochement was pursued with post-Zhivkov

---

[1] For some historical and contemporary musings on Turkey and the Balkans see J.F. Brown, 'Turkey: Back to the Balkans' in Graham E. Fuller and Ian O. Lesser, (eds), *Turkey's New Geopolitics: From the Balkans to Western China* (Westview Press/ RAND, Boulder, CO, 1993) pp. 141–62.

[2] For a brief but useful general overview of Turkey's relations with a range of Balkans countries see Şule Kut, 'Turkish Policy toward the Balkans', in Alan Makovsky and Sabri Sayari (eds), *Turkey's New World: Changing Dynamics in Turkish Foreign Policy* (WINEP, Washington DC, 2000), pp. 74–91.

[3] According to Romanian statistics there were about 2,000 Turkish companies (many of them, one assumes, very small) operating in Romania by the autumn of 1993. *Turkish Daily News*, 7 September 1993.

Bulgaria,[4] and avuncular relations were established with the smaller, poorer entity of Albania. But it was of course with the dangerous and intractable issue of the future of Yugoslavia that Turkey, like so many other states, became most engaged, especially at a diplomatic level.

The issue of Yugoslavia and more particularly the Bosnian crisis were often of rather more abstract than concrete concern for Turkey. It did not contain a direct security threat to Turkey's borders, in the way that Russian forces to the north had done, nor an indirect threat as with PKK operations in northern Iraq; the Bosnian crisis was after all not one that took place in immediate proximity to Turkish territory. Neither did turmoil and conflict in Yugoslavia completely jeopardise trade with Western Europe. It was an inconvenience that increased the cost of transport, but alternative routes were available, notably through Romania. Rather, the Bosnian issue was important to Turkey because of a range of softer issues and security challenges involving such difficult subjective factors as identity and such 'low politics' questions as refugees. Would a protracted war in the Balkans be seen in confessional terms in Turkey, and what effect would that have on self-identification and the European vocation? Would the growth of particularistic nationalisms and the collapse of the mosaic state of Yugoslavia have a deleterious effect on Turkey, itself an aggregate state comprising peoples from many different geographical origins?[5] What analogy would Bosnia offer for a range of other conflicts and areas of tension, from Nagorno-Karabakh to northern Cyprus to Kosovo? Would Turkey have to cope with a sudden influx of refugees, following other significant inflows, most notably from Bulgaria in the late 1980s? Would there be a spillover effect of the Bosnian conflict in the wider Balkans,

---

[4] On 6 May 1992 the two countries signed a Friendship, Cooperation and Security Treaty. A more specific agreement on military cooperation, the Edirne Document, was concluded in November 1992. A bilateral trade protocol was signed in Ankara in March 1993. A Military and Technical Cooperation Agreement was signed the same month.

[5] One senior Turkish diplomat, Rıza Türmen, then serving as the director-general responsible for the Council of Europe, human rights and the CSCE, likened both Bosnia and Turkey to 'marble cakes', hence making them both vulnerable to the rise of the 'new tribalism' of ethno-nationalism. Presentation at Chatham House, 2 March 1994.

perhaps sharpening existing tensions, say between Greece and Turkey? Would some or all of these issues place difficult, even insurmountable strains on existing relationships, especially within NATO?

Bosnia turned out to be a human tragedy, but it was contained in its political ramifications, for Turkey as for most other states. The cohesion of the Turkish state turned out to be stronger than perhaps it had once been feared, the Kurdish question partially excepted. Turks felt instinctive sympathy for the Bosnians, but only the radical activists on the nationalist and religious fringes tried to turn it into a critical national political issue. There was a significant refugee inflow, with estimates of up to 200,000 Bosnians seeking refuge in Turkey, but the country coped with these arrivals without there being a major domestic impact either economically or sociologically. Yet the fears at the time were real enough. This chapter will be most concerned with how Turkey set about managing these issues.

The policy predicament

In developing and applying foreign policy towards Bosnia, Ankara had two sets of concerns to address. The first was how best to manage potential domestic tensions over the issue, mindful of its emotive nature, and of the significant proportion of the Turkish population which hailed from Bosnia and the Balkans in general.[6] The second was how best to handle the issue in terms of the reemergence of Balkan politics as the epitome of chronic instability and fractiousness, and the evident combustibility of the region.

MANAGING DOMESTIC TENSIONS

For all of the notional concern about Bosnia inside Turkey, and in spite of the criticism of a range of Turkish politicians, the issue did not come to dominate the domestic political agenda in the way that was once feared. Much of the credit for this lay with the Turkish political establishment and the way in which Ankara set about managing such a delicate issue, allied with the traditional deference on

[6] Most estimates place the number of Turks of Bosnian origin at between two and four million, while it is routinely stated that perhaps around one-fifth of a population that during the crisis totalled some 60 million originated in the Balkans. (Andrew Finkle in *The Times*, 12 December 1992).

the part of public opinion towards those who presided over the state. In developing a political strategy for managing the issue, the elite adopted a three-pronged approach. First, the Turkish government, supported by the relevant state institutions, vigorously pursued the issue in its foreign policy, with the sole exception of an eight-month period of introspection; the charge of apathy or aloofness could not therefore easily be levelled against it. Second, the government organised a domestic aid effort for Bosnia, thereby showing that it was active in terms of humanitarian assistance, while also providing an avenue through which moderate activists could channel their energies. Third, Ankara also indicated, rhetorically at least, that it would be willing to contemplate active Turkish participation in the use of force in Bosnia, but only in a multilateral context; such a posture thereby helped to parry emotional calls for the immediate commitment of Turkish forces to the conflict zone.

A vigorous diplomatic campaign on behalf of the government of Bosnia was an essential part of the strategy of the Turkish government to ensure that public opinion remained reasonably content with its performance. Two elements were fundamental to this campaign. First, the Turkish government utilised every forum which provided it with a public platform at which to raise the issue. Within Western institutions like NATO, within international organisations such as the CSCE, and as part of Islamic institutions, notably the Islamic Conference Organisation (ICO), Turkey displayed considerable vigour. The energy of the foreign policy team, with foreign minister Hikmet Çetin and his chief civil servant Özdem Sanberk to the fore, helped the DYP-Social Democrat coalition government to shrug off the criticism of rival politicians for being cautious and ineffectual.

The second and arguably the most important element of this diplomatic strategy, was that it firmly wedded Turkey to a multilateral approach. By doing so, it enabled the coalition government to argue that only through the mobilisation of the major powers and international institutions could effective action be taken over Bosnia.

Moreover, this helped Turkey to steer a course away from the hazardous waters of a unilateralist approach, Ankara being able to argue that it was inappropriate and indeed counter-productive, in view of such a multilateral strategy. By the same token, Ankara was also able to argue that the apparent immobilisation of these institutions was not due to the inactivity of Turkey. This, however, was a somewhat risky furrow to plough, as it inevitably came to imply that the real reason for the lack of decisive intervention was the inactivity of Turkey's closest Western allies, with ambivalent implications about the worth of such bodies.

In retrospect, given the way that the Bosnian tragedy unfolded, it may seem hard to accept that the Turkish government could keep up this multilateral political alibi for so long. However, such a view ignores a number of factors. Turkish government rhetoric was always committed to the pursuit of a solution to the Bosnian conflict based on some notion of justice. At times, so earnest were the protestations that they were taken to obvious excess. In December 1992, for instance, the foreign minister, Hikmet Çetin, declared that Bosnia was top of Turkey's list of priorities[7]; some thirteen months later, the leader of the junior coalition partner, Murat Karayalçin, declared to a senior party meeting that Turkey would reassess its relations with its allies depending on their stand over Bosnia.[8]

Moreover, Turkey did emerge at various stages of its Bosnian diplomatic campaign with something to show for its involvement. This began with the public acknowledgement of its efforts by the Bosnian government, making it throughout the closest NATO ally the Bosnian government had;[9] continued with such gestures from its Western allies as appointing a Turkish admiral to command the fleet patrolling in the Adriatic, and including Turkey as a participant in the enforcement of the no-fly zones over Bosnia-Herzegovina; and resulted in a new willingness on the part of the international mediators to recognise and utilise a role for Turkey in the peace negotiations.[10] Towards the end of the conflict it involved a significant role in brokering and then underpinning a rapprochement between the Bosnian government and the Croats, and ultimately through subsequent participation in the peace-keeping efforts.

---

[7] *Turkish Daily News*, 22 December 1992.

[8] BBC/SWB/EE, 9 February 1994.

[9] Ivo H. Daalder, *Getting to Dayton: The Making of America's Bosnia Policy* (Brookings Institution Press, Washington, DC, 2000), p. 112.

[10] For example, note the visit to Turkey of Lord Owen and Thorvald Stoltenberg 'as it emerged that Ankara is playing a key role in seeking a rapprochement between Bosnia's warring Muslims and Croats', *Guardian*, 16 September 1993.

Finally, while Turkish policy remained broadly rooted in a multilateral approach, on the issue of weapons supplies to the anti-Serb forces Ankara was to be found much closer to the margins of such a strategy. Just three months after he retired, the former Turkish chief of staff, Doğan Güreş, admitted that Turkey had sent weapons to the Bosnian government. In response to the revelations, the Turkish general staff only issued 'lukewarm' denials.[11] The delivery of arms was strongly suspected by well informed and respected journalists specialising in foreign and security policy.[12] It was also confirmed in general terms by senior foreign policy figures in Turkey.[13] While the Turkish action was a clear breach of international law, coming as it did in defiance of the UN arms embargo against all the warring parties, it would be misleading to suggest that this placed Turkey outside an international normative consensus on the issue. It is much less likely that Turkey would have acted in such a way without at very least tacit support from the US; that the US was even unwilling to discourage Iranian weapons supplies to the Bosnian army helps to contextualise the Turkish action.[14]

It is in the third area of government action that the often measured way in which the coalition managed the Bosnian issue, and even exploited it to achieve policy objectives in other domains, can best be seen. In December 1992, the government chose to approach the Turkish Grand National Assembly (TGNA), again maximising the profile of such a move, to authorise the sending of troops to Bosnia.[15] The timing of the move, however, had less to do with the Bosnian issue than with that of Somalia. The United States had

---

[11] Original dispatch by Istanbul-based correspondent Hugh Pope to *The Independent*, 5 December 1994.

[12] For example, Semih İdiz, the former diplomatic correspondent of *Cumhuriyet* and then a senior journalist with the *Turkish Daily News*, strongly believed that Turkey had been helping the United States arm the Croats before their military action in summer 1995 to recover Krajina. Interview, 5 September 1995.

[13] Interview with foreign policy adviser to President Demirel, 10 December 1999, who referred to 'much of the Bosnian-Turkish story not having come out, especially over the supply of arms'.

[14] David Rieff notes that as the conflict continued the Bosnian army was becoming increasingly dependent on military supplies from Turkey, Iran, Pakistan and Saudi Arabia. See *Slaughterhouse: Bosnia and the Failure of the West* (Simon and Schuster, New York, 1995), p. 12.

[15] See *Newspot*, no. 92/25, 17 December 1992.

asked Turkey to send a contingent of troops to Mogadishu in order to expand the international base of an operation initiated in Washington. Ankara, ever keen to underline its new, post-Gulf crisis partnership with the US, needed to gain broad-based consent for a move that was generally unpopular in the country. The government chose to go to the TGNA under Article 92 of the constitution,[16] linking a vote on troops to Somalia with that of the issue of troops to Bosnia. While the vote on the latter met no opposition, there were 44 votes cast against dispatching troops to Somalia.[17]

The fact that the government had obtained authorisation for a possible troop deployment in Bosnia seemed to expand the options of the Turkish state. It also showed an apparent willingness to deploy troops in support of principle and international legitimacy. This willingness to commit troops on the ground was to contrast a few short weeks later with the determination of the new Clinton administration in the US not to post ground forces to Bosnia.

However, the reality in Turkey was rather different. The wording of the resolution passed by the TGNA stated plainly that any troop deployment would be 'To participate in the Peace Force (UNPROFOR) agreed under UN Security Council Resolution No 743'. In short, the resolution did not countenance unilateral military action. To underline the message a report from the Turkish military was leaked to the press which concluded that because it had no refuelling capability, Turkish aircraft could only remain over the territory of former Yugoslavia for about five minutes. The Turkish military thereby ended all further speculation that its air force could mount a military strike against Serbian positions on its own.[18]

ACTIVE IN THE BALKANS

Against such a backdrop, it was almost inevitable that Turkey would become a more active player in the Balkans region.[19] Turkey took

---

[16] This states: 'The power to authorise the…send[ing of] Turkish Armed Forces to foreign countries…is vested in the Turkish Grand National Assembly.'

[17] BBC/SWB/ME, 10 December 1992.

[18] *Turkish Probe*, vol. 1, no. 5, 15 December 1992.

[19] For a discussion of Turkey's relationship with the Balkans see Gareth Winrow, *Where East Meets West: Turkey and the Balkans* (Institute for European Defence and Strategic Studies, London, 1993).

part in the conference of Balkan foreign ministers in Belgrade in February 1988. Ankara drew Bulgaria, Romania and, eventually, Greece into its Black Sea Economic Co-operation project, a multi-lateral organisation which was formally constituted in 1992, but which was first unveiled as a Turkish initiative in the late 1980s.

Turkey's commitment to stability in the Balkans, combined with the innate caution of its foreign policy practitioners, resulted in a default policy reaction when the Yugoslav crisis began to emerge. In particular, together with the US and the EC, Turkey clung on to the status quo of a unitary Yugoslav state, well after it was any longer tenable. Perhaps Turkey found additional succour in the fact that its major Western allies also supported the policy. Once the Yugoslav army, the JNA, had moved into Slovenia on 26 June 1991 to prevent its secession forcibly, and once the fighting had spread to and inten-sified in Croatia soon afterwards, stability in Yugoslavia was at an end. The new spectre of Serbian expansionism had emerged to change the strategic landscape of the Balkans. The decision of the EC to recognise the independence of Slovenia and Croatia formally legitimised change in Yugoslavia. Turkey was belatedly released from its obligations to the *status quo ante*. Ankara was therefore free to support the independence of Bosnia-Herzegovina and Macedonia.

Turkey's desire for stability in the Balkans was as strong after con-flict broke out in the former Yugoslavia as it was before. Whereas the pursuit of stability was initially predicated on the preservation of the status quo, it subsequently became attached to the twin objectives of ending the conflict in Bosnia-Herzegovina and ensuring that that conflict did not spread to other entities, especially Macedonia. As a territorially non-revisionist power with important economic ties with Western Europe, Turkey had nothing to gain and much to lose from war in the Balkans. With a bloody insurgency taking place in south-eastern Turkey and perennial problems with its neigh-bours to the north-east and south-east, Ankara would not have wel-comed additional or protracted conflict close to its Balkan borders.

The spread of conflict to Macedonia, whether in the context of strife in Kosovo or during the Bosnian war, was always an alarming prospect for Turkey. First, it would have marked the geographical spread of the conflict in the direction of Turkey, and would have been of additional concern in view of the fact that both Greece and

Bulgaria, Turkey's two Balkan neighbours, had potentially explosive relations with Macedonia. Second, were Macedonian Slavs and Albanians to have been pitted against each other, as later became a worrying possibility during the Kosovo crisis and after, Turkey would have been in a position of great discomfort, not least because Macedonia and Albania were throughout much of the 1990s Turkey's closest friends in the Balkans. Third, the involvement of Macedonia's neighbours (and any combination of Albania, Bulgaria, Greece, and Serbia could have become drawn in) would offer the prospect of territorial revisionism affecting those Balkan states outside the former Yugoslavia. Thus would have been created the circumstances under which Turkey might have been drawn into a widening Balkans conflagration.

Turkey wanted to see the fighting stop in Bosnia–Herzegovina, but not at any price. Ankara stated that it was prepared to accept a compromise settlement in the republic provided that it was acceptable to the Bosnian government. In spite of its strong desire to see an end to the fighting, Ankara adopted such a course because of its perceived need to bolster the Bosnian government as a secularist, non-confessional entity. In working closely with the Bosnian government, Ankara was pleased to give support to a state which it identified as closely resembling itself: that is, a secular government in a country predominantly made up of Muslims. In this respect it is noteworthy that while most commentators on the issue became preoccupied with the religious affiliations of the warring parties, all official Turkish statements and publications referred to 'the Bosniaks' and 'the Bosnian government', never 'the Bosnian Muslims'.

A particular manifestation of the Turkish government's secular concerns could be seen in its attitude towards President Alija Izetbegovic. In the early 1970s, as an opponent of Communism, Izetbegovic was a political figure who had couched his opposition in terms of Islam. Indeed, he had even gone so far as to criticise the rapid and coercive secularisation process under Atatürk;[20] in the words of one senior Turkish diplomat, Izetbegovic was a Muslim conservative, almost a fundamentalist. By the early 1990s, however, he had become essentially a secular politician leading a non-confessional state. For Turkey Izetbegovic represents one of the great secularist conversions.[21]

[20] Noel Malcolm, *Bosnia: A Short History* (Macmillan, London, 1994), p. 221.
[21] Interview with senior Turkish official, Ankara, 22 April 1993.

ANALOGIES

Throughout the war Turkey was concerned at the effect that the battlefield victories of the Bosnian Serbs might have on the Bosnian government. Ankara feared that the lack of political and military success might result in the discrediting of secularism and moderation. Turkish officials long worried about the fall of the secular administration in Sarajevo and the Islamisation of Bosnian politics. In the autumn of 1993, with the devaluation of inter-confessional ties and the growing importance of the Muslim assembly in Bosnia, some of Turkey's worst fears looked as if they might soon be realised. Moreover, Iran, Turkey's 'silent' rival in the former Soviet south, was also gaining in influence in Bosnia. This steady undermining of the secularism of the Bosnian government took place at a time when the other secularist Muslim regimes most closely allied to Turkey were looking increasingly embattled. Azerbaijan sustained a string of defeats at the hands of the Armenians in spring and summer of 1993; this resulted in the ousting of the most Kemalist of Azerbaijan's aspiring leaders, Abulfez Elçibey. In the self-styled Turkish Republic of Northern Cyprus its leader Rauf Denktaş was coming under increased pressure to make concessions over the future of Cyprus, pressure which in 1993 brought him into greater friction with his domestic opposition. With the movement of political Islam growing in the Arab World and as apparently entrenched as ever in Iran, for Turkey the erosion of the position of its secular Muslim friends was a disturbing sight.

As far as Turkey was concerned the dangers inherent in the Bosnian model had already become manifest. Ankara regarded the upsurge in the war in and around Nagorno-Karabakh as a direct result of the precedent set in Bosnia. Armenia was perceived as having observed that Serbia had been able to launch and succeed in its expansionist plans. The sanctions against Serbia, which then amounted to little more than an oft-violated economic embargo, were viewed as being an insufficient deterrent to states such as Armenia. Consequently, the Turks believed, Armenia decided to launch its military campaign not only to secure the whole of Karabakh with linking corridors to Armenia, but also to take control of large swathes of Azerbaijani territory; by the end of the 1990s Armenia was accused of occupying some 20 per cent of Azerbaijani territory, aside from Karabakh. Because of Azerbaijan's military weakness, no international check was brought to bear on Yerevan, and Armenia emerged without even the economic sanctions imposed against Serbia. According to such an analysis, Ankara similarly dismissed the ability of Azerbaijan's Armenian population in Karabakh to launch and execute such a plan independent of Armenia, as it did the notion that the Bosnian Serbs might have been operating independently of Serbia proper.

From a Turkish point of view, rewarding Serbian aggression by recognising its control of a disproportionate part of Bosnia–Herzegovina, as prescribed in successive peace plans from the Vance-Owen Plan to the Dayton agreement, has made it even harder to dislodge Armenian fighters from Azerbaijani territory. The greater proximity of the conflict in the Caucasus to Turkey and the potential importance of Azerbaijan as a 'Turkic' ally make the Karabakh situation of much greater strategic importance to Ankara than that of Bosnia. There must also be the possibility that the Bosnian model will act as an incentive to other states and leaders to use military means to realise their ambitions. The Bosnian example could yet inspire similar actions elsewhere in the Balkans and the Caucasus, or perhaps in the Middle East or Central Asia. In any of these cases such conflict would be taking place in regions where Turkey claims important interests.

The policy chronology

TURKEY AS RELUCTANT ACTOR, FROM 1923[22] TO APRIL 1992

Since the foundation of the modern state in 1923, Turkey has not been a revisionist power in the Balkans. Mustafa Kemal Atatürk, the founder of modern Turkey and its dominant political figure for almost the first two decades of its existence, willingly renounced all claims to the former provinces of the Ottoman Empire. Atatürk was satisfied to consolidate the new state based on the territory of Anatolia and Eastern Thrace. This clear geopolitical vision continues to provide an ideological bulwark against territorial adventurism to the west and indeed the east of Turkey's borders. This ultimate act

---

[22] Though earlier dates could have been taken, 1923, and more particularly the Treaty of Lausanne, has been selected as it marks the securing of the international status of the modern state of Turkey.

of disengagement was later followed by relatively little interaction between Turkey and the Balkans during the era of Communism. While Turkey enjoyed better relations with Yugoslavia than the other states of the region,[23] especially once Belgrade had left the Cominform, Tito's need to preserve a strict non-alignment in order to manage relations with Moscow restricted opportunities in bilateral relations with Turkey.[24]

The regime changes that took place across the region in 1989 gave no reason for Turkey to reconsider this approach. At a time of political change in the region, and against a backdrop of new institutions and economies suffering massive contraction, the continuity in Turkey's approach to the Balkans was of great value. Though Turkey's involvement with the Balkans grew quickly with the collapse of Communism, it remained, politically, a reluctant actor in the region.

Even as the cohesion of the Yugoslav state began to weaken, Turkey maintained regular relations with Belgrade. Afterall, Ankara was generally well disposed towards Belgrade at this time, not least because of Yugoslavia's criticism of Zhivkov's policies towards the Turkish minority in Bulgaria in the late 1980s. As a *status quo* power, mindful of its own heightening Kurdish insurgency, Turkey remained fully committed to the protection of the unity and the territorial integrity of Yugoslavia.[25] Bilateral relations were emphasised and frequent official visits took place. The relationship ironically appeared to be at its most auspicious during this difficult period in April 1991, just two months before Croatia and Slovenia began the process leading to independence and federal forces intervened in

---

[23] Şule Kut describes Turkish-Yugoslav relations as being good, especially during the Tito era. See her '*Yugoslavya Bunalımı ve Türkiye'nin Bosna-Hersek ve Makedonya Politikası: 1990–1993*' (The Yugoslav Crisis and Turkey's Bosnia-Herzegovina and Macedonia Policy: 1990–1993) in Faruk Sönmezoğlu (ed.), *Türk Dış Politikasının Analizi* (Analysis of Turkish Foreign Policy) (Der Yayınları, Istanbul, 1994), p. 163.

[24] For a brief discussion of Turkish-Yugoslav relations in the first two decades of the Cold War see Ferenc A. Vali, *Bridge Across the Bosporus* (Johns Hopkins University Press, Baltimore, 1971), pp. 206–7.

[25] For example, see one of the first statements of the Turkish foreign minister, Safa Giray, after the creation of the Yılmaz government in June 1991; a statement which actually took place against a background of increasing violence in Slovenia. *Newspot*, 4 July 1991.

the former. It was during April that the chairman of the Presidential Council of Yugoslavia, Borisav Jovic, visited Turkey as the official guest of President Özal.[26] Jovic referred to 'the desire of the hosts that Yugoslavia should remain a united country'. Furthermore, Turkey proposed that Yugoslavia should be included in the development projects of the Black Sea Economic Co-operation project; both sides stated that there was no issue between them that could not be resolved peacefully.[27]

Controversial as well as co-operative subjects were discussed at such meetings. For instance, during the visit to Turkey of the Yugoslav foreign minister, Budimir Loncar, in August 1990 the issue of national minorities was addressed; the resulting communiqué rather unrealistically stated that such minorities should be the means to create greater trust, rather than suspicion, in the Balkans.[28] The two sides were, however, plainly less ill at ease when discussing economic issues. The broadening of economic ties was a non-controversial area into which both parties could channel their desire for good relations. It therefore featured prominently during all such visits between 1990 and 1992. Many of the agreements signed on broader economic matters showed the importance of Yugoslavia for Turkey in its transport and communications strategy. For instance, when the joint economic commission met in July 1990 it ended up by clinching accords on air, rail and road transport matters. As part of the common expectation of intensified transport co-operation, the use of Yugoslav rail and road networks by services from Turkey was predicted to rise by 75 per cent and 25 per cent respectively.[29] Contracts were also signed to boost bilateral trade. As late as January 1992 Turkey took delivery of the first consignment of municipal buses from a firm in Belgrade.[30]

In spite of the general reluctance of Turkey to get involved in the Yugoslav question, Ankara was clearly seen as an important player by the various parties to the problem. As senior members of the Yugoslav state visited the Turkish capital to try to maintain Ankara's

---

[26] For a commentary on the visit of the Yugoslav head of state see *Newspot*, 25 April 1991.

[27] BBC/SWB/ME, 13 April 1991.

[28] BBC/SWB/EE, 8 August 1990.

[29] BBC/SWB/EE, 2 August 1990.

[30] BBC/SWB/EE, 23 January 1992.

support for the union, so did top officials from some of the constituent republics lobby for their own interests. As with the emerging
republics during the final months of the Soviet Union, Turkey was
subject to the diplomacy of others, rather than acting as an initiator.
Senior figures from Bosnia-Herzegovina were the first from the
individual republics to see the utility of a link with Turkey. Against
a backdrop of full scale war in Croatia, Bosnian Vice-Premier Muhamed Cengic paid a one day private visit to Turkey in November
1991 to discuss the possibility of oil and humanitarian deliveries from
Turkey.[31] The Bosnian government also approached Turkey to plead
its case within NATO and with the EC.[32] The Bosnian foreign
minister, Haris Silajdzic, canvassed support for the recognition of
Bosnia-Herzegovina in Ankara in advance of its declaration by
Sarajevo.[33] The beginning of such a relationship clearly alarmed
Belgrade, as Tanjug, the official news agency, tried to spoil the
Cengic visit by attributing to him inflammatory remarks, which he
vehemently denied, about Germany and Christianity.[34] The fact
that Belgrade was unsuccessful in this tactic was revealed a month
later when Cengic visited Turkey for 12 days to discuss a variety of
different types of co-operation. He concluded the trip by describing Turkey as 'our primary partner' in the future.[35]

Macedonia also invoked the friendship of Turkey. President Kiro
Gligorov of Macedonia paid a three day official visit to Turkey in
July 1991, as fighting in Croatia intensified. He was keen to obtain
Turkish support as insurance against the disintegration of Yugoslavia.
His visit appears to have been of some considerable success. The
Turkish press quoted officials in Ankara, whether accurately or not,
as saying that 'Turkey will protect Macedonia from the countries
which would threaten it.'[36] This emerging relationship was further
consolidated by a visit from the Macedonian minister for foreign
relations, Denko Malevski, in October. He was confidently able to
assert that the two entities held 'identical stands on how to deal

[31] BBC/SWB/EE, 18 November 1991 and 20 November 1991.
[32] BBC/SWB/EE, 20 November 1991.
[33] BBC/SWB/EE, 3 January, 1992.
[34] See BBC/SWB/EE, 20 November 1991.
[35] BBC/SWB/EE, 20 December 1991.
[36] *Hürriyet*, 12 July quoted in BBC/SWB/EE, 19 July 1991.

with the crisis in Yugoslavia'. In particular, he seemed to have won the Turkish Foreign Ministry over to the idea that Yugoslavia should be reconstituted as an alliance of sovereign states.[37]

Under the impact of the lobbying of individual republics, and in a context of the fading tenability of the federal Yugoslav state, Turkish policy began to change. Ankara still held firmly to the principle of the maintenance of the territorial integrity of the Balkans countries. However, Turkey increasingly juxtaposed this basic position with a realisation of the need for what the late Turkish academic Oral Sander, writing in October 1991, described as 'a peaceful and negotiated restructuring of ethnically troubled countries'. It was as a reflection of this growing process of restructuring that Ankara took such decisions as to open a consulate in Skopje, with enlarged functions and a brief to conduct direct contacts with the Macedonians. Increasingly, it came to resemble an embassy in all but name.[38]

It was against this evolving background that Turkish diplomacy came to deal with the question of recognition. The earlier representations of the Bosnian and Macedonian governments to Ankara seemed to have paid off. Turkish policy was clearly to treat the constituent republics of Yugoslavia as a whole, rather than on a piecemeal basis. By January 1992 the Turkish prime minister, Süleyman Demirel was able to tell the Croatian foreign minister that 'Turkey will not recognise Yugoslav republics individually but in a package'.[39] Thus, while the EC adopted an ad hoc approach to the issue of recognition, giving full recognition to Croatia on 15 January 1992 but leaving Bosnia-Herzegovina as late as 6 April, Turkey recognised all four republics on 6 February. Turkey thus became only the second state, after Bulgaria, to recognise the independence of Bosnia. However, though the decision of Ankara to recognise the four together reflected an emerging special relationship between Turkey and the governments in Skopje and Sarajevo, the timing of the move reflected the inherent conservatism of Turkey. Ankara was unwilling to run ahead of the EC or the United States in formalising the break-up of Yugoslavia.

---

[37] BBC/SWB/EE, 18 October 1991.
[38] Oral Sander, 'Turkey and the Balkans', *Middle East Business and Banking*, November 1991, p. 10.
[39] BBC/SWB/EE, 14 January 1992.

Furthermore, it should be noted that neither recognition nor the outbreak of fighting in Bosnia immediately changed the reticence of the Turkish diplomatic approach. When Muhamed Cengic tried to use his relationship with Turkey to bring in Ankara as a mediator and as an advocate on the Bosnian government's behalf with the United States and France, Turkey's response was disappointing. Ankara responded by sending a fact finding mission to Belgrade under a Foreign Ministry official. The ministry was reluctant to adopt a new policy until the mission had returned.[40] It was nearly a week later that the first stirrings of Turkey's activist diplomatic engagement began, with Foreign Minister Çetin raising the Bosnian issue at the UN, the CSCE and the ICO. Even then, Ankara seemed slow to engage diplomatically, with Cetin announcing that only 'if necessary' will Turkey back its 'verbal efforts with written applications'.[41]

TURKEY AS VIGOROUS ADVOCATE, MAY 1992-JANUARY 1993

Once the scale and brutality of the conflict started to become apparent, Turkey became fully engaged, a period of what Şule Kut has called '*aktif ve yetkin diplomasili*' (active and authoritative diplomacy).[42] For Ankara, there was no doubt about the guilty party over Bosnia, it was the state of Serbia and its leader, President Slobodan Milosevic. Serbia was officially labelled as guilty of 'expansionism'; it was held responsible for 'inhuman acts' against Bosnian Muslims; Serbian officials were held to be 'directly responsible for the events in Bosnia-Herzegovina'.[43] In adopting this view Ankara dismissed the notion that the Bosnian conflict was essentially a civil war. It believed that the Bosnian Serbs would not have been able to sustain their war effort without significant and continuing assistance from the state of Serbia. By the beginning of May 1992, after a slow start, Turkey had emerged as an energetic advocate in support of Bosnia within the multilateral machinery of which it was a part. For instance, at one point in December 1992 Çetin managed to address the CSCE, the conference on Yugoslavia at Geneva and a NATO Council of Ministers meeting, all in the space of less than three days. Increasingly, however, this period became one of disillusionment as

[40] *Turkish Daily News*, 18 April 1992.
[41] *Turkish Daily News*, 24 April 1992.
[42] Şule Kut, op. cit., p. 173.
[43] *Turkish Daily News*, 28 May 1992.

Turkey's allies politely, even sympathetically, heard the passion with which Ankara argued its case only to turn their backs on the sort of substantive action being proposed.

During the first three months of this phase Turkey seemed to find some satisfaction in the international community. Nowhere was this more evident than in Turkey's attitude to the work of the United Nations. For example, Turkey expressed itself satisfied with the chairmanship statement after the Security Council meeting of 24 April, which called for the immediate cessation of the fighting in Bosnia.[44] A truce was signed on 5 May between the Bosnian presidency and the JNA. Though the fighting quickly re-erupted, Turkey welcomed the tougher approach of the international community as the UN introduced sanctions against Serbia and Montenegro on 30 May. May also saw the UN begin its relief missions for Sarajevo. At this time Ankara recalled its ambassador from Belgrade, which represented the complete breakdown of what had been for many months a worsening diplomatic relationship with Serbia.[45]

As the fighting intensified, stories about the displacement of populations and the existence of prison camps began to emerge. The international community was completely unable to make any brokered cease-fire stick. Consequently, Turkey became increasingly frustrated with the international diplomatic process. This exasperation helped encourage Turkey to move from supporting the initiatives of others to launching its own integrated plan. Thus on 7 August the Turkish government submitted an 'Action Plan for Bosnia Herzegovina' (*Bosna işin İki Aşamlı Eylem Planı*) to the Security Council.[46] The plan clearly identified the Bosnian Serb militia, supported by Serbia, as being responsible for the continued conflict. It demanded that Belgrade cease helping the Serb militia. It also stated that the attacks in Bosnia should be considered crimes against humanity. The Action Plan included a major role for international agencies, insisting that the Red Cross should take over Serb-run prison camps and that the UN should assume control of the region. Finally, it proposed the imposition of a deadline on the Serbs, threatening military action in the form of air raids on the militia and even against

---

[44] *Newspot*, 7 May 1992.
[45] *Newspot*, 21 May 1992.
[46] Unpublished plan formally dated 7 August 1992.

Serbia itself if the fighting did not end within two weeks. From this point onwards, while Ankara remained committed to working within the machinery of the international community, its policy prescriptions became increasingly divorced from the sort of measures that the major external actors would be willing to contemplate.[47]

The Action Plan proved to be Turkey's major diplomatic initiative on Bosnia-Herzegovina during its most intensive phase of activism. At the London Conference on Yugoslavia on 26–27 August 1992, the first meeting to bring all major domestic and foreign actors together, Çetin circulated the Action Plan as a conference document.[48] Indeed, as far as the Turks were concerned the plan still appeared to be on the table the following January.[49] But by the time of the London Conference Turkey's mounting frustrations appeared to have hardened its line. Çetin thus went beyond the Action Plan in his statement to the conference. In particular, he stated that all territory occupied as a result of the conflict should be given up. Furthermore, he maintained that all those who had been expelled should be allowed to return to their own homes.[50] Though this may have been a laudable statement of principle, those at the centre of peace-making felt that it completely ignored both the realities on the ground in Bosnia and the politics surrounding the conflict. It is therefore hardly surprising that the subsequent attempts on the part of the international mediators to broker a peace were at great variance with such positions, as Lord Owen and his successive UN-appointed partners addressed reality rather than principle.

The substance of Çetin's speech to the London Conference proved to be but the first of a number of public manifestations of Turkish frustration with the Western-dominated international diplomatic machinery. The staging of a Balkans Conference in Istanbul on 25 November, apparently against the advice or at least without US approval, was a second notable instance. The participants called on the UN to send troops to Kosovo, Vojvodina and the Sancak of Novipazar in Serbia, as well as to Macedonia, in order to prevent the spread of ethnic clashes. They also urged that Macedonia, whose

---

[47] For details see *Newspot*, 13 August 1992.
[48] *Newspot*, 10 September 1992.
[49] *Turkish Probe*, vol. 1, no. 9, 12 January 1993.
[50] For Hikmet Çetin's London Conference speech see *Newspot*, 10 September 1992.

recognition had been held up by Greek objections, should be generally recognised. A wide-ranging agenda even led to the recommendation that a meeting of the CSCE, the forerunner of the OSCE, should be held in the beleaguered Bosnian capital of Sarajevo.[51]

A third example was Turkey's greater diplomatic activity within the ICO in the second half of 1992 and in early 1993. The first significant move, at Turkey's behest,[52] was the convening of an extraordinary meeting of ICO foreign ministers in Istanbul on 17–18 June. The joint communiqué that resulted from the meeting laid down important policy guidelines on Bosnia for the Muslim world: blame for the conflict laid at the door of Serb leaders in Belgrade and Bosnia; demands that the JNA withdraw and Serb militias disband; full support for UN positions on the conflict; no recognition of the new Yugoslavia until UN resolutions had been implemented; and coordinated military intervention under Chapter Seven of the UN Charter should existing international sanctions prove to be ineffectual.[53] In other words, while being tough on Serbian aggression, Ankara had also been invaluable in tying Muslim states to the same multilateral ground rules that governed the formulation and implementation of its own policy.

The Istanbul meeting was not the end of Turkish diplomacy within the ICO. With Turkey by now holding the ICO presidency,[54] Ankara tried to use the emergency meeting of the organisation in Senegal in January 1993 to hinder the Vance-Owen Plan, which had been unveiled less than 10 days before. The vigour with which Ankara pursued the matter at the ICO, though at face value unhelpful to the West, was, nevertheless, a shrewd move; it prevented Islamist ideological rivals such as Iran from charging Turkey with being soft on the Bosnian issue because of its strategic alliance with the West. Ironically, it also raised Turkey's importance in Western strategic calculations, as Ankara was viewed as an effective block against the adoption of embarrassing resolutions. Even Lord Owen

---

[51] *Turkey Confidential*, no. 34, December 1992, pp. 12–13.
[52] Hasan Ünal, 'Bosnia II: A Turkish Critique', *The World Today*, vol. 51, no. 7, July 1995, p. 128.
[53] For a summary of the final communiqué see *Newspot*, 2 July 1992.
[54] Turkey held the presidency of the ICO for 18 months, relinquishing it in April 1993.

himself, who was presumably greatly irritated by the Turkish stance in Senegal, later acknowledged that Turkey was 'important for our credibility with the Islamic nations'.[55]

With Ankara's plan for limited intervention clearly moribund, in autumn 1992 Turkey switched tack. The Turkish government now began to argue that, in the absence of military help from the international community, the Bosnian state should not be deprived of the right of self-defence.[56] Indeed, by mid October Ankara had decided to concentrate its diplomatic efforts on trying to get the UN arms embargo, which hitherto had been applied to all parties to the conflict, revoked in the case of the Bosnian government.[57] By December, Turkey had formulated a simple trinity of demands: lift the arms embargo; establish safe havens; engage in limited military intervention.[58] But while Turkey's allies in the West continued to listen to the pleas of Turkish politicians and officials with respect, Turkey remained singularly unable to realise any of its central goals.

Faced with painfully slow moving activity at the international level, Turkey was at least able to busy itself with relief activity on behalf of the Bosnian population. Turkey's humanitarian effort can be divided into three parts: direct aid to Bosnians on the ground; the provision of health care to those badly injured; sanctuary to large numbers of Bosnian refugees.

Initially the Turkish government was slow to understand the importance of the provision of aid. The coalition government was criticised in early July 1992 for being slow to send relief flights to Sarajevo. One columnist in the Turkish press stung the government by noting that even Greek planes had already resumed flights since the reopening of the airport.[59] The early tardiness of the Turkish government in providing aid may have had something to do with the fact that Ankara tended to regard the Western aid effort as a substitute for real political action on Bosnia.[60] Turkey did, however,

---

[55] David Owen, *Balkan Odyssey* (Victor Gollancz, London, 1995), p. 225.

[56] *Turkish Daily News*, 29 October 1992.

[57] *Turkish Daily News*, 21 October 1992.

[58] For example see *TDN*, 17 December 1992.

[59] Mehmet Ali Birand in *Sabah*, 7 July 1992, reprinted in *TDN*, 8 July 1992.

[60] This was a view that was widely shared beyond Turkey. See Tom Gallagher, ' "This Farrago of Anomalies": The European Response to the War in Bosnia-Hercegovina, 1992–95', *Mediterranean Politics*, vol. 1, no. 1, summer 1996, p. 84.

eventually implement an aid effort. By March 1993, according to Turkish Minister of State Orhan Kilercioğlu, Ankara had disbursed $23 million worth of aid in Bosnia-Herzegovina;[61] $11.7 million was disbursed in the first four and a half months of 1993 alone.[62] Turkey felt frustration at the problems of dispersing international aid on the ground. Consequently, Ankara backed Washington's controversial decision to use cargo planes to drop consignments of aid directly to Muslim areas cut off in eastern Bosnia, which began on 28 February. Part of Turkey's aid was subsequently delivered in this way.[63]

The Turkish authorities offered hospital facilities to Bosnians wounded in the conflict. This was extended to Bosnian soldiers as well as civilians. While many of these casualties were treated in hospital in Istanbul some of the wounded were sent to other parts of the country, as far afield as Kayseri. In addition to relieving pressure on beds in the country's largest city, this also had the political benefit of demonstrating widely across the country, especially in the conservative Anatolian heartland, that Turkey was active in the provision of assistance.[64]

Turkey was also willing to give refuge to a very substantial number of Bosnian refugees. As early as April 1992 Turkey had accepted 2,000 Bosnian refugees.[65] A month later this had risen to 7,000, the bulk of whom were staying with relatives. In May formal provision began to be made for temporary housing in anticipation of the arrival of more refugees, with mayors of three cities offering to take up to 6,000 newcomers in total between them. Unlike most European countries, Turkey did not seriously attempt to put bureaucratic obstacles in the way of Bosnian refugees, which might well have elicited a backlash among Turks of Bosnian origin. By March, 1993 the number of Bosnian refugees was estimated to be in excess of 200,000.[66]

---

[61] BBC/SWB/ME, 29 March 1993.

[62] *Turkish Daily News*, 17 May 1993.

[63] *Turkish Daily News*, 11 March 1993.

[64] For example, ten wounded soldiers were sent to the Erciyes University medical hospital in Kayseri in October 1994.

[65] *Turkish Daily News*, 27 April 1992.

[66] BBC/SWB/ME, (note 61).

The opening of the doors to Bosnian refugees did not, however, exempt the Turkish government from criticism of its policy towards the new state. From May 1992 onwards, the coalition government in Turkey was criticised for different aspects of its policy. Criticism came both from the coalition's major rival for power, ANAP or the Motherland Party, and from the smaller parties, notably the Welfare Party before its electoral success of 1995; as an Islamist party, Welfare uniquely offered the Turkish electorate an alternative world view in contrast to the Kemalist consensus of the rest of the Turkish political parties.

The Motherland politicians critical of government policy tended to attack it for being conservative and over-cautious in style, and for lacking substance. For instance, one of the most consistently vocal critics on the matter, Kamran İnan, accused the government of a 'wailing wall policy', whereby Ankara's only action was to bemoan the developments in Bosnia in a multitude of foreign capitals.[67] The late Adnan Kahveci was another leading critic from the Motherland Party. He denounced government policy, accusing it of being 'passive and cowardly...[and] timid'.[68] Such criticism was not, however, exclusively confined to the issue of Bosnia. In this case Bosnia was but the latest example of the newly emerging differences in approach between a traditional, cautious, Kemalist style of foreign policy, as implemented under the coalition, and the new, assertive and interventionist policy which had been developed by Turgut Özal since the late 1980s. Indeed, İnan and the coalition were to clash again on the same basis over government policy towards Azerbaijan in spring 1993.

Criticism of coalition policy by the Welfare Party went much deeper. Islamist politicians were less concerned with issues of style than with what the matter said about the general orientation of Turkish policy. For instance, during the debate on sending Turkish troops to Somalia, Abdullatif Şener implied that Ankara was more interested in executing a US strategic plan than in intervening to end strife and starvation, and compared the positive decision with Turkish inaction on Bosnia.[69] The Welfare Party was generally much

---

[67] *Turkish Daily News*, 1 December 1992.
[68] *Turkish Daily News*, 28 July 1992.
[69] BBC/SWB/ME, 11 December 1992.

more willing to advocate the use of Turkish forces in the Bosnian conflict. For instance, the party leader, Professor Necmettin Erbakan, as rhetorically florid as ever, said that his party would form a rapid deployment force of 10,000 troops to be sent to Bosnia.[70] Otherwise, Welfare was rather short on the details of troop deployments, such as how forces would travel to Bosnia, the nature of the mission, rules of engagement and so on, issues which tended to be regarded of key importance in the minds of diplomats and military men and were significant practical obstacles to embarking on such a course.

Criticism of government policy was not, however, confined to the opposition parties. Coalition performance was also the target of influential deputies from within the ruling parties. Coşkun Kırca, the *de facto* leader of the nationalist right wing of the dominant party, the True Path Party, was an early critic of the coalition. At the beginning of May 1992 Kırca criticised the government for not having taken prompter action in seeking a meeting of the UN Security Council to take steps against Serbia for attacks on Bosnian Muslims.[71]

Dissident voices were also heard in the junior coalition member, the Social Democratic Populist Party (SHP), notably Mümtaz Soysal. Professor Soysal emerged in November 1991 as the alternative voice on foreign affairs in the SHP to his fellow deputy Hikmet Çetin, who was appointed foreign minister in the new coalition. Soysal had argued for a complete revision of Turkish foreign policy in the aftermath of the October 1991 election, the central planks of which would be reduced dependence on the US and the cultivation of a leadership role within the Third World. Soysal's revisionism was probably a key reason why he did not receive the foreign affairs portfolio himself at that time. Soysal extended his revisionism to policy over Bosnia. By the end of 1992 he was not merely criticising government policy but advocating a new basis for Turkey's advocacy of Bosnia-Herzegovina. He argued that because the Muslims of the Balkans were converted under the Ottoman Empire Turkey should declare itself to be the moral protector of these communities. He underlined this view by drawing an analogy with nineteenth

[70] *Turkish Daily News*, 18 February 1993.
[71] *Turkish Daily News*, 9 May 1992.

century France, which had demanded a similar role for itself with regard to the Christian communities of the Levant under the Ottoman Empire.[72]

TURKEY AS PASSIVE BYSTANDER, JANUARY–SEPTEMBER 1993

The death of President Özal in April 1993 and the resulting domestic party political turmoil in Turkey were clearly a major factor in distracting senior figures from the Bosnian question. First, a new president had to be chosen. Once Süleyman Demirel had been elected head of state, a further round of politicking ensued as the DYP set about choosing a new political leader, and hence a new prime minister. It was not exclusively the parties in government that were preoccupied with such happenings. Political opposition inside Turkey also became fixated with the dual leadership question, to the virtual exclusion of all else, Bosnia included.

The loss of Özal was also important in another way. Turgut Özal had been a prominent advocate for Bosnia, notably during the ICO meeting in Senegal, when, with characteristic panache, he had flown President Izetbegovic to Dakar in his private jet. Furthermore, Özal had undertaken a controversial visit to the Balkans, including Macedonia and Albania on his itinerary, a matter of just two months before his death. Some reports quoted his enemies as saying that Özal now saw himself as a 'Balkans crusader'.[73] Though Özal was by this time on the margins of political power in Turkey, a position that was clearly visible through his increasingly cavalier actions, he did still have the ability to influence the national political agenda. His demise meant that there was virtually no-one left of sufficient stature in Turkey capable of projecting the issue back into the public eye.

The death of Özal and the period of introspection that followed should not, however, obscure the fact that Turkey by April 1993 had already become a bystander as far as the Bosnian issue was concerned. By January, after months of 'intense lobbying',[74] Ankara had not made any real diplomatic headway. Disillusionment with the West was deepening. For instance, incredulity was expressed at the fact

---

[72] See *Financial Times*, 11 January 1993.
[73] *Turkish Probe*, vol. 2, no. 15, 23 February 1993.
[74] *Turkish Probe*, vol. 1, no. 9, 12 January 1993

that the Security Council was prepared to give the Serbs 30 days to comply with its no-fly resolution.[75] On 2 January the Vance-Owen Plan, to which Ankara profoundly objected on the grounds that it legitimised the seizure of territory by the Bosnian Serbs, was unveiled by its two sponsors. By the end of January, with the Vance-Owen Plan now dominating the peace process, it had become clear that Turkey was effectively a marginalised spectator of the conflict.[76]

The realisation that Turkey had been confined to the margins of influence appeared to have a corrosive effect on the morale of the Turkish diplomatic elite. This perhaps explains why senior Foreign Ministry officials seemed to run out of steam as their political masters became side-tracked by the political vacuum created by the death of Özal. If a serious loss of morale was indeed significant in subduing the diplomatic activity of the Turkish Foreign Ministry, it appears to have had two further contributory causes. First, the killing of the Bosnian deputy premier, Hakija Turajlic, in Sarajevo by Bosnian Serbs moments after seeing off a Turkish minister of state, Orhan Kilercioğlu, in January 1993 was deeply shocking for the Turks. Second, the failure of the new American president Bill Clinton, once in office, to follow up the interventionist words he proclaimed during the election campaign seemed to remove any hope that the Western approach would change. Once Clinton had dropped his plans for intervention in Bosnia, there was no longer any realistic chance that the aspirations outlined in the Action Plan and during Çetin's speech to the London Conference would be implemented. A leading Balkans specialist in Turkey, Hasan Ünal, has argued that this period of disengagement was a disaster, as in the crucial months of April and May Ankara should have been stiffening the United States against British attempts to dissuade it from a 'lift and strike' strategy towards the Bosnian Serbs.[77]

As a result of Turkey's consequent diplomatic inertia, there were only two developments of note regarding Turkey and Bosnia during this period. The first, in April, was the NATO decision that the Turkish air force should participate in the enforcement of the no-fly

---

[75] *Turkish Probe*, vol. 1, no. 10, 19 January 1993.
[76] *Turkish Probe*, vol. 1, no. 11, 26 January 1993.
[77] Ünal, op. cit., p. 129.

zone. Eighteen Turkish F-16s were subsequently assigned in two batches to Vicenza in Italy to be part of 'Operation Clear Skies'.[78] However, this was in reality nothing more than a formal, though presentationally important, gesture towards Turkey on the part of its Western allies, as Turkish planes remained part of a second group of NATO countries with their aircraft on permanent standby. Turkey had been ostentatiously put on 'the team sheet', in an important piece of public diplomacy by the core Western states. However, a gesture was really all that it was, as owing to Turkey's geographical proximity and controversial profile in the Balkans, its aircraft had, at that time, little chance of taking to the skies.[79] The second was a decision by the ICO to send a delegation of foreign ministers to major international capitals to lobby on behalf of the Bosnian government. This ultimately ceremonial gesture did not even achieve the symbolic success of the inclusion of Turkish aircraft in Operation Clear Skies.

It was not only the politicians of Turkey, however, who were side-tracked during this time. Public opinion does not appear to have been openly mobilised in support of an assertive, let alone a unilateral approach towards the issue. For all the talk of the large number of Turks of Bosnian origin, there appears to have been a marked lack of public engagement with the subject, beyond a general sympathy for the victims of the strife. Perhaps the best example of this public inertia was the demonstration in Taksim Square, Istanbul, in February 1993, which was organised under the ambiguous slogan of 'Turks to Bosnia'.[80] In the event only some 20,000 people turned up, well below the number expected by the organisers. One reason why many more did not turn out was thought to be that President Özal had tried to use the event for domestic political gain. While this is undoubtedly true, what is of key interest is that the main parties felt able to boycott the event without eliciting a popular backlash over Bosnia. Turks had chosen domestic party politics in preference to the Bosnian issue as the critical determinant of whether they would participate. As a result, the rally only attracted ultra-nationalist and Islamist support.

---

[78] *Daily Telegraph*, 19 April 1993.
[79] Interview with West European diplomat, 19 November 1993.
[80] See *Turkish Probe*, vol. 2, no. 14, 16 February 1993.

A second example of the limited interest of public opinion in Bosnia was the fact that Turkish mainstream political parties perceived there to be no cost to the political introspection caused by Özal's death and its aftermath, even at a time of continuing conflict in Bosnia. Moreover, there was no accumulation of public pressure to return to an active role over Bosnia once these domestic political issues were resolved. As one Turkish columnist remarked in early August: 'Bosnia has simply disappeared from the minds of the people ruling Turkey. Public opinion has forgotten the issue—or has been made to forget'.[81] It was therefore the end of the summer before Ankara resumed an active diplomatic role.

The general lack of public mobilisation in the Bosnian case is hardly surprising given the elite orientation of foreign policy in Turkey, and the absence of issues other than Cyprus that animate the wider population. The lack of organised public concern over Bosnia cannot, however, be attributed either to ignorance or the lack of alternative policy proposals. Bosnia became a subject of intense political debate in Turkey after the first two months or so of the conflict in the former Yugoslavia spreading to that republic—that is, once it was clear that the Bosnian Serbs were making spectacular gains at the expense of the forces of the Bosnian government. Subsequently, Bosnia was often the subject of intense political debate in the Turkish press and also on television. Bosnian politicians were frequently to be seen on television in Turkey appealing for help.[82] There was no shortage of gruesome photographs displaying massacre victims in Bosnia. Fly poster campaigns in the major cities ensured that the brutal realities of the situation were virtually unavoidable.

TURKEY AS MEDIATOR, SEPTEMBER 1993-JUNE 1994

Turkey emerged from its prolonged period of *de facto* disengagement from the Bosnian question apparently purged of its maximalist inclinations. Instead, Ankara appeared to adopt a much more modest strategy. Rather than forlornly appealing for the international

---

[81] Cengiz Çandar in *Sabah*, 1 August 1993 reprinted in *Turkish Daily News*, 2 August 1993.

[82] Kemal Kirişci, 'New Patterns of Turkish Foreign Policy Behaviour', unpublished paper presented at conference on 'Change in Modern Turkey: Politics, Economy, Society' at the University of Manchester, 5–6 May 1993, p. 15.

community to take sweeping action over Bosnia, the efforts of Ankara now appeared to be more focused on specific and limited diplomatic aims. Foremost among these was the objective of re-forging the anti-Serb alliance of the Bosnian government and Croatia and, as a necessary precursor of this, bringing an end to the fighting in Bosnia between the Muslim and Croat communities.

The seeds of this role were planted with the visit to Ankara of Croatian president Franjo Tudjman at the end of April 1993, and it was founded on mutual condemnation of the Serbs. As a result, a joint governmental goodwill mission was put together and dis-patched to Bosnia. Though the Tudjman visit in itself made little substantive difference, it was of important symbolic value. Croatia had acknowledged that Turkey was a major regional player, and one with which Zagreb was eager to strike up good relations. In return for closer bilateral relations, Tudjman offered the prospect of relin-quishing aspirations to a greater Croatia, the joint declaration attach-ing 'utmost priority' to the sovereignty, independence and territorial integrity of Bosnia. With bilateral relations now unprecedentedly high, Turkey had established the two-handed credibility necessary to begin a mediation effort.

It was, however, to be the autumn before Turkey emerged as an important mediator in the Bosnian Muslim-Croat fighting. Inter-estingly, Ankara did not take the initiative, but only responded fol-lowing the urging of both the Bosnian and Croatian governments. The fact that Turkey was a reluctant mediator may have reassured Croatia that Turkey did not have a political prescription that it would seek to thrust upon the Croats. The recent battlefield reverses for the Bosnian Croats at the hands of government forces gave the Croats an extra incentive to accept Turkey's good offices. Neverthe-less, when Çetin declared that Turkey 'did not intend to impose its views on anyone' both parties (though of course not the Serbs) appeared to accept such a statement at face value.[83]

Ankara's approach to the mediation effort began by drawing attention to the futility of the Croat-Muslim fighting, when the strategic enemy of both sides continued to be the Serbs. This view appeared to be as much a function of Ankara's antipathy towards Belgrade as a realistic appraisal of the Croat-Muslim conflict. After

---

[83] *Turkish Probe*, vol. 4, no. 45, 28 September 1993.

all, it was because the Bosnian Croats were weaker than the Serbs and continued to occupy a disproportionate amount of territory that the Bosnian government forces, now better trained and stiffened by mercenaries, turned their guns on them. Whatever the assessments, Ankara seemed to play a useful role in exploring the boundaries of a potential compromise between the two new warring parties. For example, Turkey took up the Bosnian demand for an outlet to the Adriatic Sea with Croatia.[84]

Turkey took part in two sets of high-level meetings in the context of the Muslim-Croat rapprochement, punctuated by more frequent meetings of senior officials,[85] which in particular wrestled with the difficult subject of territory. The first such tripartite summit, which featured Hikmet Çetin, was convened in Zagreb on 24 September 1993 at the invitation of the Bosnian and Croatian governments.[86] A further tripartite meeting took place in Sarajevo on 12 November 1993, including both Cetin and the Croatian prime minister, Mate Granic, the highest ranking Croat to visit the beleaguered Bosnian capital since the onset of the conflict. Though Ankara's involvement continued to be somewhat low key, a request from Paris and Bonn to Cetin to intercede with the two sides on behalf of the EC further drew attention to the useful role being played by Ankara, and generally encouraged the Turkish side.[87]

Such meetings helped both to set an example for US diplomacy and to lay the foundations on which it would soon be successful. More particularly it sent a powerful message to the hard liners on both sides that compromises would have to be made. The resulting Washington Agreement was signed in March 1994.[88] Under the

---

[84] *Turkish Probe*, vol. 4 no. 45, 28 September 1993.

[85] These tended to take place at the level of political directors within the foreign ministries of the three states involved. See, for example, the meeting in Ankara, 5–6 April, 1994.

[86] *Turkish Daily News*, 27 September 1993.

[87] *Turkish Probe*, vol. 4, no. 52, 18 November 1993.

[88] Both the representatives of Bosnia and Croatia were fulsome in their praise of Turkey once the agreement had been clinched. As Bosnian ambassador to Ankara Hajredin Somun commented: 'The Americans did not start on empty ground. The groundwork was contributed largely by Turkey'. His counterpart, Hidayet Biscevic of Croatia, was quoted as saying: 'One cannot stress enough the importance of Turkish diplomacy. We always had Turkey, particularly Foreign Minister Hikmet Çetin, to turn to when we thought the talks would break down.'

terms of the accord, the Bosnian Croats and Muslims were formally reconciled in the form of a federation, which was then to be linked to Croatia through the creation of a confederation. If the agreement was to be imperfectly implemented, that, from a Turkish perspective, was of minor importance. For Ankara the Washington Agreement was of far more symbolic than substantive importance, its main utility being in signalling the end to the conflict between the Croats and the Bosnian government. In that light it is little wonder that Turkish diplomats drew a favourable analogy with the Declaration of Principles also signed in Washington by the leaders of Israel and the PLO the previous September.[89] In recognition of the Turkish contribution to bridging the gap between the two sides, Hikmet Çetin was invited to Washington to witness the signing of the confederation accord. An end to Muslim–Croat fighting in turn opened the way to further improvement in bilateral relations between Turkey and Croatia.

Amid the brief afterglow of the Washington Agreement it fleetingly seemed as if a broader end to the conflict might be in sight, with Turkey having aspirations to repeat its mediating role honed during the Muslim–Croat rapprochement. Ankara pragmatically embraced the objective of trying to extend the Muslim–Croat federation to include the Bosnian Serbs. Both the Turkish and the Bosnian governments appealed in early April to the Serbs to join a 'united, multi-cultural and multi-religious Bosnia'. Çetin even expressed some optimism in April that a dialogue with Belgrade could be kindled. In spite of a brief flurry of diplomatic traffic, between February and April the initiative, which was never more than tentative, foundered. In turn, Ankara was unwilling to normalise relations with Belgrade until there was a satisfactory outcome to the Bosnian crisis.

The role played by Turkey during this phase was a boon both for its reputation and for its position. It was also a vindication of a more pragmatic, problem-solving approach to Bosnia, rather than the passionate but impractical rhetoric of 1992 and early 1993. Consequently, Turkey's position in the Balkans was improved and a close relationship with Croatia, that would last until the death of President

[89] Interview with Turkish diplomat responsible for the Bosnia brief, London, 25 April 1994.

Tudjman in December 1999, was forged.[90] It also boosted Ankara's credibility on a wider plane. The two international mediators were the first to appreciate Turkey's new, more practical involvement. Thorvald Stoltenberg and Lord Owen were quoted as praising Turkey for 'playing a key role in seeking a rapprochement between Bosnia's warring Muslims and Croats'.[91]

TURKEY AS A CONSOLIDATOR OF PEACE, JUNE 1994–

With Turkish leverage over both the Serbs and the Bosnian Serbs once again having been exposed as somewhat limited, Ankara's role in consolidating the peace was almost exclusively oriented towards the Muslims and Croats, and, more broadly, towards the Bosnian and Croatian governments. At the diplomatic level, the top priority subsequent to the Washington Agreement was to consolidate the relationship between the two communities. Consequently, a further three tripartite meetings followed, aimed at cementing the relationship.

The first of these was held in Ankara on 2 July 1994, shortly before Çetin stepped down as foreign minister. All sides there agreed to study ways of repairing Bosnia's war torn economy. The following summit took place in Zenica in May 1995, with Professor Erdal İnönü, then fleetingly foreign minister, representing Turkey. The three sides met again in Ankara one year later, for a summit at which they urged greater international contributions for the reconstruction of Bosnia.

The practical usefulness of these engagements seemed to reinvigorate Turkey's foreign policymakers. Increasingly President Demirel became a key player in the three-way dynamics, astutely easing his way into the policy vacuum that was opening up domestically. Demirel's involvement deepened once Çetin had ceased to be foreign minister, when prime minister Çiller virtually ignored the issue of Bosnia after one brief but eye-catching visit to Sarajevo with her Pakistani counterpart Benazir Bhutto.[92] Indeed Richard

---

[90] President Demirel would be the only foreign head of state to attend Tudjman's funeral, the Croatian leader being shunned by an international community grown weary of his authoritarian style: a mark of the good personal chemistry that characterised the two men's relationship.

[91] *Guardian*, 16 September 1993.

[92] During the visit, which took place on 2 February 1994, 250,000 copies of the Koran and DM 30,000 were distributed. Margaret Thatcher had been invited to join the trip but had politely declined, pleading prior commitments.

Holbrooke, the US envoy who was so instrumental in ending the Bosnian war, was later to pay tribute to Demirel as 'the foreign leader whom Izetbegovic probably respected the most'.[93]

Subsequently, during the first visit by a Turkish president to Zagreb in July 1994, Demirel signed a formal friendship pact with Croatia, the conclusion of which had earlier been resisted by Ankara when the two communities were at war. Turkey further sought to make a symbolic contribution through the stabilisation and confidence-building process, most notably through the rebuilding of the old bridge between the two communities at Mostar.

However, the most significant and practical way in which Turkey was to contribute to the maintenance of peace in Bosnia was through the sending of a major troop contingent to the area. Until February 1994 the UN position had been that all regional states with 'a past' should not send peace-keepers to the area. Turkey had, with some misgivings, accepted its exclusion from Unprofor on the basis of this principle. But in February Russia was allowed to send some 400 soldiers to the Bosnian capital as part of a compromise in the wake of the infamous mortar attack on a Sarajevo market square, whereby the Bosnian Serbs would agree to withdraw their heavy weapons from the high ground around the city. Turkey was outraged. It felt that Russia's position in Bosnia was analogous to its own. Ankara was therefore livid at what it perceived as the 'double standards' of the Security Council in accepting such an arrangement as part of a deal.[94] This slight was compounded by the omission of Turkey from a defence ministers, meeting at Aviano in Italy, which consisted of all the other countries with warplanes at the ready. The resentment of the Turkish side could be gauged from the bitter remarks that found their way into the public domain, such as those by the defence minister, Mehmet Gölhan, who stated that the European states were acting 'as if Turkish troops there [Bosnia] would amount to a repetition of the Ottoman occupation of Europe'.[95]

With Turkey engaged diplomatically and through reconstruction efforts on the ground, it was perhaps only a matter of time before Ankara's insistence that Turkish troops should be deployed succeeded.

---

[93] Richard Holbrooke, *To End a War* (Random House, New York, 1998), p. 294.
[94] *Turkish Daily News*, 22 February 1994.
[95] *Turkish Daily News*, 24 February 1994.

In the aftermath of widespread anger at the Bosnian Serb move against the safe area of Gorazde the time became opportune. Ankara's argument that the Bosnian Muslims needed further reassurance, the mirror image of the Russian argument back in February, became more persuasive. The bridgehead of the Washington Agreement created momentum for the further dissipation of tensions between Croats and Muslims in Bosnia. The principal Western states were also no doubt concerned to give Turkey an enhanced role following an affray involving Islamists and ultra-nationalists in a handful of Turkish cities in the immediate aftermath of the attack on Gorazde, in which the US embassy was attacked and UN premises were stoned.[96] With a handful of arguments in their favour, the UN Security Council agreed on 22 March 1994 that Turkey should dispatch 1,467 troops to take up positions between the two recently reconciled communities[97] around Zenica in central Bosnia.[98]

More than seven years later the Turkish troops at Zenica are still there, having metamorphised from an Unprofor contingent into part of an IFOR force in late 1995. If there were any lingering doubts as to the wisdom of the decision they were quickly dispelled, not least by some canny Turkish public relations. By the end of 1995 it was reported that Turkish troops in the area had delivered 30,000 food parcels and helped with the reconstruction of fifteen schools.[99] The troop contingent also participated in the provision of a wide range of health care, including even some surgical operations, for the people of the town. Subsequently, Turkey contributed a police contingent to Bosnia of about fifty, which was then strengthened by another thirty in spring 1996, based at Velika Kladusa. During this

---

[96] *Turkish Daily News,* 12 April 1994.

[97] The Croats initially preferred to have Swedish troops hold the line in this area. It was felt that in the event of a renewed confrontation Turkish troops would side against the Croats, and hence that agreeing to Turkish troops was 'another Croat concession'. In mitigation Turkey's membership of NATO was regarded as a restraining influence, while early Turkish confidence building measures, such as support for Croatia's participation in the Partnership for Peace initiative with NATO, were highly appreciated in Zagreb. Interview with Drago Stambuk, Croatian embassy, London, 25 April 1994.

[98] For details of the deployment of the 'self-sustained mechanized infantry Battalion task force', see 'Briefing Note about the Turkish Contingent Force to UNPROFOR', Turkish Ministry of Foreign Affairs, June 1994.

[99] *Turkish Daily News,* 29 January 1996.

lengthy span of time there is general agreement that the Turkish troop presence has been a success. The Welfare Party, apparently ever vigilant for ways of exploiting the Bosnian issue, organised a gift of 10 buses from the Istanbul municipality, which it controls, to its counterpart in Zenica in October 1995.

Turkey has also sought to play its part in the consolidation of peace more generally. Here, special emphasis has been placed on ensuring that the Dayton agreement, which formally brought an end to the fighting between all three sides,[100] does not collapse.[101] Ankara has interpreted its mission here in terms of helping to bolster the Bosnian state. This has primarily been achieved through the provision of training, in particular for members of the Bosnian army. Close ties between the Turkish and Bosnian military extend back to September 1994, when the commander of the Bosnian army, General Rasim Delic, paid his first official visit to Turkey.[102] Turkey and Bosnia concluded a military accord in August 1995, shortly before the military denouement in Bosnia, which provided for cooperation in a range of different areas, including training and defence industries.

Turkey's contribution to military training for Bosnian troops has taken place at a number of levels. Turkey hosted an international pledging conference on equipping and training the Bosnian military in March 1996. It was then quick to extend training assistance to the Bosnian state, too quick for some American sensibilities, the State Department spokesman Nicholas Burns gently chiding the Turks for not waiting until all foreign fighters had left Bosnia. However, Turkey's main training contribution was included in a larger effort co-ordinated by the US, and overseen by James Pardew, in his capacity as the State Department special co-ordinator. Turkey made a commitment of $2 mn for the training of federation troops at the Ankara pledging conference. Turkey in turn hosted Bosnian troops

---

[100] The Dayton peace process only became possible once the US had intervened militarily against the Bosnian Serbs. Thus, as Şule Kut has wryly observed, 'Though Turkish actions did not end the war, the fighting ended only when measures proposed much earlier by Turkey were actually taken up by the international community and, in particular, by NATO under US leadership.' See Şule Kut, 'Turkish Policy', op. cit., p. 83.

[101] Interview with General Nazihi Cakar, adviser to President Demirel, Ankara, 6 June 1997.

[102] BBC/SWB/EE, 3 September 1994.

for training in use of artillery and American M-60 tanks near Ankara, a facility that was subsequently extended to Croat troops.

In spite of the long term commitment to peace-keeping and the provision of military and technical training, official Turkish interest in Bosnia-Herzegovina quickly waned once the Dayton Agreement had been made to stick and the fighting had come to an end. This rapid devaluation of Bosnia as a foreign policy priority marked the passing of a period of exceptional circumstances. It also reflected the Turkish establishment's outlook and the relative lack of public interest at home. This rapid disengagement with Bosnia is illustrated both by aid and diplomatic matters. Aid commitments to the tune of some $80 mn made in 1996 were largely undisbursed by the end of the decade. When İsmail Cem visited Bosnia in March 1998 he was the first Turkish foreign minister to make the trip for three years. Perhaps there could be no greater example of the dwindling in bilateral relations than Bosnia-Herzegovina's decision in November 1999 to establish diplomatic relations with the Clerides government as the sole political authority on the island of Cyprus.

The Bosnian conflict clearly did not leave the world untouched. But neither did the war in Bosnia-Herzegovina draw the regional powers into a wider conflict. The same was true with regard to Turkey. Turks were appalled at the scale and nature of the killing in Bosnia, even, in some cases, to the point of perceiving dark conspiracies to be at work behind it. Turkey certainly had good reasons for wanting an end to conflict in Bosnia, based on *raison d'état* as much as humanitarian sentiment. The impact of the Bosnian crisis on Turkish public opinion and hence on policy has, however, been consistently over estimated. As with much of the rest of Europe, Turkey was able to live with the consequences of the fighting on the ground. At no time during the conflict did any of the basic tenets of Turkish foreign policy—from its Western orientation to its commitment to multilateralism and its distrust of foreign adventures—come anywhere close to being overturned.

More broadly, the events of the 1990s in the former Yugoslavia have shown that Turkey is a Balkan power. Ankara considers that it has interests in the Balkans; Balkan states, and entities that aspire to statehood, consider Turkey to be an important potential ally or an obstacle to their ambitions. While the events in Bosnia were important for Turkey, the real centre of gravity for Turkish interests in the region is to be found further to the south and east. It is Albania and Macedonia that Turkey has identified as being the most strategically important states in the region. It is with Romania and Bulgaria that bilateral relations have most rapidly improved since the end of the Cold War. It is Greece that was regarded as the old, unreconstructed rival, at least up to the earthquake diplomacy of late summer 1999; it was Serbia that came to be viewed as the new threat to order. Only if the conflict in former Yugoslavia had not been contained in Croatia and Bosnia, and had spread down through the Balkans, would Turkey have found itself much more directly affected.

CONCLUSION

This book has been written more than fifteen years since the beginning of the end of the Cold War. During that time Turkey has faced profound change on all its borders and within the international system of which it is very much a part. Regional change has included such cataclysmic events as state collapse, civil war, invasion and superpower intervention. Within the international system gone is the bipolarity of East-West antagonism, but gone too are the easy assumptions about the old way that, in a Western context at least, peoples conceived of themselves and the basis on which states acted. Turkey, of course, has not been immune to such changes. It has had to face the consequences of some of these developments, from Kurdish ethno-nationalist self-assertion through refugee inflows to costly disruptions in its foreign economic relations. But what is perhaps most remarkable about Turkey's experiences of the last decade and a half is how relatively unaffected that it has been by the instabilities and transformations that have occurred all around, and how strong has been the theme of continuity in its straddling of the worlds of the pre- and post-Cold War eras.

It should not be a surprise to discover that Turkey's success in avoiding the entanglement of its regions is due to a combination of factors. At a systemic level the emergence of the United States as the sole remaining superpower has had a marked impact on Ankara, where the respect for hard power is largely undiminished. This impact has been most pronounced within a multilateral context, where Ankara has tended to understand the compromises that had to be made in order to retain and reinvigorate the major institutions of the Western world. Thus Turkey, at the instigation of Washington, has chosen not to use its notional veto to block NATO enlargement and has chosen also to agree to the amendment of the CFE treaty, which allows Russia to station higher levels of conventional weapons near its borders.

Systemic factors have also been important in helping to shape and circumscribe Turkish actions in a variety of regional crises once they began to emerge. Mandatory UN Security Council resolutions were decisive in helping Turkey to define Iraq's invasion of Kuwait in 1990 as an international as opposed to a regional crisis. Ankara's actions were consequently channelled in a direction of international solidarity, rather than being governed by the default option of disinterest, which had come to govern its approach to intra-Middle Eastern disputes. The Bosnian crisis showed the depth of the Turkish commitment to a Western-oriented multilateralism, even in a conflict of a protracted nature, marked by great bloodshed, a commitment that was subsequently reconfirmed in the Kosovo crisis. In the Karabakh conflict too, Turkey has eschewed unilateralism, and has focused its efforts on existing international machinery, such as the Minsk process.

However, systemic factors have clearly not been the only ones of significance in shaping Turkish foreign policy during this time. Indeed, at a time of systemic uncertainty and change there have arguably been added opportunities for other factors to make their mark. Key among these have been domestic factors. In the Turkish case two elements have been especially important in this respect. First, the deep-seated domestic impulses that have provided the broader material and ideational interests and attitudes that have resulted in the development of national perceptions, approaches and strategies. Second, the individuals, institutions and processes that have been important in channelling such impulses into the generation and elaboration of policy.

In the case of the domestic impulses, emphasis in this book has been placed on historical, ideological and domestic security factors in creating the broader impetus for Turkish foreign policy. Of course, these are in many ways interlocking and reinforcing elements. Turkey's historical experiences, especially during the later Ottoman and post-First World War periods, help explain the psychology of insecurity that has often seemed to place the country beyond reassurance during the post-Cold War period. The premium placed in the young state's Kemalist ideology on an illiberal notion of secularism and an over-arching subjective Turkish identity has helped to provide a context in which alternative ideas about religion and ethno-nationalism are conceived of in narrow security-oriented terms. It is the enduring aspect of these factors and their relatively fixed nature that begins to explain the continuities in the Turkish establishment's world view.

If such factors provide a backdrop and indeed a rationality for Turkish foreign policy, it is usually the main actors and the processes characterising their interaction that result in the development and implementation of policy. Here again it is possible to identify a key component in the continuity of Turkish foreign policy by focusing on those institutions that invariably play a primary role in its creation. The Turkish military has long claimed to be the guardian of the strategic contours of Turkish foreign and security policy, as was perhaps most evident during the Islamist-led coalition in 1996–7. Such relatively homogeneous institutions as the Turkish Foreign Ministry are important in giving ballast to Turkish foreign policy and consistency in its implementation.

It would be misleading simply to reduce Turkish foreign policy to a function of the interests, outlook and priorities of the leading institutions of the state. Turgut Özal demonstrated that influential individuals can and do make a difference; it was after all his reorientation of the Turkish economy on the cusp of the 1970s and 80s that introduced foreign economic relations as an important component of foreign policy. It would also be wrong to claim that governments in Turkey have no impact on foreign policymaking, Erbakan's infamous trips to Iran and Libya and the establishment of the D-8 illustrating that this can happen even at times of great domestic ideological discordance.

The development, elaboration and implementation of foreign policy in Turkey work best when there is harmony between the government, the bureaucracy and the military, as the period of 1991–4 illustrates. Turkey was indeed fortunate to have such an experienced, effective and harmonious team in place when the post-Cold War turbulence was at its height in such places as Bosnia, Karabakh, Chechnya and northern Iraq. The years since then have confirmed that weak, incoherent, ineffectual, short-termist and chaotic government at home extracts a cost in terms of Turkey's international profile and impact, regardless of the standing of the Foreign Ministry and the military. It is under those sorts of circumstances that the military ends up playing more of a day to day role in foreign affairs, as the Karadayı diplomacy of 1997–8 during the minority Yılmaz government best indicates. And it is under those conditions of persistent domestic disharmony and introspection that Turkey, a regional actor whose relative power has grown during the post-Cold War period, has ended up punching below its weight.

A wide-ranging retrospective over fifteen years of Turkish foreign policy evokes a complex and chequered picture. A picture in which domestic factors have been of great importance, especially in areas beyond the specific contexts of international crisis or issues that are internal to rule-based multilateral institutions. One in which domestic attitudes and perceptions, moulded in a past era of predecessor state collapse and republican state creation, are strong and slow in changing. One in which key and relatively homogeneous institutions like the Foreign Ministry and the senior military are central, but in which other actors, notably leaders and governments, can and do have a bearing, thereby questioning the stereotypical image of Turkey as a rational bureaucratic actor. One in which other elements, such as the media and the ethnic lobbies, have been of generally less importance; as in most countries, there is an inverse relationship between noise and influence.

If the development and management of Turkey's foreign policy have never been quite as smooth as its diplomats and generals would have liked, the nature of its output has more often than not been characterised by continuity and caution. The three key areas of Ankara's foreign policy are, for example, substantively the same as at the height of the Cold War, not to mention the beginning of its end. First, Turkey has been a member of NATO for nearly five decades; its commitment to the alliance is as strong today as at any time in the past, which helps to explain Ankara's misgivings over the development of an exclusively European security and defence policy. Second, Turkey has pursued virtually uninterrupted a goal of membership of the EU and its previous incarnations since the late 1950s; at the 1999 Helsinki summit Turkey acquired candidate status for the Union and therefore saw its European vocation become, as David Barchard has put it, an 'active possibility'.[1] Third, Turkey has

---

[1] David Barchard, *Building a Partnership, Turkey and the European Union* (Turkish Economic and Science Foundation, Istanbul, 2000), p. 9.

been structurally involved with the Cyprus issue since the 1960 Treaty of Guarantee, Ankara becoming an active, military and diplomatic participant with the invasion/intervention of 1974.

Of course, focusing on NATO, the EU and Cyprus is not to imply that the onset of a post-Cold War period has not made an impact on Turkish foreign policy. Turkey now finds itself located in the midst of a messier, more volatile world, where there has been a multiplication of state and non-state actors. There have been rhetorical flights of fancy.[2] A new foreign policy goal of the management and diffusion of regional tensions and conflicts has emerged in the 1990s to accompany such long standing objectives as European integration and the protection of the Turkish Cypriots. But in its approach to such contingencies traditional values have continued to assert themselves. Turkey has invariably acted as a status quo power, especially in its preference for state continuity and territorial integrity and its uneasiness with revisionist sub-state groups.

In the unstable regions to which it lies adjacent Turkey has pursued this new goal of the containment of regional tensions with caution and has sought to confine the nature of its engagement. Consequently, Turkey remained a supporter of the status quo in Yugoslavia and the Soviet Union, in contrast to many fellow Europeans, virtually

---

[2] A leading example of this has been the increasing tendency in the late 1990s to refer to Eurasia, and to place Turkey as 'a pivotal state' at its centre. So, for example, the then under secretary at the Foreign Ministry, Korkmaz Haktanır, spoke thus on 1 October 1998: 'By virtue of its historical and cultural attributes and its privileged double-identity, European as well as Asian, Turkey is firmly positioned to become the strategic "Centre" of "Eurasia", (speech printed as 'New Horizons in Turkish Foreign Policy' in *Dış Politika*, nos 3–4, 1998, p. 4). This particular example of comfort rhetoric took hold in the aftermath of the Luxembourg summit of December 1997, when the Kemalist elite looked around for a device through which to maintain collective self-esteem at a time of a perceived rebuff from the main locus of their cultural-cum-political aspirations. While admittedly a good and apparently effective sound-bite, the glibness of the term 'Eurasia' is exposed by its dubious geography and poorly elaborated definition. An honest riposte came from the *Wall Street Journal* correspondent based in Istanbul, Hugh Pope, who, when asked to give a journalist's perspective at a conference on 'Building a Secure Eurasia for the 21st Century', began: 'Well, at my newspaper I should first say we don't use the word Eurasia because I don't think we know what it means.' ('The New Great Game: a Journalist's Perspective', *Insight Turkey*, vol. 2, no. 3, July–September 2000, p. 81).

until the onset of collapse. Ankara then fell back on the defence of the territorial integrity of successor states, whether those with which it might have been expected to be sympathetic, notably Azerbaijan and Bosnia, or those where it might have been thought tempted to dabble, like the Russian Federation and Serbia. While Turkey's contributions to the containment and ending of such conflicts might appear peripheral to the international relations generalist, a negative, uncooperative, irredentist or revisionist Turkey could have multiplied international complications in Bosnia or Karabakh, with the risk of turning them into different and certainly more complex conflicts. It is then not difficult to understand the geopolitical premium that American officials and security commentators placed upon Turkey in the 1990s.

Some Turkey analysts have suggested that the region of the Middle East has proved to be an exception to this general approach of caution and the strategy of limited regional engagement. This is, at the very least, a moot point. Consider then the evidence. During the Gulf crisis, Turkey's involvement stopped short of the deployment of troops to the 30-country-strong multinational force, and it chose not to become a combatant; after February 1991 Ankara avoided the temptation to exploit the disarray in Iraq to take the northern-most vilayet of Mosul, which it had claimed prior to 1926. Ankara was slow to create a *de facto* security zone in northern Iraq, only doing so for defensive purposes in the absence of the writ of the Iraqi state, the return of which it has consistently advocated.

In the arena of Arab-Israeli peace-making, Turkey has warily kept its distance, its interest only momentarily flickering when it appeared as though there might be lucrative contracts for the building of infrastructure for a Palestinian state. The emergence of the Israeli-Turkish military relationship in 1996 owed more to domestic ideological politics in Turkey than to a new regional strategy; indeed, Turkey does not have 'a Middle Eastern strategy', only policies towards its immediate neighbours and towards that other European orphan, Israel.[3] Only in 1998 with the threat to use force against Syria over the presence in Damascus of the PKK leader Abdullah Öcalan did

---

[3] The former under-secretary of the Turkish Ministry of Foreign Affairs, Özdem Sanberk, states that Turkey's aim has been to establish 'unilateral, pragmatic relations with each Middle Eastern country'.

Turkey appear prepared to abandon its cautious and limited approach to foreign policy. The fact that it never contemplated such recourse against Iran, towards which it has expressed similar complaints about the sponsorship of hostile groups, makes Syria very much the bold exception that proves the cautious rule.

This combination of the re-emphasis on a Western and specifically European vocation with the limited and guarded engagement of Turkey in adjacent regional problems also serves to rebut speculation that the end of the Cold War might lead Turkey to reorient its geopolitical focus. Such ideas first arose in respect of the emergence of a newly independent band of states in the former Soviet south. Excitement at the creation of a community of states based on 'Turkic' solidarity did not survive the crushing disappointment of the Ankara summit of October 1992. Little is heard today about the Turkic world, while non-Turkic states like Georgia have become more of a priority for Turkey than the faraway fringes of Central Asia. Similarly, in spite of Ankara's fleeting advocacy for the new state of Bosnia-Herzegovina during the war of the break-up of Yugoslavia, Sarajevo has long since ceased to be a focus of Turkey's external relations. Moreover, creative thinking in the direction of new multilateral institution building, of which the creation of Black Sea Economic Co-operation is perhaps the best example, has not been followed up with either political will or economic resources. It is the multi-member institutions, located in the centre of gravity that is the heartland of Europe, that have eclipsed such visions for Turkey as for other members.

Caution, continuity and support for the status quo all conjure up a positive image of Turkey as an actor in the post-Cold War period. It is Turkey's misfortune that the substance of these strengths has been partly modified by a style of foreign policy conduct, whether over the EU, Cyprus, Greece or 'terrorism',[4] that is best encapsulated

---

[4] The term 'terrorism' is placed in inverted commas for two reasons: first, the well documented difficulty of arriving at a commonly accepted definition of what constitutes terrorism and hence which groups and states may best be described as terroristic; second, because of the widely shared view that much of the political violence that Turkey has witnessed, especially in the east and south-east of the country since the late 1980s, has been either directly or indirectly of its own making, through its repressive responses to the upsurge in PKK violence and through its establishment and funding of the Village Guard system.

by the euphemistic term 'démarche diplomacy'.[5] Yet there is a further problem for Turkey that is ironically a by-product of this very conception of being a status quo power. While it has been argued that Turkey's nature as a status quo actor has much utility, this has been a rigid commitment to an overarching notion of the status quo, which has often bordered on the dogmatic refusal to countenance change. Turkey has not only been committed to the status quo of states, territories and regions but has also been wedded to the normative status quo of values, power and conduct. In this way Turkey has found itself increasingly out of step with a world that, in its post-Cold War variant, is changing quickly and where much of this change has been embraced as being qualitatively good.

As the new norms in foreign and domestic political conduct have accelerated during the 1990s Turkey has increasingly slipped behind in relative terms. So much so that since the end of the Cold War Turkey has taken on the appearance of being a normative anachronism. This shows particularly clearly in its ideological rigidities developed in the 1920s, its deification of a leader who died in 1938, its violent conduct towards large segments of its own population, and its contemptuous attitude towards NGOs. Turkey's nature has often appeared increasingly out of step with the new values of a new age, as its reluctant attempts to address the Copenhagen Criteria for membership of the EU help to illustrate.[6]

There is nothing immutable about Turkey's current position. Change will of course not be easy, given the embedded nature of its values and perceptions both among the elite and in wider society. However, the onset of crisis always offers the possibility of real and accelerated change, and Turkey's financial crisis of February 2001 is no exception. As ever, though, the overriding question will be: if real change does take place in Turkey, in what direction will the crisis precipitate that change? Will Turkey become a more liberal country,

---

[5] For example, the long-time Turkish ambassador in Washington in the mid 1990s, Nuzhet Kandemir, was unaffectionately and irreverently nicknamed Nuzhet Candemarche, in recognition of his tendency to lodge a continuous stream of complaints in a crusty fashion.

[6] See for example Turkey's disappointing *National Programme for the Adoption of the Acquis* (unofficial translation dated 19 March 2001), published in response to the EU's Accession Partnership of November 2000. *Turkish Probe* headlined its evaluation of the plan as: 'National Program: no surprise, but surely disappointing'.

achieving a synthetic blend of foreign policy caution and normative change? Or will it alternatively turn in on itself, with larger helpings of surly uncooperativeness displacing caution, and normative change dismissed as the latest device of those outsiders who would seek to weaken Turkey's cohesion, as a subtle step towards its eventual division? The impression remains that Turkey will follow its own timeframe, regardless of the pace of change outside its borders.

SELECT BIBLIOGRAPHY

Abramowitz, Morton, 'Dateline Ankara: Turkey After Ozal', *Foreign Policy*, vol. 91, no. 3, pp. 164–81.
———, (ed.), *Turkey's Transformation and American Policy*, Century Foundation, New York, 2000.
Agha, H.J., and A.S. Khalidi, 'The Struggle for Iraq: Saddam and After', unpublished report, St Antony's College, Oxford, 1997.
Ahmad, Feroz, *The Making of Modern Turkey*, Routledge, London, 1993.
Akder, Halis, 'Turkey's Export Expansion in the Middle East, 1980–1985', *Middle East Journal* 41, 1987, pp. 553–67.
Amnesty International, *Continuing Violations of Human Rights in Turkey*, London, 1987.
———, *Turkey, Brutal and Systematic Abuse of Human Rights*, London, 1989.
Arat, Yeşim, *Political Islam in Turkey and Women's Organisations*, TESEV/Friedrich Ebert Stiftung, Istanbul, 1999.
Aricanli, Tosun, and D. Rodrik, *The Political Economy of Turkey: Debt, Adjustment and Sustainability*, Macmillan, Basingstoke, 1990, pp. 9–36.
Athanassopoulou, Ekavi, 'Turkey and the Black Sea Initiative', *Mediterranean Politics*, 1, 1994, pp. 130–7.
———, 'Turkey and the Balkans: the View from Athens', *International Spectator*, vol. 29, no. IV, 1994, pp. 55–64.
———, *Turkey, Anglo-American Security Interests, 1945–1952*, Frank Cass, London, 1999.
Aydın, Mustafa, 'Turkey and Central Asia: Challenges of Change', *Central Asian Survey*, vol. 15, no. II, 1996, pp. 157–77.
———, (ed.), *Turkey at the Threshold of the 21st Century*, International Relations Foundation, Ankara, 1998.
———, *New Geopolitics of Central Asia and the Caucasus*, Ankara, Centre for Strategic Research (SAM Papers no. 2/2000), 2000.
Aykan, Mahmut Bali, 'Ideology and National Interest in Turkish Foreign Policy Toward the Muslim World, 1960–87', unpublished doctoral thesis, University of Virginia, 1987.
———, 'The Palestinian Question in Turkish Foreign Policy from the 1950s to the 1990s', *International Journal of Middle Eastern Studies*, vol. 25, no. 1, 1993, pp. 91–110.
———, 'Turkey's Policy in Northern Iraq, 1991–95', *Middle Eastern Studies*, vol. 32, no. 4, October 1996, pp. 343–66.

Baehr, Peter R., and Leon Gordenker, *The United Nations and the End of the 1990s*, Macmillan, London, 1999.

Bağiş, Ali İhsan, 'The Beginning and Development of Economic Relations between Turkey and Middle Eastern Countries', *Diş Politika*, vol. XII, nos 1–2, June 1985, pp. 85–96.

————, *Southeastern Anatolia Project: The Cradle of Civilisation Regenerated*, Gelisim Yayinlari/Interbank, Istanbul, 1989.

Bahcheli, Tosun, 'Turkey, the Gulf Crisis, and the New World Order' in Tareq Y. Ismael and Jacqueline S. Ismael (eds), *The Gulf War and the New World Order: International Relations of the Middle East*, University Press of Florida, Gainesville, 1994, pp. 435–47.

Bal, Idris, and Cengiz Basak Bal, 'Rise and Fall of Elchibey and Turkey's Central Asia Policy', *Diş Politika*, vol. XXII, nos 3–4, 1998, pp. 42–56.

Balkır, Canan, and Allan M. Williams, (eds), *Turkey and Europe*, Pinter, London, 1993.

Balim-Harding, Cigdem, and Ersin Kalaycioğlu, *Turkey: Political, Social and Economic Challenges in the 1990s*, E.J. Brill, Leiden, 1995 (Social, Economic and Political Studies of the Middle East, LIII).

Banuazizi, Ali, and Myron Weiner, *The New Geopolitics of Central Asia and its Borderlands*, Indiana University Press, Bloomington, 1994.

Barchard, David, *Building a Partnership: Turkey and the European Union*. TESEV, Istanbul, 2000.

————, *A European Turkey?* Centre for European Policy Reform, London 1998.

————, *Turkey and the West*, Routledge & Kegan Paul/RIIA, London (Chatham House Papers, 27), 1985.

Barkey, Henri J., 'Turkey's Kurdish Dilemma', *Survival*, vol. 5, no. 4, 1993–4, pp. 51–70.

————, 'Turkey, Islamic Politics, and the Kurdish Question', *World Policy Journal*, vol. 13, no. 1, 1996, pp. 43–52.

———— (ed.), *Reluctant Neighbour: Turkey's Role in the Middle East*, United States Institute of Peace Press, Washington, DC, 1996.

Beschorner, Natasha, *Water and Instability in the Middle East*, International Institute of Strategic Studies, London (Adelphi Paper 273), 1992.

Bhatty, Robin Land Rachel Bronson, 'NATO's Mixed Signals in the Caucasus and Central Asia', *Survival*, vol. 42, no. 3, autumn 2000, pp. 129–45.

Bishku, Michael B., 'Turkey and its Middle Eastern Neighbors since 1945', *Journal of South Asian and Middle Eastern Studies*, vol. 15, no. 3, 1992, pp. 51–71.

Blank, Stephen J., Stephen C. Pelletiere and T.W. Johnsen, *Turkey's Strategic Position at the Crossroads of World Affairs*, Strategic Studies Institute, US Army War College, Carlisle, 1993.

Bölükbası, Süha, 'Turkey Challenges Iraq and Syria: the Euphrates Dispute', *Journal of South Asian and Middle Eastern Studies*, vol. 16, no. iv, 1993, pp. 9–32.

Borovali, A. Fuat, 'The Bosnian Crisis and Turkish Foreign Policy', *Diş Politika* vol. XVII, no. 3–4, 1993, pp. 74–87.

————, 'The Caucasus Within a Historical-Strategic Matrix: Russia, Iran and Turkey', *Diş Politika*, vol. XVIII, unnumbered, 1994, pp. 23–48.

Boulden, Jane, *Peace Enforcement: The United Nations Experience in Congo, Somalia and Bosnia*. Praeger, Westport, CT, 2001, forthcoming.

Boutros-Ghali, Boutros, *Unvanquished: a US-UN Saga*, I.B. Tauris, London, 1999.

Brewin, Christopher, 'Turkey and the European Union', *Cambridge Review of International Affairs*, vol. 10, no. 1, 1996, pp. 30–50.

Brown, L. Carl (ed.), *Imperial Legacy: The Ottoman Imprint on the Balkans and Middle East*, Columbia University Press, New York, 1996.

Buğra, Ayşe, *Islam in Economic Organisations*, TESEV/Friedrich Ebert Stiftung, Istanbul, 1999.

Buszynski, Leszek, *Russian Foreign Policy after the Cold War*, Praeger, Westport, CT, 1996.

Buzan, Barry, and Thomas Diez, 'The European Union and Turkey', *Survival*, spring 1999, pp. 41–57.

Çakır, Ruşen, *Ne Seriat, Ne Demokrasi*, Siyahbeyaz, Istanbul, 1994.

Çarkoğlu, Ali, Mine Eder and Kemal Kirişci, *The Political Economy of Regional Cooperation in the Middle East*, Routledge, London, 1998.

Carley, Patricia M., 'Turkey and Central Asia: Reality comes calling' in A.Z. Rubinstein and O.M. Smolansky (eds), *Regional Power Rivalries in the New Eurasia: Russia, Turkey, and Iran*, M.E. Sharpe, Armonk NY, 1995, pp. 169–97.

Celik, Tasemin, *Contemporary Turkish Foreign Policy*, Praeger, Westport, 1999.

Cengizer, Altay, 'Turkey and the European Community at the Threshold of Customs Union', *Diş Politika*, vol. XVII, no. 3–4, 1993, pp. 65–73.

Center for Strategic Research (various authors), *Seminar on Russia and the NIS*, Proceedings (SAM Papers 1/96), Ankara, 1996.

Chislett, W., *Turkey: A Market for the 21st Century*, Euromoney Publications, London, 1999.

Clogg, Richard, *A Concise History of Greece*, Cambridge University Press, 1992.

Cornish, Paul, 'European Security: the End of Architecture and the New NATO', *International Affairs*, vol. 72, no. 4, October 1996, pp. 751–69.

Coufoudakis, V., 'Turkey and the United States: the Problems and Prospects of a Post-War Alliance', *Journal of Political and Military Sociology*, 9, 1981, pp. 179–96.

Couterier, Kelly, *US-Turkish Relations in the Post-Cold War Era*, Friedrich Ebert Stiftung, Istanbul, 1997.

Daalder, Ivo H., *Getting to Dayton. The Making of America's Bosnia Policy*, Brookings, Washington DC, 2000.

Dağı, İhsan D., 'Turkey in the 1990s: Foreign Policy, Human Rights, and the Search for a New Identity', *Mediterranean Quarterly* vol. 4, no. iv, 1993, pp. 60–77.

Dannreuther, Roland, 'Russia, Central Asia and the Persian Gulf', *Survival*, vol. 35, no. 4, winter 1993, pp. 92–112.

Dean, Jonathan and Randall Watson Forsberg, 'CFE and Beyond: The Future of Conventional Arms Control', *International Security*, vol. 17, no. 1, summer 1992, pp. 76–121.

Demirel, Süleyman, 'Turkish Foreign Policy at the Threshold of the 21st Century', *Dis Politika*, vol. XVIII, unnumbered, 1994, pp. 1–21.

Denktaş, Rauf, 'The Crux of the Cyprus Problem', *Perceptions*, vol. VI, no. 3, Sept.–Nov. 1999.

Deringil, Selim, *Turkish Foreign Policy during the Second World War*, Cambridge University Press, 1989.

Dilligil, Turhan (ed.), *Erbakancilik ve Erbakan*, Arkadas-Adas?, Ankara, 1996?

Dodd, C.H. (ed.), *Turkish Foreign Policy: New Prospects*, Eothen Press, Huntingdon, 1992.

——, 'Confederation, Federation and Sovereignty', *Perceptions*, vol. IV, no. 3, Sept.–Nov. 1999, pp. 23–38.

Dunlop, John B., *Russia Confronts Chechnya: Roots of a Separatist Conflict*, Cambridge University Press, 1998.

Eaton, Robert S., *Soviet Relations with Greece and Turkey*, Hellenic Foundation for Defence and Foreign Policy (Occasional Papers 2), Athens, 1987.

Economist Intelligence Unit, *Turkey on Trial: Political Uncertainty in Turkey and its Implications for Business and International Relations*, London, 1990.

Eren, Nuri, *Turkey, NATO and Europe: a Deteriorating Relationship?*, Atlantic Institute for International Affairs, Paris, 1977.

——, 'Turkey—the Middle East: New Risks—New Opportunities', *Diş Politika*, vol. X, no. 1–2, 1983, pp. 135–53.

Eralp, Atila, 'Turkey's Role in Political Dialogue in the Mediterranean Region', *Perceptions*, vol. 2, no. 1 1997, pp. 99–103.

——, Muharrem Tunay and Yesolada Birol (eds), *The political and Socioeconomic Transformation of Turkey*, Praeger, Westport, CT, 1993, pp. 193–213.

Evin, Ahmet O., 'Turkey-EU Relations on the Eve of the IGC: The Social and Cultural Dimension', *Diş Politika*, vol. XX, no. 1–2, 1996, pp. 35–54.

Eyal, Jonathan, 'NATO's Enlargement: Anatomy of a Decision', *International Affairs*, vol. 73, no. 4, October 1997, pp. 695–719.

Falkenrath, Richard A., 'The CFE Flank Dispute, Waiting in the Wings', *International Security*, vol. 19, no. 4, spring 1995, pp. 118–44.

Fromkin, David, *A Peace to End all Peace*, Avon Books, New York, 1989.

Fuller, Graham E., 'Turkey and the Middle East Northern Tier' in Laura Guazzone (ed.), *The Middle East in Global Change: the Politics and Economics of Interdependence versus Fragmentation*, Macmillan, Basingstoke, 1997, pp. 43–57.

——, and Ian O. Lesser, *Turkey's New Geopolitics: From the Balkans to Western China*, Westview Press/RAND, Boulder, CO, 1993.

Gall, Carlotta, and Thomas de Waal, *Chechnya: Calamity in the Caucasus* New York University Press, 1998.

Gallagher, Tom, '"This Farrago of Anomalies": The European Response to the War in Bosnia–Herzegovina, 1992–95', *Mediterranean Politics*, vol. 1, no. 1, summer 1996, pp. 76–94.

GAP Regional Development Administration, *Agricultural Commodities Marketing Survey: Planning of Crop Pattern and Integration and Crop Patterns*, Ankara, 1992.

——, *GAP Action Plan 1995*, Ankara, 1995.

——, *Latest State in* [sic] *Southeastern Anatolia Project*, Ankara, 1999.

Gozen, Ramazan, 'The Turkish-Iraqi Relations: From Cooperation to Uncertainty', *Dis Politika*, vol. XIX, nos 3–4, 1995, pp. 49–99.

Graham-Brown, Sarah, *Sanctioning Saddam: The Politics of Intervention in Iraq*, I.B. Tauris, London, 1999.

Gresh, Alain, 'Turkish-Israeli-Syrian Relations and their Impact on the Middle East', *Middle East Journal*, vol. 52, summer 1998, pp. 188–203.

Gruen, George E., 'Dynamic Progress in Turkish-Israeli Relations', *Israel Affairs*, vol. 1, no. 4, summer 1995, pp. 40–70.

Gunter, Michael M., 'Turkey and the Kurds: New Developments in 1991', *Journal of South Asian and Middle Eastern Studies*, vol. 15, no. 2, 1991, pp. 32–45.

————, *The Kurdish Predicament in Iraq: a Political Analysis*, Macmillan, London, 1999.

Gürel, Şükrü, Samil Unsal, and Yoshihiro Kimura, *Turkey in a Changing World— with Special Reference to Central Asia and the Caucasus*, Institute of Developing Economies, Tokyo, 1993.

Gureş, General Doğan, 'Turkey's Defence Policy: the Role of the Armed Forces and Strategy, Concepts and Capabilities', *Royal United Services Institution Journal*, vol. 138, no. 3, 1993, pp. 1–6.

Gurun, Kamuran, *The Armenian File: The Myth of Innocence Exposed*, Rustem & Bro. and Weidenfeld & Nicolson, Nicosia, London, 1985.

Guvenen, Orhan, 'A Frame Approach to Economic Development and Peace in the Middle East Through Cooperation on Natural Resources, Trade and Joint Ventures', *Dis Politika*, vol. XVIII, no. 1994, pp. 120–33.

Hale, William, *Turkish Foreign Policy, 1774–2000*, Frank Cass, London, 2000.

————, 'Turkey, the Middle East and the Gulf Crisis', *International Affairs*, vol. 68, no. 4, October 1992, pp. 679–92.

Haktanır, Korkmaz, 'New Horizons in Turkish Foreign Policy', *Diş Politika*, vol. XXII, nos. 3–4, 1998, pp. 1–9.

Harris, George S., *Troubled Alliance: Turkish-American Problems in Historical Perspective, 1945–1971*, American Enterprise Institute, Washington, DC, 1971.

————, *Turkey: Coping with Crisis*, Westview Press, Boulder CO, 1985.

Henze, Paul, *Turkey: Toward the Twenty-First Century*, RAND, Santa Monica, 1992.

Heper, Metin, *The State Tradition in Turkey*, Eothen Press, Beverley, England, 1985.

————, and Ahmet Evin, (eds), *Politics in the Third Republic*, Westview Press, Boulder, CO, 1994.

Heper, Metin, Ayse Oncu, and Heinz Kramer (eds), *Turkey and the West: Changing Political and Cultural Identities*, I.B. Tauris, London, 1993.

Holbrooke, Richard, *To End a War*, Random House, New York, 1998.

Human Rights Foundation of Turkey, *1996 Human Rights Report*, Ankara, 1998.

Human Rights Watch (under original name of Helsinki Watch), *Turkey: New Restrictive Anti-Terror Law*, New York, 1991.

Human Rights Watch, *Weapons Transfers and Violations of the Laws of War in Turkey*, New York, 1995.

————, *Violation of Free Expression in Turkey*, New York, 1999.

Hunter, Shireen T., *Turkey at the Crossroads: Islamic Past or European Future?*, Centre for European Policy Studies, Brussels, 1995 (CEPS Paper 63).

————, *Central Asia Since Independence*, Praeger, Westport, CT, 1996.

Hyman, Anthony, 'Moving out of Moscow's Orbit: the Outlook for Central Asia', *International Affairs*, vol. 69, no. 2, April 1993.

İmset, İsmet, *The PKK: A Report on Separatist Violence, 1973–1992*, Turkish Daily News Publications, Ankara, 1992.

Inalcik, Halil, 'Turkey and Europe: a Historical Perspective', *Perceptions*, vol. 2, no. 1, 1997, pp. 76–92.

Inbar, Efraim, 'The Turkish-Israeli Entente: The New Power Alignment in the Middle East', unpublished paper, 2000.

Jenkins, Gareth, *Context and Circumstance: The Military and Politics*, International Institute for Strategic Studies, London, (Adelphi Paper 337), 2001.

Kalaycıoğlu, Sema, 'Turkey's Economic Relations with Third Countries in the Aftermath of her Accession to the European Customs Union', *Turkish Review of Middle East Studies*, 9, 1996/7, pp. 81–96.

Karaosmanoğlu, Ali, and Seyfi Taşhan, *Middle East, Turkey and the Atlantic Alliance*, Foreign Policy Institute, Ankara, 1987.

Karaosmanoğlu, Ali, 'Turkey's Security and the Middle East', *Foreign Affairs*, vol. 62, no. 11, 1983, pp. 157–75.

———, 'Turkey's Security Policy in the Middle East', *Dış Politika*, vol. X, no. 1–2, 1983, pp. 3–17.

———, 'The South-East European Countries and the CSCE, CFE Negotiations', *Dış Politika*, vol. XVI, no. 3–4, 1992, pp. 13–28.

Kedourie, Sylvia, *Turkey: Identity, Democracy, Politics*, Frank Cass, London, 1996.

Kirişci, Kemal, 'The End of the Cold War and Changes in Turkish Foreign Policy Behaviour', *Dış Politika*, vol. XVII, no. 3–4, 1993, pp. 1–43.

———, 'Turkey and the Kurdish Safe-Haven in Northern Iraq', *Journal of South Asian and Middle Eastern Studies*, vol. 19, no. 3, 1996, pp. 21–39.

———, 'Turkey and the United States: Ambivalent Allies' in Barry Rubin and T. Keaney (eds), *US Allies in a Changing World*, Frank Cass, London, 2000.

——— and Gareth M. Winrow, *The Kurdish Question and Turkey: An Example of a Trans-State Ethnic Conflict*, Frank Cass, London, 1997.

Kolars, John R., and W.A. Mitchell, *The Euphrates River and the Southeast Anatolia Development Project*, Southern Illinois University Press, Carbondale, 1991.

Kramer, Heinz, 'The Cyprus Problem and European Security', *Survival*, vol. 39, no. 3, autumn 1997, pp. 16–32.

Kut, Gün, 'Burning Waters: The Hydropolitics of the Euphrates and Tigris', *New Perspectives on Turkey*, no. 9, fall 1993, pp. 1–18.

Kuniholm, Bruce, 'Turkey and the West', *Foreign Affairs*, vol. 70, no. 2, 1991, pp. 34–48.

Kyle, Keith, *Cyprus*, Minority Rights Group, London (Report #30), 1984.

Landau, Jacob, *Pan-Turkism in Turkey: From Irredentism to Cooperation*, Hurst, London, 1995.

Lesser, Ian O., *NATO Looks South*, RAND, Santa Monica, 2000.

———, and Ashley J. Tellis, *Strategic Exposure. Proliferation Around the Mediterranean*, RAND, Santa Monica, 1996.

Lewis, Bernard, *The Emergence of Modern Turkey*, Oxford University Press, 1961.

Liel, Alon, *Turkey in the Middle East, Oil, Islam, and Politics*, Lynne Rienner, Boulder, CO, 2001.

Lieven, Anatol, *Chechnya: Tombstone of Russian Power*, Yale University Press, New Haven, CT, 1998.

Lochery, Neill, 'Israel and Turkey: Deepening Ties and Strategic Implications, 1995–1998', *Israel Affairs*, vol. 5, no. 1, autumn 1998, pp. 45–62.

Loewendahl, Ebru, *'Promises to Keep': The Reality of Turkey-EU Relations*, Action Centre for Europe, Charley, Laucs, 1998.

Lynch, Dov, *Russian Peacekeeping Strategies in the CIS*, Macmillan/RIIA, London, 2000.

Malcolm, Noel, *Bosnia: A Short History*, Macmillan, London, 1994.

Makovsky, Alan, and Sabri Sayari (eds), *Turkey's New World: Changing Dynamics in Turkish Foreign Policy*, WINEP, Washington, DC, 2000.

Manisalı, Erol, *Turkey's Place in the Middle East*, Middle East Business & Banking Publications, Istanbul, 1989.

———, *Turkey and the Balkans: Economic and Political Dimensions*, Middle East Business and Banking Magazine Publications, Istanbul, 1990.

———, *Avrupa Cikmazi. Turkiye-Avrupa Birligi Iliskileri*, Otopsi, Istanbul, 2001.

Mango, Andrew, *Turkey: the Challenge of a New Role*, Praeger, Westport, CT, with the Center for Strategic and International Studies, Washington, DC, 1994.

Mastny, Vojtech, and R. Craig Nation (eds), *Turkey Between East and West: New Challenges for a Rising Regional Power*, Westview Press, Boulder, CO, 1996.

Mayall, Simon, *Turkey: Thwarted Ambition*, Institute for National Strategic Defence, Washington, DC (MacNair Paper 56), 1997.

McDowall, David, *A Modern History of the Kurds*, I.B. Tauris, London, 1996.

McGwire, Michael, 'NATO Expansion: a Policy Error of Historic Importance', *Review of International Studies*, vol. 24, no. 1, January 1998, pp. 23–42.

Mesbahi, Mohiaddin (ed.), *Central Asia and the Caucasus after the Soviet Union: Domestic and International Dynamics*, University of Florida Press, Gainesville, 1994.

Menon, Rajan, 'After Empire: Russia and the "Near Abroad"' in Michael Mandelbaum (ed.), *The New Russian Foreign Policy*, Council on Foreign Relations, New York, 1998.

Migdalovitz, Carol, *Cyprus: Status of UN Negotiations*, Congressional Research Service Issue Brief, Washington, DC, 1998.

Ministry of Foreign Affairs, *Southeastern Anatolia Project Investment Opportunities*, Ankara, 2000.

Mufti, Malik, 'Daring and Caution in Turkish Foreign Policy', *Middle East Journal*, vol. 52, winter 1998, pp. 32–50.

Müftüler-Bac, Meltem, *Turkey's relations with a Changing Europe*, Manchester University Press, 1997.

Naff, Thomas, and Ruth Matson, *Water in the Middle East: Conflict or Cooperation*, Westview Press, Boulder, CO, 1984.

Nugent, Neill, 'Cyprus and the European Union: A Particularly Difficult Membership Application', *Mediterrean Politics*, vol. 2, no. 3, winter 1997, pp. 53–76.

Nye, Joseph S., 'The US and Europe: Continental Drift?', *International Affairs*, vol. 76, no. 1, January 2000, pp. 51–9.

Oktem, Kerem, 'The Power of Dams: Great Infrastructure Projects and State Politics in the Middle East', unpublished dissertation, Oxford, 2001.

Olcay, H. Bulent, 'The Euphrates-Tigris Watercourse Controversy and the 1997 Convention on the Law of the Non-Navigational Uses of International Watercourses', *Diş Politika*, vol. XXII, no. 3–4, 1997, pp. 48–81.

Olson, Robert (ed.), *The Kurdish Nationalist Movement in the 1990s*, University Press of Kentucky, Lexington, 1996.

Oncu, Ayşe, Çağlar Keyder and Saad Eddin Ibrahim, (eds), *Developmentalism and beyond: Society and Politics in Egypt and Turkey*, American University in Cairo Press, 1994.

Öniş, Ziya, 'Turkey in the post-Cold war era: in Search of Identity', *Middle East Journal* vol. 49, no. i, 1995, pp. 48–68.

———— and James Riedel, *Economic Crises and Long-Term Growth in Turkey*, The World Bank, Washington, DC, 1993.

Onur Öymen, 'Turkey's European Foreign Policy', *Perceptions*, vol. 2 no. i, 1997, pp. 7–14.

Ostergaard-Nielsen, Eva, 'The Political Participation of Turkish Immigrants in Europe and in Denmark', *Les Annales de l'autre Islam: Turcs d'Europe…et d'ailleurs*, Institut des Langues et Civilisations Orientales, Paris, 1995.

Owen, David, *Balkan Odyssey*, Victor Gollancz, London, 1995.

Oxford Business Group, *Emerging Turkey 1999*, London, 1998.

Park, William, 'Turkey's European Union Candidacy: From Luxembourg to Helsinki—to Ankara?', *Mediterranean Politics*, vol. 5, no. 3, autumn 2000, pp. 31–53.

Peres, Shimon, *The New Middle East*, Element, Shafesbury, England, 1993.

Pettifer, James, *The Turkish Labyrinth: Ataturk and the New Islam*, Viking, London, 1997.

Pipes, Daniel, *The Hidden Hand*, St Martin's Griffin, New York, 1996.

Pope, Hugh and Nicole, *Turkey Unveiled: Atatürk and After*, John Murray, London, 1997.

Pope, Hugh, 'The New Great Game: A Journalist's Perspective', *Insight Turkey*, vol. 2, no. 3, July–Sept. 2000, pp. 81–4.

Poulton, Hugh, 'Turkey as Kin-State: Turkish Foreign Policy towards Turkish and Muslim Communities in the Balkans' in Hugh Poulton and Suha Taji-Farouki (eds), *Muslim identity and the Balkan state*, Hurst, London, 1997.

Poulton, Hugh, *Top Hat, Grey Wolf and Crescent: Turkish Nationalism and the Turkish Republic*, Hurst, London, 1997.

Rieff, David, *Slaughterhouse, Bosnia and the Failure of the West*, Simon & Schuster, New York, 1995.

Robins, Philip, *Turkey and the Middle East*, Pinter/RIIA, London, 1991.

————, 'Between Sentiment and Self-interest: Turkey's Policy towards Azerbaijan and the Central Asian States', *Middle East Journal*, vol. 47, no. 4, pp. 393–610.

————, *Partners for Growth: New Trends in EC-Turkish Cooperation*, Forum Europe, Brussels, 1993.

————, 'Turkish Foreign Policy Under Erbakan', *Survival*, summer 1997, pp. 82–100.

————, 'Turkey: Europe in the Middle East, or the Middle East in Europe?' in B.A. Roberson (ed.), *The Middle East and Europe: The Power Deficit*, Routledge, London, 1998.

Robinson, Richard, *The First Turkish Republic, A Case Study in National Development*, Harvard University Press, Cambridge, MA, 1963.

Rouleau, Eric, 'Turkey: beyond Atatürk', *Foreign Policy*, 103, 1996, pp. 70–87.

Rustow, Dankwart A., *Turkey, America's Forgotten Ally*, Council on Foreign Relations, New York, 1987.

Sander, Oral, 'Turkey and the Turkic World', *Central Asian Survey*, vol. 13, no. 1, 1994, pp. 37–44.

Sasley, Brent, 'Turkey's Energy Politics in the Post-Cold War Era', *Middle East Review of International Affairs*, vol. 2, no. 4, December 1998.

Sayarı, Sabri, 'Turkey: the Changing European Security Environment and the Gulf Crisis', *Middle East Journal*, 46, 1992, pp. 9–21.

———, 'Turkey's Islamist Challenge' in *Middle East Quarterly*, vol. 3, no. III, 1996, pp. 35–43.

Schick, Irvin C., and Ertugrul Ahmet Tonak (ed.), *Turkey in Transition*, Oxford University Press, 1987.

Sezer, Duygu Bazoğlu, *Turkey's Security Policies*, International Institute of Strategic Studies, London, 1981 (Adelphi Paper 164).

Shapland, Greg, *Rivers of Discord: International Water Disputes in the Middle East* Hurst, London, 1997.

Shulman, Debra Lois, 'Periphery to Prominence: The Evolution of Turkish-Israeli Relations, 1948–1998', unpublished MPhil thesis, Oxford University, 1999.

Simons, Geoff, *The United Nations: A Chronology of Conflict*, Macmillan, London, 1994.

Sirman, N., and Andrew Finkel (eds), *Turkish State, Turkish Society*, Routledge, London, 1990.

Sönmezoğlu, Faruk (ed.), *Turk Dis Politikasinin Analizi*, Der Yayinlari, Istanbul, 1994.

Stavridis, Stelios, 'Double Standards: Ethics and Democratic Principles in Foreign Policy: The European Union and the Cyprus Problem', *Mediterranean Politics*, vol. 4, no. 1, spring 1999, pp. 95–112.

Stephen, Michael, 'How the International Community Made a Cyprus Settlement Impossible' *Perceptions*, vol. VI, no. 1, March–May 2001, pp. 61–78.

Taşhan, Seyfi, 'Turkey and the European Community: a Political Appraisal', *Diş Politika*, vol. X, no. 1–2, 1983, pp. 18–28.

———, 'Contemporary Turkish Policies in the Middle East: Prospects and Constraints', *Diş Politika*, vol. XII, no. 1–2, June 1985, pp. 7–21.

———, 'Turkey: From Marginality to Centrality', *Diş Politika*, vol. XVI, no. 3–4, 1992, pp. 1–12.

———, 'The Caucasus and Central Asia: Strategic Implications', *Diş Politika*, vol. XVII, no. 3–4, 1993, pp. 44–64.

———, 'A Turkish Perspective on Europe-Turkey Relations on the Eve of the IGC', *Dis Politika*, vol. XX, no. 1–2, 1996, pp. 55–68.

Toksoz, Mina, *Turkey to 1992: Missing Another Chance?*, Economist Intelligence Unit, London (Special Report 1136), 1988.

Turkish Embassy (various authors), *Water and Development in South-East Anatolia: Essays on the Ilisu Dam and GAP*, London, 2000.

Ünal, Hasan, 'Bosnia II: A Turkish Critique', *The World Today*, vol. 51, no. 7, July 1995.

Vali, Ferenc A., *Bridge across the Bosporus*, Johns Hopkins Press, Baltimore, MD, 1971.

Vassiliev, Alexei, 'Turkey and Iran in Transcaucasia and Central Asia' in Ehteshami, Anoushiravan (ed.), *From the Gulf to Central Asia: Players in the new Great Game*, University of Exeter Press, 1994.

White, P.J., 'Turkey: from Total War to Civil War?' in P.J. White and W.S. Logan (eds), *Remaking the Middle East*, Berg, Oxford, 1997, pp. 225–57.

Williams, Michael C., *Civil-Military Relations and Peacekeeping*, International Institute of Strategic Studies, London (Adelphi Paper 321), 1998.

Winrow, Gareth M., *Where East Meets West: Turkey and the Balkans*, Institute for European Defence and Strategic Studies, London, 1993.

———, 'Turkey and the Former Soviet Central Asia: A Turkic Culture Area in the Making?' in K. Warikoo (ed.), *Central Asia-Emerging New Order*, Har-anand, New Delhi, 1994.

———, 'Turkey and the Newly Independent States of Central Asia and the Transcaucasus', *Middle East Review of International Affairs*, 2, 1997.

———, *Turkey and the Caucasus: Domestic Interests and Security Concerns*, RIIA, London, 2000.

Zurcher, Erik, *Turkey: A Modern History*, I.B. Tauris, London, 1993.

INDEX